W9-CKH-213

CHICAGO POLITICS WARD BY WARD

David K. Fremon

CHICAGO POLITICS WARD BY WARD

Indiana University Press

BLOOMINGTON & INDIANAPOLIS

Library of Congress Cataloging-in-Publication Data

Fremon, David K.
  Chicago politics, ward by ward.

  Includes index.
  1. Chicago (Ill.)—Politics and government—
1951-   . I. Title.
F548.52.F74   1988   977.3'11043   87-46094
ISBN 0-253-31344-9
ISBN 0-253-20490-9 (pbk.)
1 2 3 4 5 92 91 90 89 88

Contents

Dedicated with love to Sonja,
who put up with an often-grumpy writer

PREFACE

The idea for this book came during a Saturday morning in October 1985. I was driving to a daylong conference that promised to be nothing if not boring. At the time I was working for a community newspaper and grumbling about how difficult it was to contact city officials and obtain basic information about Chicago. Then the idea hit: why not put together the facts and numbers that a political writer needs, all in one book? I entered the conference, stayed just long enough to be seen by the right people, and fled to a café to outline my nascent book.

One point emerged almost instantly—a political almanac could end up a dry recitation of facts and figures that ignores the heart of the city. One could read the name of a man who represents the 6th Ward or 23rd Ward or 30th Ward. But who lives out there? *What* is out there? Why is the 18th Ward different from all others? How, if at all, do the surroundings determine the sort of politician elected to office?

Before I could write a book about Chicago, I decided I had to journey around every ward in the city and see just what is there. It took the better part of two months, visiting one or two wards a day, traveling on every street in the city.

What is out there? Quite a bit. We have the large buildings and museums, the world-famous theaters, restaurants, and nightclubs that can be discovered in many another guidebook. There are the huge businesses, many famous nationwide, and ma-and-pa stores whose owners harbor the American dream of wealth and success.

We have neighborhoods—hundreds of smaller foci of stores and businesses, which together make up the metropolis. They provide a continuous social and economic flow. Some are thriving, some are suffering; some once suffering are now thriving and others are declining after having seen better days. But all have something to offer. Even North Lawndale, subject of a Pulitzer Prize–winning series describing urban decay, shows signs of hope.

Most of all, there are homes—condominiums and mansions, Queen Anne and graystone and balloon-frame homes, suburban-style homes and bungalows. Entire wards consist of little but street after street of residences, which makes for nice living if not necessarily interesting driving.

Finally, Chicago abounds in little-known and sometimes hidden treasures. It may be a one-of-a-kind business, unique entertainment, or even an imaginatively painted garage. These small, often quirky attractions may not make the newspapers but nonetheless prove that the creative spirit is alive in the Windy City. Granted, one's knowledge of Chicago politics is not enhanced by the awareness of the existence of a huge cigar-store Indian at 63rd and Kedzie— but maybe one's appreciation of the city's wondrous diversity is.

Descriptions of each ward include not just the lay of the land, but also recent (and sometimes not-so-recent) political history. A sense of perspective is vital when considering the modern Chicago political scene. Many of the current political leaders are the product of organizations and philosophies that have endured for decades. Others emerged in direct protest to the *ancien régime*.

The ward narratives feature the two major political offices in each ward, alderman and Democratic committeeman. Often the same person holds both positions, but the positions themselves are different. An alderman is a legislative representative with a firmly delineated set of duties. He votes on proposed ordinances and budgets in the city council. In effect he serves as mayor of the ward, seeing to the streets, alleys, and sidewalks of the ward.

The committeeman, on the other hand, is an unpaid party representative with few delineated duties. Yet for years the Democratic committeemen held the real power in most wards. The reason was patronage. The Democratic machine depended on an army of precinct workers whose civil service-exempt jobs depended on how well they performed on election day (in many cases it could be argued that their real job was that of precinct captain, and that non-taxing city jobs merely provided a legal manner of paying for the political work).

Someone had to serve as conduit through which the requests for city jobs could be handled. By custom, the role (and thus life-or-death power over city jobs) fell to the committeeman. No law required this to be the case. Thus when Mayor Richard J. Daley wished to emasculate a committeeman, he turned the patronage power over to someone else in the ward. Ralph Metcalfe lost his 3rd Ward patronage when he defied Daley in 1975. The mayor awarded jobs in the 5th Ward, but not through Committeeman (and Daley critic) Alan Dobry.

Politicians have another important reason for running for Democratic committeeman. Unlike legislative positions (alderman, state representative, senator, etc.), where campaign funds are subject to disclosure laws, the Democratic committeeman is a party job in which contributions need not be revealed.

Candidates thus may build up huge war chests away from public scrutiny. Longtime 47th Ward Democratic committeeman Ed Kelly, unopposed for years, has such a chest estimated in the millions. When Manuel Torres ran for 26th Ward alderman in the important 1986 special election, he simultaneously ran for committeeman against a weak candidate. Torres was required to reveal his aldermanic election funds. But we will never know how much money was funneled to him through a committeeman campaign fund.

Republicans have committeemen too. But Republicans for years have held no real power in Chicago, former alderman Dick Simpson notes. "That's why a Republican committeeman in Chicago is as influential as a garbageman," he comments, a quote which when printed provoked an irate response by a garbageman.

The Shakman decree, which outlawed most political hiring and firing, reduced most committeemen's strength. Yet they retain some powers, among them being selection of election judges, slating of party-backed candidates, and replacement of state legislators from the party who have left office during their term. They also retain residual loyalty from those workers who got their jobs through them. An incumbent alderman challenges a committeeman or committeeman-backed candidate at his peril, as defeated aldermen in the 8th, 12th, 20th and 45th wards learned in 1987.

In addition to ward descriptions, the book also offers maps and tables on each ward. The tables include:

Census data: Alderman Edward Vrdolyak in the waning days of the 1983 Democratic primary said of the election, "It's a racial thing." The media censured Vrdolyak for his remark, but election results have proved him correct.

Chicago elections, now more than ever, are racial things. Whites tend to vote for whites. Blacks tend to vote for blacks (the 5th Ward being a notable exception). Hispanics have shown in recent elections that given the chance they will support one of their own. Asians, assuming they settle somewhere in numbers large enough to allow representation, likely will follow the same pattern.

Two sets of percentages are given: total population figures of non-Hispanic whites, blacks, Hispanics, and others (Asians, American Indians, Eskimos, Aleuts, etc.) and voting age populations for those groups. A major decrease from total population to voting age population of a particular group indicates the abundance of children. Such disparities are most visible among the Hispanic community.

Census figures listed are taken from the city's statistical abstract and reflect populations of the present wards from the 1980 census. They do not and cannot reflect any racial changes that have taken place since the census.[1]

Census tracts: Chicago's wards, like other legislative districts, are transitional by nature. Every ten years they must be redistricted to reflect one person-one vote requirements. Thus a long-term overview of a community could not be based on ward numbers alone.

The Social Science Research Committee of the University of Chicago identified seventy-five community areas in the 1930s, based on such considerations as common settlement and history, local institutions, and natural boundaries. Some of those designated communities have undergone changes which make unity all but non-existent (the Near North Side, for example, includes both the wealthy Gold Coast and impoverished Cabrini-Green high rises). Other community areas are best known to local residents by other names (those just south and west of the Loop consider themselves part of Pilsen, not the Lower West Side). Yet the community designations have a purpose. They provide a stable unit by which to measure racial and economic change. Census tracts from the communities offer a close-up on any sub-area within the community.

Detailed census data is beyond the scope of this book. Census tracts are offered for those who wish to pursue further information, which can be found in the *Local Community Fact Book: Chicago Metropolitan Area* (Chicago Review Press, 1984).

Community newspapers: At best, community newspapers can be the most reliable source of political information anywhere. Whereas metropolitan dailies must spread a staff throughout the city, community papers generally restrict themselves to a few wards. Reporters there can hear the gossip, chat with the precinct captains, and obtain more inside information than their megapaper counterparts. At worst, community papers can be uninforming or misinforming. Some live in fear of offending the local alderman. Others are owned and operated by the local alderman. For some, objectivity is an unknown word.

The community newspaper sections include those papers circulating in a given ward, without rendering judgment on their comparative worth in political coverage. Each list, as much as possible, is limited to those papers which offer political news (although changing editorial philosophies may alter political emphasis).

Chicago also has a lively foreign-language press, including more than a dozen Spanish-language papers. These Hispanic newspapers generally cover Hispanic politics throughout the city and are listed in the wards where they circulate. Other foreign-language papers concentrate more on national affairs or news from the homeland, although they may provide stories on politicians of their nationality.

Three other papers, not community newspapers, provide extensive political coverage. The *Reader* (11 E. Illinois, 828–0350) frequently prints in-depth political stories, mostly with a liberal slant. The *Windy City Times* (3223 N. Sheffield, 935–1790), aimed at the gay and lesbian community, features political events, mostly those pertaining to the gay community. *All-Chicago City News* (1140 W. Montrose, 275–3822), published by Harold Washington ally Walter "Slim" Coleman, provides political news from around the city—none of it critical of the late mayor or his allies.

Aldermen and committeemen: Each alderman is featured with a brief biography, list of city council committees on which he or she serves, city hall and ward office telephones (as of December 1987), and results of the 1987 aldermanic election and any special elections which took place since 1983. Similar information is given for Democratic committeemen.

Mayoral elections: The 1983 mayoral primary and general elections proved a watershed in Chicago politics, in which entire wards quit allegiances of the past. New voting patterns formed which generally continued into the 1987 elections (except in some wards altered by the 1986 remap). Primary and general election results of both years show the similarities and contrasts of the recent elections.

No book is a solo effort, certainly not this one. Special thanks are extended to many reporters, writers, and editors, especially Jorge Casuso, Manuel Galvan, Carl Franz, Joe Garcia, Jane Harrison, Ben Joravsky, Dick and Debbie Stein, and others who requested anonymity; Deanna Bertoncini, provider of sound editing advice; Chris McCarthy, for his computer help; Tom Boyden and Robert Kennedy, who navigated and offered insightful comments during tours around the wards; the staff of the Municipal Reference Library; too many politicians, aides, and political operatives to mention, for answering what might have seemed extremely trivial questions; and most of all my parents, Joe and Irene Fremon, who offered unfailing encouragement throughout the book's writing.

NOTE

1. Population data given for whites, blacks, and Hispanics in the ward summaries is derived from statistics compiled by attorneys in the ward remap lawsuit. The lawsuit concerned itself only with blacks and Hispanics; since Asians, native Americans, and "others" do not appear anywhere in the city in numbers large enough to make representation a legal issue, those groups were not enumerated separately. In some cases those groups appear to have been counted with the white population.

Another problem emerged in some predominantly black wards: totals of blacks, whites, and Hispanics exceeding 100 percent. This may be explained due to the doubling factor of Hispanics. Although attempts were made to count Hispanics separately from non-Hispanic blacks and non-Hispanic whites, there are some (Caribbean blacks, for example) who have listed themselves in more than one category.

I have used two methods of computing the "Asian and other" population. Where the black, Hispanic, and non-Hispanic white totals added up to less than 100 percent, I subtracted the total from 100 percent and called the difference "Asian and other." In those wards where totals of the three major groups exceeded 100 percent, I counted all

Asians, Pacific islanders, and native Americans in census tracts belonging to the affected wards and included that number in the census data ("Asian and other" totals did not exceed one percent in any of the latter wards).

In any case, it must be remembered that the census data represent the 1980 population of the various wards and do not reflect demographic changes since that time. Such data are provided here to show relative racial and ethnic distribution as seen from the last census, not to measure present population distribution.

The
Race
for
Mayor

Council Wars

"HAROLD! HAROLD!" came the booming cry at Donnelley Hall the night of April 15, 1983. Thousands applauded as the newly elected Harold Washington, who would soon take office as Chicago's first black mayor, shouted, "You want Harold? Well, heeere's Harold!"

Downtown, at the Palmer House Hotel, followers of Republican candidate Bernard Epton waited well into the evening for their man to speak. An obviously testy Epton made a brief appearance, said it was too early to predict results and promised to return later. He never did.

Elsewhere, there were other, less public meetings taking place. Democratic regulars, faced with the reality of their second consecutive mayoral election defeat, plotted how to regain power.

The 1987 mayoral election was already beginning.

Instead of offering an olive branch to his recent opponents, Washington waved a red flag. His inaugural address, anything but conciliatory, promised the ouster of employees hired during the waning days of the Jane Byrne administration and reform "while there's still time"—only a slight rewording of Bernard Epton's "before it's too late."

Washington's aldermanic allies, most notably veteran Wilson Frost, crowed about their upcoming takeover of the Chicago City Council. Aldermen who had opposed Washington during the election would fall into line, they figured. After all, the council always backed the mayor before.

Not this time. A minor alderman, Aloysius Majerczyk, declared that he would not automatically support the new mayor. Majerczyk lacked the clout to lead a rebellion, but a more powerful ally, Edward Vrdolyak, seized this discontent and quickly formed an unwavering coalition.

Vrdolyak's bloc included himself and Fred Roti, who represented multiethnic wards; council patriarch Vito Marzullo, an Italian representing a ward by now overwhelmingly Mexican; twenty-two white aldermen representing white ethnic wards (Patrick Huels, Majerczyk, John Madrzyk, Edward Burke, Frank Brady, Robert Kellam, Michael Sheahan, Frank Stemberk, William Krystyniak, Michael Nardulli, George Hagopian, Theris Gabinski, Richard Mell, William Banks, Frank Damato, Thomas Cullerton, Anthony Laurino, Patrick O'Connor, Roman Pucinski, Gerald McLaughlin, Eugene Schulter, and Bernard Stone); two Lakefront aldermen (Bernard Hansen and Jerome Orbach); and the council's lone Hispanic, Miguel Santiago. Another white ethnic alderman, Joseph Kotlarz, later became the twenty-ninth member of the bloc.

Washington's bloc, equally unified, included all sixteen black aldermen

(Bobby Rush, Tyrone Kenner, Timothy Evans, Eugene Sawyer, William Beavers, Marian Humes, Perry Hutchinson, Anna Langford, Allan Streeter, Clifford Kelley, Niles Sherman, William Henry, Wallace Davis, Ed Smith, Danny Davis, and Frost), many of whom came from the ranks of the Regular Democratic Organization yet realized it would be dangerous to oppose a mayor who won 99 percent of the black vote; four white liberals (Lawrence Bloom, Martin Oberman, Marion Volini, and David Orr); and Burton Natarus, a product of the regular organization whose committeeman, deposed County Chairman George Dunne, was an ardent Vrdolyak foe.

Realizing that his forces lacked the numbers to gain control of city council committees, Washington tried to postpone a reorganization vote at his first council meeting. Natarus moved for immediate adjournment. The mayor adjourned the meeting and left the chamber.

Vrdolyak charged to the podium and took over the meeting. By the time he gaveled it closed, every one of his allies had a committee chairmanship, including Ed Burke of the powerful Finance Committee. Washington claimed the council coup was illegal, but the courts (major players in the Washington administration's first term) ruled that the city council could organize itself as it pleased.

The "Eddies," Vrdolyak and Burke, carried the load for the anti-Washington "Vrdolyak 29." Outgoing, charismatic Vrdolyak led the attack on the mayor's proposals. Burke, a master of parliamentary procedure and council finances, handled the detail work. The other twenty-seven majority-bloc aldermen, for the most part, went along for the ride.

This alignment guaranteed stalemate. Vrdolyak's bloc had enough votes to pass every controversial proposal, yet lacked the two-thirds needed to override the inevitable Washington veto.

If this process had been followed quietly—majority vote, then mayoral veto—the Chicago impasse would have gained no more attention than an Icelandic parliament meeting. But the personal animosity and circus atmosphere that attended the meetings caused headlines throughout the world. The *Wall Street Journal* described Chicago as "Beirut on the Lake." Local comedian Aaron Freeman in a nightclub routine parodying the movie *Star Wars* gave the political struggle a lasting nickname—"Council Wars."

The Vrdolyak-bloc strategy included making city government look foolish by objecting to almost anything Washington or his allies proposed. Thus Frank Stemberk moaned about separation of powers after a Washington aide allowed a filmmaker and children inside council chambers to shoot a documentary. Thus two hefty aldermen staged an impromptu sit-in when administration officials planned to convert an aldermanic office into a press room. Thus when Washington described activist Dorothy Tillman as an "alderwoman" in his nomination of her to replace convicted 3rd Ward alderman Kenner, Rules Committee chairman Stemberk refused the nomination because there is no such word as "alderwoman." Thus Burke declared the office of mayor vacant after Washington failed to file a routine ethics statement on time.

Not that Vrdolyak's faction held any monopoly on pettiness. Washington delayed construction of a new library in Richard Daley's Bridgeport neighborhood. He vetoed construction of a new soccer field—the sort of community project considered an alderman's divine right—in Vrdolyak's 10th Ward.

Council Wars reached a new low during one particularly heated session. Vrdolyak made remarks which questioned the mayor's masculinity. Washington responded by offering Vrdolyak "a mouthful of something you don't want."

After a while Council Wars began to wear thin, and the Vrdolyak bloc abandoned most cheap theatrics (although Vrdolyak provoked Washington ally Slim Coleman during a 1985 meeting by calling him "the funeral director of the Nazi party"). Nevertheless, attacks on any and all Washington programs continued.

The majority-bloc aldermen's most potent weapon was inaction, a weapon used to block most Washington nominations to city boards and commissions. The mayor's nominations were sent to the appropriate council committees, where the opposition-bloc chairmen refused to hold hearings on them. Some sixty "hostages" thus languished, most of them nominees to commissions which carried little political clout. But they also included park board nominees needed by Washington to oust a major antagonist, parks boss Ed Kelly.

The two factions fought a six-week battle over the 1984 budget (such budgetary disagreements characterized the first three years of Washington's term). At first the council majority refused to let Washington rescind a property tax cut. Washington threatened massive layoffs, including police and firemen, and refused to budge from that position. Eventually, the Vrdolyak bloc yielded.

One product of the budget compromise was the creation of even more city council committees. The fifty-member Chicago City Council grew from twenty-nine to thirty-seven standing committees in late 1983. The U.S. House of Representatives, with 435 members, has only twenty-two standing committees.

The Cook County Democratic party, at Vrdolyak's urging, endorsed presidential candidate Walter Mondale in November 1983. Soon afterward the *Tribune* disclosed that Vrdolyak had conducted a secret meeting with two top White House officials. Vrdolyak at first denied such a meeting. Later he claimed that he and the Ronald Reagan staffers talked only about 10th Ward issues, not politics.

Few people believed White House chief of staff James Baker and political director Edward Rollins would confer with a Chicago alderman and limit discussion to Southeast Side alleys and sewers. Republican sources claimed that Vrdolyak sought to shake down the Grand Old Party. Vrdolyak offered to throw local support to Mondale, believed to be the weakest possible Democratic challenger. Negotiations halted when he claimed that he needed money to pull off the organization endorsement.

The chairman of the Democratic party cavorting with Republicans? Harold Washington received a perfect campaign tool in his attempt to oust Vrdolyak as party boss by electing new, friendlier Democratic ward committeemen in 1984. But he failed to use it. Washington allies Jesus Garcia and Robert Remer won committeeman elections, and several pro-Washington blacks displaced those who earlier opposed him. Yet anti-Washington sentiment proved more popular than anti-Republican feelings among the white ethnic Democratic committeemen. Vrdolyak carried the committeemen's weighted votes over token opponent John Stroger by a two-to-one margin.

After the committeeman elections, the battle switched to another front—control of city contracts. The Shakman court decree, which outlawed political hiring and firing, removed most city jobs from political influence. Issuance of contracts, however, remained a way to reward friends and punish enemies. Burke and Vrdolyak sought control over city contracts by demanding approval power over them. Washington offered the council review of contracts, nothing more. The ensuing disagreement became a six-week battle in the summer of 1984.

The Vrdolyak faction threatened to block three megaprojects—expansion of O'Hare Airport, construction of a southwest rapid transit line, and reconstruction of the Jackson Park elevated line—unless the mayor gave in. Eventually, a compromise was reached where the council won approval rights of contracts over $100,000, review rights of lesser contracts.

At one point, Council Wars took its show on the road. CBS reporter Ed Bradley arranged an interview with Washington during the Democratic convention in San Francisco. Unbeknownst to the mayor, Bradley also invited Vrdolyak for a simultaneous interview. The county chairman remained affable and glib while Washington groused at Bradley. Advantage, Vrdolyak.

The rival factions called a truce until after the presidential election. Then a number of events combined to give Washington psychological momentum.

Turning Points

Harold Washington's city council foes might not have loved Dorothy Tillman. But they could not in good faith deny her aldermanic nomination after she beat two opponents for Democratic committeeman in 1984 by a two-to-one margin. The council confirmed her shortly thereafter.

Tillman had to run for the office in a 1985 special election. Few doubted the Washington-backed incumbent would win, but a less-than-convincing victory would be an embarrassment to the mayor.

Eight opponents faced Tillman, including Kenner ally James "Skip" Burrell. Washington invited Burrell to his apartment, reportedly to ask him to leave the race. During the conversation, he made disparaging remarks about Tillman. Burrell taped the conversation, and the tape ended up at the *Tribune*, which published the remarks regarding Tillman. Third Ward voters became indignant—not at Tillman, but at a candidate who dared invade the privacy of the mayor in his own home.

Another major battle took place in the spring of 1985. When federal Community Development Block Grants, designed to help social programs in economically disadvantaged areas, became available, Washington submitted a list of proposed recipients to the council. The majority bloc revised Washington's CDBG request to include funds for projects (mainly street repairs) in middle-income (and therefore ineligible) communities. Stemberk requested deletion of funds to thirty Hispanic agencies, a move which pushed many Hispanics against the Vrdolyak bloc. Others proposed funds for "instant" community groups which had not gone through the application process. Washington, Vrdolyak, and Burke broke a month-long impasse by approving the original CDBG requests plus others sought by majority-bloc members. Majority-bloc aldermen took home funds to repair WPA-built streets in outlying wards, with the money coming from motor tax funds.

No sooner had the block grant feud subsided than a $125 million bond issue battle over street repairs appeared. Majority-bloc aldermen held for ransom funds which covered infrastructure repairs in all fifty wards. Burke complained about the small property tax increase needed to finance the bond issue. Others viewed the battle as purely political. The *Tribune* editorialized, "It isn't that tiny tax increase that worries the Eddies. It's the loss of all those potholes and dangerous sidewalks. The more broken ankles and car axles, the more they can whine about a do-nothing mayor." Mell conceded the political nature of the obstruction. "I will sacrifice a vote that probably won't be popular in my community for the good of the (anti-Washington) coalition," he claimed.

For once, the mayor went on the offensive. He took the press on a guided tour of streets to be repaired, including a 19th Ward street that became a small lake after heavy rains. The resultant publicity worked to Washington's advantage, and the bond issue passed.

Not all issues went the mayor's way. Nation of Islam leader Louis Farrakhan denounced Judaism as "a gutter religion" in 1984. Majority-bloc aldermen jumped on this opportunity to embarrass Washington. They introduced a resolution denouncing the controversial Farrakhan. The resolution was an obviously political one; even some Jewish leaders called for an end to denunciations and name-calling. Yet the black mayor refusing to repudiate a black extremist was an image that did not help Washington in the Jewish community.

Some moves caught their perpetrators empty-headed. An administration official removed a creche from city hall in 1984, causing Burke to call Washington "the grinch who stole Christmas." The manger scene made its way back into the display.

Washington received a more devastating Christmas present in 1985— charges of widespread corruption within his administration. An FBI "mole" named Michael Raymond, posing as a representative for a company vying for city bill collection contracts, reportedly offered bribes to a number of city officials, including several pro-Washington aldermen, in a probe known as "Operation Incubator."

Raymond's reported go-between was the Washington administration's chief liability. Clarence McClain, a former Washington aide, had been fired early in Washington's term after reports surfaced of his previous vice convictions. Any time antiadministration politicians wished to rebuke Washington's carefully nurtured reformer image, all they had to do was invoke the name of Clarence McClain.

Washington appointed former U.S. Attorney Thomas Sullivan to head an investigation of the case. At first the mayor squelched Sullivan's report, on grounds that he was forbidden by law to make it public. However, a copy leaked to the *Sun-Times*, which published excerpts in October 1986.

The report said that former deputy revenue director John Adams accepted $10,000 from Raymond in 1984 and offered "inside information" to McClain, who was working closely with Raymond's collection company. Adams's boss, Charles Sawyer, took $2,500 in the form of a campaign contribution for his brother, 6th Ward alderman Eugene Sawyer.

Instead of acting decisively with Adams and Sawyer, the administration wavered. Chief of staff Ernest Barefield, corporation counsel James Montgomery, mayoral advisor Ira Edelson, and Sawyer knew of the bribe-taking in August 1985. Yet none of the four reported the information to authorities. Adams was allowed to keep his job until early 1986. Sawyer was relieved of his duties in January 1986 but not fired until Washington received the Sullivan report in October of that year.

Operation Incubator cast a pall over much of 1986 for Washington allies. But the mayor was not greatly hurt by the disclosure. His enemies weren't going to vote for him anyway. Hard-core Washington loyalists viewed the probe as a glorified smear campaign, and the aldermen implicated in wrongdoing (Humes, Hutchinson, Kelley, and Wallace Davis) were known as marginal Washington allies at best. And Raymond's checkered past (he was convicted of weapons and parole violations and suspected in the disappearance of three people in Florida) made many good-government types question the ethics of using him to entrap others. Most important, while the report blasted administration members, it failed to implicate the mayor in any corruption.

Gloom and apprehension over the bribery investigation soon were replaced by joy from another source. If Operation Incubator made for an unhappy Christmas for Washington, events in a local courtroom made for a very happy new year.

The Remap

Every redistricting is a gerrymandering of sorts. Those in charge of drawing the new maps go out of their way to help themselves and hurt their enemies, (usually) within the limits of the law. To Mayor Jane Byrne, blacks were the enemy in 1981. Even though the black vote decided her victory over Democratic regular Michael Bilandic in 1979, she turned her back on it shortly after taking office. Instead, Byrne veered on a more conservative course, hoping to attract white ethnic voters who might otherwise favor undeclared 1983 mayoral candidate Richard Daley.

Former alderman Tom Keane drew the new council map for Byrne in 1981. It kept the number of black majority wards at seventeen, the same as during the 1970 remap, even though blacks by 1980 formed the majority in nineteen wards of the old map.

Hispanics were considered too unpredictable to be reliable votes. As a result the Pilsen and Little Village Mexican communities on the Near Southwest Side were split among four wards. West Town, Humboldt Park, and Logan Square, predominantly Puerto Rican areas on the Near Northwest Side, were split into six wards.

In past generations, the minorities might have accepted the remap with resignation. This time they took it to court. U.S. district court judge Thomas McMillan ruled in December 1982 that Keane's map was discriminatory and ordered a new map drawn.

Still not satisfied with the McMillan remap, the black and Hispanic plaintiffs took their case higher. The court of appeals ruled in May 1984 that the 1982 map did not go far enough in remedying the Keane map's discrimination. The Supreme Court declined to hear the case twelve months later and sent it back to the district court to arrange the new ward boundaries. Both sides agreed to a compromise map in November 1985.

The ward map battle was lost, but the "29" could still survive if special elections were not ordered in wards set to be altered by the remap. City council (majority-bloc) attorney William Harte argued before district court judge Charles Norgle that since the midterm point had been passed, special elections were prohibited by state law. Norgle disagreed and on December 31 ordered special elections to coincide with the March 1986 primaries.

Seven wards were redrawn to provide for black or Hispanic "super-majorities" (65 percent minority population)—the Southwest Side 15th and 18th Wards, the West Side 37th, the Near Southwest Side 22nd and 25th and the Near Northwest Side 26th and 31st. Vrdolyak-bloc aldermen served all these wards; Washington allies needed to win four of them to wrest council control.

Washington all but conceded two wards: Kellam's half-black, half-white 18th, where whites maintained a definite majority among registered voters; and Santiago's 31st Ward, where no strong independent organization had emerged. Likewise, three wards were considered certain wins for the mayor: the 22nd, where Committeeman Jesus Garcia faced token challenges; and the black 15th and 37th. That left two Hispanic wards up for grabs: the 25th, still a regular Democratic stronghold; and the 26th, whose alderman and committeeman both had been redistricted out of the ward.

Majority-bloc members Kellam and Santiago were reelected, and Vrdolyak ally Juan Soliz won without a runoff in the 25th. Washington stalwarts Garcia and Percy Giles (37th) also got clear majorities. The 15th failed to insert a Washington ally right away only because a solidly black majority split its vote among a number of candidates.

Control of city government came down to the 26th Ward. Washington supporter Luis Gutierrez and Vrdolyak backer Manuel Torres were the only two candidates on the ballot. Gutierrez claimed a paper-thin victory. But the board of elections ruled that an obscure write-in candidate named Jim Blasinski garnered exactly enough votes to force a runoff.

Chicago's best and brightest from both factions paraded for their candidates during the two-week runoff campaign. Washington, Garcia, Danny Davis, Tillman, and state senate nominee Miguel del Valle stumped for Gutierrez. Byrne, Daley, and Burke openly campaigned for Torres. Vrdolyak remained officially neutral, but his car made frequent stops at Torres headquarters.

Torres might have destroyed himself the night before the runoff. During a TV debate on a Spanish-language station, Torres spoke English, thus annoying much of the ward's Hispanic community. Gutierrez won the runoff by a definite though not resounding margin.

Thus freed from a hostile city council, Washington set to work. He and his allies realigned the council committees and put veto-proof majorities on all of them. Burke was allowed to keep the Finance Committee chair, but real power was transferred to a Budget Committee headed by Evans.

The newly arranged council wasted little time in confirming the "hostages," some of whose nominations had been in committee so long that their designated terms had expired. The takeover of power became complete when two of those new appointees combined with an existing park board member to strip power from Washington archfoe Kelly.

With a friendly city council at his side, Washington now could pass any measure he saw fit. One of those was a record $79.9 million (later pared to $54 million) property tax hike in September 1986. Washington claimed the tax hike was necessary because of a decrease in federal revenue sharing funds. Foes jumped on a move bound to win enemies in both the Bungalow Belt and the Lakefront.

There were plenty of foes.

The Campaign

Everyone agreed on one major point: Washington, because of his impenetrable base among blacks and white liberals, was unbeatable in any race that included two white candidates. Anti-Washington forces would have to unite behind one candidate. But who?

Throughout the spring of 1985, Congressman Dan Rostenkowski's name was bandied about by regular Democrats. Rosty might have enjoyed the attention, but he nurtured his own dream—to succeed retiring Thomas "Tip"

O'Neill as Speaker of the House. Rostenkowski declined any party draft for mayor.

Likewise, other commonly heard names popped up during that time: 41st Ward Alderman Roman Pucinski, popular among Chicago's huge Polish community but seemingly incapable of making a dent elsewhere; Ed Kelly, one of Washington's most outspoken foes; Richard Daley, still believed to be harboring mayoral ambitions.

And then there was former mayor Jane Byrne, not the first choice of most party regulars but one who would not be removed from the race. Byrne preempted the field by declaring in mid-1985, more than a year before any other major candidate. The strategy was obvious. Now any other candidate entering the Democratic primary would be perceived as a "spoiler," a code word meaning a white candidate who would split the white vote and thus assure Washington's reelection.

Her declaration brought little new fire to the campaign. The former mayor slipped back into the low-key campaigning she liked best—accepting any and all invitations and campaigning one-on-one at small social events. Her speeches were not the strident attacks of yore, but calmly delivered visions of a revived, happier Chicago complete with a 1992 World's Fair and Chicagofests.

She lost ground with an important constituency in mid-1986. Byrne as mayor courted the gay community, an affluent bloc not shy when it came to campaign contributions. Yet when Washington introduced a gay rights bill, the former mayor remained silent, citing Joseph Cardinal Bernardin's opposition to the measure. Even though Washington did little for the bill's passage (several black aldermen otherwise terrified of bucking the mayor defied him on this vote), he was seen as a major backer of gay rights while Byrne was villified.

Washington remained coy on his options. He could seek reelection as a Democrat, facing Byrne and possibly others in a primary. Or he could run as an independent, versus the winners of both the Democratic and Republican primaries.

Daley allies wanted Harold Washington out, but likewise had no use for Jane Byrne in city hall. They came up with a means of eliminating both potential nemeses—a nonpartisan mayoral ballot.

Chicago aldermen are elected on a nonpartisan basis. All candidates (no matter what their party label) run against each other. If no one achieves a majority, the top two compete in a runoff. Southwest Side congressman William Lipinski led the drive to apply the same rules to mayoral elections, starting in 1987.

The strategy served two purposes. Since all candidates would be bunched together, Washington could not run as an independent and thus force a two-on-one confrontation. Byrne also could be eliminated; a nonpartisan primary might amount to a white-versus-white battle to face Washington in a runoff. Daley's followers felt their man could outpoll Byrne.

Needless to say, the proposed nonpartisan ballot attracted opposition from all fronts. Washington backers charged it was an attempt to change the rules in the middle of a campaign in order to remove a duly elected mayor who happened to be black. Byrne voiced the same objections as Washington allies, although she had added reason to oppose a nonpartisan vote. Through her early declaration, she had staked out the role of "white Democratic candidate" and saw no need to give up that advantage. The Republicans, miniscule force though they were, likewise opposed a nonpartisan ballot. They saw unknown candidate Bernard Epton come close to winning in 1983. Although no Republican stood a chance in a nonpartisan field against well-known Democrats, the Republicans envisioned a possible victory in a one-on-one partisan election against Washington.

Despite Byrne's opposition, the nonpartisan ballot was seen as an anti-Washington move. Supporters of the proposal collected more than 210,000 petitions in mid-1986—far more than the 140,000 needed to put a nonpartisan mayoral referendum on the November 1986 ballot.

Washington allies, unable to challenge a sufficient number of signatures, used another approach to avoid such a referendum. Illinois law allowed only three nonbinding referenda on any given ballot. Washington's newly won council majority packed the November ballot with three meaningless referenda—concerning casino gambling, utility rate increases, and an elected school board. The important issue—a new election process for the mayor—was kept off the ballot. Even Burke expressed admiration at the strategy.

Potential foes were not deterred by the nonpartisan defeat. Vrdolyak refused to rule out a candidacy. Daley showed no desire to seek the mayor's office himself, but ally Tom Hynes was believed interested in running under the Daley banner.

Washington feared Hynes most. The county assessor, a two-term "Mr. Clean" in an office which virtually invites corruption, controlled the loyalty of a large voting bloc, plus the ability (shared by all county assessors) to attract large campaign contributions.

At first, the mayor indirectly attacked Hynes. A campaign newspaper run by a Washington ally endorsed most Democrats in the 1986 general elections—but not Hynes. That strategy drew fire from prominent Democrats who kept their distance from the Council Wars. Washington, who still considered a run as a Democrat, ended up endorsing all Democrats—even Hynes.

The 1986 elections carried an upset—the victory of Democrat-turned-Republican James O'Grady over longtime sheriff Richard Elrod. Heartened by this win, Republicans opened their doors and awaited the stampede of big-name Republicans expected to seek the mayoral nomination.

Reality set in two days later. Former governor Richard Ogilvie, eternally a rumored mayoral candidate, made his perennial noncandidacy official. Former U.S. Attorney Dan Webb, the other Great Republican Hope, likewise expressed his regrets. O'Grady, fresh off his sheriff win, refused the temptation to enter the mayoral struggle.

Nonetheless, many other names floated as Republican hopefuls: Wallace Johnson, the banker whom Byrne crushed in the 1979 general election; Frank

Ranallo, retired railroad engineer and perennial candidate; State Senator Walter Dudycz; former state representative Susan Catania; school board president George Munoz; Illinois Commerce Commission member Ray Romero; Chicago Bear safety Gary Fencik; former alderman Bill Singer; former congressman Donald Rumsfeld; Ed Howlett, son of former Illinois secretary of state Michael Howlett; Michael Galvin, a member of the United Republican Fund; Terry Savage, WBBM-TV financial reporter; Northwestern University professor Louis Masotti; former World Fair Authority director John Kramer; appeals court judge Joel Flaum; and Cook County Clerk Stanley Kusper, a Democrat.

Epton sought vindication from a press he felt had treated him unfairly the last time. He was the choice of the "New Republicans," former Democratic organization members who took over Republican organizations in several Near Northwest Side wards.

Most committeemen, however, backed a "blue-ribbon" choice—Don Haider, a Northwestern University associate professor of public management. If anything, Haider was known for the $29 million property tax overcharge blamed on him while city budget manager during the Jane Byrne administration.

Epton mounted an unspirited campaign for the nomination. He filed petitions but chose not to fight a challenge which knocked him off the ballot.

Three minor candidates managed to survive on the Republican ballot: Ken Hurst, 39th Ward committeeman and a perennial candidate; 35th Ward committeeman Chester Hornowski, a cop more interested in his simultaneous aldermanic campaign than the mayoral one; and Ray Wardingley, a.k.a. "Spanky the Clown," another perennial candidate.

One Democrat loomed as a serious Republican nominee: State Senator Jeremiah Joyce, an ally of Daley and Hynes. The nomination was his for the taking; Joyce had more voters in his 19th Ward base than the Republicans did in the entire city. Republican leaders, however, had little use for him because he would not pledge to remain in the race no matter who won the Democratic primary. Besides, Joyce was too conservative for Lakefront liberals, and a Daleyite candidate needed Lakefront votes to win.

Hynes surprised most observers by taking himself out of the race in mid-November. Two weeks later, Vrdolyak announced his candidacy.

From time to time, he had made overtures to the Lakefront, promoting issues such as a condominium garbage rebate. Vrdolyak's law-and-order campaign overture, however, was aimed at the Bungalow Belt rather than the Condo Belt. As he would throughout the campaign, Vrdolyak downplayed race as an issue. Yet white audiences understood references to (predominantly black) public schools, where "you can get gang jackets, dope, and birth-control devices but no education."

A week later, Hynes reversed his earlier position. At the urging of Daley and Rostenkowski, he entered the fray. Joyce withdrew to become Hynes's campaign manager.

Both new entrants kept their ballot options open. Vrdolyak said he would file as a Democrat unless two other persons (meaning Washington and Byrne) entered the primary. Hynes said he would run as an independent. Washington kept mum, holding enough petitions to run either as Democrat or independent. Ultimately he filed as a Democrat.

Vrdolyak grabbed the Solidarity party label used by Adlai Stevenson in his 1986 gubernatorial election. When a Polish-American announced plans to oppose Vrdolyak as a write-in, the Illinois Solidarity party was forced into primary participation. Hynes speculated that Vrdolyak could receive enough primary votes to deny Byrne the Democratic nomination (in fact Vrdolyak received only a handful of primary votes).

Hynes still planned to run as an independent. When Washington backers threatened to challenge primary ballots of Hynes supporters who signed his independent petition (a state law prevented independent petitioners from voting in a primary), Hynes formed an ad hoc party known as Chicago First.

Their third-party candidacies put Hynes and Vrdolyak in awkward positions, since neither had much to do until the general election. Vrdolyak (as did almost every other white ethnic political leader) endorsed Byrne in the primary.

Hynes felt it was improper to endorse an opponent in a primary. Instead, he put out television advertisements to remind voters that he existed. Some were lightly humorous ads that played on his image as an unexciting politician (in one ad, his son fell asleep listening to Dad talk; another promised a city run so smoothly "you won't even know I'm there," spoken while the candidate faded away).

Jane Byrne did not fade away. Although her campaign appearances remained subdued yet positive, she took her attack to the airwaves. Her most controversial ad featured a lightning bolt literally splitting the city, exposing Harold Washington as a grim-faced black bogeyman. Another ad hit Washington on tax increases. Washington allies sought to have the ad pulled from local television stations, claiming it was untrue. The stations refused to stop that ad.

Washington's allies inadvertently reinforced Byrne's image of a town rent by racial woes. Judge Eugene Pincham declared "Any (black) man south of Madison Street who doesn't vote for Harold Washington ought to be hung." Alderman Tillman opined that any white Lakefronters who didn't vote for Washington opposed him because of race. Washington eventually disavowed both remarks, but did himself no favors when he said that Byrne "reminds me of Hitler, the Big Lie."

But on the whole, the primary (and ensuing general election) campaign did not degenerate into the open racial antagonism of 1983. An ad hoc watchdog committee known as CONDUCT (Committee on Decent Unbiased Campaign Tactics) monitored racist or potentially racist actions. CONDUCT recorded numerous complaints, some of them admittedly minor (Byrne was reprimanded for discussing "the Gold Coast to the Soul Coast," even though such black politicians as Jesse Jackson and Danny Davis had used the phrase for years). But the committee's presence probably kept down at least openly racial attacks.

Byrne, like Washington, fell victim to foot-in-mouth disease. She referred to Puerto Ricans as aliens, and pro-Washington Hispanics wasted no time in pointing out that Puerto Ricans are U.S. citizens. It was an apparently innocent error but embarrassing for a candidate already under siege for her lack of support of the ward remap (while Washington put himself in the forefront of the remap fight).

Washington took another step in the courtship of the Hispanic vote, one of the few blocs not considered welded to one of the candidates. He followed the advice of a Hispanic search committee and backed Gloria Chevare, a Puerto Rican attorney, for city clerk. Chevare opposed incumbent Walter Kozubowski, a generally respected Burke ally whom Washington nonetheless described as "a nerd."

The mayor reached out to white ethnics, even though that bloc was all but conceded to Byrne. He backed a home equity program which would insure (white) homeowners against property value losses stemming from racial change. Washington hinted support of a linked development program, which would tax large downtown developments and transfer those revenues to outlying communities.

Byrne tried to campaign in the black community but with little success; most black churches would not invite her to speak. She finally got one invitation. Rev. Jesse Butler, father of 27th Ward aldermanic candidate Sheneather Butler, let the former mayor address his congregation. (The address probably did Byrne little good, although it might have been the factor that won the younger Butler her election.)

She lost face on another important front—the Lakefront. When strong winds combined with already high shoreline to close Lake Shore Drive by flooding three Sundays before the primary, Byrne appeared at the scene and challenged the mayor to reopen the drive. Washington also appeared and promised to reopen it as soon as possible.

Byrne might have hoped for a repeat of 1979, when another act of God (a huge blizzard) helped her defeat incumbent Michael Bilandic in the primary. This time city crews worked through the night and cleared the drive in time for morning rush hour. Washington looked like a mayor who could get things done; Byrne appeared as an opportunist who almost hoped for disaster in order to help her cause.

Both candidates argued on a number of fronts: taxes, crime, lakefront erosion. But one had to listen hard to hear comments from either on a continuing problem, the sorry state of the Chicago Housing Authority. The CHA in January 1987 lost $7 million in funding because officials missed a deadline for the awarding of contracts. Embattled CHA boss Renault Robinson resigned. But Byrne's CHA record, under controversial director Charles Swibel, was less than stellar. If Washington gained no points from the CHA shakeup, he likewise lost few.

The former mayor challenged the present mayor to a television debate. Washington, with a lead estimated at somewhere between comfortable and commanding, was in no hurry to face her. The two sides never agreed to conditions; Washington wanted a live audience, while Byrne sought a debate in a television studio. Byrne bought air time, anticipating a debate. When it failed to come about, she used the time for a half-hour campaign commercial.

Washington got his live audience during a February rally held at the University of Illinois at Chicago Pavilion. More than 10,000 supporters greeted him, including "Freedom Riders" from the South who came to Chicago for election day precinct work.

The mayor saved his coup de grace for the campaign's final days. An ethics ordinance introduced by Orr had languished in the council since early 1985. Washington forces had had the votes to pass it ever since the special elections. But it had been held until mid-February for two reasons: an ethics bill passed at this time could provide a striking contrast between Washington and Byrne and otherwise recalcitrant aldermen would be pressured to back such a bill during their own reelection campaigns. The ethics measure passed, 49–0.

Polls taken shortly before election day showed Washington with a lead approaching 15 percent. The seemingly hopeless race may have kept many would-be voters at home. Not only white ethnic wards but also black wards voted in numbers lower than 1983 (Richard Mell's 33rd Ward being one of the few exceptions).

It might have been a victory, but no one called it a landslide. Washington won 53 percent of the vote to 46 percent for Byrne. A third candidate, Lyndon LaRouche follower Sheila Jones, received only .23 percent.

Washington, as expected, won near-unanimous totals in the black community (close to 99 percent in all-black wards). He made gains over the 1983 general election, albeit slight ones, in Northwest Side wards (although no improvement on the Southwest Side). The mayor showed strongest gains in the Hispanic communities. Byrne won an estimated 50 percent of the vote here four years ago to only 13 for then-challenger Washington. This time Hispanics (thanks to solid support from Puerto Ricans) voted for Washington in numbers roughly equal to the citywide percentage. Byrne also lost ground on the Lakefront, where she took all six wards by healthy margins in 1983. Washington won three wards and came close in two others (ironically falling behind only in the once-liberal 43rd Ward).

With Byrne out of the way, the other challengers revved up their campaigns in earnest. Hynes attacked Vrdolyak day after day. The Hynes campaign strategy involved driving home the point that Vrdolyak could not possibly win the election, thus forcing his departure, and convincing anti-Washington voters that a vote for Haider would be wasted.

Vrdolyak, however, would not be moved. His aggressive campaign pushed blue-collar issues: crime, the poor state of the schools, and tax increases. Vrdolyak argued that he, not Hynes, had been in the vanguard of Washington attackers over the last four years. Furthermore, he charged that Hynes and the Daleyites were the real spoilers ("It's rule or ruin with [the Daleyites]," Vrdolyak commented).

Haider lacked funds for any kind of television advertising, but he became a master of the television news segment and thus gathered his share of free publicity. Haider's campaign was heavy on visuals—poses of him wearing his trademark red nylon jacket, standing beside broken parking meters and eroded lakeshore, or riding an elephant.

Washington early in the campaign played the cool, cautious incumbent. His television ads emphasized the wonderful place that Chicago had become. His ubiquitous campaign posters showed a smiling Washington, arms outstretched in front of the Picasso. Behind him was a throng of happy Chicagoans, oh-so-carefully chosen to show proper racial, gender, and age balance.

Hynes and Vrdolyak carried two different outlooks into the campaign. Hynes tried to walk a fine line. On the one hand, he had no desire to villify black folk hero Washington (black votes might be necessary in future campaigns; some theorized that Hynes was using this longshot campaign as a rehearsal for a future run, perhaps for the U.S. Senate in 1990). However, he also had to play to his white ethnic, blue-collar constituency.

Vrdolyak, as active leader of the Washington opposition, had little to lose by criticizing the mayor. Yet he made attempts at attracting black and white liberal votes. One Vrdolyak ad, supposedly set in the Robert Taylor homes, pictured a black hand at a polling place with a voice questioning what Washington had accomplished. A similar ad, aimed at Lakefront independents, showed a white hand and a voice wondering out loud, "What's an old liberal like me going to do?"

At first, Hynes took the high road, stressing his honesty and government experience. His candidacy gained the support of such committeemen as Lipinski, Cullerton, Howard Carroll, Ann Stepan, Thomas Lyons, and even Vrdolyak's friend Burke.

But "Mr. Nice Guy" failed to make an impression on the public at large. After Washington criticized Hynes for working part-time with a law firm which performed city bond work, Hynes went on the attack. "His history and record are one of sleaze," he said of Washington. "He surrounds himself with grafters and corrupters." The assessor resurrected a favorite Bernard Epton issue—Washington's nonpayment of income taxes and temporary suspension of his law license.

Washington's campaigners savored the opportunity to return the fire. They took Hynes to task for his office's low percentage of women and minorities. They noted patronage, including Joyce's brother, Sheahan's wife, his campaign manager's daughter, and his wife's cousin on the assessor's office payroll.

Vrdolyak escaped that kind of censure. The Washington strategy involved giving him a pass—so as not to force him out of the running and risk a one-on-one battle with Hynes.

By mid-March, the race appeared to have ground to a halt. Hynes and Vrdolyak were going for the "silver medal," the gold being conceded to Washington. The 1987 general election could be described by a word scarcely imagined during the last four years—dull.

With a lopsided Washington victory assured if his three challengers remained on the ballot, it appeared obvious that either Hynes or Vrdolyak would have to withdraw in order to prevent the mayor's reelection. Which one should go? The *Sun-Times* announced its decision: Vrdolyak. The paper, in a March 12 editorial, argued that "his continued candidacy would serve only negative ends," that it would muddy up the campaign so as to prevent the presentation of issues by the only two candidates with a chance of winning, deprive Washington of a chance at a mandate, undercut Hynes's chances of rallying Washington opposition, and hurt Vrdolyak's chances in future elections.

It backfired. Vrdolyak called the editorial "beyond reason, beyond logic, beyond good taste." Instead of being an object of scorn, Ed Vrdolyak became an object of sympathy.

Less than two weeks later, the *Sun-Times* exploded another bomb. "Hynes charges Vrdolyak met with mob boss," read the March 23 headline. A closer examination of the story revealed a much less definite charge. "I have heard that Ed Vrdolyak met with Joseph Ferriola. I believe that such a meeting took place and that his candidacy for mayor has received encouragement as a result of it," Hynes was quoted in the story. He declined further comment.

The Hynes statement was carefully worded to avoid a possible lawsuit. At the same time, it was so vague as to be almost meaningless. Vrdolyak produced records detailing his whereabouts at the times of the alleged meetings. The *Sun-Times* failed to bring forth any witness to substantiate the mobster story. Vrdolyak later brought a lawsuit against the newspaper.

If the editorial backfired on Hynes, the mobster story blew up in his face. Vrdolyak's populist campaign started taking hold not just in the Northwest Side, but also in Hynes's Southwest Side base. It even split ward organizations. Committeeman Ed Kelly of the 47th Ward endorsed Hynes, yet several of his precinct captains worked for Vrdolyak.

Kelly suffered a more serious defection. Eugene Schulter, a quiet alderman considered in Kelly's pocket for many years, broke from his mentor shortly before the election to back the mayor. Bernard Hansen of the neighboring 44th Ward also endorsed Washington late in the campaign. Recent opponent Byrne made an endorsement. Washington allowed the word "mandate" to slip into his campaign vocabulary.

Hynes and Vrdolyak had one final chance—to perform so convincingly in a March 31 debate that the other would "blink" (Chicagoese for quitting the race). Washington agreed to a debate with his three rivals, if each would sign an agreement that he would remain on the ballot through the election.

Opinions varied on who "won" the debate. Some said smooth, aggressive Vrdolyak. Others said that Haider, who presented issues well and with humor, came out best. Washington presented a stiff, boring recitation of statistics recounting his administration's glories—the opposite of his usually colorful and fiery debate style. Yet Washington won the debate merely by doing nothing scandalous enough to lose it.

All but the most partisan observers agreed: Hynes lost the debate, and lost it badly. His bland performance showed up in the polls. A WBBM-TV preelection survey showed Washington with 53 percent support, Vrdolyak overtaking Hynes for second at 16 percent, Hynes with 11 percent, and Haider at 5.

Hynes nonetheless shocked the city by withdrawing from the race less than forty hours before the polling places opened. He withdrew, he said, "so

HAROLD WASHINGTON. Born: April 15, 1922. Died: November 25, 1987. Career: B.A., Roosevelt University, 1949; J. D., Northwestern University, 1954; Assistant City Prosecutor, 1954–58; Arbitrator, Illinois Industrial Commission, 1950–64; Illinois House of Representatives, 1965–77; Illinois Senate, 1977–81; U.S. Representative, 1981–83.

the people of Chicago could have a clear choice." Hynes aides claimed he left only because he realized he could not win, although many observers felt that he withdrew to avoid the embarrassment of a third-place finish.

"They'll have to add another chapter to *Profiles in Courage*," said Lipinski of Hynes after the announcement. The *Sun-Times* offered a different view, calling the withdrawal "tardy and selfish" because it came too late to afford remaining candidates time to mount a meaningful challenge.

Even so, Chicago saw an instant campaign. Hynes posters disappeared immediately, to be replaced by Vrdolyak ones. Vrdolyak persuaded a printer to work all night and produce 300,000 palm cards.

Haider also campaigned with renewed vigor. Governor James Thompson, reclusive through most of the election, accompanied Haider on a hand-shaking expedition during the campaign's final day.

The Hynes withdrawal shifted the position of some of his erstwhile supporters. Pucinski, a recent convert to Hynes, endorsed Vrdolyak after the withdrawal. Stepan and Attorney General Neil Hartigan endorsed Washington. Most of the former Hynes backers kept their mouths shut.

Washington workers entertained visions of capturing many of those Hynes votes, particularly along the Lakefront. Optimistic partisans talked of a 60 percent rout. He won the election, but not with any mandate. Washington carried 53 percent of the vote to 42 percent for Vrdolyak and 4 percent for Haider.

The mayor made distressingly few gains over the 1983 general election or the 1987 primary. His vote total showed only a 13,000 increase over the primary, and a .11 percent loss overall. As expected, he received near-unanimous votes in black precincts, but made few if any inroads in white ethnic ones. His gains over the primary in Hispanic wards were offset by percentage losses along the Lakefront.

But those figures could be hashed out another time. Tuesday, April 7, 1987, belonged to Harold Washington, the first Chicago mayor since Richard J. Daley to be reelected. He entertained a Navy Pier throng of supporters with a delightfully off-key rendition of "Chicago, Chicago, That Toddlin' Town," as happy as any man has the right to be.

1983 Democratic primary:

Harold Washington	424,131	(36%)
Jane Byrne	387,986	(34%)
Richard Daley	344,590	(30%)

1983 general:

Harold Washington	668,176	(52%)
Bernard Epton	619,926	(48%)

1987 Democratic primary:

Harold Washington	587,594	(53%)
Jane Byrne	509,436	(47%)

1987 general:

Harold Washington	600,290	(53%)
Edward R. Vrdolyak	468,493	(42%)
Donald H. Haider	47,652	(4%)

The
Fifty
Wards

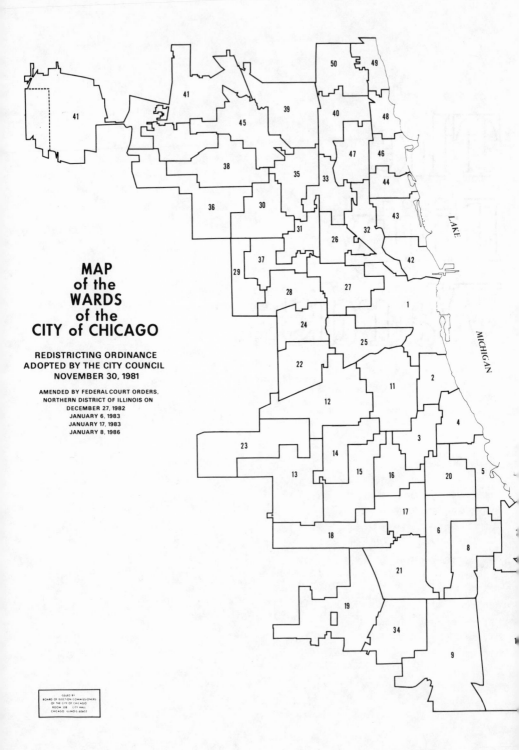

MAP
of the
WARDS
of the
CITY of CHICAGO

REDISTRICTING ORDINANCE
ADOPTED BY THE CITY COUNCIL
NOVEMBER 30, 1981

AMENDED BY FEDERAL COURT ORDERS,
NORTHERN DISTRICT OF ILLINOIS ON
DECEMBER 27, 1982
JANUARY 6, 1983
JANUARY 17, 1983
JANUARY 8, 1986

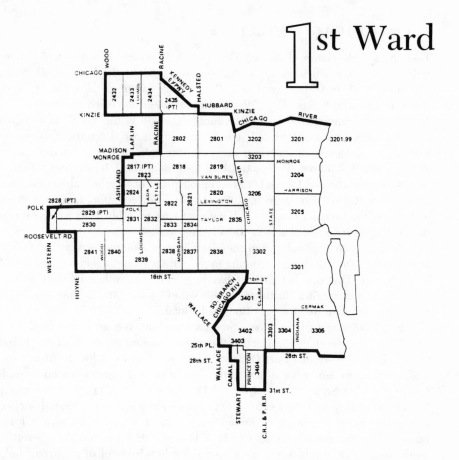

TOURISTS VISITING CHICAGO may view some of the most breathtaking sights of any American city. On a clear day Lake Michigan shines like a sapphire on the city's eastern boundary. The famed Loop provides a bustling testimonial to economic vibrancy, including the corner of State and Madison, arguably the busiest intersection in the world, and Sears Tower, unarguably the world's tallest building.

If Chicago is the City of the Big Shoulders, it is also a city of world-renowned culture. The Chicago Symphony Orchestra is considered by many to be the finest anywhere. Four museums of international fame—the Art Institute, Field Museum of Natural History, Shedd Aquarium, and Adler Planetarium—lie in the Loop or hug the shoreline.

A visitor may fly into Meigs Field, then head for a convention at McCormick Place or a seminar at the University of Illinois at Chicago or the nearby Medical District. If that visitor is lucky, he or she may arrange for tickets to see the 1986 Super Bowl champion Bears play at Soldier Field.

Anyone may see all of the above sights—without leaving Chicago's First Ward.

Few places on earth offer the variety of activities available in the 1st Ward.

Take the simple matter of dining. One may feast on *souvlaki* in Greek Town, Italian beef sandwiches on Taylor Street, soul food on the Near South Side, Mandarin duck in Chinatown, or Polish sausages from an all-night open-air stand on Maxwell Street. First Ward residents need never go hungry.

Once the undisputed home of Chicago's wealthy, the 1st Ward is again drawing upper-class residents to live in or near downtown. Recently constructed apartments in Dearborn Park and Printers Row help anchor the revitalization of the South Loop area. Renovated buildings near the UIC campus, such as the Jackson Boulevard District, draw the offspring of former Italian residents who fled to the suburbs years ago. Presidential Towers offers high-rise living just west of the Loop for professionals willing to pay monthly rents which exceed the per capita incomes of several developing nations.

If there is an "up" side, then there is a "down" side to the ward, both past and present. The 1st Ward was home to the nation's largest skid row, just west of the Loop. This derelict district has largely been displaced but is still in evidence. An area not so fortunate is the Valley, a once Italian and now black ghetto near Racine Avenue and Roosevelt Road.

Focal point of Chicago ever since its founding, the area now in the 1st Ward has been the stage for much of the city's historical drama. Indians chased settlers from the original Fort Dearborn, just south of the Chicago River, and massacred them near what is now 18th and Calumet. Someone tossed a bomb into Haymarket Square (Randolph and Desplaines), igniting an 1886 tragedy known as the Haymarket Riot. Mrs. O'Leary's cow (according to legend) kicked over a lantern in a barn on DeKoven Street, starting the 1871 Chicago Fire. Jane Addams welcomed the poor to Hull House at Halsted and Polk, a settlement house that would serve as a model for hundreds of other urban help centers. The Everleigh sisters welcomed the rich to their "house" (one of the world's most opulent bordellos) at 21st and Dearborn. Gangster Al Capone worked out of the Lexington Hotel at Michigan and Cermak, where millions of television viewers in 1986 watched reporter Geraldo Rivera unearth a couple of beer bottles while looking for treasures in Capone's vault.

If these aren't enough, the ward also offers a potpourri of other attractions: Maxwell Street, which on Sundays houses the last major outdoor flea market in the city (the nearby police station was the one shown in "Hill Street Blues"); the Prairie Avenue Historical District south of 18th Street, Chicago's first Gold Coast; Quinn Chapel at 24th and Wabash, the oldest black church in the city; Tri-Taylor, a historical district of 1890s homes near Ogden, Western, and Harrison; the former home of Chess Records at 2120 S. Michigan, where Sam Cooke, Chuck Berry, and the Rolling Stones recorded in the early years of rock and roll; the *Chicago Defender* at 24th and Michigan, perhaps the nation's most influential black newspaper; the former Chicago Coliseum at 15th and Wabash, rebuilt from a Confederate prison and site of many national conventions; the pastel colored Illinois Library for the Blind and Disabled at Roosevelt and Blue Island; and the embankment north of the Chicago and North Western Railway tracks, decorated with murals depicting nearly extinct animals.

The variety so evident throughout the 1st Ward does not extend to the ward's politics. The 1st Ward is irrevocably tied to the Regular Democratic Organization, which aggressively resists any attempt at outside intervention. This is not to say that 1st Ward politics has been dull; nothing could be further from the truth. In fact, the ward spawned two of the most colorful figures of Chicago history, Michael "Hinky Dink" Kenna and "Bathhouse John" Coughlin, rulers of the Levee vice district at the turn of the century.

Pint-sized Hinky Dink, a saloon keeper, ran the ward and fixed the pay rate at fifty cents per vote. Bathhouse (he got his name from his original place of employment) was a rowdy, boisterous sort, composer of such "songs" as "Oh, Why Did They Build That Lousy Lake So Close to That Beautiful Burg?" and "She Sleeps by the Drainage Canal." He originated the system of moving vagrants from polling place to polling place and having them cast multiple ballots, a system described in pseudo-Latin as "Hobo floto voto." Every year these two statesmen sponsored the First Ward Ball, an extravaganza of politicians, prostitutes, and pickpockets that only occasionally stopped short of orgy.

Hinky Dink and Bathhouse are generally viewed as living cartoon characters. Yet both were astute men in their time. Were they to appear today, they probably would have made their fortunes through law, insurance, or real estate—more acceptable means of entry into the 1980s political arena.

Nowadays when the 1st Ward is mentioned two words come into mind: crime syndicate. Many have charged that reputed crime syndicate boss Tony Accardo is the real ruler of the ward. Even the ward's boundaries reflect the syndicate's influence. The southern border extends to 26th Street except for one small peninsula which extends to 31st Street—and not coincidentally, takes in the fortresslike home of reputed mob boss Angelo LaPietra at 30th and Princeton.

Nor has Committeeman John D'Arco done much to discourage speculation of links between 1st Ward Democrats and organized crime. Committeeman since 1952, he has frequently been seen in the company of gentlemen routinely described with the word "reputed" prefacing their occupations and names. "D'Arco has never bothered to deny that he is a political appendage of the Mafia, probably because he knows that nobody would believe him," wrote Mike Royko in his 1971 book *Boss*.

D'Arco served as a state representative in the 1940s, as part of the "West Side bloc" of lawmakers which opposed reform and anticrime legislation. He became alderman in 1951. Following in a 1st Ward tradition that dated back to Hinky Dink and Bathhouse, he also owned a lucrative Loop insurance business on the side.

His reputed Mafia connections may have caused D'Arco to lose his alderman job—but not for the reasons one might think. D'Arco and mob boss Sam "Momo" Giancana were eating lunch together in late 1962. A less-than-subtle FBI agent approached them. "Ho ho ho, it's Moe," he said to Giancana. Then he turned to D'Arco, saying, "And good afternoon to you, John." A startled D'Arco instinctively shook the agent's hand, and Giancana immediately stormed out of the restaurant. The following day, D'Arco checked himself into a local hospital and announced that he would not seek re-election as alderman.

Anthony DeTolve, Giancana's nephew by marriage, originally was slated to succeed D'Arco but left the ticket shortly before the 1963 election. A last-minute replacement, Mike FioRito, won the election but was forced out of office when it was determined that he didn't even live in Chicago.

Mayor Richard J. Daley then urged D'Arco to come up with a higher-level candidate. The ward boss found such a man, young banker Donald T. Parrillo, who took office in 1964. In fact, Parrillo turned out to be too high class. He resigned from the council in 1968, claiming that being 1st Ward alderman was harmful to his reputation.

Fred Roti succeeded Parrillo and still represents the ward in the city council. A former state senator (1950–56), he chose not to seek reelection because of a redistricting, then worked a number of city jobs. Roti, son of former alderman Bruno Roti, has been known to keep several of his family members on city payrolls.

Although generally a quiet alderman, Roti has an important voice on the city council floor. Since he votes first, his vote is a cue for the other machine aldermen. At least once during the Daley years, he voted "aye" when the proper machine vote was "no." Other aldermen followed his lead until Daley floor leader Tom Keane reminded Roti that the "no" vote was the correct one. Roti then changed his vote to "no," and the other errant aldermen followed suit.

Roti, chairman of the influential Buildings Committee, is always unopposed on the ballot (the last serious independent to run here was activist Florence Scala in 1963), Likewise, D'Arco has not been challenged at the polls.

Harold Washington did not show any inclination toward opposing the 1st Ward Democratic organization. Washington allies talked one would-be Roti challenger into withdrawing from the 1987 aldermanic race. Two others were knocked off the ballot.

Roti, in turn, refrained from attacking the late mayor, and cast his vote for Washington's council reorganization after the 1987 election. Although he generally supported the council's Vrdolyak bloc, Roti was not an outspoken Washington critic. On one major issue, the ward remap, he broke ranks with the former "29" to support the mayor.

That dissenting vote may have come from a sense of self-preservation rather than of ideology. Even before the remap, Roti's ward was one in which the majority of voters were from minority groups. Now the 1st Ward's voting age population is 36.9 percent black, 16.2 percent Hispanic, and 11.3 percent Asian and other nonwhite groups, which if brought together in a well-run campaign would be enough to topple the veteran alderman.

Yet after Washington's death Roti joined the white ethnic bloc of aldermen which eventually elected Eugene Sawyer acting mayor. He maintained the role he has kept for years—that of a majority-bloc alderman willing to remain as far in the background as possible.

REDISTRICTING: A federal judge ruled that the neighboring 25th Ward must be redistricted so as to provide a Hispanic "super-majority." The most logical place to gain the necessary Hispanic population was from the precincts of heavily Mexican Pilsen lying in the 1st Ward. The 1st lost six precincts in the south and one in the southwest corner to the 25th. A racially mixed precinct in the northwest corner of the ward went to the 27th.

In return the 1st gained a racially mixed precinct (part of the Tri-Taylor District) from the 25th, seven Hispanic precincts from the 32nd, and four precincts just west of the Loop that were until recently part of the 27th. Acquisition of the latter four precincts was a coup for Roti. At one time they were skid row precincts. But with the advent of such developments as Presidential Towers, they now represent some of the most valuable property in Chicago.

MAYORAL: Thanks mainly to strong support in the black precincts, Harold Washington won 7,705 votes (42 percent) in the 1983 Democratic primary, to 7,539 (41 percent) for (Roti-backed) Jane Byrne and 3,210 (17 percent) for Richard Daley.

Byrne did well in predominantly Hispanic, Italian, and upper-income neighborhoods, plus winning by resounding margins in Chinatown (Washington got a total of only 5 votes in two Chinatown precincts). But overwhelming Washington votes in the black precincts (including a 478-vote plurality in the Near South Side 13th Precinct) spelled the difference for a Washington victory.

Washington, aided by the Democratic label, easily carried the ward in the general election, 13,033 votes (63 percent) to 7,782 for Republican Bernard Epton.

Byrne retained her strength in the Italian and upper-income areas in the 1987 Democratic primary. Washington made some gains in Chinatown and held his opponent to single-digit totals in the Valley, to win 59 percent of the vote. The mayor kept a similar percentage in the general election against Ed Vrdolyak and Don Haider.

CENSUS DATA: Population (1980): 61,716. 27.50 percent white, 43.22 percent black, 18.85 percent Hispanic, 10.43 percent Asian and other. Voting age population: 35.69 percent white, 36.82 percent black, 16.23 percent Hispanic, 11.26 percent Asian and other.

CENSUS TRACTS: See ward map.

COMMUNITY NEWSPAPERS:
Bridgeport News, 3252 S. Halsted (927–3118)
Chicago Metro News, 2600 S. Michigan (842–5950)
Downtown and Lakeshore News, 17 E. Monroe (346–6884)

Near North News, 26 E. Huron (787–2667)
Near West Side Gazette, 1335 W. Harrison (243–4288)
New City, 161 W. Harrison (663–4685)
North Loop News, 800 N. Clark (787–5396)
South Loop News, 711 S. Dearborn (922–4168)

ALDERMAN: Fred B. Roti. Elected 1968. Born December 18, 1920. Career:
B.A., DePaul University; state senator, 1951–57; inspector, Department of
Sewers, 1957–68.
Committees: Buildings (chairman); Budget and Government Operations; Com-
mittees, Rules, Municipal Code Revision, and Ethics; Finance; License;
Traffic Control and Safety; Zoning.
City hall telephone: 744–3063, 744–3074.
Ward office: 100 N. LaSalle (236–2792).
1987 election:
Fred B. Roti, unopposed.

DEMOCRATIC COMMITTEEMAN: John D'Arco. Elected 1951. Born March 27, 1912.
Career: state representative, 1945–51; alderman, 1951–63.
Ward office: 100 N. LaSalle (236–2792).
1984 election:
John D'Arco, unopposed.

MAYORAL ELECTIONS:

1983 Democratic primary:

Harold Washington	7,705	(42%)
Jane Byrne	7,539	(41%)
Richard Daley	3,210	(17%)

1983 general:

Harold Washington	13,033	(63%)
Bernard Epton	7,782	(37%)

1987 Democratic primary:

Harold Washington	11,926	(59%)
Jane Byrne	8,368	(41%)

1987 general:

Harold Washington	12,179	(60%)
Edward Vrdolyak	7,245	(36%)
Donald Haider	977	(5%)

$\mathcal{2}$nd Ward

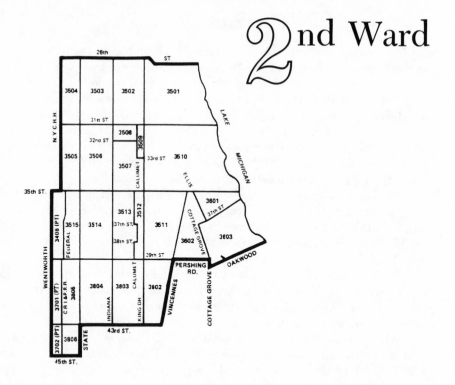

WHEN HAROLD WASHINGTON declared his election victory on April 12, 1983, it climaxed a revolution in black Chicago politics. That revolution began fifty years ago in the Near South Side's 2nd Ward.

The 2nd Ward is the heart of the area once called "Bronzeville"—a strip extending south from Roosevelt Road to 43rd Street and from Cottage Grove Avenue west to the present-day Dan Ryan Expressway. It was the first major black urban center in the United States. If Bronzeville was an appropriate cradle for a black revolution, its first hero was an unlikely one—a peg-legged politician named William Levi Dawson.

There were black politicians in Chicago before Dawson. Oscar DePriest in 1915 became the first black Chicago alderman and later the first northern black elected to Congress. Arthur Mitchell succeeded him in 1934. But Dawson was the first black to carve a local political empire.

Known by some as "the Booker T. Washington of Chicago Politics," Dawson believed in working within the system. It was an approach that served him and his constituents well. Black leaders point with pride that Dawson got his people into city and post office jobs which created the base for a black middle class.

Those same leaders will admit, if pressed on the issue, that Dawson controlled the South Side's lucrative policy racket. As a lawyer, he frequently defended gamblers prominent in the numbers game. He might have been a hero, but few called Dawson a saint.

Nonetheless, he rose to a position of power unmatched at that time by any black man in the United States. Originally a Republican, Dawson switched to the Democrats in the 1930s. He served in Congress from 1942 until his death in 1970. More important, he became 2nd Ward committeeman and undisputed boss of black politics in Chicago. He was seen as one of the kingmakers who helped put Richard J. Daley on the mayor's throne in 1955.

Dawson relished his leadership role. Friday nights he convened "Dawson College," meetings of the city's black political leaders, at his headquarters. He often ended his speeches with "Walk along, little children, and don't you worry, 'cause there's a big camp meeting at the end of the road."

The results Dawson produced on election day proved that he was worth every penny thrown in his direction. Time after time he delivered huge South Side pluralities in the five wards (2nd, 3rd, 4th, 6th, 20th) he controlled. In 1963, the black vote generated by Dawson gave Daley his victory over Republican Ben Adamowski.

But was Dawson really all that powerful? Probably not. He fought for patronage jobs but never civil rights. He was careful never to overstep his boundaries with higher-ranking Democratic leaders. To use the language of his time, Dawson knew his place.

What powers he had were eroded when Daley took over. The new mayor centralized all patronage, making himself (not Dawson) the one who would decide which blacks got city jobs. He installed Ralph Metcalfe as 3rd Ward committeeman over Dawson's bitter objections.

Daley in the early 1960s built Lake Meadows and Prairie Shores, middle-class high-rise complexes, and expanded the Illinois Institute of Technology— moves which displaced hundreds of middle-class black residents. William Harvey, the ward's alderman, fought the displacement. Dawson did nothing.

Longtime alderman Harvey won a seat on the county board in 1968. Former social worker Fred Hubbard succeeded him as the result of a special election the following year. Hubbard was elected as an independent but wasted no time in joining the party regulars.

Two years later Hubbard disappeared, taking $100,000 in federal job funds and leaving behind a string of gambling debts. He was caught, served a prison term, and kept a low profile until 1986, when he was arrested for allegedly propositioning a thirteen-year-old girl at a school where he was teaching under an assumed name.

William "Butch" Barnett, a glorified coatholder under Dawson, warmed the council seat from 1972 until 1983. He was replaced by a man of vividly contrasting background. Dawson might have turned over in his grave had he seen who won the 1983 aldermanic election—Bobby Rush, formerly a director of the Black Panthers.

Barnett and Rush were the two leaders in the seven-person field. Barnett and the regulars controlled the vote in the poverty-ridden Stateway Gardens, Robert Taylor Homes, and other southern precincts. Rush captured pluralities in Lake Meadows and Prairie Shores with large enough margins to force a runoff.

Rush took the runoff handily, thanks to the coattails of Harold Washington. He gained fifty or more votes over his February showing in all but three precincts. Barnett, on the other hand, lost votes in sixteen precincts despite a much less crowded field. A year later, Rush won the rubber match, easily defeating Barnett for Democratic committeeman. The two met again in the 1987 aldermanic election. Although Barnett maintained strength in the high rises, Rush defeated him and three others with 55 percent of the vote.

Much has been made of Rush's Black-Panther-in-a-Three-Piece-Suit image, but in fact Rush has been anything but strident on the council floor. He generally is considered an effective representative of his community and one of the council's few real reformers.

That concern may show itself in the Energy and Environmental Protection Committee, which Rush now chairs (he took control after former chairman Michael Nardulli chose not to seek reelection in the 1986 special election). Rush has proposed a new city Department of Energy and Environmental Control to handle matters such as hazardous waste disposal on the Southeast Side.

Rush's 2nd Ward is one of the poorest in the city, if not the poorest. It is the site of 38 percent of all the public housing in the city. The relative affluence of middle-class high rises in the northeastern quadrant is more than balanced by the poverty of the ward's west side.

Such poverty is visible to anyone driving along the Dan Ryan Expressway, which for all practical purposes is the ward's western boundary. Building after building of graffiti-marred high rises, the Stateway Gardens (35th Street to Pershing Road) and the northern buildings of the Robert Taylor Homes form the southwestern part of the ward. Another CHA project, the low-rise Dearborn Homes, makes up the northwest corner. Between the CHA complexes lies the Illinois Institute of Technology.

Michigan, Indiana, Prairie, and Calumet avenues form the center of the ward. These streets, along with King Drive, are broad and spacious, a reminder of the days when they were the home of the (white) wealthy. At one time large houses dominated the area. Now the 2nd has one of the lowest percentages of single-family dwellings of any ward.

One of the streets retains its earlier elegance. Calumet Avenue between 31st and 33rd, an area known as "The Gap," is home to a growing number of young black professionals.

Stately Olivet Baptist Church at 31st and King Drive stands as a monument to the ward's racial history. In 1919 a major race riot occurred when a black swimmer accidentally crossed from the 27th Street (black) to the 29th Street (white) beach and was pelted with stones by white bathers. Olivet Church, which had the largest black congregation in the city, aided riot victims and helped bring peace to the area. Ironically, the beaches are near what is now the only integrated part of the ward.

A more ironic racial monument also lies within the 2nd Ward. Stephen A. Douglas, "The Little Giant," is buried at 35th Street and Lake Park Avenue, near what was once his estate. Douglas, best remembered for his debates against

Abraham Lincoln, authored the 1854 Kansas-Nebraska Act, which allowed the spread of slavery into those territories.

REDISTRICTING. The 2nd Ward's boundaries were not altered by the 1986 remap.

MAYORAL. Harold Washington won the 2nd Ward with an overwhelming 80 percent of the vote in the 1983 primary. Jane Byrne, running with the support of Barnett, limped home a poor second with 3,244 votes (16 percent); only in one South Commons precinct and one Taylor Homes precinct did she gain 100 votes. Richard Daley, with 803 votes (4 percent), finished a distant third.

Incredible though it may seem, Washington captured 98 percent of the vote here in the general election, yet ten wards gave him higher percentages. Republican Bernard Epton got more than 100 votes in the only precincts (33 and 48) with significant white populations, yet Washington amassed more than 300 votes in each of those precincts. Elsewhere, Epton reached double figures in only seven other precincts.

Washington captured 98 percent of the vote in both the primary and general elections of 1987. His opponents got most of their votes in the integrated precincts.

CENSUS DATA: Population (1980): 60,141. 5.90 percent white, 91.90 percent black, .77 percent Hispanic, 1.43 percent Asian and other. Voting age population: 8.72 percent white, 87.87 percent black, .70 percent Hispanic, 2.51 percent Asian and other.

CENSUS TRACTS: See ward map.

COMMUNITY NEWSPAPERS:
  Chicago Independent Bulletin, 2037 W. 95th (783–1040)
  Chicago Metro News, 2600 S. Michigan (842–5950)

ALDERMAN: Bobby Rush. Elected 1983. Born November 23, 1946. Career: B.A., Roosevelt University, 1974; insurance agent, Prudential Insurance Co.; associate Dean, Daniel Hale Williams University; financial planner, Sanmar Financial Planning Corp.
Committees: Energy, Environmental Protection, and Public Utilities (chairman); Aviation; Budget and Government Operations; Capital Development; Historical Landmark Preservation; Finance; Human Rights and Consumer Protection; Intergovernmental Relations; License; Ports, Wharves, and Bridges.
City hall telephone: 744–6836, 744–9867.

Ward office: 3426 S. Martin Luther King Dr. (225–3444).
1987 election:

Bobby Rush	9,989 (55%)	Jeffery L. Roberts	1,501	(8%)
William Barnett	3,991 (22%)	Deotis Taylor	386	(2%)
Jerry D. Brown	2,295 (13%)			

DEMOCRATIC COMMITTEEMAN: Bobby Rush. Elected 1984.
1984 election:

Bobby Rush	8,292 (64%)
William Barnett	4,609 (36%)

MAYORAL ELECTIONS:

1983 Democratic primary:

Harold Washington	12,608 (80%)
Jane Byrne	3,244 (16%)
Richard Daley	803 (4%)

1987 Democratic primary:

Harold Washington	19,100 (97%)
Jane Byrne	492 (3%)

1983 general:

Harold Washington	22,749 (98%)
Bernard Epton	558 (2%)

1987 general:

Harold Washington	20,018 (98%)
Edward Vrdolyak	296 (1%)
Donald Haider	194 (1%)

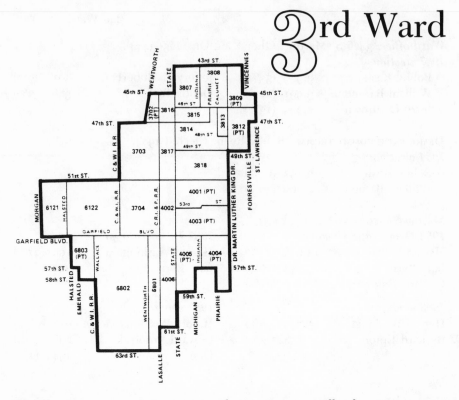

HIGH-RISE APARTMENT BUILDINGS that serve as unofficial prisons, over-crowded schools which fail to teach, commercial strips filled up with boarded-up buildings or taverns, ramshackle houses—these are the images that many whites have of black Chicago. It is a misleading picture when applied to much of the South Side. Unfortunately, much of it is accurate when describing the 3rd Ward.

Chicago's most impoverished community lives within the twenty-eight high-rise buildings known as the Robert Taylor Homes. The graffiti and scorches outside the buildings describe the squalor that lies within. From their inception in the 1950s, the Robert Taylor Homes and other high-rise public housing projects had their critics. Yet both white and black politicians favored them—whites because the high rises helped keep blacks out of their wards, blacks because they provided concentrations of easily controllable votes.

Roosevelt University urbanologist Pierre deVise, in a 1984 report, claimed that ten of the sixteen poorest neighborhoods in the United States are located in Chicago Housing Authority projects. Three of the four poorest are divisions of the Taylor Homes located in the 3rd Ward.

Mid-South Taylor Homes (from 47th to 51st Street), with a per capita income of $1,339, is the neighborhood deVise claims is the poorest in the nation. Eighty percent of the residents live below the poverty line, most in female-headed households. Nor is the poverty cycle likely to be broken soon. More than half of the residents of 3rd Ward Taylor apartments are children under fifteen years of age.

Those children most likely will go to DuSable High School at 49th and Wabash, a school which produces some of the lowest test scores in the city. The 1984 senior class tested in the 21st percentile in math. Other classes that year failed to attain even the 20th percentile in either reading or math tests. One student in eight dropped out of DuSable during the 1984–85 school year, most of them pregnant girls. DuSable moved to cut its teen pregnancy rate in 1985 and gained nationwide attention. The school offered contraceptives from its clinic, an action which attracted protests from Right to Life activists.

If the Taylor Homes are the most visible examples of 3rd Ward poverty, they are not the only ones. East of the Dan Ryan Expressway (which roughly bisects the ward), areas that years ago were delightful now are destitute. In many blocks, vacant lots outnumber developed ones.

At the turn of the century, 47th Street near Grand Boulevard (now Martin Luther King Drive) was one of the centers of Jewish society. By the mid-1920s, blacks had moved in and made the Grand Boulevard area the city's most important black business and entertainment center, "the Harlem of Chicago." Grand Boulevard began deteriorating in the 1940s and has never been the same.

Today 47th Street is a collection of flea markets, pawn shops, wig and discount clothing stores, fast food outlets, and taverns. Near King Drive most of the stores are closed, boarded, or barred. The Met Theatre at 46th and King bills itself as "where the good pictures play," although it appears that no pictures, good or bad, have played there for years.

The 51st Street business strip is similar to 47th Street, although not quite as busy. A new shopping center at Wentworth and Garfield may perk up the southeastern part of the ward, where the major industry appears to be storefront religion.

Is it any wonder that this area is a worldwide capital of the blues? The legendary Checkerboard Lounge (423 E. 43rd St.) is located in the 3rd Ward— along a stretch of 43rd Street also named Muddy Waters Drive, after the late, beloved Chicago bluesman.

To be fair, the east side of the ward is not entirely depressing. King Drive, thanks to the beautification efforts of Alderman Dorothy Tillman, is a positive example of what cleanup programs can accomplish. Michigan Avenue in the southern part of the ward is an impressive boulevard with three-story brownstone and graystone buildings, the closest thing the ward has to elegance. The George Cleveland Hall branch library at 48th and Michigan is one of the most attractive in the city. The 5500 block of Perry contains colorfully painted frame houses; it is one of the few isolated bright spots in the ward.

Another bright spot, for a different reason, is at 46th and State—Parker House Sausage Company, one of the largest black-owned businesses in the city. Three blocks away is another site of importance in the black community—the headquarters of the Urban League at 45th and Michigan.

West of the expressway, the ward takes on a different character. Frame houses there look like those of many other cities (this area was not subject to the city fire codes enacted after the 1871 fire and thus not required to have fireproof housing). The homes are plain but livable, rundown but hardly blown out, weary but not dead.

Ralph Metcalfe once ruled this ward. A South Side athletic hero (he finished second in the 100-meter dash in the 1936 Olympic games—only a fraction behind winner Jesse Owens), he served as alderman before being elected to Congress in 1970, after William Dawson's death.

Even though Dawson and Metcalfe led neighboring wards, there was no love lost between them. Richard Daley handpicked Metcalfe to replace Dawson's man as committeeman in 1952. Three years later Metcalfe became alderman.

Metcalfe had one attribute Daley especially liked—his Catholicism. Daley chose Catholics as his black ward leaders. Corpus Christi Parish (49th and King Drive) was the major black proving ground during the Daley years.

Dawson opposed the Metcalfe appointment for several reasons. His public one was Metcalfe's political inexperience (Metcalfe had been working as a hotel manager). But Dawson also feared Metcalfe as a potential rival. Metcalfe had his own (athletic) popularity base. He did not come up through Dawson's organization and had only marginal ties to the congressman. Open rivalry never came about, but Metcalfe remained Daley's, not Dawson's, man.

Years later, in 1972, Metcalfe broke with Daley. Two prominent South Side dentists, one of them Metcalfe's finance chairman, were beaten up by police. An irate Metcalfe demanded that Daley meet with him in his (Metcalfe's) office. The mayor refused. Metcalfe extracted his revenge in the November elections by leading a black revolt against Democratic candidates. As a result, the Democratic state's attorney nominee lost to Republican Bernard Carey, and Republican Senator Charles Percy outpolled challenger Roman Pucinski.

The rebellion was anything but typical for Metcalfe, for years a solid organization man. In the 1963 election, he carried his ward for Daley over Benjamin Adamowski by 18,852 votes—the largest plurality in the city. Metcalfe behaved more like a ward boss than a reformer. He operated the Democrat Club, reportedly *the* gambling place on the South Side. His office was located above the club. Since the Democrat Club was a members-only key club, a constituent had to pay in order to see the alderman.

A young lawyer named Harold Washington worked for Metcalfe as a precinct captain and won praise for his organization of a Young Democrats group. Metcalfe slated him for a state representative job in Springfield—perhaps as a boot upstairs to get a possible challenger out of the way.

Tyrone Kenner replaced Metcalfe as alderman in 1971 and took over as committeeman upon Metcalfe's death in 1978. A former policeman, Kenner made no pretense of reform.

Kenner took over the real power even before Metcalfe died. Metcalfe in 1975 supported independent Alderman William Singer for mayor, while Kenner stuck with Daley. The victorious Daley afterward gave Kenner the ward's patronage powers, leaving Metcalfe as party head in name only.

Not even the specter of extortion charges was enough to defeat Kenner in 1983, as he bested civil rights activist Dorothy Tillman and Washington aide Sam Patch. Kenner escaped a runoff by 134 votes. The victory was not enough to keep Kenner out of trouble, though. He was convicted in May 1983 of extortion, mail fraud, conspiracy, and obstruction of justice. Mayor Washington nominated Tillman to replace him.

That nomination became one of the more heated battles of the stormy early Council Wars. Alderman Bernard Stone refused to support Tillman because she once allegedly called him an obscene name. When Washington submitted the nomination he described her as an "alderwoman." Rules Committee chairman Frank Stemberk refused to accept the nomination because there is no such word as "alderwoman."

Tillman, with Washington backing, won a convincing victory in the 1984 Democratic committeeman election. Party regulars finally yielded on the appointment and confirmed Tillman in May 1984.

The 1985 special aldermanic election was supposed to be a routine Tillman ratification, but an incident shortly beforehand turned it into a major Washington electoral and psychological victory. Washington invited one of Tillman's eight opponents, James "Skip" Burrell, to his apartment three weeks before the election and asked Burrell to withdraw from the race. During the conversation, the mayor made disparaging remarks about Tillman.

Burrell, a precinct captain under Kenner, taped the conversation, reportedly for evidence if the mayor offered him anything to leave the race. Washington made no such offer. Somehow (no one has ever claimed blame or credit) the tape made its way to the *Tribune*, which published excerpts and later, the entire conversation. If the intention of the tape provider was to embarrass the mayor, it produced the opposite effect. Public sympathy fell behind the mayor (presumably people felt that everyone, even a mayor, has the right not to be recorded in the privacy of his own home).

Tillman's opponents in the special election included such worthies as Burrell, storefront minister M. Earle Sardon, real estate agent and "buppie" (black yuppie) Johnnie Gettings, and Philander S. Neville, Jr., attorney and self-proclaimed "problem buster." She outpolled them with 81 percent of the vote.

Burrell was indicted on felony eavesdropping charges but died in May 1986 before he could go to trial.

Alderman Dorothy Tillman is known for two things: her hats (she is always seen wearing one of more than two hundred that she owns) and her aggressive defense of the Washington administration (when an opposition-bloc alderman suggested that Washington signed his political death warrant by approving a property tax increase, Tillman retorted, "He'll be around next year, but a lot of you won't!") After Washington's death she remained equally outspoken for neighboring alderman Tim Evans as the rightful heir to the Washington legacy.

Two persons challenged Tillman in 1987 including former state representative Jerry Washingon, a Kenner ally. She rolled over them by at least a four-to-one margin in every precinct.

REDISTRICTING: Two precincts at the western end of the ward were removed from the 11th Ward and added to the 3rd as a result of the 1986 remap.

MAYORAL: Harold Washington won a landslide victory (84 percent of the vote) in the 1983 Democratic primary, winning every precinct. Jane Byrne scored 13 percent (but no more than eighty-seven votes in any precinct). Richard Daley won 3 percent—a tie for his lowest percentage in the city.

Washington took a near-unanimous victory, 99.1 percent, in the general election. Republican Bernard Epton received so little support that Socialist Workers party candidate Ed Warren beat him in three precincts and tied him in seven others.

In 1987, Washington again won 99 percent in both primary and general elections, Even Byrne, considered to be his strongest foe, failed to attain ten votes in any precinct.

CENSUS DATA: Population (1980): 60,207. .42 percent white, 99.20 percent black, .80 percent Hispanic. Voting age population: .36 percent white, 99.51 percent black, .56 percent Hispanic.

CENSUS TRACTS: See ward map.

COMMUNITY NEWSPAPERS:
Bridgeport News, 3252 S. Halsted (927–3118)
Chicago Independent Bulletin, 2037 W. 95th St. (783–1040)
Chicago Metro, 2600 S. Michigan (842–9590)

ALDERMAN: Dorothy J. Tillman. Appointed 1984, elected 1985. Born 1948. Career: civil rights worker, community organizer.
Committees: Housing (chairman): Budget and Government Operations; Claims and Liabilities; Economic Development; Education; Finance; Human Rights and Consumer Protection; Land Acquisition, Disposition, and Leases; Traffic Control and Safety; Zoning.
City hall telephone: 744–0584, 744–0585.
Ward office: 4650 S. Martin Luther King Dr. (373–3228).
1985 special election:

Dorothy J. Tillman	7,883	(81%)	Jackie Brown	113	(1%)
James "Skip" Burrell	788	(8%)	Ella Evans	88	(1%)
M. Earle Sardon	444	(5%)	Robert A. Palmer	69	(1%)
Philander S. Neville, Jr.	188	(2%)	Marlene Copeland	55	(1%)
Johnnie B. Gettings	157	(2%)			

1987 election:
Dorothy J. Tillman   13,498   (79%)
Jerry Washington   2,713   (16%)
Cleaophas Ingram   855   (5%)

DEMOCRATIC COMMITTEEMAN: Dorothy J. Tillman. Elected 1984.
1984 election:
Dorothy J. Tillman   7,166   (64%)
Tyrone T. Kenner   3,148   (28%)
Myron C. Meredith   904   (8%)

MAYORAL ELECTIONS:

1983 Democratic primary:
Harold Washington   17,068   (84%)
Jane Byrne   2,613   (13%)
Richard Daley   672   (3%)

1983 general:
Harold Washington   24,472   (99%)
Bernard Epton   178   (1%)

1987 Democratic primary:
Harold Washington   19,914   (99%)
Jane Byrne   232   (1%)

1987 general:
Harold Washington   20,769   (99%)
Edward Vrdolyak   113   (1%)
Donald Haider   100   (0%)

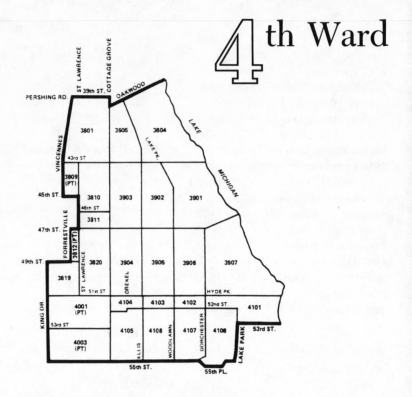

ALDERMAN CLAUDE HOLMAN was a city hall legend. At almost any time, Holman was liable to stand up and shout, "God bless Richard J. Daley, the greatest mayor in the history of the world, the best friend the black man ever had," or words to that effect. The man now serving as 4th Ward alderman also thought the incumbent mayor was the best friend the black man ever had in city hall. This alderman is Timothy Evans, who served as city council floor leader for Mayor Harold Washington.

Both aldermen's fates are ironic. Holman, originally selected because of his blue-ribbon credentials, devolved into little more than a buffoon. He became one of the "Silent Six," black aldermen who refused to criticize the ruling Democratic organization, Evans, considered a puppet during Daley years, became the point man for Washington and led the charge against many of his former allies during Washington's first term.

Holman first gained attention as an attorney representing workers in a dispute with International Harvester Corporation. Daley picked Holman in 1955 to run the ward, which was then half white. The poorer precincts in the north always went with the machine, but Daley wanted someone with a good reputation to appease the ward's white voters.

There was no love lost between 2nd Ward boss William Dawson and Holman. Dawson correctly saw the Holman selection as yet another attempt by Daley to dilute his South Side empire. Dawson went to the Democratic

Central Committee and asked that Holman's patronage powers be stripped. The committee refused the request.

Holman died in the spring of 1973. Evans, then an assistant corporation counsel, won the election to succeed him that November. The ward's precinct captains pushed for Evans as alderman and Ward Superintendent Frederick McVoy as committeeman. Daley vetoed the McVoy selection and placed Evans in both posts.

Evans slipped almost unnoticed through the Daley, Bilandic, and Byrne years. He was accused of being more interested in his private law practice than his city council duties. Despite his tenure, Evans was forced into a runoff in 1983. He carried the machine-oriented northern precincts by the expected large margins. But schoolteacher Toni Preckwinkle, attorney Michael Smith, and five other candidates made inroads into southern Hyde Park and Kenwood precincts. Preckwinkle carried traditionally independent Hyde Park precincts in the runoff, but Evans more than balanced that edge with strong showings in the northern precincts. He won, 11,203 to 8,503.

With the Harold Washington election, Timothy Evans became a "born-again" reformer. Whether this newfound independence stemmed from a genuine inclination toward reform that was bottled up during the previous administrations, or whether it came from supporting the group with the upper hand, is not known. Preckwinkle supporters claimed the latter and made another run at Evans in 1987, a race that also included free-lance writer Excell Jones. The Independent Voters of Illinois backed their 4th Ward officer. Washington did not discourage Preckwinkle's candidacy, believing that a hot aldermanic race would spur voting in the mayoral primary. It wasn't close. Preckwinkle carried one Hyde Park precinct and did well in a few others, but Evans scored lopsided wins in the rest of the ward.

Washington bypassed more experienced black aldermen to make Evans his right-hand man. Evans was relatively young, articulate, and telegenic—three qualities which may have explained the late mayor's choice.

After the 1986 special elections, Evans was a logical choice to assume the chair of the council's important Finance Committee. Some Washington allies, however, balked at removing Washington nemesis Edward Burke from that post. Instead, a new Budget Committee was created which assumed most of Finance's power. Evans headed that committee.

Evans and fellow Washington ally Lawrence Bloom now hold the two most important council committee chairs, Evans at Finance and Bloom at Budget. Each serves as vice-chairman of the other's committee, although their loyalty to Harold Washington greatly exceeded their love for each other.

Because of his leadership in the council, Evans was viewed as the heir apparent to Washington among the "movement" blacks, Lakefront whites, and independent Hispanics who formed the heart of the Washington coalition. Even though all signs indicated Evans was the resounding choice of the black community to replace Washington as acting mayor, that apparent message was lost on six black aldermen who backed his rival, 6th Ward alderman Eugene Sawyer. Evans lost the city council election for acting mayor, 29–19. Had those six black votes (including Sawyer's) swung to Evans, he could have been elected mayor.

Evans all but declared his 1989 candidacy the night of his loss to Sawyer. Although others in the eventual Evans bloc (Danny Davis, Larry Bloom) entertained their own thoughts of becoming mayor, there appears little doubt that Evans will run in the upcoming special election and most likely will gain the support of erstwhile Washington backers.

His ambition leaves Evans in a city council dilemma. He remains in charge of Finance (Sawyer promised not to jostle council committees), and both he and Sawyer have sworn to continue what they perceive as the Washington agenda. But such cooperation cannot be comfortable for either of these once (and possibly future) antagonists.

The area Evans represents provides a sharper contrast between rich and poor than any other ward in the city, except perhaps the 42nd. No other ward has wealth and poverty in such proximity.

North of 47th Street, in the area known as Oakland, the ward is a continuation of the impoverished 2nd and 3rd Wards. The northwest corner, especially, is the type of area people leave in order to enter CHA high rises. Iron bars are standard furnishings on first and second-floor windows of the buildings that are occupied. Many other buildings are unoccupied, burned, and gutted.

Holy Angels Church at Oakwood and Vincennes was one of those buildings that burned. Prior to its 1986 destruction, Holy Angels was the largest black Catholic parish in the country. Its pastor, Rev. George Clements, gained nationwide fame by personally adopting three sons.

A different sort of "religious organization" is located a few blocks away, at Drexel and Oakwood—the El Rukns. A fortresslike Masjid Al Malik Temple serves as headquarters for the El Rukns, variously described as a Muslim sect, the city's largest street gang, or a full-fledged black mafia.

South of 47th Street and east of Cottage Grove, the ward becomes elegant. This is the Kenwood-Hyde Park area, which most people associate with the neighboring 5th Ward. In fact many of the precincts were part of the 5th Ward, redistricted by party regulars into the 4th in an unsuccessful attempt to dilute the power of independents.

Kenwood is the officially designated community east of Cottage Grove between 43rd and 51st Streets. The area south of 47th houses the single-family mansions that once were homes to Chicago's upper crust. Industrialists Gustavus Swift and Martin Ryerson lived in Kenwood. So did John G. Shedd (who donated the aquarium), poet Edgar Lee Masters, and architect Louis Sullivan.

Religion has always been a visible influence, and a walk through the ward shows the diversity: the K.A.M. Isaiah Israel Congregation at 51st and Greenwood, oldest Jewish congregation in Chicago; Muhammad Mosque at 47th and Woodlawn, two blocks north of onetime Black Muslim leader Elijah Muhammad's former home; the Church of the Latter Day Saints at 54th and University. Perhaps the most influential pulpit of recent years is at 50th and Drexel—

TIMOTHY C. EVANS

national headquarters of Operation PUSH, formerly directed by Rev. Jesse Jackson.

Kenwood south of 47th Street and the 4th Ward portion of Hyde Park are well integrated, but the area is especially recognized as a center of the black elite. Kenwood Academy at 51st (Hyde Park) and Harper, one of the finest public schools in the city, is located here. Nearby stands Provident Hospital (King Drive and 51st), the first black hospital in Chicago. Across the street from the hospital is Washington Park, which forms the southwest corner of the ward.

The southern part of the ward is the northern portion of Hyde Park, home of many University of Chicago students but little of the university itself. However, the 4th Ward includes the second "home" of many U of C types—Jimmy's Woodlawn Tap at 55th and Woodlawn, long renowned as a college watering hole and intellectual center.

REDISTRICTING: The 4th Ward was not affected by the 1986 remap.

MAYORAL: Harold Washington was an easy victor in the 4th Ward during the 1983 mayoral primary. He won pluralities in every precinct but the 30th (where he and Richard Daley each got 110 votes). Daley and Jane Byrne each received more than 100 votes in only two other precincts (the 38th and 45th), both also integrated Hyde Park precincts. Overall, Washington got 78 percent of the vote, to 13 for Byrne and 9 for Daley.

Likewise, Washington coasted to a 94 percent win in the general election. The Hyde Park 30th, 38th, and 45th (in which Washington eked out a 390–360 win) precincts were the only ones in which Bernard Epton received more than 100 votes.

Washington won every precinct in both primary and general elections in 1987, with opponents virtually shut out everywhere except Hyde Park. The mayor achieved nearly identical totals in both elections—19,720 in the primary, 19,766 in the general election.

CENSUS DATA: Population (1980): 60,051. 17.71 percent white, 79.01 percent black, 1.35 percent Hispanic, 1.93 percent Asian and other. Voting age population: 22.16 percent white, 74.56 percent black, 1.33 percent Hispanic, 1.95 percent Asian and other.

CENSUS TRACTS: See ward map.

COMMUNITY NEWSPAPERS:
Chicago Independent Bulletin, 2037 W. 95th St. (783–1040)
Chicago Metro News, 2600 S. Michigan (842–5950)
Chicago Spectator, 5454 S. South Shore (549–8288)
Hyde Park Herald, 5240 S. Harper (643–8533)
Observer, 1563 E. 63rd St. (493–0557)

ALDERMAN: Timothy C. Evans. Elected alderman 1973. Born June 1, 1943. Career: B.A., University of Illinois, 1965; J.D., John Marshall Law School, 1969; assistant corporation counsel, 1969–71; deputy commissioner, Chicago Department of Investigations; chief hearing officer, Cook County, Illinois Secretary of State office, 1973.
Committees: Finance (chairman); Budget and Government Operations (vice-chairman); Committees, Rules, Municipal Code Revision, and Ethics; Capital Development; Housing; Land Acquisition, Disposition, and Leases; Municipal Code Revision; Zoning.
City hall telephone: 744–3380, 744–3381.
Ward office: 4759 S. Cottage Grove (373–5965).
1987 election:
Timothy C. Evans   15,027 (77%)
Toni Preckwinkel   4,113 (21%)
Excell M. Jones   397   (2%)

DEMOCRATIC COMMITTEEMAN: Timothy C. Evans. Elected 1973.
1984 election:
Timothy C. Evans, unopposed.

MAYORAL ELECTIONS:

1983 Democratic primary:

Harold Washington	17,927	(78%)
Jane Byrne	3,112	(13%)
Richard Daley	1,961	(9%)

1983 general:

Harold Washington	24,278	(93%)
Bernard Epton	1,984	(7%)

1987 Democratic primary:

Harold Washington	19,720	(95%)
Jane Byrne	981	(5%)

1987 general:

Harold Washington	19,766	(93%)
Edward Vrdolyak	946	(4%)
Donald Haider	540	(3%)

5th Ward

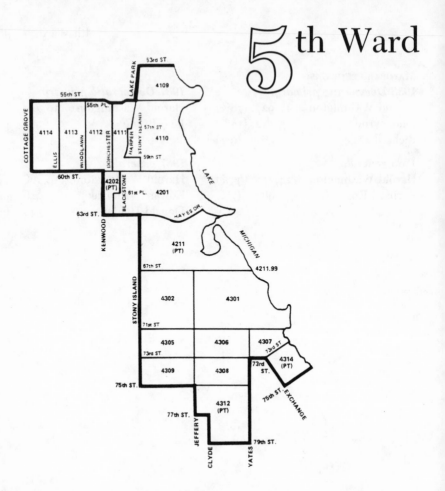

HYDE PARK BEGAN as a well-to-do suburb, named after the upper-class community of London. A developer named Paul Cornell created the area in the 1850s, centered around the Hyde Park House hotel at 53rd Street and the lake. The town, extending from 39th to 63rd Streets, was incorporated in 1861. Later, the southern boundary was extended to 138th Street, the current southern city limit.

Geographically, Hyde Park Township was annexed to the city in 1889. Politically, Hyde Park has never really joined the city. The community known as Hyde Park (51st to 60th Streets east of Cottage Grove) has long been an antimachine hotbed. Hyde Park's 5th Ward is synonymous with independent politics.

One contributing factor to the ward's nontraditional political outlook (at least nontraditional by Chicago standards) is the University of Chicago. An ivory-tower village in the City of the Big Shoulders, the University of Chicago dominates the local scene. The large, Gothic Rockefeller Chapel at 58th and Woodlawn (named after John D. Rockefeller, the school's patron) and Gothic/Tudor-style Cobb Hall at 58th and Ellis are the largest buildings, most visible from the boulevard known as the Midway Plaisance. More than physically imposing, the university is undeniably one of the intellectual centers of the United States, home to fifty-three Nobel Prize winners.

But one University of Chicago accomplishment overshadows all others. Scientist Enrico Fermi in 1942 produced the first controlled chain reaction. It took place under the stands of the old Stagg Field football stadium, near the present Regenstein Library.

That Stagg Field is not the current playing grounds at 55th and Cottage Grove. The University of Chicago was at one time a Big Ten football power, producing stars such as the first Heisman Trophy (1935) winner, Jay Berwanger. But university president Robert Maynard Hutchins considered sports frivolous and dismantled the football program overnight. The school plays intercollegiate football now—against Lake Forest and Ripon Colleges, not Michigan and Ohio State.

The university also has had an impact on its neighbors, with actions not universally praised. The school in the 1950s and 1960s bought up surrounding land and demolished many of the buildings, thus forming a buffer between itself and an encroaching black population. That action, while criticized by many, deterred white flight and may have helped preserve Hyde Park as the most integrated community in Chicago. Statistics, however, are deceptive. While the community as a whole is 31 percent black, the areas around the university are almost 90 percent white.

Hyde Park is more than the university. Blocks around the school feature an outdoor museum of American architecture, highlighted by Frank Lloyd Wright's Robie House at 58th and Woodlawn. The Del Prado Apartments (formerly Hyde Park Hotel) lie on the northern boundary of the ward. At one time this was an overnight resting place for the wealthy. Nearby is Hampton House Condominium, which boasted a most notable resident—Mayor Harold Washington.

A different, and more unusual, set of "residents" also call Hyde Park home—South American parrots apparently brought up to Chicago by a local resident and later released. The birds have adapted to the Chicago climate and now live near 53rd and Lake Shore Drive.

The 5th Ward takes in more than Hyde Park. Its Jackson Park played host to the 1893 Columbian Exposition, a world's fair of a magnitude scarcely imaginable today. Patrons rode on Mr. Ferris's giant wheel and gaped at the raciness of exotic dancer Little Egypt. Only one building remains from the fair's "White City." The Fine Arts Palace served as the original home of the Field Museum until that museum moved to Grant Park. Now the building houses the Museum of Science and Industry at 57th and Lake Shore Drive—Chicago's most visited tourist attraction.

South of sprawling Jackson Park, the ward also takes in South Shore all the way to 79th Street—an area once heavily Jewish but now almost entirely black. At one time graceful, South Shore underwent a period of decay after the massive white flight of the 1960s. Now it appears to be on the way back up. The once-grand South Shore Country Club has been refurbished and sold to the Chicago Park District. South Shore Bank at 71st and Jeffrey by reinvesting in the community has spearheaded local renovation.

All of Hyde Park used to be in the 5th Ward. But the community was split down the middle after the 1981 redistricting. It was a blatant attempt by party regulars to dilute the white vote and spell defeat for white independent Larry Bloom by putting him into an overwhelmingly black ward.

The ploy didn't work. Bloom ran in 1983 against six blacks (including machine-backed Frank Bacon and redistricted 7th Ward incumbent Joseph Bertrand) and one white opponent (Lyndon LaRouche supporter Robert Moon). He won handily with 64 percent of the vote. A firm Harold Washington ally, Bloom was the first aldermanic candidate endorsed by the mayor in the 1987 election. That quick backing might have scared off would-be challengers; Bloom ran unopposed. Bloom is successful because he goes out of his way to represent all of the ward. Although a Hyde Park lawyer, he maintains his ward office at 71st and Clyde—in the black South Shore section of the ward.

Larry Bloom is the latest in a long string of liberal independent 5th Ward aldermen. It is a chain that goes all the way back to Paul Douglas in the 1940s. The intellectual Douglas was hardly a favorite among his city hall brethren. When at age fifty-one he volunteered for Marine combat duty as a private, 43rd Ward alderman Paddy Bauler shouted, "Good riddance to bad rubbish!"

Democratic party chairman Jacob Arvey made a surprising move in 1948 by slating Douglas for the Senate. He was part of a "blue-ribbon ticket," expected to lose handily to Republican incumbent C. Wayland Brooks as Republican Thomas Dewey was predicted to oust President Harry Truman.

Tribune headlines ("Dewey Defeats Truman" in the early editions) notwithstanding, both Truman and Douglas won their elections. If Chicago Democratic party leaders were not enthused by having Douglas in the Senate, at least they had the consolation of having the maverick alderman out of the city council.

Douglas was replaced by Robert Merriam, another independent, who helped create a crime investigation committee in the city council. Merriam is best remembered as Richard Daley's first mayoral opponent. A lifelong Democrat, Merriam nonetheless opposed Daley as a Republican in 1955. Strange as it may seem now, he put up a creditable fight; Daley's win was no sure thing. Merriam carried the middle- and high-income wards (twenty-one in all) and won 581,255 votes. Daley took that election with 708,222 votes. The new mayor was so pleased by that victory that he ordered license plate number 708222 for the rest of his life.

The most legendary of 5th Ward aldermen, Leon Despres, succeeded Merriam. Despres spent his entire aldermanic career as an outspoken Daley foe, and most of those years as the council's lone independent. As a result, he frequently found himself on the short end of forty-nine-to-one votes.

This is not to say that Despres never got results from his proposals. Daley at times liked Despres's ideas. When he did, the Despres resolution would be outvoted. The same resolution, slightly reworded, would be introduced afterwards by Daley floor leader Tom Keane, and would pass overwhelmingly.

Harold Washington was more respectful of Despres. The former alderman now serves as city council parliamentarian.

Ross Lathrop succeeded Despres and served only one term. He and Lakefront aldermen Martin Oberman and Dick Simpson served as the only voices of protest against Daley and successor Michael Bilandic in the mid-1970s.

The 5th Ward also boasts the most unlikely of Democratic committeemen—a research chemist named Alan Mora Dobry. A veteran of the Independent Voters of Illinois-Independent Precinct Organization, Dobry was first elected in 1976. Many of Dobry's ideas are not shared by his peers on the Democratic Central Committee. For example, he does not bother to maintain a ward office, out of the belief that the alderman is the people's elected legislative representative and thus the one to whom residents should take their problems.

Likewise, Dobry's platform is anathema to the typical ward committeeman. He calls for an end to patronage and slating of candidates, and a halt to funds for primary candidates—positions which have not endeared him to party regulars.

As an opponent of the patronage system, Dobry never handled the city jobs which were the committeeman's due; those were parceled out through other 5th Ward Democrats. Such a deprivation has made no difference at election time. Dobry has proven so popular that party regulars did not even bother to oppose him in 1984.

REDISTRICTING: The 5th Ward was unchanged by the 1986 redistricting.

MAYORAL: Over the years, the 5th Ward has been the one least likely to vote for a machine candidate. Even liberal Democrat-turned-Republican Richard Friedman carried the ward in 1971—one of only two wards Friedman won. William Singer took the ward in the 1975 Democratic primary. Two years later, Harold Washington beat incumbent Michael Bilandic in the primary. Bilandic also lost here in 1979 against Jane Byrne in the primary.

The 5th Ward supported its former state representative, state senator, and congressman in the 1983 Democratic primary. Harold Washington carried it easily, with 77 percent of the vote. Byrne got 13 percent and Richard Daley 10 percent, their votes coming mainly from Hyde Park. One precinct, the high-rise 24th located across from the Museum of Science and Industry, split the vote almost evenly among the candidates: 135 for Daley, 118 for Washington, and 105 for Byrne.

The general election was an unexpected confrontation: Hyde Parker Harold Washington and former Hyde Parker Bernard Epton pitted against each other. Epton, a state representative from Hyde Park during the years of cumulative balloting, certainly was no stranger to 5th Ward residents. Yet Washington swamped him, taking 91 percent of the vote. Epton failed to carry a precinct but achieved respectable totals in the Hyde Park community.

It was an ironic loss for Epton. Generally considered to be a moderate to liberal Republican, he was thrust into the role of "white ethnic" candidate in an election heavy with racial overtones. But had either Byrne or Daley won the Democratic primary, Epton would have run as the liberal indepen- dent candidate. Undoubtedly he would have carried the 5th Ward—and little else in the city.

Washington swept every precinct in the 1987 elections, with 95 percent of the vote in the primary and 92 percent in the general elections. His opponents did best in Hyde Park but not impressively anywhere.

CENSUS DATA: Population (1980): 60,215. 21.37 percent white, 75.36 percent black, .96 percent Hispanic, 2.31 percent Asian and other. Voting age popu- lation: 25.05 percent white, 71.87 percent black, 1.00 percent Hispanic, 2.08 percent Asian and other.

CENSUS TRACTS: See ward map.

COMMUNITY NEWSPAPERS:
  Chatham Citizen, 412 E. 87th St. (487–7700)
  Chicago Independent Bulletin, 2037 W. 95th St. (783–1040)
  Chicago Metro News, 2600 S. Michigan (842–5950)
  Chicago Spectator, 5454 S. South Shore (549–8288)
  Hyde Park Herald, 5240 S. Harper (643–8533)
  Observer, 1563 E. 63rd St. (493–0557)

ALDERMAN: Lawrence S. Bloom. Elected 1979. Born November 4, 1943. Career: B.A., University of Chicago, 1965; J.D., University of Chicago, 1968; attor- ney.
Committees: Budget and Government Operations (chairman); Finance (vice- chairman); Committees, Rules, Municipal Code Revision, and Ethics; His- torical Landmark Preservation; Housing; Intergovernmental Relations; Land Acquisition, Disposition, and Leases; Municipal Code Revision; Special Events and Cultural Affairs; Traffic Control and Safety.
City hall telephone: 744–6832, 744–3195.
Ward office: 2106 E. 71st St. (667–0900).
1987 election:
Lawrence S. Bloom, unopposed.

DEMOCRATIC COMMITTEEMAN: Alan Mora Dobry. Elected 1976. Born 1927. Ca- reer: Ph.D., University of Chicago, 1950; research chemist.
Ward office: 5623 S. Drexel Ave. (373–5965).
1984 election:
Alan Mora Dobry, unopposed.

MAYORAL ELECTIONS:

1983 Democratic primary:		
Harold Washington	18,471	(77%)
Jane Byrne	3,188	(13%)
Richard Daley	2,359	(10%)

1983 general:		
Harold Washington	24,738	(91%)
Bernard Epton	2,455	(9%)

1987 Democratic primary:		
Harold Washington	22,354	(95%)
Jane Byrne	1,196	(5%)

1987 general:		
Harold Washington	22,543	(92%)
Edward Vrdolyak	1,256	(5%)
Donald Haider	642	(3%)

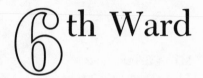

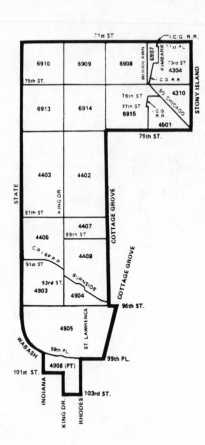

MANY NORTH SIDE whites picture the South Side as one long, uninterrupted black ghetto, fraught with deteriorating high rises inhabited by gun-toting junkies and teenage welfare mothers. Sad to say, those images are part of black Chicago. But there is a whole other South Side, a huge area of homes filled with families who worry about car payments, go to the occasional movie, and work hard to provide a better life for their children—just like their North Side counterparts.

Such an area is the 6th Ward, in the heart of the South Side. The 6th is a revolver-shaped ward, pointing southward, with its handle formed by the rectangle of State, 71st, Stony Island, and 79th, the barrel roughly formed by State, 79th, Cottage Grove, and 95th.

This is not an area that outsiders visit—not so much because of danger or deterioration, but instead because it is a residential area that lacks tourist sights. The most notable point of interest is Chicago State University at 95th and King Drive, a basketball powerhouse whose team won seventy-three consecutive home games. And those passing the corner of 75th and King Drive can spot a Sinclair dinosaur sign in front of a former gas station; dinosaur signs are otherwise extinct in the city.

People live well here, especially by the standards of the rest of black Chicago. The great downtown streets—State, Wabash, Michigan—are mere residential streets here. They flow through neighborhoods such as Park Manor and Chatham, home of a burgeoning black middle class. Germans, Swedes, Irish, and Italians were the earliest settlers, forming a solidly white community and remaining until World War II. But after the Supreme Court in 1948 struck down restrictive covenants, which had kept blacks out of the area, the latter moved in fast. By 1960 neighborhoods which once had had a handful of blacks now had only a handful of white residents.

Black migration by no means meant deterioration. Those who entered Chatham and Park Manor were the bourgeoisie—most notably teachers and other civil servants—who had the wherewithal to escape the Bronzeville ghetto. Their spiritual descendants also live here, although the new generation may be bankers or corporate executives as well as postmen or policemen.

Those bankers need not travel far. Seaway National Bank (87th and Champlain) and Independence Bank of Chicago (79th and Cottage Grove) are located here—the largest and third-largest black-owned banks in the nation, respectively.

Homes in the ward are investments, not just abodes, and homeowners keep the houses and streets immaculate. Chatham could serve as the setting for *Leave It to Beaver*—or, more aptly, *The Bill Cosby Show*.

That same attractiveness does not describe the ward's shopping strips, the main ones being 71st and 79th streets, Cottage Grove and Stony Island avenues. Although unusual shops like the Boutique Afrika on 83rd Street (a boutique and soul food restaurant) occasionally appear, by and large the stores are taverns, clothing stores, or fast food restaurants which make up most black business areas. Even in the more affluent neighborhoods, black business strips lag behind black residences in quality of development.

Robert Miller, owner of a chain of funeral parlors, ran the 6th Ward as alderman from 1959 until 1967. A coarse southerner, he did not suit the more dignified Park Manor residents. They revolted and almost elected another funeral parlor director, A. A. "Sammy" Rayner, in 1963.

Rayner, a Republican, campaigned continuously after his loss and beat Miller in 1967. It was the first time in Chicago that a black independent beat a black party regular. His election, plus that of William Cousins in the neighboring 8th Ward, showed Daley's weakness among blacks who did not owe their living to the machine.

Rayner was nothing if not colorful. Soon after being sworn in he took a tour of Russia. He showed up once at the city council wearing an African dashiki.

Democratic party regulars regrouped following the Miller defeat. They replaced him as committeeman in 1968 with Eugene Sawyer, a former high school biology teacher and chemist in the city water department.

Rayner at first decided not to seek reelection in 1971 but changed his mind, waging a last minute write-in campaign that went nowhere. He reemerged in 1978. When Democratic bosses slated unpopular Alderman Bennett Stewart to replace recently deceased Ralph Metcalfe in Congress, Republicans removed their nominee and replaced him with Rayner. He polled nearly 40 percent of the vote in a district where Republicans just don't exist.

Sawyer won the 1971 aldermanic election and was reelected four times without difficulty. Prior to 1987 he appeared destined to be remembered in his ward as a "nuts and bolts" alderman who offered good constituency services. He led a strong ward organization which boasts among its alumni state comptroller Roland Burris.

If anything, Sawyer was best known outside the 6th Ward because of his family ties. Brother Charles, city revenue director under Washington, was implicated in the Operation Incubator probe (although never charged with wrongdoing) for accepting $2,500 from "mole" Michael Raymond and donating it to Eugene's ward organization. Charles Sawyer was relieved of duties in early 1986 but fired only after a report by former U.S. Attorney Thomas Sullivan was made public in October of that year (Eugene Sawyer was one of the few aldermen who refused to cooperate with Sullivan).

Even though Sawyer was the first alderman to endorse Harold Washington in 1982, he never completely relinquished his Regular Democratic Organization ties. After the Edward Vrdolyak faction took over the city council following the 1983 election, Sawyer was installed as president pro tempore in an unsuccessful attempt to win over his vote. Sawyer retained the position when Washington gained control of the council (although due to Washington's perfect attendance at council meetings, Sawyer wielded the gavel only when the mayor went to the bathroom) and also gained chairmanship of the Rules Committee—although both positions were due more to his tenure as longest serving black alderman than to any status as a Washington confidant.

After Washington's sudden death in late 1987, Sawyer burst into public view as one of the frontrunners to succeed him. Most Harold Washington backers in the council supported his rival, Timothy Evans. The bulk of Sawyer's support came from white ethnic aldermen who had fought Washington throughout the Council Wars years and from black aldermen better known for regular organization ties than reform initiatives.

In the end, the city council election for acting mayor came down to one vote—Sawyer's own. He held enough council support to be elected acting mayor. But had he withdrawn his candidacy and supported Evans, other black aldermen (none of whom could support a white candidate for mayor and expect to survive in politics) would have had to follow his lead. All signs indicated that the black community favored Evans (even though Evans foes decried such events as a Saturday morning Operation PUSH meeting and a Monday evening Harold Washington memorial service as well-orchestrated Evans rallies, the fact remains that during the period between Washington's death and the city council election there was no significant outpouring of public support for Sawyer). And the gathering of 5,000 persons inside and outside city hall the night of the election must have contributed to Sawyer's indecisiveness about accepting a job that was his for the taking. Finally he decided to claim the chief executive position, reportedly after watching Evans declare in a television interview that Sawyer lacked the votes to win.

Instead of being hailed as the new acting mayor, Sawyer became the object

EUGENE SAWYER

of intense scrutiny. Another brother, Ernest, a Chicago Transit Authority official, was shown to be the administrator of a contract issued to a businessman who gave $4,000 to Sawyer's 6th Ward Regular Democratic Organization. A son was found to hold a park district job, a daughter worked with the city, a sister held a county job. Sawyer said that all were hired before the Shakman decree that outlawed much patronage, and that all performed their jobs well. But even though Sawyer declared "Patronage is dead, dead, dead," at least sixteen of Sawyer's relatives and associates were found to dine at the public trough.

He did not have time to warm the mayoral chair (still draped in memory of Washington) before another story broke. Newspapers claimed that Sawyer received a $20,000 fee in 1977 from an attorney who ultimately gained a favorable zoning change through him. He at first said that he did not remember the incident clearly, although skeptics wondered aloud how someone could forget a sum of money that exceeded his aldermanic salary ($17,500) of that year. Sawyer at first admitted that he got "about $20,000" from the lawyer in question. Later he issued a terse statement in which he said the fee was $30,000, not $20,000; he got the money in 1978 and 1979, not 1977; and that the money came for assisting in a purchase of Arizona real estate, and was unrelated to the zoning change.

Sawyer, replacing a man who achieved admiration bordering on veneration in the black community, faced a nearly impossible struggle. Some tried to portray him as a man who could unify black and white aldermen. Yet blacks who voted for Evans, despite offering lip service support, remained suspicious of the man elected by the remnants of the "Vrdolyak 29." And white ethnics who at first saw him as a candidate easy to defeat in a 1989 special election were not about to do anything that would help him build a popularity base.

Nonetheless Sawyer prevailed in his first major test—passage of the 1988 city budget with a property tax increase ($60 million) not far removed from a compromise figure favored by Washington before his death. He secured the necessary votes after meeting with leading aldermen during a five-hour recess. One of the aldermen swayed to Sawyer was Richard Mell, who led an anti-tax hike coalition of aldermen when Washington was alive.

Speculation arose that council members opposed to a property tax increase might delay the appointment of Sawyer's hand-picked aldermanic successor, well-liked City Council Sergeant-at-Arms Ron Robinson, for fear that Robinson's vote might be decisive against them in determining the budget. But Robinson was confirmed by a 46–0 vote. A former teacher and principal, Robinson most likely will continue as alderman in the Sawyer tradition—a faithful executor of basic services in the ward, and an almost invisible presence outside of it.

REDISTRICTING: The 6th Ward was unchanged by the 1986 redistricting.

MAYORAL: Harold Washington received his third highest percentage here in the 1983 primary—86.9 percent. Jane Byrne received 3,075 votes (10 percent) and Richard Daley only 987 (3 percent). No ward gave Daley a lower percentage than the 6th.

Washington crushed Bernard Epton in the general election. He received 35,052 votes to 240 for Bernard Epton—a 34,812 vote difference, Washington's largest margin in the city.

Other predominantly black wards experienced a drop in voter turnout for the 1987 primary, but not the 6th. It was the only black ward to attract an 80 percent turnout, and virtually all of those voters (99 percent) selected Harold Washington. Those numbers were duplicated in the general election. In both cases, the 6th gave Washington more votes than any other ward in the city.

CENSUS DATA: Population (1980): 60,576. .92 percent white, 98.31 percent black, .78 percent Hispanic. Voting age population: .57 percent white, 98.04 percent black, .59 percent Hispanic.

CENSUS TRACTS: See ward map.

COMMUNITY NEWSPAPERS:
Chatham Citizen, 412 E. 87th St. (487–7700)
Southend Citizen
Chicago Independent Bulletin, 2037 W. 95th St. (783–1040)
Chicago Metro News, 2600 S. Michigan (842–5950)
Daily Calumet, 181127 Williams, Lansing (821–1200)
Observer, 1563 E. 63rd St. (493–0557)

ALDERMAN: Ronald Robinson. Appointed 1987. Born 1930. Career: B.A., Chicago Teachers College, 1958; M.A., Roosevelt University, 1961; teacher, assistant principal, Thomas Jefferson School, 1958–65; personnel worker, Board of Education, 1965–69; director, Career Opportunities Program, Board of Education, 1970–72; principal, James McCosh School, 1972–86; sergeant-at-arms, City Council, 1987.
Committees: Aging and Disabled; Budget and Government Operations; Committees, Rules, Municipal Code Revision, and Ethics; Economic Development; Education; Finance; Local Transportation; Municipal Code Revision; Special Events and Cultural Affairs; Zoning.
City hall telephone: 744–6868, 744–5689.
Ward office: 8026 S. Cottage Grove (994–3900).
1987 election:

Eugene Sawyer	21,383 (75%)	Adrianne Pace	1,993 (7%)
Jules R. Packnett	3,607 (13%)	Milton M. Waters III	1,517 (5%)

DEMOCRATIC COMMITTEEMAN: Eugene Sawyer. Elected 1968. Born 1935. Career: B.A., Alabama State University, 1956; high school biology teacher, 1956–57; chemist, Department of Sewers; alderman, 1971–87; acting mayor, 1987- .
1984 election:
Eugene Sawyer, unopposed.

MAYORAL ELECTIONS:

1983 Democratic primary:

Harold Washington	26,979 (87%)
Jane Byrne	3,075 (10%)
Richard Daley	987 (3%)

1987 Democratic primary:

Harold Washington	31,302 (99%)
Jane Byrne	294 (1%)

1983 general:

Harold Washington	35,052 (99%)
Bernard Epton	240 (1%)

1987 general:

Harold Washington	36,676 (99%)
Edward Vrdolyak	182 (1%)
Donald Haider	117 (0%)

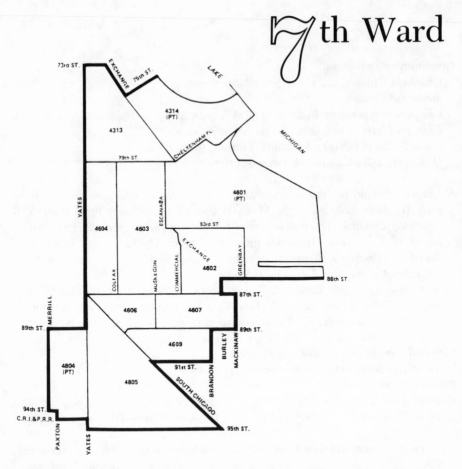 7th Ward

JOEL GARREAU IN *The Nine Nations of North America* describes "The Foundry"—old, decaying cities around the Great Lakes, where heavy industry that once provided thousands of jobs is dying, leaving a shattered local economy in its place.

Garreau had areas such as Chicago's 7th Ward in mind when he wrote about the Foundry. The U.S. Steel (now USX) South Works plant at the east end of the ward, which once provided the economic base, has been reduced to skeleton level. Nearby Wisconsin Steel closed in 1980. All too many of the ward's residents are left with unappealing choices: unemployment, underemployment, or migration.

Economic woes have taken their toll in a number of ways. Business areas, not attractive even in the best of times, are now also blighted by closed stores. Even local Catholic churches have been hit. Three of them—Sts. Peter and Paul at 91st and Exchange, St. Joseph at 88th and Saginaw, and St. Patrick's Church at 95th and Commercial in the nearby 10th Ward—shut their doors for good in the spring of 1986, due to declining attendance.

The community known as South Chicago forms the midsection of this ward.

Originally an independent town, it became part of Chicago when the city annexed the Village of Hyde Park in 1889.

From almost the beginning, South Chicago lived up to its reputation as "industrial heart of the Midwest." Forge works, railroad works, iron and steel works all located here. Docks, food processing plants, and grain elevators also provided jobs. Foremost was the Carnegie Steel Company, which became South Works when U.S. Steel was formed in 1901. It was said, "If you couldn't find work in South Chicago, you didn't want to work."

Immigrants streamed to South Chicago from the four corners of Europe for grueling but high-paying jobs. Swedes and Germans came first, followed by Poles, Bohemians, Slovenians, Lithuanians, Serbs, and Croatians. As each new ethnic group moved in, the preceding group moved up in affluence and increasingly left the neighborhood.

By the early 1900s, a new group joined the Slavs. Mexicans were imported from the Southwest by the steel companies in 1910, originally as strikebreakers. That move was a limited success, as many of the Mexicans sided with the strikers.

South Chicago is home of the oldest Mexican community in Chicago. But it is far from the largest (Pilsen and Little Village have higher Hispanic percentages), and far from the most organized. In the 1960s the area had two significant population centers. When those two groups worked together for an independent candidate (John Chico, for delegate to the 1970 constitutional convention) party regulars nipped such a coalition in the bud. The Hispanic neighborhoods were split into the 7th and 10th wards after the 1970 redistricting.

Even though Mexican-Americans may be the most visible ethnic group in the ward, they are not the majority. When the numbers are added up, this is a black ward. The northern part of the ward is the south end of South Shore— not so long ago an exclusive Jewish neighborhood, now nearly all black. This section includes the lakeside Rainbow Park, plus 79th Street—a black shopping strip of chicken and chitlins restaurants, blues, gospel, and jazz record stores.

At about 83rd Street, the atmosphere changes from black to Mexican. But the ambience here is different from, say, Pilsen. Mexican-Americans here do not consider themselves a disadvantaged minority; they instead see themselves as an ethnic group, like Serbs or Italians. Bars here have Old Style signs that advertise "cold beer," not "cerveza fria."

White ethnics still abound in South Chicago, and coexist with the Mexicans. Most visible symbol of their intermingling is St. Michael's Church at 83rd and South Shore, which contains shrines of both the Polish Black Madonna and the Mexican Our Lady of Guadalupe.

From Burley east to Green Bay, 83rd to 86th Street is a little area called The Bush. This neighborhood got its name because at one time it consisted of sandy beach plus a few bushes. That shrubbery has been replaced by grimy-looking frame houses.

The ward also contains seven precincts southwest of South Chicago Avenue—a middle-class neighborhood known as Stony Island Heights. These precincts are almost entirely black, with small Hispanic populations only in the 12th and 33rd precincts.

In a ward where the United Steel Workers of America election is more important to many residents than a city council election, it is not surprising that the aldermen have never shone as citywide leaders. Seventh Ward voters have asked for little from their elected officials—and often have gotten it.

Nicholas P. Bohling, a tomato-nosed Republican, held sway in the ward for nearly thirty years (1943–71). Since then, the 7th has had a revolving door of political representatives.

Edward Wilinski, a Pole, won the special election to succeed Bohling in 1972. A federal court, however, ruled that the ward's boundaries were gerrymandered to minimize black influence. The result was yet another special election in 1973. Black candidate Gerald Jones, a sociology instructor who was as much a party loyalist as Wilinski, won that race.

That unrequested hiatus gave Wilinski's forces a chance to recoup their strength. They did in 1975, and Wilinski regained the aldermanic seat.

Wilinski lasted only one term. Joseph Bertrand, city treasurer and Democratic committeeman since 1972, replaced him on the party slate in 1979.

Like other black leaders favored by Mayor Richard J. Daley (i.e., Ralph Metcalfe, Claude Holman), Bertrand was a devout Roman Catholic. Some theorize that the mayor handpicked black Catholics because they at least had a spiritual, if not racial, bond with him. No less a Catholic leader than John Cardinal Cody recommended Bertrand, a bank president and former All-American basketball player.

Daley tapped Bertrand for city treasurer in 1975. But Bertrand's clout died with Daley. Mayoral successor Michael Bilandic dumped Bertrand from the ticket and replaced him with another black, Cecil Partee.

Wilinski, a favorite of neighboring 10th Ward alderman Edward Vrdolyak, tried twice without success to upend Bertrand. A 1976 write-in campaign for committeeman failed miserably. Three years later, despite the support of such black leaders as Partee and Alderman Wilson Frost (34th), Wilinski lost the aldermanic race by 1100 votes.

Vrdolyak ultimately extracted his revenge. Bertrand was redistricted out of the ward by the 1981 remap (his house is 1/2 block inside the 5th Ward). Bertrand's refusal to move back into the 7th left the race wide open in 1983. Ironically, one of his bodyguards won that race.

William Beavers, a twenty-one-year Chicago policeman, lobbied unsuccessfully for Harold Washington's endorsement before the February election. He survived a field of eleven to a runoff and beat 1980 committeeman winner Ray Castro, a Vrdolyak ally.

In a runoff that followed strict ethnic lines, Beavers won 8,488 to 7,288. Beavers (now endorsed by Washington) carried the black precincts. Castro won the Mexican and white ethnic vote.

Beavers made a run for committeeman in 1984. His main target was Castro. Even though the incumbent was the first Hispanic committeeman, his Vrdolyak affiliation kept many citywide Hispanic groups from rushing to his aid.

Utter lack of political organization and voter enthusiasm manifested itself in the 1984 Democratic committeeman election. Four candidates vied for the post; none was able to survive ballot challenges by the others.

This turn of events led to a write-in election, which Beavers won, with 2,980 votes. He beat Castro (2,143), Johnny Acoff, Jr. (407), Henry Martinea (128), and John Doe (2 votes). If no candidate had received 1,500 votes, the party's central committee would have chosen the committeeman, which undoubtedly would have been Castro, the regulars' choice.

Few aldermen are more invisible at city council meetings than William Beavers. And his record at home hardly frightened away challengers; nine persons filed nominating petitions against him, and four remained on the ballot.

Rumors of Beavers's involvement in the Operation Incubator probe circulated during the campaign, although he never was indicted. Both metropolitan dailies instead endorsed William King, Jr., an investigator for the Equal Employment Opportunity Commission. Yet Beavers captured a surprising 58 percent of the vote. David Vargas, the only Hispanic in the race, fared well in South Chicago precincts. Craig A. Ford, an official with the Department of Housing and Urban Development, did well in his South Shore base.

REDISTRICTING: No changes were made in 7th Ward boundaries by the 1986 redistricting.

MAYORAL: Harold Washington took the ward in the primary by a comfortable but not overwhelming margin: 65 percent (12,147 votes) to 22 percent (4,061) for (Vrdolyak and Castro-backed) Jane Byrne and 13 percent (2,393) for Richard Daley. Washington carried the black precincts; the others won the Mexican areas.

Washington also claimed victory in the general election: 17,304 votes (82 percent) to 3,776 for Bernard Epton. His percentage and plurality were not as high as totals in wards with greater black majorities, but they were impressive nonetheless, including unanimous (600–0 and 480–0) totals in two precincts.

Those same percentages persisted in the 1987 elections. Washington won 84 and 83 percent of the vote in the Democratic primary and general election, respectively, winning every area except the South Chicago Hispanic and white ethnic precincts.

CENSUS DATA: Population (1980): 59,906. 11.33 percent white, 58.40 percent black, 30.09 percent Hispanic, .18 percent Asian and other. Voting age population: 14.72 percent white, 58.03 percent black, 26.55 percent Hispanic, .80 percent Asian and other.

CENSUS TRACTS: See ward map.

COMMUNITY NEWSPAPERS:
Chatham Citizen, 412 E. 87th St. (487–7720)
Chicago Independent Bulletin, 2037 W. 95th St. (783–1040)
Chicago Metro News, 2600 S. Michigan (842–5950)
Daily Calumet, 18127 Williams, Lansing (821–1200)
El Dia, 2648 S. Kolin (277–7676) (Spanish)
El Imparcial, 3610 W. 26th St. (376–9888) (Spanish)
El Informador, 1821 S. Loomis (942–0295) (Spanish)
Impacto, 3507 W. North Ave. (486–2547) (Spanish)
La Voz de Chicago, 8624 S. Houston (221–9416) (Spanish)
La Opinion, 2501 S. East Ave., Berwyn (Spanish)
Observer, 1563 E. 63rd St. (493–0557)
South East News, 9318 S. Phillips (978–2233)

ALDERMAN: William M. Beavers. Elected 1983. Born 1937. Career: Loop Junior College; officer, Chicago Police Department, 1962–83 (on leave).
Committees: Police, Fire, and Municipal Institutions (chairman); Land Acquisition, Disposition, and Development (vice-chairman); Aviation; Budget and Government Operations; Claims and Liabilities; Capital Development; Economic Development; Finance; Intergovernmental Relations; Streets and Alleys.
City hall telephone: 744–6833, 744–3127.
Ward office: 2552 E. 79th St. (731–1515).
1987 election:

William M. Beavers	9,775	(58%)	William C. King Jr.	1,230	(7%)
David Vargas	3,204	(19%)	Charles J. Stewart	1,163	(7%)
Craig A. Ford	1,557	(9%)		

DEMOCRATIC COMMITTEEMAN: William M. Beavers. Elected 1984.
1984 election (all write-in votes)

William M. Beavers	2,980	(51%)	Henry Martinea	128	(2%)
Raymond Castro	2,143	(37%)	Louise Brown	33	(1%)
Johnny Acoff Jr.	407	(7%)	Others	123	(2%)

MAYORAL ELECTIONS:

1983 Democratic primary:

Harold Washington	12,147	(65%)
Jane Byrne	4,061	(22%)
Richard Daley	2,393	(13%)

1987 Democratic primary:

Harold Washington	15,447	(84%)
Jane Byrne	2,825	(16%)

1983 general:

Harold Washington   17,304 (82%)

Bernard Epton   3,776 (18%)

1987 general:

Harold Washington 16,072 (84%)

Edward Vrdolyak   3,049 (16%)

Donald Haider   108   (1%)

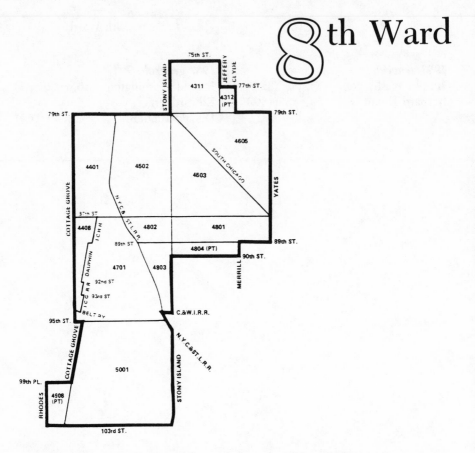

THE BEST WAY to describe Chicago's ethnic settlement pattern is to imagine a giant wagon wheel, with the center located in the Loop and spokes radiating out into the suburbs. Each spoke of the wheel represents a different ethnic group.

Earliest arrivals of each group settled toward the city's center. As they, or their descendants, became more prosperous, they moved out, along the spoke, toward the city's outskirts and eventually the suburbs. Germans moved north, Poles moved northwest, Italians west, Bohemians southwest, and so on.

Blacks, to some extent, followed that pattern. Earliest black settlement was in the Near South Side, and the logical flow pattern dictated that they move southward in the city.

For many years they met with an obstacle: restrictive housing covenants which kept them out of many South Side neighborhoods. The Supreme Court in 1948 ruled such restrictions illegal, and blacks then started a rapid outward migration.

Whites in comfortable middle-class areas such as the present 8th Ward were beset by unscrupulous real estate speculators who preyed on their fears of neighborhood deterioration and decreased property values. These specula-tors bought homes from whites at low prices, then sold them for high prices to blacks. As a result of this "panic peddling," neighborhoods that were 95 percent white and 5 percent black in 1950 have the opposite percentages now— if, indeed, there are any whites left at all.

The black displacement of whites is all but complete. However, the deterioration foreseen by doomsayers never came about. The 8th Ward neighborhoods are what they were in the 1950s—comfortable, middle-class areas. The main difference between then and now is the pigmentation of the homeowners.

If not affluent, the 8th Ward at least shows signs of stability. Avalon Park, on its northwest side, is a modestly prosperous area once known as Penny-town—after a store owner named Penny who sold homemade popcorn balls to local kids. The park itself, at 85th and Woodlawn, was once the site of a body of water named Mud Lake. Nearby at 87th and Clyde is Chicago Vocational School.

South of 95th Street, the homes take on the look of a suburban housing development. They border Olive-Harvey College at 103rd and Woodlawn, one of the City Colleges of Chicago.

In the southwest corner of the ward is Gately Park, which includes a high school football field. Political football was played there in 1986, as Mayor Harold Washington vetoed city funds to repair the field. Washington claimed that the Chicago Park District, which owns Gately, is responsible for its upkeep.

Between Avalon Park and 95th Street is an area called Burnside, the smallest officially designated community in the city. Centering around the now-closed Burnside Foundry at 92nd and Kimbark, it once served as home for working-class Poles and Hungarians who toiled in the local railroad shops and yards.

Other sights reinforce the ward's overall middle-class image. Stores on 87th Street, a busy commercial strip, include many catering to the white-collar professions of the ward's residents—a beauty supply store, a teacher supply store, a police uniform store. And a home at 83rd and Ridgeway displays perhaps the ultimate black middle-class icon—a white jockey lawn ornament.

Symbol of the community's hopes is the former Avalon Theatre at 79th Street just east of Stony Island. The Moorish rococo building, certainly the most distinctive in the ward, was at one time a movie theater in the Balaban-Katz chain. It is now restored as a black performing arts center, and renamed the New Regal Theatre, after a once-famous entertainment palace at 47th and King Drive.

The ward west of the Chicago Skyway is mainly residential, but the area to the east has its share of unusual attractions. Rev. John C. Connor Fellowship Hall now occupies the Moorish building at 79th, South Chicago, and Stony Island that is a smaller replica of the Avalon Theatre. Yahweh Temple occupies a storefront church on Stony Island just north of 79th Street. Conquering Lion Records at 79th and Drexel holds perhaps the city's top collection of reggae records.

Just south of 79th Street on South Chicago Avenue is another Chicago institution—the WGN Flag Company, which preceded the radio station and has resisted all attempts by the broadcasting conglomerate to change its name.

The most famous 8th Ward politician is one who never got elected. Cub immortal Ernie Banks was so popular, it was said, that he could run for mayor. But even his popularity could not get him elected as a Republican against Democratic regular James A. Condon in 1963.

Four years later, a challenger defeated Condon. William Cousins, a Harvard-educated lawyer, originally was a Republican but bolted that party after the 1964 Barry Goldwater nomination. He won as an independent Democrat; "Unbowed, unbossed, and unbought" was his motto. Tall, courtly, and dignified, Cousins created a strong ward organization. He formed many block clubs and once held a "prom" for older residents of his ward.

Cousins, a reform-minded alderman and administration foe, served until he fell victim to one of Mayor Richard Daley's favorite adages: "If you can't beat them, offer them a judgeship." Cousins took the bait in 1976.

His successor was Marian Humes, then an ally of Democratic committeeman John Stroger. Humes was a onetime teacher and aspirant to the chairmanship of the Education Committee. Humes made headlines several times in early 1986, mostly for reasons not of her own choosing. She was one of four aldermen implicated that January as having accepted money from FBI "mole" Michael Raymond during an undercover investigation, and was indicted in early 1987. Humes admitted she took $5,000 from Raymond but said she later returned it by registered mail.

In May 1986, with control of city council committees and executive appointments on the line, Humes took a walk from a pivotal council meeting, reportedly to attend to personal legal business. Her "unexcused" absence sent shock waves through the ward, and angry constituents left no doubt of their disapproval.

Keith Caldwell, a Cook County jury supervisor and son-in-law of former state representative Lewis Caldwell, was Stroger's choice against Humes in the 1987 aldermanic election. Caldwell captured 57 percent of the 1987 aldermanic vote and all but one precinct.

John Stroger, Democratic committeeman, has held that post since 1968. Even though first elected with the support of party regulars, he was not considered to have a strong party organization (he ran and lost twice against Cousins for alderman, and finished well out of the running in a 1980 congressional primary against Washington and incumbent Bennett Stewart). In 1983 Stroger was the only major black politician to back State's Attorney Richard Daley in the Democratic primary; Daley carried only 5 percent of the ward's vote.

Nonetheless, Stroger appears secure. A Cook County commissioner since 1970, he was one of only three county commissioners endorsed by both regular Democrats and Harold Washington in the March 1986 primary. Only county board president George Dunne and well-known soul singer Jerry Butler finished with more votes in both the primary and general elections.

After the primary, Stroger mounted a symbolic challenge to Edward Vrdolyak for the party chairmanship. As expected, he received the votes of blacks and other anti-Vrdolyak committeemen but still lost by a two-to-one margin.

In late 1986 Washington-allied committeemen called for a meeting of the Democratic Central Committee. When Chairman Vrdolyak refused to convene such a meeting, the rebel group met anyway and declared Stroger municipal chairman—a declaration not taken seriously outside the rebel group's ranks. When the party voted George Dunne Cook County chairman in 1987, Stroger yielded the municipal chairmanship to his longtime friend.

REDISTRICTING: The ward was unchanged by the 1986 redistricting.

MAYORAL: Ever since the black middle-class migration of the 1950s, the 8th has consistently been one of the strongest antimachine wards. It ranked in the top ten wards in 1971 for Richard Friedman, Daley's 1971 Republican challenger. In 1975 the combined vote for white liberal William Singer and black State Senator Richard Newhouse surpassed the Daley vote. Harold Washington carried the ward in the 1977 Democratic primary.

As with other predominantly black middle-income wards (6th, 21st, 34th), Harold Washington carried the 8th by a huge margin in the 1983 primary—86 percent, leaving 9 percent for Jane Byrne and 5 percent for Daley.

Only two other wards—the 6th and 21st—provided higher pluralities in the general election than the 8th. Washington won it by 30,648 votes, with 99 percent of the total vote.

Likewise, Washington clobbered Jane Byrne in the 1987 Democratic primary, Edward Vrdolyak and Donald Haider in the general election—with just short of 99 percent of the vote in each case.

CENSUS DATA: Population (1980): 59,928. 2.53 percent white, 96.13 percent black, .99 percent Hispanic, .65 percent Asian and other. Voting age population: 2.02 percent white, 96.11 percent black, .80 percent Hispanic, 1.07 percent Asian and other.

CENSUS TRACTS: See ward map.

COMMUNITY NEWSPAPERS:
Chatham Citizen, 412 E. 87th St. (487–7700)
Chicago Independent Bulletin, 2037 W. 95th (783–1040)
Chicago Metro News, 2600 S. Michigan (842–5950)
Chicago Standard News, 518 Parnell Ave., Chicago Heights (755–5021)
Daily Calumet, 18127 Williams, Lansing (821–1200)
Observer, 1563 E. 63rd St. (493–0557)
Southend Citizen, 412 E. 87th St. (487–7770)

ALDERMAN: Keith A. Caldwell. Born 1935. Career: B.A., Northeastern Illinois University, 1967; U.S. Marine Corps; regional manager for pharmaceuticals, 3M Company; jury supervisor, Cook County.

Committees: Municipal Code Revision (vice-chairman): Budget and Government Operations; Capital Development; Historical Landmarks Preservation; Finance; Housing; Intergovernmental Relations; Police, Fire, and Municipal Institutions; Special Events and Cultural Affairs.

City hall telephone: 744–3075, 744–3098.

Ward office: 8539 S. Cottage Grove (874–3300).

1987 election:

Keith A. Caldwell	14,753	(58%)	Bryan A. Moore	879	(3%)
Marian Humes	6,031	(23%)	Joseph C. Faulkner	677	(3%)
Mulbe Dillard	2,018	(8%)	Jeff Carroll, Jr.	491	(2%)
Henrene Honesty	1,224	(5%)			

DEMOCRATIC COMMITTEEMAN: John H. Stroger, Jr. Elected 1968. Born May 19, 1929. Career: B.S., Xavier University of New Orleans, 1952; J.D., DePaul University, 1965; teacher and basketball coach, 1952–53; assistant auditor, City of Chicago Municipal Court, 1953–55; personnel director, Cook County Jail, 1955–59; examiner, Illinois Department of Financial Institutions, 1963–70; Member, Cook County Board of Commissioners, 1970– .

County office telephone: 443–6396.

Ward office: 8539 S. Cottage Grove (874–3300).

1984 election:

John H. Stroger, Jr., unopposed.

MAYORAL ELECTIONS:

1983 Democratic primary:

Harold Washington	23,946	(86%)
Jane Byrne	2,426	(9%)
Richard Daley	1,325	(5%)

1987 Democratic primary:

Harold Washington	28,714	(99%)
Jane Byrne	388	(1%)

1983 general:

Harold Washington	31,106	(99%)
Bernard Epton	458	(1%)

1987 general:

Harold Washington	29,847	(99%)
Edward Vrdolyak	340	(1%)
Donald Haider	102	(0%)

9th Ward

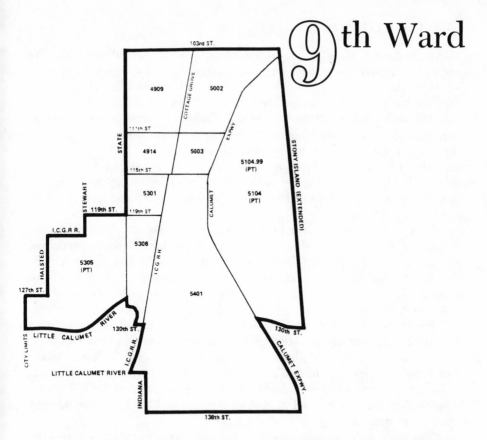

SMILING CHILDREN'S FACES greet visitors at "Welcome to the 9th Ward," a mural at 103rd Street and Cottage Grove Avenue. The mural may be deceptive. In many ways, life is bleak in this Far South Side ward.

For too many of the ward's residents, the work has gone. The scaling down of the U.S. Steel South Works plant in recent years and the 1980 Wisconsin Steel closing have taken away the jobs that, most likely, will never return.

Environmental concerns also seem to affect this ward more than any other. The sprawling Altgeld Gardens CHA project made headlines in 1986 when high levels of asbestos were found in some of the buildings, and residents made vociferous demands that the toxic substance be removed. Those in the southwest portion of the ward faced health tests after five cases of lead poisoning were attributed to a nearby recently closed paint plant. Residents of Maryland Manor, eight homes near 134th Street and the Calumet Expressway, for years drank well water before discovering cyanide, benzene, and toluene in it. Manor residents obtained hookups to Lake Michigan water in 1986.

The current situation is ironic, because the ward houses what was once considered the "ideal" community—Pullman, a company-owned town which flourished in the late 1800s. Railroad magnate George Pullman built his town out of what was an open prairie in 1880, and named it after himself. Pullman, the town, provided modern quality housing, plus such amenities as schools, a library, a theater, and Green Stone Church. a nondenominational place of worship. (One amenity not covered was taverns, since Pullman did not allow workers' bars inside his town. Beer baron Joseph Schlitz filled that void by building taverns on Front Street, just outside Pullman town limits).

Although foreign sociologists voted Pullman the "most perfect" town in the world, there were rumblings of discontent. Workers were unhappy because they were not allowed to buy their own homes. Pullman's philosophy that all aspects of his community should make a profit led to high prices at the company store and even a borrowing fee at the library. Pullman's employees showed their displeasure by voting in 1889 (over Pullman's objections) for annexation to the city of Chicago.

Pent-up frustrations came to a head a few years later. During the 1893 depression, Pullman lowered workers' salaries. He did not make corresponding cuts in rents or store prices. The workers voted to strike in May 1894—a strike that drew worldwide attention, violence, and, ultimately, federal troops as strikebreakers. The strike was quelled and young labor leader Eugene Debs jailed for his protests.

Pullman died in 1897, so despised that his family buried his coffin under a solid block of concrete and steel girders—to deter would-be grave robbers.

The former town of Pullman (between 111th an 115th Streets, Cottage Grove and Langley) was named a national landmark in 1970 and still retains its old-time charm. A onetime stable is now an equally appropriate fuel stop—a tasteful gas station. A small malt shop at 112th and St. Lawrence appears lifted intact from the 1950s.

Pullman's 37th and 14th precincts are white (resolutely so, one gets the feeling). The rest of the ward is as solidly black.

North Pullman (103rd to 111th Streets, Cottage Grove to Lake Calumet), once the site of the Pullman manufacturing plants and some workers' homes, is one of the latter neighborhoods. Another is Roseland (Cottage Grove to State, 103rd to 115th Streets), originally settled by the Dutch. The most prominent building there is Mendel Catholic High School (111th and Indiana), at one time a trade school operated by Pullman.

South of Roseland is Kensington, originally a separate village, described as "The Pearl of South Chicago" by a wall sign at Front and Kensington. Burned out buildings, vacant lots, and broken signs indicate a faded jewel. One Kensington store is significant—Brady's, a store at 118th and Michigan specializing in imported Caribbean foods for the Haitians, Belizeans, and Jamaicans living on the Far South Side.

West Pullman constitutes the southwest part of the ward. This area was not related to George Pullman's community except that late nineteenth-century speculators wished to capitalize on the fame of the Pullman village. At one time a small business strip occupied 123rd Street just west of West Pullman Park. Now most of the stores are closed.

The center of the ward is industrial, from 115th to 130th Streets, bounded by Cottage Grove and Lake Calumet. A Sherwin Williams paint plant dominates the local scene.

Unlikely neighbors share the land between 130th Street and the Little Calumet River: to the west, Eden Green, a private townhouse and apartment complex; to the east, Altgeld Gardens, a mammoth public housing project that is home to some 5,300 people in 1,500 apartments.

If the 9th Ward is problem-laden, the unsteady political situation has done little to alleviate those ills. The 9th has elected three different aldermen in the last four elections.

Alderman Robert Shaw and his predecessor, Perry Hutchinson, faced off in those four elections. Both entered the 1975 race and split the black vote, thus assuring the reelection of machine-backed alderman Alexander Adducci. Shaw and Hutchinson ran again in 1979. Shaw, with a better organization and backing of powerful alderman Wilson Frost, won this race.

Shaw made himself known as the most vocal backer of aldermanic pay raises. More important, he introduced legislation which would have scrapped the city's civil service hiring. That motion failed, but it enabled then-mayor Jane Byrne to extract a compromise which obtained civil service exemptions for one-third of city employees.

Byrne was the big issue in the 1983 election. Shaw stood by the mayor until the final days of the campaign. Hutchinson backed Harold Washington. Hutchinson and Shaw were the top finishers in the ten-person race and met in a runoff. This time Hutchinson won handily. He repeated his victory over Shaw in the following year's committeeman election.

For the first two years of the Washington term, Hutchinson appeared to be best remembered as the man who proposed relocation of the 1992 Chicago World's Fair to industrial Lake Calumet. Events in late 1985 and early 1986 shoved Hutchinson into the headlines. An FBI probe in late 1985 alleged that four aldermen, including Hutchinson, accepted bribes from "mole" Michael Raymond. Hutchinson admitted that he took $28,500 from Raymond but said that $8,500 of that money went to pay a staffer's salary and the balance paid for supplies at two ward schools.

Even more dangerous to Hutchinson was his failure to stay for a key city council meeting in May 1986. His early departure (reportedly to attend a doctor's appointment) prevented the Washington bloc from obtaining the majority it needed to change council committee chairmanships and free "hostage" appointments.

The black community voiced its displeasure with Hutchinson in no uncertain terms, and the chastened alderman responded at the next meeting. Hutchinson was brought to City Hall in an ambulance and transported to the chamber in a wheelchair so that he could cast deciding votes—one of the most dramatic (or melodramatic) moments in city council history.

Shaw and Hutchinson faced off again in 1987, along with nine others. As in 1983, loyalty to Harold Washington was the main issue. Hutchinson once again attacked Shaw for his loyalty to then-mayor Jane Byrne in 1983. Shaw counforcharged that Hutchinson had enlisted the aid of pro-Vrdolyak precinct captains, a statement Hutchinson described as "about as real as the hairpiece that (Shaw) wears."

Hutchinson showed strength in Pullman and northern precincts, while Shaw carried Altgeld Gardens, Kensington, and Roseland. But more than 40 percent of the voters chose a candidate who was Neither of the Above. Shaw won the runoff by a 53–47 percent margin.

Perry Hutchinson remained the ward's Democratic committeeman (he beat Shaw in 1984), but Shaw's aldermanic win showed Hutchinson's vulnerability. Events after the election also hurt. A federal grand jury indicted him in connection with Operation Incubator. Hutchinson also was indicted in an unrelated case, involving an alleged insurance swindle.

In 1988, for the first time in years, a 9th Ward election took place without either Robert Shaw or Perry Hutchinson. Shaw's twin brother, William, a state representative, was a committeeman candidate. Robert Shaw voted for Eugene Sawyer as acting mayor instead of Timothy Evans, citing a poll he conducted. Many observers saw the committeeman election as a referendum on Robert's Sawyer vote.

REDISTRICTING: The 1986 city council remap made no changes in the 9th Ward.

MAYORAL: Harold Washington won handily here (80 percent), although several other black wards gave him higher percentages. Jane Byrne's vote total (15 percent, mainly from Pullman) was one of her best totals in any of the black wards, probably because of Shaw's backing. Richard Daley received 5 percent of the vote.

Washington took 94 percent of the vote in the general election. As expected, the white enclave of Pullman was the major source of Republican Bernard Epton's vote.

Harold Washington won 95 percent of the vote both in the 1987 primary and general election. His only weak spot was Pullman, where neighbor Ed Vrdolyak is affectionately known as "Bro."

CENSUS DATA: Population (1980): 6.12 percent white, 89.15 percent black, 4.81 percent Hispanic. Voting age population: 7.61 percent white, 86.89 percent black, 4.51 percent Hispanic.

CENSUS TRACTS: See ward map.

COMMUNITY NEWSPAPERS:
Chicago Independent Bulletin, 2307 W. 95th St. (783–1400)
Chicago Metro News, 2600 S. Michigan (842–5950)
Chicago Standard News, 518 Parnell Ave., Chicago Heights (755–5021)
Daily Calumet, 18127 Williams, Lansing (821–1200)
Southend Citizen, 412 E. 87th (487–7700)

ALDERMAN: Robert Shaw. Elected 1987. Born July 31, 1937. Career: Malcolm X College; bailiff, Cook County Courts; affirmative action executive, Illinois Department of Labor; alderman, 1979–83.

Committees: Ports, Wharves, and Bridges (chairman); Aviation; Budget and Government Operations; Buildings; Claims and Liabilities; Committees, Rules, Municipal Code Revision, and Ethics; Economic Development; Finance; Intergovernmental Relations; Special Events and Cultural Relations.

City hall telephone: 744–6838, 744–3061.

Ward office: 723 W. 123rd St. (785–3200).

1987 election:

Robert Shaw	6,447	(31%)	James A. Meredith	1,142 (6%)
Perry Hutchinson	5,716	(28%)	James "Jim" Owens	890 (4%)
Richard J. Dowdell	2,045	(10%)	Randolph Norris	718 (3%)
Bernard C. Taylor	1,417	(7%)	Johnny J. O'Neal	459 (2%)
Edna "Bonnie"	1,186	(6%)	William A. Wilson	396 (2%)
McCullough			Heron Lee O'Neal	306 (1%)

1987 runoff:

Robert Shaw	10,872	(53%)
Perry Hutchinson	9,587	(47%)

DEMOCRATIC COMMITTEEMAN: Perry Hutchinson. Elected 1984. Born October 18, 1943. Career: J.D., Kent College of Law; aide to State Rep. Lewis Caldwell, 1972–77; Delta Airlines, 1977–79; Allstate Insurance, 1979–83.

Ward office: 743 E. 103rd St. (264–4900).

1984 election:

Perry Hutchinson	9,164	(61%)
Robert Shaw	5,078	(34%)
Omar Faruq	854	(6%)

MAYORAL ELECTIONS:

1983 Democratic primary:

Harold Washington	17,691	(80%)
Jane Byrne	3,391	(15%)
Richard Daley	1,174	(5%)

1987 Democratic primary:

Harold Washington	21,237	(95%)
Jane Byrne	999	(4%)

1983 general:

Harold Washington	24,076	(94%)
Bernard Epton	1,521	(6%)

1987 general:

Harold Washington	22,012	(95%)
Edward Vrdolyak	1,036	(4%)
Donald Haider	113	(0%)

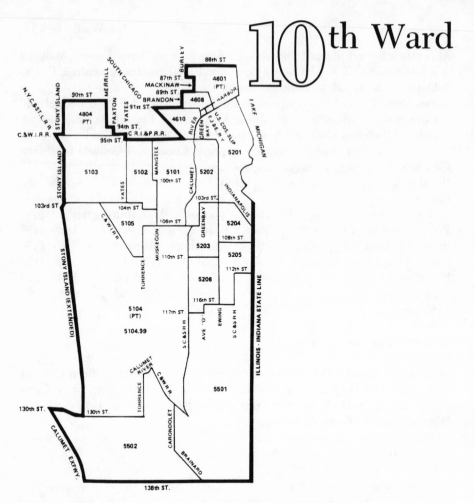

"HOG BUTCHER FOR THE WORLD, TOOL MAKER, STACKER OF WHEAT . . . CITY OF THE BIG SHOULDERS." Carl Sandburg in his poem *Chicago* described a tough, brawny, lusty city. He was not referring to the downtown skyscrapers where suit-clad businessmen deal in government or service industries. Instead, Sandburg described the Chicago exemplified by the Southeast Side 10th Ward.

Things are big here, massive and industrial: the gigantic Wisconsin Steel plant, at one time home to thousands of workers, since 1980 home to none; the Torrence Avenue Ford plant; a man-made mountain range of salt, coal, and scrap iron hills at 92nd and Jeffrey; a railroad car graveyard at 135th and Avenue O; giant lift bridges on the Calumet River, near grain elevators; the huge Chicago Skyway bridge cutting through the northeast sector of the ward; Chicago's only sawmill, at Buffalo and Brainard.

This is the Chicago where areas are known as Irondale and Slag Valley. Steel City National Bank is a large financial institution. Streets named Commercial and Exchange offer testimony that people came here to make a buck, not admire the scenery.

Even the empty spaces are huge. Nearly one in five acres in the 10th Ward are vacant land. The 10th claims the largest parcel of vacant land in the city—a 24.5 million-square-foot (562 acre) site at 116th and Torrence.

Don't let those large expanses of empty grass fool you. The William Powers Wildlife Preserve, near Wolf Lake in the far southeast corner, is a legitimate preserve. A marshland at Constance from 95th to 103rd Street, known locally as "The Prairie," is a major resting place for migratory waterfowl. But many other green spaces are garbage or toxic waste dumps, not parks.

Waste disposal is a major issue here; the Far South Side 9th and 10th Wards house one of the highest concentrations of landfills in the United States. A June 1987 *Sun-Times* series detailed many of the environmental problems of the Paxton Lagoons, Paxton Landfill, Alburn Incinerator, U.S. Drum, and other 10th Ward sites. Congressman Gus Savage (D-2) moved to halt relicensing of two other dumps, C.I.D. Landfill (138th and the Calumet Expressway) and S.C.A. Chemical Services (117th and Stony Island), until a possible link could be researched between the presence of waste facilities and unusually high incidence of cancer in Far South Side Communities.

For many, environmental woes are matched by economic ones. The steel industry, once the bulwark of the Southeast Side, has all but disappeared. Wisconsin Steel (106th and Torrence) closed in 1980, costing 3,000 jobs plus many others in steel-related businesses. U.S. Steel (now USX) has trimmed itself to a bare-bones level. Of the major steel companies only Republic Steel (114th and Avenue O) remains. Republic Steel was the site of a major Chicago tragedy—the 1937 Memorial Day Massacre. Striking workers picketed the plant on the holiday. Police fired on them, and ten were killed.

Its relative isolation might have explained why the 10th Ward was the setting for two other sensational Chicago tragedies. The body of a Hyde Park boy named Bobby Franks was found near Wolf Lake in 1924—along with glasses belonging to Nathan Leopold, one of his killers. Leopold and Richard Loeb, two young University of Chicago graduates, confessed to killing Franks in an attempt to commit the "perfect crime." The "thrill kill," as well as Clarence Darrow's eloquent defense, provided headlines throughout the year. An even grislier story broke 42 years later. A drifter named Richard Speck murdered seven student nurses in their dormitory at 100th and Calhoun.

Rather than a homogeneous entity, the 10th Ward may be considered a collection of diverse villages:

South Chicago: The 10th Ward includes the southeast sector of South Chicago, many old frame buildings which have taken in generations of coal dust. The busy 91st and Commercial area and its statue of Christopher Columbus is part of the 10th Ward. The already established Mexican population here constructed Our Lady of Guadalupe Church (91st and Brandon), Chicago's first Mexican-built church, in 1928.

Directly to the east lies Calumet Park, south and east of the Calumet River which separates South Chicago from the rest of the ward. Calumet Park was formed from landfill generated from the slag of nearby steel mills. Its fieldhouse contains one of the largest model railroads in the world.

Pill Hill: Once known as the South Side home of doctors (hence the name), the neighborhood at the northwest corner of the ward now serves as one of the most affluent black areas in Chicago.

Pill Hill also contains two South Side landmarks: the Vernon Park Church of God (91st and Stony Island), whose associate minister, Addie Wyatt, was one of Harold Washington's most visible supporters; and Helen Maybell's Soul Queen Restaurant (90th and Stony Island), where a sign on the wall gives the motherly warning, "You may eat all you want, but you must pay for all you take."

Jeffrey Manor and Merrionette Manor: These are two other black middle-class neighborhoods in the northwest corner of the ward, occupying the area originally known as Irondale. Racial tensions erupted during the 1950s in the Trumbull Park Chicago Housing Authority project just south of Jeffrey Manor. A black family who moved there in 1953 faced a barrage of insults and threats from white neighbors that continued for almost three years. Today the area is Mexican and black.

Slag Valley: The Rock Island railroad tracks separate lily-white Slag Valley (to the east) from the blacks and Hispanics who make up the rest of the community known as South Deering. Slag Valley, located between 95th Street and the Calumet, is the oldest part of South Deering.

Hegewisch: A small town feel permeates this, Chicago's most isolated neighborhood. Baltimore Avenue, with its grocery stores and cafés and the small former movie theater, looks more like a main street in La Salle County than southeast Chicago. Only police cars and CTA buses (and Eastern European, as opposed to WASP, names on businesses) remind the visitor that he or she is in the city.

Island Homes: The 22nd Precinct is composed of Island Homes (132nd and Avenue F), Chicago's only trailer park.

East Side: Newcomers to Chicago may scoff that Lake Michigan is the east side of Chicago. But veteran Chicagoans know the East Side as the neighborhood between the Calumet River and the Indiana state line, where avenues are denoted by letters instead of names.

Once a "suburb" for more well-to-do workers of South Chicago plants, the East Side today is a neighborhood dominated by the children of Serbian, Croatian, Polish, Italian and Mexican immigrants. A black man who moved here in 1984 found his garage burned within days of his arrival. The man and his family moved immediately.

The southern portion of the East Side consists of the Fair Elms development, postwar housing that is new by Chicago standards. Two sights distinguish Fair Elms from the average suburban tract. One is St. Simeon Mirotocivi Serbian Orthodox Church (114th and Avenue H), a striped and checkered church modeled after a Serbian monastery. The other is a nearby house at 115th and Avenue J, described as a Taj Mahal among the bungalows, equipped with a tennis court, swimming pool, and TV satellite dish. It belongs to one Edward

Robert Vrdolyak, formerly the alderman of the 10th Ward.

Vrdolyak's larger-than-life home is appropriate. No other figure has dominated Chicago politics more in the post-Daley generation. "The Coffee Rebellion," "Fast Eddie," "The Evil Cabal," "The 29," "Council Wars"—all these Chicago household terms are attributable to the colorful politician. Even after vacating his city council seat and the county Democratic chairmanship, he casts a gigantic shadow over the local scene.

Already a successful personal injury lawyer in 1967, Vrdolyak made known his intentions of running for alderman. Incumbent John Buchannan talked him out of the race. They struck a deal; Vrdolyak would back Buchannan for alderman, and Buchannan would support Vrdolyak for Democratic committeeman.

Vrdolyak kept his end of the bargain, but Buchannan instead supported the reelection of incumbent committeeman Stanley Zima. Even so, Vrdolyak squeaked by Zima in 1968. He became the first challenger from outside the regular Democratic organization to defeat an incumbent committeeman in fifty years.

From his committeeman office he assembled a powerful ward organization and opposed Buchannan in 1971. Columnist Mike Royko commented in a mock endorsement, "The two used to be pals but now they hate each other, and I don't blame either one of them. Vote for the one you hate least." The voters chose Vrdolyak.

An unwritten city council rule is, "Freshmen are seen and not heard." Vrdolyak broke that rule. He and several of the younger aldermen (Edward Burke, Clifford Kelley, Wilson Frost) led the "coffee rebellion," so called because they plotted strategy over cups of coffee at a nearby hotel. These "young turks" were not seeking political reform; they wanted a share of the political power kept in a stranglehold by Finance Committee chairman Tom Keane. Vrdolyak called off the rebellion, but not before securing himself a seat on the powerful Finance Committee.

Daily News reporter Jay McMullen bestowed upon Vrdolyak a nickname he still owns—"Fast Eddie." In part, the name was given because of Vrdolyak's quick rise to influence. But detractors claim he earned it because of his adroitness at remaining one step ahead of the law. Vrdolyak has never been convicted of a crime, or even indicted. But over the years, he has been involved in a number of questionable incidents:

—Vrdolyak precinct captains hustled accident victims after a 1972 Illinois Central train wreck. Such a maneuver, though not illegal, violated legal ethics;

—Critics described Vrdolyak's home as "The house that clout built." A *Tribune* report claimed that he received 30,000 free bricks from a contractor (as a "housewarming gift"), plus free electrical work and a substantial discount on plumbing;

—In 1974 he helped approve a zoning change for a local financial institution, soon after selling the affected property to that institution at a huge profit;

EDWARD R. VRDOLYAK

—He and several partners purchased fifty Marina City condominiums at bargain basement rates shortly before a strengthened condo conversion law passed in 1977. He later rushed through the council an ordinance which had the effect of allowing owner Charles Swibel to retain control of parking spaces at Marina City.

Vrdolyak bucked Mayor Richard Daley in 1974 when he ran for county assessor against organization-backed Tom Tully. The Democratic primary was a rout; Vrdolyak carried only his 10th Ward. In early days Daley would have punished such effrontery, but he allowed a repentant Vrdolyak back into the fold.

He held no major position after Daley's death. Yet Vrdolyak came under attack from maverick 1979 mayoral candidate Jane Byrne as leader of a "cabal of evil men," along with Burke and 1st Ward committeeman John D'Arco. Byrne won that election and maintained her feud with Vrdolyak for several months afterward.

Byrne appeared, to the surprise of many, at a Vrdolyak barbecue that summer. Soon afterward the newly elected mayor made peace with the cabaleros. Some analysts awarded Vrdolyak co-mayor status. Others hinted that he, not Byrne, wielded the real power.

The Byrne-Vrdolyak combine wrested the Democratic chairmanship from an unprepared George Dunne in 1982. Dunne, an ally of State's Attorney Richard Daley, held the Daley Southwest Side base, plus most suburban committeemen. Vrdolyak took most of the rest, including (ironically) all but one of the black committeemen.

At first the Vrdolyak chairmanship was viewed as a tonic for the Democrats. Vrdolyak mounted a highly publicized "Punch 10" (straight Democratic) campaign which some analysts credited for the strong city showing of gubernatorial candidate Adlai Stevenson. Others countered that a strong turnout among blacks, not related to "Punch 10," was the main reason for Stevenson's showing.

That governor's race made little difference. The real reason for Vrdolyak's elevation to party chairman was to boost Byrne's reelection bid. It nearly worked. Two Vrdolyak allies on the county board mounted a revolt against President George Dunne. Combining with suburban Republicans, they formed a veto-proof majority and reorganized board committees to stifle Dunne. Eventually, Dunne got his powers back, but the infighting neutralized a potentially influential Daley ally during the primary campaign.

A remark attributed to Vrdolyak sunk Byrne's campaign. Speaking to precinct captains the Saturday before the primary, Vrdolyak was quoted as saying, "It's a racial thing," and that a vote for Daley would serve as a vote for Harold Washington. His remarks drove Byrne-leaning blacks and white liberals into the Washington camp, perhaps in numbers large enough to cost the mayor renomination.

Even though giving lip service to Washington during the general election, he worked behind the scenes for Bernard Epton, the Republican nominee. After Epton's loss, Vrdolyak united twenty-eight white ethnic and one Hispanic aldermen to form an impenetrable (yet not veto-proof) council majority—the "29."

The Vrdolyak bloc's 29–21 council majority lasted three years—until 1986 special elections replaced four Vrdolyak stalwarts with black and Hispanic Washington allies. The new 25–25 council split proved just as rigid as the old 29–21 one, but Washington gained the edge because he cast tie-breaking votes.

Vrdolyak did not escape challenges in his own backyard. Miriam Balanoff, who previously had beaten a handpicked ally for a state representative position, opposed Vrdolyak himself for alderman in 1983. Despite a spirited campaign and the endorsements of both Harold Washington and Richard Daley, she received only one-third of the vote, mainly from the black precincts. The two met again in the 1984 Democratic committeeman election, with similar results.

Miriam Balanoff won election as circuit court judge in 1986, largely because of intense Washington campaigning in her behalf (bar associations rated her not qualified, and Vrdolyak campaigned hard against her). The Balanoff family nonetheless continued to be an irritation to Vrdolyak.

In most wards (especially those dominated by regular Democrats), the alderman has two top assistants. One is the ward secretary, chosen by the alderman himself. The other is the ward superintendent, who heads the local department of Streets and Sanitation. The mayor appoints the ward superintendent, usually upon the recommendation of the alderman. But in 1986, Washington placed Miriam Balanoff's son, Clement, in the 10th Ward spot.

Tenth Ward voters faced another battle in the Vrdolyak-Balanoff feud in 1987, but this time with two different contestants. When Edward Vrdolyak announced his candidacy for mayor in December 1986, he endorsed his older brother Victor for alderman.

The brothers offer a striking contrast in personalities. Glib, outgoing Edward "struts like a peacock among the mudhens on the Council floor." Victor is silent to the point of being taciturn.

Yet the "other" Vrdolyak also had a colorful record. A career policeman who once served as deputy superintendent, Victor served as a human political football during the early months of the Jane Byrne administration, when the mayor fought with her brother. An expert hostage negotiator, Victor dealt with a Croatian terrorist holding an airplane at O'Hare in 1979. Byrne (who saw to his demotion from deputy superintendent) called him off the case.

Victor resigned from the force soon afterward and set up a security company. Not surprisingly (given the realities of Chicago politics), the company received many choice contracts, including security for the expansion of McCormick Place.

The Victor Vrdolyak anointment did not meet with universal approval. Glenn Dawson, a former state senator and presumed heir apparent to the council seat, abandoned the Vrdolyaks and worked as Clem Balanoff's campaign manager. That defection made little difference. Victor Vrdolyak won easily, with roughly the same percentage (61) as his brother in his races against Balanoff's mother.

No one expects Victor Vrdolyak to waver from his brother's wishes in the city council. Some have speculated that he will resign and allow Edward to reenter the body. But if he quits, acting mayor Eugene Sawyer can nominate his successor (most likely Clement Balanoff), a choice that would last until 10th Ward voters have a chance to reelect Ed Vrdolyak—which, no doubt, they would.

Ed Vrdolyak may not want that seat. He resigned as Democratic party chairman in June 1987 and formally joined the Republicans that September. A month later he gained Republican slating for Clerk of the Circuit Court, an obscure but patronage-heavy office from which he can launch what most observers view as an inevitable 1989 or 1991 mayoral challenge.

Vrdolyak took most of his organization with him, including brother Victor (who became the first avowed Republican alderman since John Hoellen in 1975) and State Representative Sam Panayotovich. The Democratic Central Committee appointed Clement Balanoff committeeman in late 1987, thus putting him in charge of the only ward where the existing Republican organization is stronger than the Democratic one.

REDISTRICTING: The 10th Ward was unaffected by the 1986 ward remap.

MAYORAL: Even though Alderman Ed Vrdolyak served as Jane Byrne's floor leader throughout most of her term, his home ward delivered less than impressively for her in the 1983 Democratic primary. She carried the ward with 54 percent of the vote (mostly from white strongholds such as the East Side). Harold Washington took his 24 percent of the vote mainly from the black northwest corner. Richard Daley won 22 percent of the vote.

Washington picked up some of that Daley vote in the general election, but Bernard Epton won with 66 percent (in precincts coinciding almost precisely with Vrdolyak's strongholds against Balanoff).

Harold Washington received roughly the same number of votes in the 1987 Democratic primary and general elections (8,971 and 9,052), almost all of them from the Pill Hill and Jeffrey Manor areas.

The anti-Washington vote saw an increase in the general election. More than 3,000 additional anti-Washington voters turned out April 7, most of them contributing to a 68 percent victory for local hero Ed Vrdolyak.

CENSUS DATA: Population (1980): 60,184. 55.48 percent white, 27.20 percent black, 16.73 percent Hispanic, .59 percent Asian and other. Voting age population: 60.11 percent white, 24.88 percent black, 13.98 percent Hispanic, 1.03 percent Asian and other.

CENSUS TRACTS: See ward map.

COMMUNITY NEWSPAPERS:
  Daily Calumet, 18127 William St., Lansing (821–1200)
  El Dia, 2648 S. Kolin (277–7676) (Spanish)
  El Imparcial, 3610 W. 26th St. (376–9888) (Spanish)
  El Informador, 1821 S. Loomis (942–1295) (Spanish)
  Hegewisch News, 3150 W. 133rd (646–1100)
  Impacto, 3507 W. North Ave. (486–2547) (Spanish)
  La Opinion, 2501 S. East Ave., Berwyn (795–1383) (Spanish)
  La Voz de Chicago, 8624 S. Houston (221–9416) (Spanish)
  South East News, 9381 S. Phillips (978–2233)

ALDERMAN: Victor A. Vrdolyak. Elected 1987. Born July 14, 1932. Career: DePaul University; Thornton Community College; Wright Junior College; Lewis University; Chicago Police Department, 1963–79; president, AIC Security Company, 1979– .
Committees: Claims and Liabilities (vice-chairman); Aging and Disabled; Housing; License; Special Events and Cultural Affairs.
City hall telephone: 744-3078, 744-5687.
Ward office: 9618 S. Commercial Ave. (347-8181).
1987 election:
  Victor Vrdolyak   15,991   (61%)
  Clement Balanoff   10,223   (39%)

DEMOCRATIC COMMITTEEMAN: Clement Balanoff. Appointed 1987. Born April 16, 1953. Career: Ripon College; organizer, Steelworkers Old Timers Foundation; aide to Congressman Esteban Torres; aide to Congressman Matthew Martinez; ward superintendent, Department of Streets and Sanitation.
Ward office: 9211 S. Ewing (374–8081).

1984 election:

Edward Vrdolyak	17,121	(73%)
Miriam Balanoff	6,332	(27%)

MAYORAL ELECTIONS:

1983 Democratic primary:

Jane Byrne	15,005	(54%)
Harold Washington	6,560	(24%)
Richard Daley	6,242	(22%)

1983 general:

Bernard Epton	19,651	(66%)
Harold Washington	10,105	(34%)

1987 Democratic primary:

Jane Byrne	14,396	(61%)
Harold Washington	8,971	(38%)

1987 general:

Edward Vrdolyak	19,906	(68%)
Harold Washington	9,052	(31%)
Donald Haider	241	(1%)

11th Ward

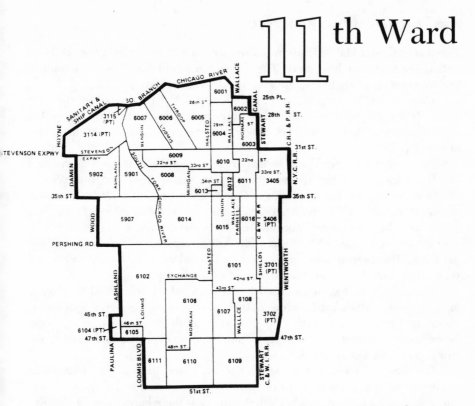

A DRIVE THROUGH BRIDGEPORT is a journey back in time. Street after street of frame houses and brick bungalows line neatly maintained blocks. Aged but sturdy and stately Roman Catholic churches provide a physical as well as spiritual anchor. Ruddy-faced Irish kids play along the streets, much as their ancestors had for generations.

One such lad of an earlier age, young Richard Daley, lived in the heart of Bridgeport, at 36th and Lowe. Undoubtedly he, like any other curious boy, explored his neighborhood. He saw the stockyards a few blocks south in neighboring Canaryville, where many of his friends' fathers worked (and which later would house the International Amphitheater, scene of grandiose livestock shows, at 42nd and Halsted). Or maybe he wandered west a few blocks and threw stones into the South Fork of the South Branch of the Chicago River—known locally as "Bubbly Creek," because fermented animal carcasses thrown into the river occasionally produced effervescence. Then he might have crossed Bubbly Creek into McKinley Park, a slightly more well-to-do area. Part of this area was known as "Ducktown," because it frequently was flooded.

If he saved his money, he traveled a few blocks east to newly built Comiskey Park, "Base-Ball Palace of the World," which towered over the Bridgeport neighborhood. He rooted for White Sox heroes such as spitball pitcher Ed Walsh, cocky second baseman Eddie Collins, and the immortal Shoeless Joe Jackson. On his way back home, he might have passed taverns like Schaller's

Pump at 37th and Halsted, where bartenders similar to Finley Peter Dunne's fictional Mr. Dooley held sway. The White Sox might have been one topic of conversation. Equally likely, the men inside were talking politics.

Canaryville, Bridgeport, and McKinley Park together make up the 11th Ward. It is fitting that a ward in the center of the city (37th and Honore has been determined to be Chicago's geographical center) should be at the center of city politics.

Bridgeport was an old city neighborhood even when Daley was growing up. It got its start in the 1830s when settlers, mainly Irish, arrived to build the newly approved Illinois-Michigan Canal. These settlers built houses along the south branch of the river, an area known as "Hardscrabble." It also was known as "Cabbage Patch," because residents grew cabbage in their gardens. "Bridgeport" came about because a low bridge crossing the river at Ashland prevented barges from passing. Traders had to unload at that spot, and reload their goods onto barges on the other side of the bridge.

Slaughterhouses soon emerged in the area. Many combined in 1865 to form the Union Stock Yards, which at their peak covered 400 acres with cattle, sheep, and pigs waiting to meet their doom. As the stockyards grew, so did other industries such as breweries, foundries, steel mills, and brickyards. Bridgeport boomed in the late 1800s.

Germans who entered Bridgeport at the same time as the Irish often got the more skilled positions in the meat packing industry. But the Irish had one major advantage over other ethnic groups—their knowledge of the English language. This, plus the freedom to seek office denied them in English-controlled Ireland, led many of them along the path to politics.

Chicago elected its first Irish Catholic mayor when Richard Daley was a youngster. Edward Dunne, who served from 1905 to 1907, was Chicago's first "ethnic" mayor, a sign that the older ethnic groups were coming of age in politics. Even then, the area was highly political. "It was taking your life in your hands to campaign against Dunne in Bridgeport or Back of the Yards," Carter Harrison II commented.

(Dunne was not the city's first Irish mayor. That honor went to one John Hopkins, who served in the 1880s. Hopkins is best remembered for stalling the Ogden Gas franchise until his personal bank account was fattened.)

A Bridgeport neighbor became mayor in 1933. Ed Kelly took office shortly after the death of Anton Cermak. He was chosen by Democratic leader Patrick Nash, a fellow 11th Ward resident who assumed the party chairmanship upon Cermak's death.

Forty years after his tenure, the verdict on Kelly is still open. Foes called him a corrupt ward boss who made Chicago into a "modern day Gomorrah." Allies cited his role in developing Lake Shore Drive, the State Street subway, and the CTA, plus his work (while with the South Park Board) in bringing about Grant Park, the Field Museum, Shedd Aquarium, and the Adler Planetarium.

No one disputes Kelly's role in strengthening the Democratic machine. He did so in part by taking in money from organized crime (reportedly $20 million per year from gambling alone).

Kelly secured the black vote for the Democrats. He gave symbolic support (Joe Louis was made "mayor" for ten minutes), but he also slated blacks for high positions. Arthur Mitchell was tapped for Congress in 1934 and William Dawson for 2nd Ward alderman in 1939.

He lubricated the Democratic machine with New Deal funds. President Franklin Delano Roosevelt went along with Kelly, in part because of the huge pluralities Kelly always delivered.

By 1947, Kelly's corruption had become too hot for party leaders to handle. They needed a reformer and found one in Bridgeport native Martin Kennelly. The millionaire owner of a moving company, Kennelly served mainly as a figurehead. He made attempts at reform, such as the introduction of a civil service system, but was not very successful. A crackdown on the South Side's policy racket served only to infuriate black political boss William Dawson, who demanded his removal.

Daley, meanwhile, quietly moved to the top. He assumed the chairmanship of the Cook County Democratic party's central committee in 1953, assuring that he could have himself slated for mayor a year later.

Eugene Kennedy in his book *Himself!* noted that Daley as mayor "kept things as they were in Bridgeport, while he refashioned the face of downtown Chicago; he maintained one in the mood of another age while he could not modernize the other fast enough."

"Maintaining the mood" meant, among other things, the exclusion of blacks, a pattern that exists to this day. Critics charge that Daley built the Stevenson and Dan Ryan expressways in their particular sites to act as a barrier between Bridgeport-Canaryville and nearby black neighborhoods. Two black students who moved to an apartment near Daley's house in 1964 were met with such hostility that they were forced to leave. The most overt symbol of Bridgeport's racial hostility was an iron gate at 42nd Street. The locked gate made access impossible from the black Fuller Park neighborhood to the east. The gate was removed in 1982.

Daley never forgot Bridgeport; unlike his predecessors, he did not move out of the neighborhood. And he saw to it that his Bridgeport buddies reached powerful spots in local government: Robert Quinn, fire commissioner; Ed Quigley, sewer department chief; Edward Bedore, budget director; Tom Donovan, patronage chief; Matt Danaher, clerk of the circuit court; and Danaher's successor, Morgan Finley.

Throughout the Daley years, the 11th Ward lacked notable city council representation (Mike Royko once wrote, "This is the mayor's ward. Why does it need an alderman?"). Danaher served there before rising to the circuit court position. He was replaced in 1969 by Michael Bilandic, another quiet soul.

Bilandic nonetheless assumed leadership of the important Finance Committee after imprisonment of predecessor Tom Keane in 1975. When Daley died in 1976, Bilandic (because of his 11th Ward connection) was chosen by his fellow aldermen as interim mayor. He won a special election in 1977 and ran again in 1979.

It is not inconceivable that party leaders planned to let Bilandic babysit the mayoral throne until Daley's son Richard came of appropriate age. Bilandic would then be rewarded with a judgeship, Daley could occupy the fifth floor office, and the party could revert to the status quo.

Bilandic ultimately won his seat on the bench, but otherwise 11th Ward Democrats never saw the hoped-for state of affairs. A heavy blizzard engulfed Chicago a month before the 1979 election, causing havoc for both car owners and CTA riders. Bilandic's moves, in retrospect, were precisely the wrong ones. He commissioned a $90,000 snow removal study which said, in effect, "When it snows, remove it." Blacks, the group most dependent on public transportation, often saw trains roar past them as they shivered at frozen el stops.

During one speech, Bilandic compared his critics with those who crucified Jesus Christ, sent Jews to the gas chambers during the Holocaust, enslaved blacks, mistreated Polish peasants, oppressed Latin Americans, and fomented unrest in Iran. It was a remarkable speech, one which managed to offend almost every major ethnic group in Chicago.

The weather broke on primary day in 1979—and so did the 11th Ward stranglehold on the mayor's office. The machine got its normal vote out, but that total was outnumbered by thousands of blacks and independents who chose maverick politician Jane Byrne.

Four years later, Bridgeport's real "favorite son," Richard M. Daley, entered the mayoral race. Although he finished third in the Democratic primary, the 78 percent vote total he received in the ward indicated the esteem with which the Daley name is still held there.

The younger Daley assumed the 11th Ward Democratic committeeman post upon his father's death but gave it up when he became state's attorney in 1980. A brother, John, now holds that position.

John Daley's life has not been without controversy. When it was disclosed in 1973 that Mayor Daley steered lucrative insurance contracts to John and a brother, the mayor responded by suggesting that critics kiss his posterior. The following year newspapers found that John had failed his insurance examination but got his license due to misgrading by the examiner.

In 1975 John Daley again made headlines by marrying the daughter of a reputed mob figure. One columnist commented, "In most cities when the son or daughter of the mayor is going to be wed, the news is covered in the society page. In Chicago, from the day of the announcement . . . the story has belonged exclusively to the crime reporter."

Ward secretary Patrick Huels replaced Bilandic in the city council. He conducted an almost invisible campaign and refused to talk with reporters. The *Tribune* commented before the election, "(Huels) lives in Bridgeport and was chosen for the City Council by State Sen. Richard M. Daley, ward committeeman and son of the late mayor. Mr. Huels' other known qualifications are that he moves, speaks and breathes. It's not certain he needs them." Yet he won the 1977 special election by a ten-to-one margin over an opponent who felt that no one should run unopposed.

Even though the 11th Ward has been shut out of the mayor's office for the last three elections, Huels remains a silent member of the city council. Yet he receives only token opposition at election time. In 1987, he ran unopposed.

Demographic changes may alter the power structure in future years. Hispanics, dispersed fairly evenly throughout the ward, account for nearly one-quarter of the population. Blacks, almost all living south of 47th Street and in the eastern tier of precincts, make up 12 percent of the population. Chinese have spilled over from Chinatown into northern Bridgeport, joining the Lithuanians, Poles, Italians, Mexicans, and Irish who call the area home.

These minorities may declare independence from the Irish-run 11th Ward Regular Democratic Organization, although (with the exception of blacks) there appears little inclination for them to do so. But even if all groups unite behind party regulars, one thing appears certain: the 11th Ward will never again see the overwhelming political power it had during the Kelly, Kennelly and Daley years.

Redistricting: Three precincts south of 51st Street were transferred to the 3rd Ward. In turn the 11th gained two precincts at the southwest corner which previously belonged to the 14th Ward.

Mayoral: As expected, Bridgeport's Richard Daley won a landslide vote in the 1983 primary—78 percent of the vote, the largest number received by either white candidate in any ward. Harold Washington received 13 percent of the vote and Jane Byrne, 9 percent.

Daley remained officially neutral in the general election, although many of his precinct captains pushed for Bernard Epton. Election results showed the racial split found in many other wards. Some predominantly black southern and eastern precincts went 100 to 1 for Washington. Epton's percentages outside the black areas were not quite so convincing, but they were enough to give him 74 percent of the ward's vote.

Ironically, onetime Daley nemesis Jane Byrne in 1987 outpolled favorite son Daley's 1983 total, with 80 percent of the vote. The Vrdolyak-Haider combination drew a similar percentage in the general election. As in 1983 Harold Washington's strength was found in the black precincts.

Census data: Population (1980): 58,489. 64.10 percent white, 12.61 percent black, 21.71 percent Hispanic, 1.58 percent Asian and other. Voting age percentage: 68.68 percent white, 11.35 percent black, 18.15 percent Hispanic, .82 percent Asian and other.

CENSUS TRACTS: See ward map.

COMMUNITY NEWSPAPERS:
Back of the Yards Journal, 4625 S. Ashland (927–7200)
Bridgeport News, 3252 S. Halsted (927–3118)
Brighton Park & McKinley Park Life, 2949 W. 43rd (523–3663)
El Heraldo, 3734 W. 26th St. (521–8300) (Spanish)

ALDERMAN: Patrick Huels. Appointed 1976, elected 1977. Born August 26, 1949,
Career: B.A., Christian Brothers College, 1971; staff member, Committee
for Environmental Control, 1971–76.
City hall telephone: 744–6663, 744–6664.
Ward office: 3659 S. Halsted (254–6677).
1987 aldermanic election:
Patrick Huels, unopposed.

DEMOCRATIC COMMITTEEMAN: John Daley. Appointed 1980. Born December 5,
1946. Career: B.A., Loyola University; aide to circuit court clerk Matt Danaher, 1969–71; insurance agent; state representative, 1985–.
Ward office: 3659 S. Halsted (254–6677).
1984 election:
John Daley, unopposed.

MAYORAL ELECTIONS:

1983 Democratic primary:
Richard Daley   21,239 (78%)
Harold Washington   3,586 (13%)
Jane Byrne   2,552   (9%)

1987 Democratic primary:
Jane Byrne   17,874 (80%)
Harold Washington   8,971 (19%)

1983 general:
Bernard Epton   20,574 (74%)
Harold Washington   7,200 (26%)

1987 general:
Edward Vrdolyak   16,186 (78%)
Harold Washington   4,460 (20%)
Donald Haider   432   (2%)

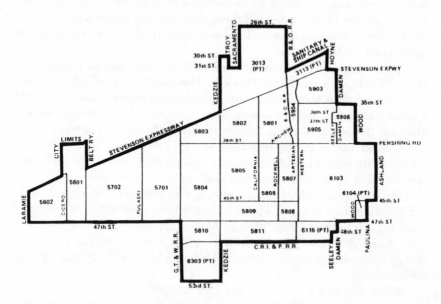

12th Ward

NOT ALL POLITICAL SQUABBLES in Chicago were Harold Washington versus Edward Vrdolyak affairs. In fact, one of the liveliest battles in the city was the seemingly endless civil war in the Southwest Side's 12th Ward, a war that now appears to be resolved.

On one side there was Aloysius Majerczyk, political maverick and two-term alderman. The opposing faction may be called the House of Swinarski. Its current standard bearer is Robert Molaro, the ward's Democratic committeeman.

For years the Swinarskis held all the control in this Brighton Park-Archer Heights ward. Theodore served in the state house of representatives from 1948 to 1956. He made an unsuccessful state senate attempt that year, but won election as Democratic committeeman.

Eight years later, he again ran for the senate. This time he won. Or did he? Republicans claimed Swinarski could not be sworn in because he failed residency requirements at the time of the election. The courts agreed. Donald Swinarski shook his fist at Senate Majority Leader W. Russell Arrington and vowed "I'll be back!"

He kept his promise. Swinarski won an election in 1970 and quickly became chairman of the senate Elections Committee.

Meanwhile, Theodore's son Donald entered the political picture. He ran for alderman and defeated six other candidates in 1967. Almost from the beginning, the younger Swinarski engendered controversy. His political enemies claimed that the insurance executive actually lived in Oak Lawn. Swinarski admitted to owning the suburban residence but claimed he kept it as a summer home and weekend residence for raising his sixteen St. Bernard dogs. Swinarski maintained that he, his wife, and three children (and presumably, the sixteen St. Bernards) lived in a second-story apartment above his campaign head-quarters on Archer Avenue.

Three years later he was arrested early one morning on a beach at Key West, Florida, with a woman not his wife. The couple was charged with indecent exposure and illicit sexual intercourse. Swinarski claimed he was unable to find a motel and that he and the woman were fully clothed. The charges were later dropped; the arresting officer commented only that he had "a weak case."

Donald Swinarski won reelection in 1971, then tried for the state senate the following year. The elder Swinarski, having made his point with Arrington and the other Republicans, stepped aside in favor of his son.

Once in Springfield, Donald continued his controversial ways. A member of the senate Insurance and Financial Institutions Committee, he admitted to receiving a loan from a man he later helped appoint to the state Savings and Loan Board. Afterward he told of plans to seize control (through appointments) of state agencies regulating savings and loans and then selling favorable rulings for payoffs.

But it was an income tax charge that scuttled Donald Swinarski. He was convicted in 1975 of understating his 1969 income tax by $7,800—one-third of his total income that year. That conviction led to Donald Swinarski forfeiting his state senate seat. Thus Theodore and Donald Swinarski became the first father and son team ever to be removed from the General Assembly.

Even after his conviction, Donald left with a bang and not a whimper. As was a common custom in those days, he collected his two-year legislative salary in advance. Attorney General William Scott had to file a lawsuit to recover the balance of the salary.

Meanwhile George Kwak, a cousin of Donald's by marriage, won the special election to replace him as 12th Ward alderman. A 1974 *Tribune* report described him as "another say-nothing, do-nothing administration alderman." His moment in the sun occurred in 1975, when a judge ordered him to demolish a half-finished home he started building in the 11th Ward.

Kwak defeated the same challenger both in the special election and the 1975 race—a former policeman named Aloysius Majerczyk, who ran as a Re-publican. The elections board ruled that Majerczyk could not run as long as he remained a cop. Rather than fight a protracted battle against the board, he quit the police force.

Third time proved to be the charm for the insurgent Majerczyk. He trounced Kwak in 1979. Rather than offer a peace pipe to Committeeman Theodore Swinarski, he reportedly threatened the ouster of Swinarski's pa-tronage workers.

Theodore Swinarski, having beaten Majerczyk for committeeman in 1980, sought to regain the aldermanic chair for the family in 1983. Majerczyk out-polled him the February election. A third candidate's vote forced a runoff, which Majerczyk won by a narrow margin.

Majerczyk observed (correctly, if the April election returns were any indication) the he would lose few votes in his white ethnic ward by opposing the (black) Democratic mayoral nominee, Harold Washington. He became the first alderman to declare open support for Republican Bernard Epton. Most other white aldermen followed suit, either overtly or covertly.

After the election Majerczyk was the first alderman to declare that he might not work with Washington. Alderman Edward Vrdolyak consolidated opposition to the new mayor, but Majerczyk did not play a major role in the antiadministration bloc.

In fact, Majerczyk tried without success to consolidate power in his own ward. Swinarski retired as committeeman in 1984 and backed a thirty-five-year old attorney named Robert Molaro. Two other candidates (one of them former congressman John "Mr. Bingo" Fary) also entered the race.

The election fight became a fistfight two days before the election as Majerczyk and his supporters exchanged blows with Molaro supporters in a tavern. Majerczyk may have won that battle, but he lost the electoral war.

Majerczyk's most notable moment came in early 1986. He led the city council in a protest against the French film *Hail Mary*. He called the Jean-Luc Goddard film blasphemous, although admitting that he had never seen it.

The committeeman election showed that Majerczyk had, at best, a tenuous grip on his city council seat. Perhaps that is why he sought a spot on the Metropolitan Sanitary District board in the March 1986 Democratic primary. His major campaign promise was construction of a replica of Fort Dearborn along the Cal-Sag Canal.

Ordinarily an incumbent alderman is considered a shoo-in for this relatively minor county post. Yet Majerczyk finished seventh in an eight-candidate race—further evidence of his lack of clout.

Three challengers appeared on the 1987 aldermanic ballot against Majerczyk: Mark Fary, an aide to State Senator Timothy Degnan, nephew of the late congressman and the Molaro-backed candidate; Republican David Zwolinski; and Ronald McKee, a black candidate.

Majerczyk might have signed his political death warrant in the summer of 1986. He missed the city council meeting at which a record property tax increase was improved. His absence was important, because the increase passed, 25–24. Had he appeared, the 25–25 vote would have forced Harold Washington into the spotlight by casting the deciding vote for the increase. Not coincidentally, Washington placed a Majerczyk ally as ward superintendent just before that council meeting.

The alderman claimed that he was in Canada on a moose-hunting vacation. Zwolinski later took advantage of that confession, parading through city hall with a friend who was wearing a moose costume and carrying an empty six-pack of Moosehead beer.

Majerczyk did well in Brighton Park, and McKee scored with the ward's few black voters. Otherwise, Fary swept the ward. He won 58 percent of the vote.

Fary, Majerczyk, and Zwolinski all campaigned on an anti-Washington platform; no pro-Washington candidate could hope to win here. Yet once in office, Fary (who bears a facial resemblance to a young Mike Ditka) has shown himself to be a pragmatist. He voted for the city council reorganization, a vote which gained him vice-chairmanship of the Committee on Aviation.

Molaro found himself in the headlines in the summer of 1986 as the earliest public supporter of a nonpartisan mayoral ballot. Other committeemen worked behind the scenes to collect petitions for a referendum to make the 1987 mayoral election nonpartisan (and thus increase the odds of Harold Washington facing only one white opponent). He became the "leader" of the drive by default. When a political columnist asked about this petition drive, Molaro was the only committeeman not to ask that his remarks be off the record.

One could be forgiven for suspecting that Molaro lacks clout among his Democratic peers. In late 1987 he cited party loyalty as he sought backing for the county recorder of deeds slot (he said, "I stood fast all the way. It's time I got rewarded"). Molaro failed to receive the party nod. When a death created a vacancy on the board of tax appeals, he sought that post. Once again he was thwarted.

The 12th is a very solidly white ethnic ward. Poles predominate. In fact, one stretch of 43rd Street has been renamed in honor of the most famous Polish visitor, Pope John Paul II Drive. The pope celebrated mass at nearby Five Holy Martyrs Church in 1979.

Archer Avenue, a prosperous-looking business strip of chain stores and car dealerships, is the major thoroughfare here. It roughly bisects the ward, northeast to southwest.

Industry can be found here and there. Campbell Soup has a plant at 35th and Maplewood. Santa Fe Railroad's Piggy Back Terminal occupies the space between Pershing and 43rd, Kedzie and Central Park. The Central Manufacturing District, an early industrial park organized by a local railroad, is located between Pershing and 43rd, Ashland and Western. Smaller factories may be found on 47th Street west of Archer.

Most of the year the northwest corner lot at 47th and Damen is vacant, playing host only to Little League baseball teams. But in August it comes to life as the setting for Chicago's biggest carnival. In past years it was known as the Back of the Yards Free Fair. Now it it called the Chicago County Fair.

Despite the above attractions this is mainly a residential ward. Brick bungalows line most of the streets, the housing interrupted only by a corner store or tavern.

The eastern half of the ward forms the Brighton Park community, named after a long-gone racetrack at the present-day site of McKinley Park (Western and Pershing). The western half is known as Archer Heights, although nothing suggesting high ground exists in the area. In fact, 44th Street east of Cicero is one street without curbs or drainage. After a heavy rain or snow melt, standing water covers much of the street—hardly the sign of high ground.

Although the 12th Ward contains areas many consider solidly white ethnic, there are also sizable minority populations. Hispanic stores, churches, and bars are visible in the southeast section of the ward, part of the Back of the Yards neighborhood.

A black anomaly can be found on the far western end of the ward. This is the Le Claire Courts CHA housing project, which in the summer of 1986 became the first CHA project to allow tenants to manage a project's day-to-day affairs.

Finally, the 12th Ward has perhaps the most unusual precinct in the city, at 26th and California—Cook County Jail.

REDISTRICTING: The 12th Ward suffered only minor changes from the 1986 remap. It lost one northern precinct to the 22nd Ward and gained one from the 25th.

MAYORAL: Even though Aloysius Majerczyk won reelection as alderman of the 12th Ward in 1983, his mayoral choice (Jane Byrne) did not fare as well. Richard Daley of the neighboring 11th Ward (backed by Theodore Swinarski) won 59 percent of the primary vote (carrying every white precinct but one) to 33 percent for Byrne and 8 percent for Harold Washington.

In the general election, Harold Washington won only 15 percent of the vote—a number almost exactly equal to the black voting age percentage. Hispanic precincts, housing what is often perceived as a swing vote, went solidly for Epton.

Harold Washington received slightly less than 16 percent of the vote in the 1987 Democratic primary and picked up about one percentage point in the general election. As in 1983, his major strength lay in the black precincts.

CENSUS DATA: Population (1980): 60,674. 66.57 percent white, 13.87 percent black, 17.38 percent Hispanic, 2.18 percent Asian and other. Voting age population: 70.97 percent white, 13.07 percent black, 14.58 percent Hispanic, 1.38 percent Asian and other.

CENSUS TRACTS: See ward map.

COMMUNITY NEWSPAPERS:
Back of the Yards Journal, 4625 S. Ashland (927–2700)
Bridgeport News, 3252 S Halsted (927–3118)
Brighton Park & McKinley Park Life, 2949 W. 43rd (523–3663)
El Heraldo, 3734 W. 26th St. (521–8300) (Spanish)
Lawndale News, 2711 W. Cermak (247–8500)

Southtown Economist, 5959 S. Harlem (586–8800)
Southwest News-Herald, 6225 S. Kedzie (476–4800)

Alderman: Mark J. Fary. Elected 1987. Born 1956. Career: DePaul University, University of Illinois at Chicago; assistant to Congressman John Fary; member, National Democratic Committee on Ethnic Heritage; aide to State Senator Timothy Degnan.

Committees: Aviation (vice-chairman); Energy, Environmental Protection, and Public Utilities; Health; License; Police, Fire and Municipal Institutions; Ports, Wharves and Bridges.

City hall telephone: 744–3040, 744–3068.

Ward office: 4204 S. Archer Ave. (254–4600).

1987 election:

Mark J. Fary	12,000	(58%)
Aloysius A. Majerczyk	4,578	(22%)
David T. Zwolinski	3,186	(15%)
Ronald E. McKee	819	(4%)

DEMOCRATIC COMMITTEEMAN: Robert Molaro. Elected 1984. Born 1950. Career: B.A., Loyola University; J.D., John Marshall Law School; attorney.

Ward office: 4204 S. Archer Ave. (254–4600).

1984 election:

Robert Molaro	10,055	(56%)
Aloysius Majerczyk	4,871	(27%)
Stanley Kedzior	1,613	(9%)
John Fary	1,450	(8%)

MAYORAL ELECTIONS:

1983 Democratic primary:

Richard Daley	13,510	(59%)
Jane Byrne	7,633	(33%)
Harold Washington	1,750	(8%)

1983 general:

Bernard Epton	21,059	(85%)
Harold Washington	3,838	(15%)

1987 Democratic primary:

Jane Byrne	17,524	(84%)
Harold Washington	3,261	(16%)

1987 general:

Edward Vrdolyak	16,186	(80%)
Harold Washington	3,337	(17%)
Donald Haider	657	(3%)

13th Ward

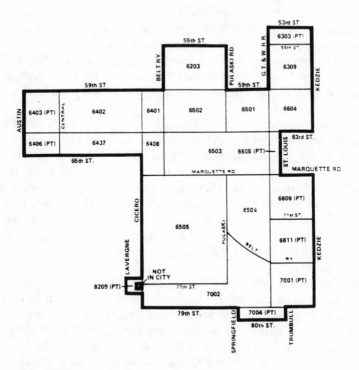

IT APPEARED DESTINED to be the world's busiest airport, and at one time the Southwest Side's Midway Airport fulfilled that prophecy. But technology unforeseen during its construction dealt a cruel blow. Midway's runways were not long enough to accommodate the large jets which soon accounted for most commercial air traffic. Those jets went to the Northwest Side's O'Hare Field, an airport then located in open spaces.

The air situation became so desperate that Midway closed to commercial flights during the 1960s. Today, the airport is rebounding strongly. One airline, Midway Airlines, is based out of the airport. Another Chicago-based airline, United, resumed service to Midway in early 1987. The southwest rapid transit line, when complete, should further increase air traffic.

Even discounting the airport, the 13th covers a diverse and relatively prosperous area. The bulk of the ward is bounded by 59th and 79th streets, Kedzie on the east and Cicero on the west. A western portion (which includes Midway) extends to Austin Avenue between 59th and 63rd streets. It forms the city limit at Cicero (south of 63rd) and 63rd (west of Cicero).

Huge factories and a railroad yard dominate the southwest sector of the ward. Many of these plants pertain to the food industry. Tootsie Rolls are made at 74th and Cicero, and Nabisco cookies are produced at 73rd and Kedzie.

Accompanying soft drinks may be consumed from Sweetheart cups manufactured at 76th and Kostner.

The southwest part of the ward also houses gigantic Ford City, Chicago's largest shopping district outside the Loop. Built in 1965, Ford City was the first Chicago shopping center built in response to the malls which were already sprouting up in the suburbs. It contains 125 stores.

Ford City has not spelled death to existing shopping strips. Lively shopping areas exist along Kedzie, Pulaski, and Cicero avenues, 55th, 79th, and 63rd streets. The latter displays banners declaring itself "The Main Street of Southwest Chicago."

These strips produce a myriad of sights. Kedzie at 59th Street has both an Oriental gift shop and the Colony Theater, scene of rock concerts. Middle Eastern bakeries may be found along 79th Street. Pulaski between 59th and 63rd streets is by itself a veritable cornucopia of sights. Where else in Chicago can one find an Irish specialties shop (59th Street), Dove Ice Cream and Candies (at 60th Street, birthplace of the nationally famous Dove Bar), Izzy Rizzy's House of Tricks (a magic shop at 61st Street), and the Balzekas Museum of Lithuanian Culture (at 65th)? If those are not enough, there is always the White Owl Cigar Store at 63rd and Pulaski, where a titanic cigar store Indian looms over the intersection.

That big Indian provided a stark contrast with what once was the most unusual attraction in the ward. The former Midget's Club at 4016 W. 63rd Street was just that—a bar operated by and for (but not limited to) midgets.

Other features of interest dot this ward: Richard J. Daley College at 74th and Pulaski; St. Gall Church, a pie wedge-shaped church liberally adorned with stained glass windows at 55th and Kedzie; the western half of Marquette Park, from Kedzie to Central Park between Marquette Drive (67th) and 71st street.

Illinois House Speaker Michael Madigan has served as Democratic committeeman here since 1972. One of the most respected of Illinois politicians, even by foes, Madigan runs what some call the most disciplined ward organization, from top to bottom, in Chicago.

Madigan is a household name throughout Illinois and perhaps second most powerful politician in the state. However, his spotlight has not shone on recent 13th Ward aldermen. Perhaps the last notable one here was John Egan, who served from 1947 to 1962 and later headed the Metropolitan Sanitary District.

A more typical 13th Ward alderman was Casimir "Casey" Staszcuk, who was first elected in 1967. Staszcuk was one of those quiet, pro-administration aldermen, the types likely to make headlines only when accused of some sort of malfeasance.

That was the case with Staszcuk. He and 23rd Ward alderman Joseph Potempa, both Republicans, were indicted in May 1973 on bribery charges stemming from zoning changes within their wards. Then-U.S. Attorney Jim Thompson surveyed the condition of his party in Chicago and lamented, "There are three Republican aldermen in the council and now two-thirds of them have been indicted."

Staszcuk was convicted on nine counts of bribery that June. John Madrzyk, a Health Department official, soon afterward defeated Republican real estate broker Charles Janulas in a special election for the aldermanic post. He has served ever since.

The *Tribune* in a 1981 story facetiously called Madrzyk the city's best alderman. "John Madrzyk of the Southwest Side's 13th Ward is cheerful, conscientious, interested, and awake," the article commented.

Virtually unknown outside his own ward, Madrzyk nonetheless is a controversial figure inside it. That controversy stems from the extensive downzoning that has taken place in the ward since 1978. Such downzoning has affected almost every piece of commercial property along his ward's business strips.

Madrzyk maintains that zoning is being restricted in order to keep out enterprises such as adult book stores, taverns, and pool halls. His foes contend that he arranged the downzoning in order to maintain control over businesses in the ward. They also charge that he has preyed upon racial fears by claiming to make downzoning changes in order to discourage blacks from entering the ward.

Blacks shop in the ward, particularly in Ford City. But they certainly don't live here. Census figures from 1980 counted only 57 blacks in a population of 61,249—.09 percent of the ward's people. Nor have they been encouraged to move here. This ward contains the site (at 60th and Kedvale) of the former Airport Gardens housing project. When black families moved there in 1946, they met with such hostility that they fled. The strong white reaction against integration influenced the Chicago Housing Authority to limit its construction of new public housing to black ghetto neighborhoods.

Downzoning was not a major issue in the 1987 aldermanic election. No strong opposing organization exists here; few pols want to tangle with the powerful Madigan. Only two persons challenged Madrzyk: city electrician James O'Connell, the Republican-backed candidate; and Art Jones, a man with a history of involvement in right-wing causes. Even though both the *Tribune* and *Sun-Times* attacked Madrzyk as a Mike Madigan puppet, the incumbent swept all precincts and took 83 percent of the vote. He received more votes (27,209) than any other aldermanic candidate in the city.

REDISTRICTING: The 13th Ward gained one precinct south of 79th Street from the 18th Ward—a one-block-wide precinct extending from Springfield to Trumbull.

MAYORAL: Michael Madigan kept a low profile in the 1983 Democratic primary. However, precinct captains spread the message that "a vote for (Richard) Daley is a vote for (Harold) Washington." Jane Byrne gained a respectable 46 percent of the vote in the Democratic primary. Richard Daley took the ward with 53 percent of the vote, but it was far less than the victory needed in a ward considered part of his home turf.

Despite Madigan's open endorsement of Washington, this overwhelmingly white (95.5 percent of the population) ward carried proportionally for Bernard Epton with the biggest voter turnout of any ward in the city. He won 95.98 percent of the vote in the general election, his best percentage in the city. Yet awesome as that percentage may seem, eleven wards gave Washington higher percentages.

The 13th once again proved the anti-Washington champion in 1987. Jane Byrne received 31,727 votes here, the highest ward total of any candidate other than Washington in either the primary or general election. Her margin over Washington (30,429) was the largest of any challenger. Only the 23rd Ward gave Byrne a higher percentage than the 95.81 percent she got here.

Vrdolyak fared almost equally well in the general election, with 31,108 votes and 93.33 percent. Washington and Republican Don Haider split almost evenly the remaining vote.

CENSUS DATA: Population (1980): 61,249. 95.58 percent white, .09 percent black, 3.42 percent Hispanic, .91 percent Asian and other. Voting age population: 96.02 percent white, .11 percent black, 2.79 percent Hispanic, 1.08 percent Asian and other.

CENSUS TRACTS: See ward map.

COMMUNITY NEWSPAPERS:
  Clear-Ridge Reporter, 6221 S. Kedzie (476–4800)
  Southtown Economist, 5959 S. Harlem (586–8800)
  Southwest News-Herald, 6225 S. Kedzie (476–4800)

ALDERMAN: John Madrzyk. Elected 1973. Born January 4, 1939. Career: U.S. Army, 1957–59; purchasing and inventory control supervisor, Chicago Board of Health, 1959–73.
Committees: Aviation; Finance; Land Acquisition, Disposition, and Leases; Special Events and Cultural Affairs; Traffic Control and Safety.
City hall telephone: 744–3076, 744–3058.
Ward office: 6500 S. Pulaski (581–8000).
1987 election:

John S. Madrzyk	27,209	(83%)
James J. O'Connell	4,658	(14%)
Arthur Joseph Jones	1,055	(3%)

DEMOCRATIC COMMITTEEMAN: Michael Madigan. Elected 1972. Born April 19, 1942. Career: B.A., University of Notre Dame; J.D. Loyola University; attorney; state representative 1970-.

Ward office: 6500 S. Pulaski (581–8000).
1984 election:
Michael Madigan, unopposed.

MAYORAL ELECTIONS:

1983 Democratic primary:

Richard Daley	17,854	(53%)
Jane Byrne	15,388	(46%)
Harold Washington	239	(1%)

1983 general:

Bernard Epton	34,893	(96%)
Harold Washington	1,460	(4%)

1987 Democratic primary:

Jane Byrne	31,727	(96%)
Harold Washington	1,298	(4%)

1987 general:

Edward Vrdolyak	31,108	(93%)
Harold Washington	1,123	(3%)
Donald Haider	1,092	(3%)

14th Ward

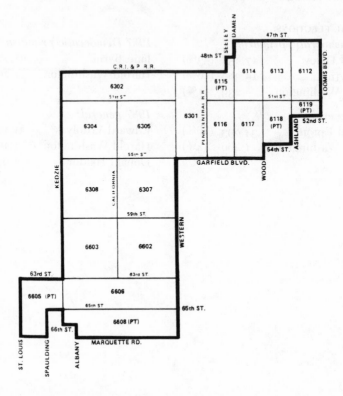

"THE IRISH SETTLED in Chicago around the 1840s to build a canal, live in the shanties, and work in the industries that followed their strong backs," Mike Royko wrote in *Boss*. "This area became known as Back of the Yards, because of its greatest wonder—the stock yards. Then the nation's busiest slaughterhouse, it gave meat to the nation, jobs to the South Side and a stink to the air that was unforgettable."

Others soon joined the Irish. Germans and Poles, taking their traditional European animosities with them, settled nearby. Lithuanians, Slovaks, Czechs, Russians, Ukrainians, and Jews arrived a few years later. Each group built its own churches or synagogues, often massive structures.

Hours were long, work was hard, and wages were irregular. Rats and other vermin abounded. This was the area Upton Sinclair described in his muckraking 1905 book *The Jungle*.

It also was an area that helped itself out of the doldrums. A community organizer named Saul Alinsky and a local resident, Joseph Meeghan, set up the Back of the Yards Council in the 1930s. This council organized youth activities and worked to improve community conditions. Half a century later, it still is one of the most respected grass roots groups in Chicago.

Back of the Yards at one time coincided with Chicago's 14th Ward. The ward extended roughly from Ashland Avenue east to State Street, 47th south to 63rd Street. As with the neighboring 11th, its population might have been polyglot, but political control was solidly Irish.

Through the years and the redistrictings, the 14th Ward has moved westward, away from Back of the Yards (and some say, always one jump ahead of an encroaching black population). Today the ward is an irregularly shaped mass, the bulk of it bordered by Western on the east, Kedzie on the west, the Rock Island railroad on the north, and Marquette Road on the south, plus a northeastern chunk bordered by Western, Garfield Boulevard on the south, Loomis on the east, and 47th Street on the north.

It's a ward big enough to contain Mexican stores at 47th and Ashland, a Byzantine Catholic church at 50th and Seeley, French restaurants and groceries on 63rd Street from Kedzie to St. Louis, a Rumanian Pentecostal church at 59th and California, Arabic groceries, bakeries, and even a photographer on 63rd Street from California to Kedzie, Nativity of the Blessed Virgin (a Ukrainian Catholic church) at 50th and Paulina, a Polish bar (complete with "Zimne piwo"—"cold beer"—sign) at 49th and Wolcott, and the 6511 Club on South Kedzie—a bar where folk musicians with traditional Irish instruments hold jam sessions on Friday nights.

Especially west of Western Avenue, the 14th Ward consists of blocks with row after row of bungalows, large Catholic churches, and busy shopping streets with many ethnic stores—in short, your quintessential Southwest Side ward.

One thing has not changed in the 14th Ward despite the many geographical and ethnic changes: the Irish still run it.

In the case of Irish politicians from the 14th and 11th Wards, familiarity bred contempt. Fourteenth Ward pols continuously tried, invariably without success, to oust their 11th Ward foes.

James McDermott ruled the ward for many years, as both committeeman (first elected in 1932) and alderman (1933). A close ally of 19th Ward alderman John Duffy, McDermott was one of the leaders of the anti-Ed Kelly-Patrick Nash faction. McDermott became a circuit court judge in 1947. In his place he named Clarence Wagner to fill both alderman and committeeman posts.

Wagner in 1950 became chairman of the Finance Committee. He (and through him, McDermott) led the "grey wolves," a pack of aldermen who were the real rulers of the city during the years Mayor Martin Kennelly was cutting ceremonial ribbons.

Following the 1952 election debacle (Dwight D. Eisenhower's landslide buried most local Democrats), the Democrats appeared ready to make a change. Wagner and McDermott were ready to challenge the 11th Ward choice for party chairman, Richard J. Daley.

When the central committee met in the spring of 1953, Wagner moved to adjourn for two weeks. This ploy was designed to give McDermott and Duffy the chance to round up the necessary votes to give the "South Side Irish" the chairmanship. In the meantime, Wagner set off to Canada for a fishing trip. He never made it. Wagner was killed in an automobile accident in Minnesota. With him died the chances for a 14th Ward party takeover. Richard Daley became party chairman in 1953 and two years later, mayor—positions he held for the rest of his life.

A rough-hewn cop named Joseph Burke was chosen as Wagner's successor. Burke attended not only the city council meetings but also the other truly important events of the ward—the weddings and wakes that aldermen consider political as well as social obligations. By his side at these affairs, saying the proper words and learning the ropes of the trade, was Burke's son Edward.

The younger Burke undoubtedly dreamed of putting these aldermanic lessons to use one day. But he probably had no idea that he would use them as early as he did. Joe Burke died of cancer in 1968—when Edward was only twenty-five years old.

Ed Burke's first election was his toughest. The dust had not settled on his father's coffin before party leaders moved to name a successor. Burke, realizing that the next party leader might hold power for a generation, called in a lifetime worth of chits. In a secret vote of sixty-five precinct captains, he won the committeeman seat (and assurance of party slating for alderman) over a veteran precinct captain by 3 1/2 votes.

Thus armed, he trounced six opponents for alderman in a 1969 special election. That was his first and last contested aldermanic race. A token opponent faced him in 1971. Burke has been unopposed for alderman or committeeman since then.

The younger Burke soon proved a sharp contrast to his late father. He was nattily attired and articulate. While some aldermen nodded through city council meetings, he studied Roberts Rules of Order. By some accounts, he was even the council's best piano player.

Burke made himself known, first as one of the members of the city council's ill-fated "coffee rebellion" of the early 1970s and later as a constant bidder for higher office. He sought without success county clerk and congressional posts. After Daley's passing in late 1976, Burke sent up trial balloons for mayor in the ensuing special election—trial balloons which turned out to be lead balloons.

Mayor Jane Byrne in 1980 perceived Richard Daley, the late mayor's son, as her major 1983 foe. She endorsed Burke against Daley for state's attorney.

Burke spent part of his time giving away whistles to aid women threatened with rape and much of his time denying that he was the "Jane Byrne" candidate. He received only 37 percent of the vote in that year's Democratic primary.

But in the city council he received power he never could have attained in most of those posts. Following the Harold Washington election, Burke engineered the dumping of Wilson Frost as Finance Committee chairman and took over the job himself. He was considered second only to Alderman Edward Vrdolyak among the anti-Washington bloc.

He also assumed the role of vocal point man for anti-Washington attacks. By most accounts, he relished it. Burke attacked the Washington transition team's report of racial bias in the city (while firing seven black members of his committee). He complained that Washington was not making appointments from throughout the city (without mentioning that previous administrations included a disproportionate number of city heads from Southwest Side wards— including the 14th). He led a fight to stop Washington from laying off 700 patronage workers; sought council approval for all contracts over $50 million; and most notably, attempted to have Washington removed from office because the mayor filed an ethics statement three weeks late.

These attacks came from a man who himself had become the target of controversy. At the time of his father's death, he was a policeman and law student. But instead of pounding a beat, young Burke had a posh assignment in the state's attorney's office. During the Vietnam war, after his hardship deferment was rejected, Burke (many say through his connections) bypassed others for a slot in a nearby Army Reserve unit. In 1977 he chaired a committee which permitted huge fare increases for Checker and Yellow Cabs. He was accused in 1985 of taking part as an attorney in lawsuits against the city.

The 1986 special elections and subsequent city council realignment killed much of Burke's influence. He retained chairmanship of the Finance Committee, but important budgetary decisions were implemented through a Budget Committee chaired by 4th Ward alderman Timothy Evans. Burke lost the Finance chair after the 1987 election; he now serves as vice-chairman of the Committee on Police, Fire, and Municipal Institutions.

After Washington's reelection Burke appeared to be a leader without a constituency, a disheartened spokesman for a group of nine or ten aldermen (most of them from the Southwest Side) who remained hard-core anti-Washington votes.

But after Washinton's death, Burke resumed his stature as one of the most powerful aldermen. He took himself out of the race for acting mayor and opted for Eugene Sawyer, despite protests from Southwest Siders who wanted a white successor to Washington. Burke was credited with organizing a prayer service among Sawyer-backing aldermen that bolstered the reluctant candidate's spirits the night of the meeting.

Why did Burke, an ardent Harold Washington foe and a man disliked in the black community perhaps even more than Vrdolyak, support a black alderman to replace Washington? For many, that question has not been answered satisfactorily. Was it because the pragmatic Burke simply realized that the numbers were not there to elect a white mayor? Or were there other motives? Foes pointed to a television report from the night before the election which alleged that Washington foes Burke, Vrdolyak, and former Chicago Housing Authority director Charles Swibel met the afternoon of the mayor's death and plotted how to install Sawyer (for whatever reason) on the mayoral throne.

Burke's future remains uncertain. His efforts for Sawyer notwithstanding, he appears unlikely to attract the black votes he would need to attain higher office. But he faces no opposition in the 14th Ward.

EDWARD BURKE

REDISTRICTING: One of the side effects of the 1986 remap was the strengthening of the white vote in wards near those mandated for black "super-majorities." In that sense, one of the chief beneficiaries of the 1986 remap was Alderman Edward Burke. His 14th Ward lost two northeast Hispanic precincts to the 11th Ward, one black and three Hispanic precincts to the 15th Ward— precincts which might have caused him electoral problems at a future date. In return, the 14th received twelve white precincts west of Western, from 59th Street to Marquette Boulevard.

MAYORAL: Jane Byrne (Burke's choice) and Richard Daley split the vote almost evenly in the 1983 Democratic primary. Byrne captured 47 percent of the primary vote, and Daley won 45 percent (mainly in the western precincts). Daley captured twenty-six precincts, Byrne twenty-five. Washington carried only 8 percent of the vote—and most of that in precincts now removed from the ward.

Harold Washington carried only 16 percent of the vote against Bernard Epton in the general election—again, most of that in black and Hispanic precincts no longer part of the ward.

Despite demographics less favorable to him, Harold Washington did not lose much ground in the 1987 Democratic primary. He carried 14 percent of the vote.

Burke at first did not endorse longtime ally Vrdolyak in the general election. Instead he mouthed support for Thomas Hynes, whom conventional wisdom dictated was the only candidate who could defeat Washington. Burke switched to Vrdolyak once Hynes withdrew from the campaign, and Vrdolyak carried the ward with 81 percent. Republican Don Haider drained 3 percent from a potential Vrdolyak vote.

Washington showed a slight gain in the general election, due largely to Hispanics in the Back of the Yards precincts who traditionally vote for the Democratic nominee.

CENSUS DATA: Population (1980): 61,963. 73.87 percent white, .52 percent black, 23.72 percent Hispanic, 1.89 percent Asian and other. Voting age population: 79.89 percent white, .43 percent black, 16.16 percent Hispanic, 3.52 percent Asian and other.

Census tracts: See ward map.

COMMUNITY NEWSPAPERS:
Back of the Yards Journal, 4625 S. Ashland (927–7200)
Bridgeport News, 3252 S. Halsted (927–3118)
El Heraldo, 3734 W. 26th St. (521–8300) (Spanish)
Southtown Economist, 5959 S. Harlem (586–8800)
Southwest News-Herald, 6225 S. Kedzie (476–4800)

ALDERMAN: Edward M. Burke. Appointed 1968, elected 1969. Born December 29, 1943. Career: B.A., DePaul University, 1968; J.D., DePaul University, 1968; officer, Chicago Police Dept., 1965–68.
Committees: Police, Fire, and Municipal Institutions (vice-chairman); Budget and Government Operations; Committees, Rules, Municipal Code Revision, and Ethics; Energy, Environmental Protection, and Public Utilities; Finance; Intergovernmental Relations.
City hall telephone: 744–6126, 744–6143.
Ward office: 2650 W. 51st St. (471–1414).
1987 election:
Edward Burke, unopposed.

DEMOCRATIC COMMITTEEMAN: Edward M. Burke. Appointed 1968, elected 1972.
1984 election:
Edward Burke, unopposed.

MAYORAL ELECTIONS:

1983 Democratic primary:			*1987 Democratic primary:*		
Jane Byrne	10,403	(47%)	Jane Byrne	19,961	(86%)
Richard Daley	9,912	(45%)	Harold Washington	3,147	(14%)
Harold Washington	1,669	(8%)			

106 / CHICAGO POLITICS

1983 general:

Bernard Epton	20,117	(84%)
Harold Washington	3,864	(16%)

1987 general:

Edward Vrdolyak	17,766	(82%)
Harold Washington	3,342	(15%)
Donald Haider	585	(3%)

15th Ward

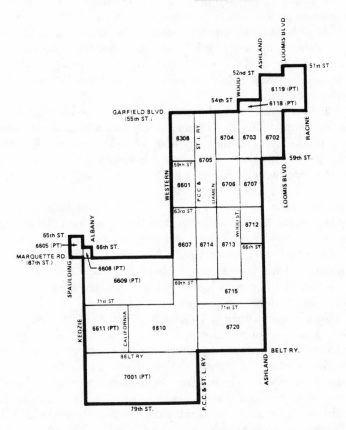

IN THEORY, a 1963 fair housing ordinance assured that any qualified Chicagoan may buy a house anywhere he or she wishes. But in Chicago, theory often differs from practice.

Especially on the Southwest Side, blacks have met with resistance when attempting to move into all-white neighborhoods. That resistance has often been physical, ranging from rocks thrown through windows to garages or even houses set afire.

Blacks have moved into previously all-white neighborhoods. But on the South Side, the end result has not been integration. "Block-busting" real estate agents often offered one or two whites on a block inflated prices for their homes, which the agents then sold to blacks. The agents then frightened remaining whites by spreading rumors of an imminent black takeover of the block. Whites sold their houses at low prices, and these houses were resold to blacks at huge profits. Houses for sale were those adjacent to black neighborhoods. Thus blacks never escaped the ghetto; they only expanded it.

It is a migration pattern which has hurt both whites and blacks. Whites sold houses for a loss and abandoned streets where many lived for decades. Blacks, even after paying inflated prices for the housing, suffered other hardships. Businesses often followed the white customers out of the neighborhoods. "Redlining," the policy by which insurance companies denied coverage to entire geographical locations, deterred bank loans. Those few white families who remained in the neighborhood suffered the same deprivations as the blacks, and eventually left. As a result, neighborhoods which had been all white became all black within a decade.

A major avenue usually served as a dividing line between white and black Chicago on the South Side. This avenue would be an undeclared, but very real, barrier. Ashland Avenue for many years served as this invisible Maginot line. Now the boundary is Western Avenue. A few blacks have moved to streets just west of Western; whether the white flight pattern will continue remains to be seen.

Nowhere has the racial tension along this border zone been more visible than in the Marquette Park area now part of the 15th Ward. Martin Luther King led demonstrators here in the 1960s and was pelted by a stone while marching to Gage Park; he later declared, "The people of Mississippi ought to come to Chicago to learn how to hate." Neo-Nazis made their headquarters here in the 1970s, and neo-Nazi leader Frank Collin received 10 percent of the vote in the 1979 aldermanic election.

Even in the summer of 1986, a Ku Klux Klan rally in Marquette Park drew an estimated 3,000 spectators and 500 policemen. A group of black counter-demonstrators was asked to leave by police, for their own protection.

Despite the negative publicity of the Marquette Park rally, cooler heads generally have prevailed in recent years. Both black and white groups have worked to ease racial tensions. Yet race dominates politics here, more than in any other ward. And a racial change in this ward's representation helped change the power balance in the entire city.

This is the ward that elected Francis X. Lawlor, Chicago's only priest-alderman, in 1971. Lawlor, a longtime high school teacher, organized block clubs to prevent blockbusting. The liberal John Cardinal Cody viewed Lawlor's actions as racist and arranged his transfer to Tulsa, Oklahoma. When Lawlor returned to Chicago without archdiocese permission, Cody expelled him.

Shortly before the 1971 election, Alderman Joseph Kriska's death left a city council opening. Paul Sheridan, incumbent 16th Ward alderman, was the party regulars' choice. Sheridan was moved into the 15th Ward by a redistricting.

Ordinarily aldermen take great pains not to redistrict incumbents out of their wards. In this case they did Sheridan a favor. He narrowly (and some claim, illegally) defeated black activist Anna Langford in 1967. The mainly white 15th Ward provided friendlier territory. However, Sheridan didn't count on the populist appeal of Lawlor. The priest defeated him by a two-to-one margin.

Once in office, Lawlor did not become the race-monger that some feared. In fact, he worked closely with Langford in a short-lived but well-publicized alliance for orderly neighborhood change. He was part of the council's seven-person anti-Daley bloc. He cast opposition votes along with two blacks (Langford and William Cousins), three Lakefront liberals (Leon Despres, William Singer, and Dick Simpson), and a North Side Republican (John Hoellen)—strange bedfellows indeed.

Nonetheless, Lawlor was first and foremost a spokesman for whites who feared an onrush of blacks into their neighborhoods. He proposed an antipanic peddling ordinance which would have limited Federal Housing Authority mortgage insurance to 5 percent of the homes in any census tract—an effort to limit the influx of low-income (black) buyers into his ward.

Lawlor declined to seek reelection in 1975. Instead, he ran an unsuccessful race as a Republican for the congressional seat vacated by the death of John Kluczynski.

Democratic regulars wasted no time in retaking Lawlor's seat. Kenneth Jaksy, an ally of committeeman and state senator Frank Savickas, easily won the 1975 special election. He warmed the 15th Ward's council seat for the next four years. Jaksy filed to run again in 1979 but met with what appeared to be a surprise challenger—Frank Brady, the ward secretary.

Brady's filing, in fact, was not a challenge to the established order but an insurance policy against another takeover from outside the organization. Savickas sought, and received, a Senate leadership post. Jaksy quit the race to become his assistant. Brady, who later said he would have withdrawn had Jaksy remained a candidate, became the regulars' choice. He defeated two opponents, with 68 percent of the vote.

Frank Brady was a luckless alderman from the beginning. Days after being sworn in, he was shot by robbers and left for dead in front of his home. He spent most of the next year recuperating.

Brady won reelection in 1983, although it took him a runoff to defeat Richard Daley-backer Michael Hogan. Even though the ward as remapped in 1981 was 60 percent black, demographics and comparative voter turnout all but assured victory for a white candidate.

Blacks and Hispanics charged that the 1981 ward map unfairly discriminated against them by diluting their voting strength. Ultimately, the courts agreed. Seven wards were ordered redrawn to provide for black or Hispanic "super-majorities." One of those wards was the 15th.

The new lines of the 15th Ward virtually assured a black alderman. The ward changed from 60 to 74 percent black. Brady's home was redistricted out of the ward.

Even before the remap, black dissatisfaction with Brady was high. Many charged that he ignored the black eastern side of his ward. Others noted that he kept two ward offices, a "black" one on Western Avenue and a "white" one on Kedzie.

Other aldermen in new "super-majority" wards (Frank Stemberk in the 22nd Ward, Michael Nardulli in the 26th, Frank Damato in the 37th) opted to run for at-large seats on the county board. Despite long odds against him, Brady moved into the revised 15th Ward and campaigned for reelection.

A crowded field of black candidates opposed him. There were Nathan Brady, a former park district landscape engineer; Marlene Carter, a secretary at the University of Illinois and one of the leaders of the remap fight; Rev. Connie Crawford, associate pastor of a local church and director of a day care center; Claude Jackson, a grocer and currency exchange operator; Annette Moore, founder of a shelter for homeless women; William Neal, a security consultant and locksmith; and David Whitehead, a real estate broker who ran against Brady in 1983.

Mayor Harold Washington at first favored Crawford. But questions about her residency (her husband, a doctor, owned several apartments, fueling allegations that she lived outside the ward) led him to withdraw that backing. He endorsed Carter only a few days before the election.

While the Washington endorsement aided Carter, it was not enough to provide her victory in the March special election. She polled 43 percent of the vote to 38 for Brady. The other candidates received enough to force a runoff.

The 26th Ward also held an April runoff, one which gained the attention of the entire city. Unlike that hotly contested election, the one in the 15th Ward was a foregone conclusion. Brady's cause was considered so hopeless that Committeeman Savickas got married the Sunday before the election and spent that election day on his honeymoon.

Election returns mirrored precisely the racial composition of the ward. Every black precinct but two gave Carter at least 100 votes, often holding Brady to single-digit totals. The reverse held true in the white precincts. Only one precinct went for the winner by less than a five-to-one tally. Three Hispanic precincts in the northeast corner went for Carter by huge margins.

Carter failed to consolidate power during her brief term. As a result, she faced eleven challengers in the 1987 aldermanic race. Larry Williams, a Brady ally, got most of the white vote. Jackson and newcomer Virgil Jones fared well in West Englewood precincts. Carter dominated in the rest of the ward, including the three Hispanic precincts. Her 39 percent fell short of the vote needed to win outright. She beat Williams in a runoff that mirrored racial lines.

Marlene Carter was a reliable Washington ally. Only once did she buck him. Carter supported the third-party gubernatorial bid of the Rev. Charles Koen, a black minister, instead of Washington's choice, Adlai Stevenson. Koen later was ruled off the ballot. But Carter did not follow the lead of most Washington allies and support Timothy Evans for acting mayor. She voted for Eugene Sawyer, reportedly because of anger at death threats aimed at her and her family from Evans's supporters.

A committeeman election also was scheduled for the 15th Ward, but Savickas successfully challenged all his opponents and ran unopposed. Given the racial percentages, the present polarization, and the likelihood of improved black organization by 1988, Savickas appears doomed to defeat unless he wins all the white votes and two or more challengers split the black vote.

The 15th Ward, racially speaking, is two wards in one. But even beyond the black-and-white ethnic split, the areas they inhabit have two very different histories. East of Western, the 15th Ward takes in the poverty-stricken community known as West Englewood. This was an extension of the then-prosperous Englewood community. The Depression and postwar white flight devastated the community. Many of the houses are abandoned. Storefronts, if occupied, are taken by churches. Hope appears to be the major industry.

Nonetheless, the ward's east side does have its positive features, including two of the better high schools in the city. St. Rita High School at 63rd and Claremont, known for its perennially strong football teams, is also an academic power. Lindblom High School, at 62nd and Wolcott, annually produces reading scores which put it among the top three public schools in the city. The Boulevard Art Center, at Garfield and Honore, is considered one of the finest in Chicago. It lies across Garfield Boulevard from another artistic monument—St. Basil's, a Byzantine-style church.

West of Western Avenue is the community designated as Chicago Lawn. Unlike Englewood, much of Chicago Lawn did not see development until the 1920s. Eccentric real estate millionaire Hetty Green once owned much of the land. She allowed it to remain open prairie, dotted by the occasional cabbage patch. Green sold the land in 1911, and after World War I the area became the center of a real estate boom. Suddenly hundreds of brick bungalows and two-flats appeared. The area tripled in population during the 1920s.

The atmosphere today is decidedly Lithuanian. Marquette Park is the world's largest such community outside Lithuania. One example of Lithuanian pride, the Darius-Girenas statue, stands at California and Marquette Boulevard. It honors two fliers who in 1933 attempted a nonstop flight from New York City to Kaunas, Lithuania, but crashed in a German forest 400 miles short of their goal.

Heart of the neighborhood is Lithuanian Plaza Court, a stretch of 69th Street between Western and California. The Basilica of the Blessed Virgin Mary, a twin-spired example of Lithuanian architecture at Washtenaw, high-lights the neighborhood. Lithuanian Plaza Court also includes a United Lithuanian Relief office, a playhouse, a flower shop, the headquarters of a soccer club, plus Lithuanian taverns and restaurants.

In addition to all things Lithuanian, the area also features Quigley South Seminary, a large campus at 77th and Western. Further west, on Columbus Avenue, the ward houses the M & R Double Drive-In, which claims to be the world's largest drive-in complex.

REDISTRICTING: Major adjustments were made to the 15th Ward to make it conform to the black "super-majority" mandated by a federal court. Eleven precincts on the northwest side between Kedzie and Western, Marquette and 59th Street were transferred to the 14th Ward. Brady complained because these included some of the ward's most prosperous areas.

In turn, the 15th received two largely industrial precincts between the

Belt Railway and the 79th Street, previously belonging to the 18th Ward; five black precincts north of 59th Street and east of Western from the 14th Ward; and three predominantly Mexican precincts, part of the Back of the Yards neighborhood at the ward's far northeastern corner, also from the 14th.

MAYORAL: Committeeman Frank Savickas and Alderman Frank Brady supported Mayor Jane Byrne in the 1983 Democratic primary. Even so, she and Richard Daley more or less split the white vote. Byrne had 28 percent of the vote, Daley 24 percent, most of their votes coming from white areas. Harold Washington took the ward with 48 percent of the vote, almost all from the black precincts.

Washington got 61 percent of the vote against Bernard Epton in the general election—a number that reflected almost exactly the black population in the ward. The vote split sharply along the racial divisions of the ward.

In 1987, Harold Washington won both elections, with 78 and 79 percent of the vote. The mayor carried the black and Hispanic precincts, his opponents the white ones.

CENSUS DATA: Population (1980): 61,567. 19.63 percent white, 74.29 percent black, 5.36 percent Hispanic, .72 percent Asian and other. Voting age population: 25.67 percent white, 67.87 percent black, 4.90 percent Hispanic, 1.76 percent Asian and other.

CENSUS TRACTS: See ward map.

COMMUNITY NEWSPAPERS:
Back of the Yards Journal, 4625 S. Ashland (927–7200)
Bridgeport News, 3252 S. Halsted (927–3118)
Southtown Economist, 5959 S. Harlem (586–8800)
Southwest News-Herald, 6225 S. Kedzie (476–4800)

ALDERMAN: Marlene Carter. Elected 1986. Born 1945. Career: community worker; secretary, University of Illinois at Chicago, 1975–86.
Committees: Aging and Disabled (chairman); Health (vice-chairman); Aviation; Budget and Government Operations; Claims and Liabilities; Economic Development; Education; Energy, Environmental Protection, and Public Utilities; Finance; Police, Fire, and Municipal Institutions; Special Events and Cultural Affairs.
City hall telephone: 744–6850, 744–6854.
Ward office: 6823 S. WESTERN (476–0475).
1986 special election:

Marlene C. Carter	4,841 (43%)	Nathan Bradley	467	(4%)
Frank J. Brady	4,299 (38%)	Annette Moore	283	(3%)

| Connie Crawford | 532 | (5%) | William A. Neal | 209 | (2%) |
| Claude Jackson | 530 | (5%) | David Whitehead | 117 | (1%) |

1986 special runoff:

| Marlene C. Carter | 10,723 | (66%) |
| Frank J. Brady | 5,546 | (34%) |

1987 election:

Marlene C. Carter	7,522	(39%)	David Whitehead	361	(2%)
Larry Williams	3,568	(18%)	Willie J. Curtis	339	(2%)
Virgil E. Jones	3,263	(17%)	Darryl J. Robinson	289	(1%)
Claude Jackson	2,401	(12%)	Theodore E. Robinson	239	(1%)
Annette Moore	514	(3%)	Tommie Grayer, Sr.	214	(1%)
Nathan Bradley	440	(2%)	Richard Hodge	182	(1%)

1987 runoff:

| Marlene C. Carter | 12,208 | (63%) |
| Larry Williams | 7,301 | (37%) |

DEMOCRATIC COMMITTEEMAN: Frank D. Savickas. Elected 1974. Born May 14, 1935. Career: Wilson Junior College; state representative, 1967–71; state senator, 1971–.

Ward office: 6743 S. Western (434–3800).

1984 election:

Frank Savickas	8,056	(53%)
Marlene Carter	5,521	(37%)
Nathan Bradley	1,487	(10%)

1986 special election:

Frank D. Savickas, unopposed.

MAYORAL ELECTIONS:

1983 Democratic primary:

Harold Washington	11,143	(48%)
Jane Byrne	6,405	(28%)
Richard Daley	5,431	(24%)

1987 Democratic primary:

| Harold Washington | 17,768 | (78%) |
| Jane Byrne | 4,965 | (22%) |

1983 general:

| Harold Washington | 15,954 | (61%) |
| Bernard Epton | 10,168 | (39%) |

1987 general:

Harold Washington	18,426	(79%)
Edward Vrdolyak	4,602	(20%)
Donald Haider	278	(1%)

16th Ward

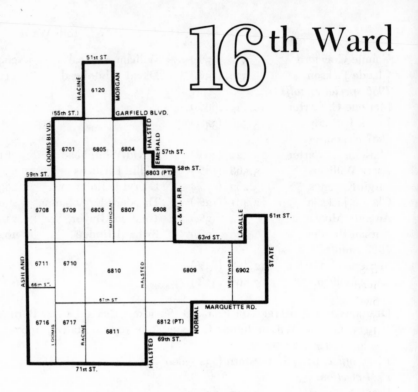

To many Chicagoans Englewood is little more than the name of the last stop on an elevated line. But in years past the South Side community was a major hub, a commercial district second only to the Loop. Its onetime prosperity and subsequent decline is a good example of the sociological changes which have beset many older cities.

The community now centered at 63rd and Halsted started before the Civil War, growing up around the railroad lines that crisscrossed the area. Residents, mainly German and Irish railroad workers, called it Junction Grove. Later developers, hoping that a name change would upgrade the area's image, re-named it Englewood, after a prosperous town in New Jersey.

After the war, Englewood showed modest growth. Standard Oil's works to the east and the stockyards to the north provided jobs. Cook County Normal School (later changed to Chicago State University) became an educational attraction. This affluent suburb joined the city in 1889.

That modest growth turned into a boom after the 1893 Columbian Exposition as the Jackson Park rapid transit line added to an already good local transportation system. With the completion of the Englewood elevated line in 1907, the area became the shopping mecca of the South Side.

Englewood was the forerunner of suburban shopping malls, except that shoppers used the rails (interurban trains, electrified streetcars, or the el) instead of automobiles to go there. One building, the Beeker-Ryan Building at the northeast corner of 63rd and Halsted, was even the forerunner of Water

Tower Place and Century Plaza. It was a vertical shopping center which included stores, a saloon, and a Chinese restaurant.

Beeker-Ryan sold out to Sears Roebuck in 1929. Five years later the giant retailer closed the building and moved into a huge building nearby. Sears thrived during the Depression, but many Englewood banks and smaller businesses suffered.

Events that took place after World War II hastened the district's decline. New residential construction ceased in Englewood, leaving only aging and often decaying housing stock. Families now had the chance to spend the money that was saved during the war. As often as not, they spent it on cars that transported them to newly built houses in the suburbs.

Meanwhile another change was taking place in Englewood. Blacks had always lived in the Englewood area in two small settlements near Racine Avenue and Stewart Street (which were part of the Underground Railway). As blacks moved to Chicago during World War II, those settlements grew rapidly. This growth, accompanied by the white exodus to the Southwest Side or the suburbs changed a 2 percent black area (1940) into the 100 percent black area that exists today.

By 1960, the once prosperous shopping area was in danger of becoming an urban ghost town. Drastic action was called for, and innovative measures took place. The Englewood Businessmen's Association and other community leaders sought and received aid from the Department of Urban Renewal. Developers altered the shopping strip in an effort to attract new shoppers and hold onto the ones already there. The Englewood shopping area was converted into a pedestrian mall, and several nearby homes were torn down to provide for parking lots.

The change did not prove effective. Newly opened suburban or Southwest Side shopping centers such as Ford City and Evergreen Plaza drew business away from Englewood. Eventually even retail giants such as Sears and Wieboldt's also fled to the suburbs.

Today the Englewood shopping strip may not be desolate, but it is still far from prosperous. It contains a number of small shops—the clothing and wig stores and fast food outlets found at other South Side business strips, not the sorts of businesses that would attract shoppers from the suburbs or elsewhere in the city. Business owners are likely to be Korean, Jewish, or Arab, not black. Englewood's shopping area may be undergoing yet another change. A 1987 proposal would eliminate the pedestrian mall and reopen Halsted for vehicle traffic.

Housing in Englewood, aided by such groups as the Neighborhood Housing Service, is going through a slow but steady improvement. But even the most enthusiastic of community boosters admit there is still much work to be done.

If Chicago's wards had names instead of numbers, the 16th Ward would be named Englewood. It centers on the shopping mall and contains the communities designated Englewood and West Englewood, plus a little territory to the north.

The 16th extends north to 51st Street, between Racine and Morgan and cuts through Garfield Boulevard (55th Street). This was the Gold Coast of the Stockyards community. Bridgeport and Canaryville residents derisively called their fellow immigrants who moved here the "lace curtain Irish."

Nowadays vacant lots and closed stores are not uncommon sights in the ward's northern tier. A bar at 52nd and Racine calls itself the Rich Man Poor Man Lounge; the appearance of the neighborhood indicates that the latter outnumber the former among the clientele.

A different form of Irish "elite" made its home a few blocks away. Ragan's Colts, the largest and fiercest street gang in the city during the early 1900s, had its headquarters at 5528 S. Halsted. "Hit me and you hit 2,000" was the motto of this "social athletic club."

Violence also marked a building in what is now the eastern portion of the ward. No home in this area was more elaborate than H. H. Holmes's castle at the southeast corner of 63rd and Wallace. None had a more sordid history. The eccentric Holmes, as it turned out, was Chicago's first mass murderer. He confessed to having killed 28 persons there; he may have slain 100 more.

Two politicians have dominated the 16th Ward political scene in the last generation—two highly contrasting politicians. The first was James "Bulljive" Taylor, a former Catholic Youth Organization Gold Gloves boxer who ruled the ward (and much of the South Side) as committeeman during the 1970s. Foes called him a bully and a buffoon. Yet he obtained more influence than any other black politicians during the Jane Byrne administration, serving as her liaison with the black community. Taylor received his nickname after two women charged he demanded sexual favors in exchange for a tavern license. When faced with this accusation, Taylor claimed he was "bulljiving" the women.

Anna Riggs Langford was the second politician. She now serves on the city council as chairman of its Rules Committee. Yet before her 1983 election, she appeared likely to be remembered as a local perennial candidate.

A longtime civil rights activist (she participated in Mississippi voter registration drives in 1964 with Dr. Martin Luther King) and clerk typist in the Secretary of State's office, she made her first run for alderman in 1967 as an independent against white candidate Paul Sheridan. Comedian Dick Gregory also ran his independent mayoral campaign out of her headquarters. Sheridan won that election by thirty-seven votes. Langford claimed that the election was stolen by party regulars—not an irrational charge considering that the ward's population was 87 percent black at the time.

Langford came back four years later. This time she won by 700 votes. Langford thus became (with the 48th Ward's Marilou McCarthy Hedlund) the first woman to be elected alderman.

She wasted little time in blasting her fellows, calling the city council a "sterile organization." They returned the favor; Alderman Vito Marzullo (25th) called her a "crybaby."

However, she was a woman of action as well as words. Langford worked closely with a neighboring alderman, Fr. Francis X. Lawlor (15th) to ease racial tensions between his ward's white residents and the black ones.

That 1971 win was her last for a long time. She ran for Democratic committeeman in 1972 against Taylor (who was the state representative and ward superintendent as well as committeeman). The board of elections claimed "forgeries and illegalities" and chased her off the ballot.

Taylor chased Langford out of the council in 1975. He backed a quiescent party regular, Eloise Barden, a woman Mayor Daley referred to as "the church-going lady." Barden soundly defeated Langford.

The indomitable Langford tried again the following year, this time for the state senate seat being vacated by the retiring Cecil Partee. She lost this one by 2,000 votes and claimed that Taylor engineered vote fraud.

Langford charged that her opponent was "not able to speak or vote his convictions because of his ties to the machine." The foe? A state representative named Harold Washington.

In 1977 Langford made a surprising move. A longtime independent, she made her peace with party regulars. She claimed her quarrel was with Daley, and not the party organization. Political observers speculated that she was seeking party slating for the congressional seat then held by Morgan Murphy, but such an offer never came her way.

Langford challenged Barden again in 1979, with no more success than before. In 1980, she ran for circuit court judge—and lost that election.

By 1982, Anna Langford was running out of offices to seek. She dropped hints that she might run for mayor in 1983, but withdrew as onetime adversary Washington entered the race. Instead she supported Washington, now firmly ensconced in independent ranks. He returned that support. This time Langford (backed by Washington) defeated Barden (endorsed by Taylor) for alderman in 1983.

Taylor, meanwhile, was no shrinking violet. Mayor Jane Byrne named him a deputy chief of staff, and he became unquestionably the most influential black in her administration. When Harold Washington was elected to Congress in 1980, local committeemen also appointed Taylor to replace him in the state senate. Washington threatened to keep his seat in the legislature rather than allow archfoe Taylor to replace him.

He served in both offices until 1983. A redistricting squeezed him out of the state senate. After Bryne lost the 1983 mayoral primary, Taylor bailed out as her assistant. But he did not have to go job hunting. State Representative Taylor Pouncey, a James Taylor ally (less kindly souls used the word "flunky") who replaced his mentor in the state house, suddenly claimed illness and resigned. Taylor was appointed to replace Pouncey.

Perhaps it was inevitable that Langford and Taylor would meet on the electoral field of war. At any rate they did in the 1984 Democratic committeeman race. That election also featured reputed influence peddler Clarence McClain, making it one of the most colorful groups of candidates ever to grace the same ballot. Washington remained neutral; some perceived his noninvolvement as a tacit endorsement of longtime associate McClain. Nonetheless, Langford won a solid victory.

Langford planned to retire in 1987 and support her son for alderman. The son, however, left the city. She ran again, and her lackluster campaign captured only 34 percent of the vote against Taylor and eight other candidates. Taylor and Langford met again in the runoff. This time the alderman campaigned seriously, and won by a two-to-one margin.

Of all the black aldermen, Anna Langford took the most heat for the support of Eugene Sawyer as acting mayor to replace Harold Washington. Few expressed surprise that aldermen such as Robert Shaw or William Henry, with their machine ties, would fall into an alliance with white ethnic aldermen. But Langford, a longtime activist, disappointed many of her constituents by not supporting Timothy Evans, the choice of most Washington allies. Langford defended her vote as realistic politics, saying that her ward was more likely to get services if she backed the obvious winning candidate. The seventy-year-old Langford will not face possible voter wrath for her decision. She announced she would not seek another term as alderman. Likewise she declined to file petitions for committeeman in the 1988 election. But one of those who did file was—who else?—James Taylor.

REDISTRICTING: The 16th lost four precincts in the northwest corner to the 15th Ward. It gained two northern precincts formerly in the 11th Ward.

MAYORAL: Jane Byrne, in part due to Taylor's help, performed better in the 16th than in any other all-black ward in 1983. By any other standard her total was unimpressive. Byrne received 19 percent of the vote and Richard Daley, 4 percent. Harold Washington took 77 percent of the vote.

Washington outpolled Bernard Epton 116 to 1 in the general election, 25,654 to 221 for the hapless Republican. His totals dropped imperceptibly in the 1987 elections, to just under 99 percent of the vote. Donald Haider received only eighty-six votes here, the Republican's second-lowest total in the city.

CENSUS DATA: Population (1980): 59,710. .74 percent white, 98.18 percent black, 1.32 percent Hispanic. Voting age population: .60 percent white, 97.90 percent black, 1.10 percent Hispanic, .40 percent Asian and other.

CENSUS TRACTS: See ward map.

COMMUNITY NEWSPAPERS:
Chatham Citizen, 412 E. 87th St. (487–7700)
Southwest News-Herald, 6225 S. Kedzie (476–4800)

Alderman: Anna R. Langford. Elected 1983. Born October 27, 1917. Career: B.A., Roosevelt University, 1946; J.D., John Marshall Law School, 1956; attorney; Secretary of State's office; alderman, 1971–75.

Committees: Committees, Rules, Municipal Code Revision, and Ethics (chairman); Aging and Disabled; Beautification and Recreation; Budget and Government Operations, Buildings; Education; Finance; Human Rights and Consumer Protection; License; Streets and Alleys; Zoning.

City hall telephone: 744–3069, 744–3184.
Ward Office: 1249 W. 63rd St. (434–5535).

1987 election:

Anna R. Langford	6,369	(35%)	Clarence C. Barry	582	(3%)
James C. Taylor	3,168	(17%)	Lee Ethel Stowers	412	(2%)
James A. Tyson, Jr.	2,735	(15%)	Jamesetta Dixon	395	(2%)
Samuel Reid	2,662	(15%)	Walter Action Jackson	370	(2%)
Eugene Davis	1,329	(7%)	Robert L. Campbell	265	(1%)

1987 runoff:

Anna R. Langford	12,536	(66%)
James C. Taylor	6,330	(34%)

Democratic committeeman: Anna R. Langford. Elected 1984.
1984 election:

Anna R. Langford	5,844	(41%)
James C. Taylor	4,381	(31%)
Clarence L. McClain	2,631	(19%)
Jack Wright	1,302	(9%)

Mayoral elections:

1983 Democratic primary:

Harold Washington	16,604	(77%)
Jane Byrne	4,061	(19%)
Richard Daley	747	(4%)

1987 Democratic primary:

Harold Washington	24,493	(99%)
Jane Byrne	268	(1%)

1983 general:

Harold Washington	25,654	(99%)
Bernard Epton	221	(1%)

1987 general:

Harold Washington	21,954	(99%)
Edward Vrdolyak	154	(1%)
Donald Haider	86	(0%)

1️⃣7️⃣th Ward

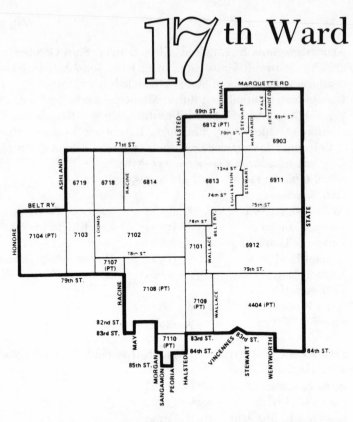

HISTORIANS LOOKING BACK on Harold Washington's 1983 election may cite the Operation PUSH-led boycott of Chicagofest as the precipitating move toward black electoral unity. But even before Chicagofest, black awareness was heightened by a special election in the South Side 17th Ward. The protagonist in this June 1982 drama was an unexpected one: Alderman Allan Streeter, who originally was seen as the most docile of city hall votes.

This ward had exhibited traces of independence in the past. Charles Chew bucked the machine to win as alderman in 1963 and served as Daley's only black council critic. The shiny-pated Chew beat the machine once more for a state senate chair. Once elected to the legislature, he quickly made peace with his erstwhile rivals and became known for his string of Cadillacs.

William Shannon, the ward's committeeman and a go-along Democrat, replaced him as alderman in 1967. Shannon never avoided strong electoral challenges, and in 1979 he lost. Tyrone McFolling, an independent Democrat, beat him for alderman that year and committeeman a year later.

His tenure in office was a short one. McFolling, complaining of a bad back, resigned as both alderman and committeeman in late 1980. The timing following McFolling's illness was, to say the least, interesting. A recently enacted state law required the mayor to fill aldermanic vacancies which occurred within twenty-eight months of the next aldermanic election. McFolling's resignation took place barely within the twenty-eight-month limit.

This is where Alan Streeter entered the scene. William Parker, an ally of

South Side boss James Taylor, was chosen committeeman. Parker tapped Streeter, a longtime precinct captain and head of the city's lead poisoning control unit, to run for alderman.

(McFolling exhibited remarkable recuperative powers, by the way. Within weeks of his resignation he became well enough to accept a post with the Department of Streets and Sanitation.)

Streeter appeared destined to languish as yet another of many obscure "aye" votes in the council. Two events changed his fate.

Streeter's appointment was challenged almost immediately. A number of 17th Ward residents, with the backing of North Side alderman Ivan Rittenberg (40th), sued to force a special election to fill out the unexpired term. Judge Thomas McMillan in early 1982 granted that request.

Ordinarily, the court ruling would be seen as a Byrne defeat. Because of a 1981 development, Byrne and her allies seized it as a chance for victory.

Byrne, who won in 1979 due to the black vote, sought to shore up support with white ethnics who otherwise might back her main rival, State's Attorney Richard M. Daley. Thus when the terms of two black school board members expired, she nominated two white anti-busing activists to replace them. The nominations were referred to the Education Committee, of which Streeter was a member.

Streeter, angered by what he perceived as a slap to the black community, announced that he was going to vote against the nominations. However, when the vote came around, he changed his mind and backed them. Parker supposedly had offered him patronage jobs if he went along with those appointments.

Extra patronage jobs, if indeed offered, never came through. Streeter voted against the appointments when they reached the full council floor. This vote signaled all-out war in the 17th. Byrne dumped three top black Streets and Sanitation officials in the ward and replaced them with whites. Streeter filed a class action suit just before the special election, charging that Byrne was withholding services from the ward. He also attacked his predecessor, Mc-Folling, whom he claimed was collecting absentee ballots from alleged voters whose addresses turned out to be abandoned buildings on vacant lots.

Jewel Frierson, a labor leader, was the regulars' choice against Streeter. Seven other candidates also appeared on the ballot, many believed to be planted by the regulars in hopes of draining votes from the incumbent. Streeter beat Frierson, 46 to 41 percent, but lacked the majority needed to avoid a runoff.

Byrne hit Streeter with her strongest shot before the runoff. She called a WGN reporter at his home and told him that Streeter was the target of federal bribery and kickback investigations. The ploy backfired on the mayor. U.S. Attorney Daniel Webb looked into the matter and found Byrne's allegations "of no merit."

This runoff, by now regarded everywhere as a black referendum on Jane Byrne, drew canvassers from across the city. Some were black precinct captains who when accompanied endorsed Frierson but when alone urged votes for Streeter. The result was not even close. Streeter won with 56 percent of the vote.

With that election decided, Streeter has returned to the background. He won alderman and committeeman races in 1983 and 1984 without much difficulty. Streeter captured every precinct in the 1987 aldermanic election, most by lopsided margins.

Only once has he reassumed the spotlight. That occurred in 1984, when Nation of Islam leader Louis Farrakhan was accused of making anti-Semitic remarks. Other aldermen sought to denounce the fiery leader; Streeter defended him. That defense was due, in part, to Farrakhan being a constituent of Streeter's. The minister's newspaper, *The First Call*, is headquartered on 79th Street just east of Halsted. Dark-suited and bow tie-clad youths scurrying in and out of the building with newspapers are a common sight.

Otherwise the 17th is in many ways a typical South Side black ward. It is mainly residential, filled with block after block of comfortable but unassuming homes and block club signs at the end of the street welcoming visitors yet proscribing dos and don'ts. The main business strip, 79th Street, contains a variety of stores and also a variety of Missionary Baptist churches.

The area made nationwide headlines in late 1984. Ben Wilson, basketball star of Simeon High School (83rd and Vincennes) and considered by many the best prep player in the country, was shot to death by two reputed street gang members near the school. Wilson's slaughter produced citywide outrage and stimulated creation of an antigang program which so far has had questionable success.

One 17th Ward sight deserves special mention. The southeastern corner of the ward is blessed with Winnaconna Park near 79th and Stewart, a charming oasis with a pond crossed by picturesque little bridges. Not far away, at 81st and Harvard, a garage mural depicts the park and two teenagers dancing to the music from a "boom box" radio. They aren't the only ones. Five little green men crawl out of a flying saucer and break dance to the music. The garage, like the park, are two of the hidden gems of the city.

REDISTRICTING: The 17th Ward lost three southern precincts to the 18th Ward under the 1986 redistricting.

MAYORAL: Galvanized by the Streeter win, the 17th continued its rejection of Jane Byrne in the 1983 Democratic primary. The mayor received only 13 percent of the vote and showed no real strength anywhere in the ward. Richard Daley obtained only 3 percent. Harold Washington reaped the other 84 percent of the vote.

As was the case in other all-black wards, Harold Washington received more than 99 percent of the vote in the general election against Bernard Epton. Likewise in 1987, Harold Washington received 99 percent of the vote in both the Democratic primary and the general election.

CENSUS DATA: Population (1980): 58,234. .59 percent white, 99.02 percent black, .80 percent Hispanic. Voting age population: .35 percent white, 99.52 percent black, .43 percent Hispanic.

CENSUS TRACTS: See ward map.

COMMUNITY NEWSPAPERS:
Chatham Citizen, 412 E. 87th St. (487–7700)
Chicago Independent Bulletin, 2037 W. 95th St. (783–1040)
Chicago Metro, 2600 S. Michigan (842–5950)

ALDERMAN: Allan Streeter. Appointed 1981, elected 1982. Born March 8, 1934. Career: Wright Junior College; U.S. Army; foreman of fueling operations, United Air Lines; director of lead poisoning control program, Chicago Board of Health.
Committees: Health (chairman); Beautification and Recreation; Budget and Government Operations; Energy, Environment Protection, and Public Utilities; Finance; Land Acquisition, Disposition, and Leases; Local Transportation; Police, Fire, and Municipal Institutions; Streets and Alleys; Traffic Control and Safety.
City hall telephone: 744–6827, 744–3064.
Ward office: 7605 S. Halsted (224–1550).
1987 election:

Allan Streeter	16,429	(74%)
Clyde Martin	4,434	(20%)
Mildred R. Embry	1,261	(6%)

DEMOCRATIC COMMITTEEMAN: Allan Streeter. Elected 1984.
1984 election:

Allan Streeter	10,002	(62%)
Albert Gaston, Jr.	6,132	(38%)

MAYORAL ELECTIONS:

1983 Democratic primary:

Harold Washington	21,559	(84%)
Jane Byrne	3,224	(13%)
Richard Daley	799	(3%)

1983 general:

Harold Washington	29,264	(99%)
Bernard Epton	206	(1%)

1987 Democratic primary:

Harold Washington	24,493	(99%)
Jane Byrne	254	(1%)

1987 general:

Harold Washington	25,539	(99%)
Edward Vrdolyak	126	(0%)
Donald Haider	99	(0%)

18th Ward

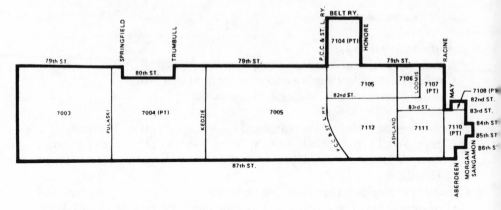

CHICAGO, AS ANY urban sociologist will tell you, is the most segregated major city in the nation. There exist, for all practical purposes, two Chicagos—one black, one white. Anyone who wants to see that dichotomy firsthand should visit the rectangular piece of real estate that is the Southwest Side's 18th Ward.

The 18th Ward, bordered roughly by 79th Street, Cicero, 87th, and Racine, is split down the middle by Western Avenue, the unofficial but very real dividing line between black and white neighborhoods on the Southwest Side. To the east lie the black precincts, to the west, the white ones.

East of Western the ward contains attractive houses, some brightly painted and others with fake stone facades. Particularly nice are the houses between Ashland and Damen south of 83rd Street, an area once called the Grove. This part of the ward, although mainly occupied by single-family houses, also has a few multiunit buildings. A few small factories operate near railroad tracks at Leavitt Avenue.

As in much of the black South Side, there is limited business development. Racine Avenue, for example, has the barber and beauty shops, taverns, and fast food outlets that comprise much of the business in black neighborhoods.

One major social service center exists in the east half of the ward—the Abraham Lincoln Center at 87th and Wolcott.

Western Avenue is solidly commercial in its eight-block run through the 18th Ward. It is the only meeting ground for many blacks and whites in the ward.

Those blacks that cross over into the "white" part of the ward are likely to be Bogan High School students. The school at 79th and Pulaski has been the scene of occasional racial tensions.

West of Western the ward is almost entirely residential. Multiunit buildings are interspersed among single family homes. All are of brick construction.

Churches and religious institutions are highly visible in this sector of the ward. Luther South High School occupies a large campus at 87th and Kedzie.

Queen of Martyrs Church stands at 83rd and St. Louis; a section of St. Louis is also named Fr. William P. Murphy Drive in honor of a late pastor. The corner of 87th and Kolin houses the Hometown Christian Church—one of several fundamentalist churches increasingly visible in outlying white ethnic areas.

The western side of the ward also has businesses, but hardly the same type that abound on the east side. Kedzie, for instance, has antique stores, video stores, candy and pastry shops. Other businesses include a casket company at 79th and Francisco and the Collar and Leash dog motel at 81st and Columbus.

A social help center also exists on the 18th Ward's west side—the Special Children's Center at 83rd and Kostner.

Given the disunity between the two halves of the ward, it could be argued that the 18th needs two aldermen. That may be the case, but it is allowed only one, just like any other ward. That alderman happens to be Robert Kellam.

As can be expected given the local geography, open housing has long been an issue in this racially divided ward. James Murray, first elected alderman in 1954, was called upon by Mayor Richard J. Daley to draft a city fair housing ordinance in the early 1960s. The law itself lacked teeth, but Daley used it to pacify black leaders who wanted stronger civil rights legislation. Sixteen white aldermen opposed the ordinance, the most ever to defy Daley on any measure. Murray's connection with the ordinance amounted to political suicide. He declined to seek reelection to the council in 1967. Daley slated him for circuit court judge in 1966. Murray won, although he failed to carry his own ward.

Edward Hines, a longtime city and county employee, was given the party nod to replace Murray. He defeated his first opponent, an anti-open housing activist. Hines himself noted that the fair housing ordinance was law, but declined to take a further position. Hines served until his death in 1977, leaving behind a general record of nonaccomplishment.

Kellam, a veteran precinct captain and employee of the Traffic and Safety Commission, won a special election in a runoff after Hines's death. He has not been vocal on open housing or anything else.

George Eddings, a black assistant principal, faced Kellam in the 1983 aldermanic election. The incumbent crushed his challenger. The two then met in another aldermanic race—a year earlier than Kellam desired.

The 18th Ward was one of seven altered by a court decree to provide for black and Hispanic majorities. Judge Charles Norgle ordered a special election here to coincide with the March 1986 primary elections. Kellam complained without success that such an election was not necessary in his ward, since the boundary changes were minor ones.

Blacks composed 50.03 percent of the revised 18th Ward. Even so, demographics still favored Kellam. Whites make up 51.44 percent of the voting age population, and better organization plus higher turnout virtually assured Kellam's reelection.

In addition to Eddings, the other candidates included former state representative Monica Faith Stewart (who got Mayor Harold Washington's belated and half-hearted endorsement); Charles Marble, a CHA executive; Chester Marks, an insurance broker; Bruce Crosby, a political consultant; Doris Nogaj, a founder of Advocates for the Disabled and Elderly and the only other white candidate; and community activist Eldora Davis.

Most political observers expected Kellam, the only major white candidate, to score an easy victory. Even Washington all but conceded this particular election. Kellam won 12,666 votes to 4,720 for Stewart and 2,461 for all others.

Kellam won again in 1987, not without difficulty. Three white candidates challenged him and Davis, enough to keep the veteran alderman from a majority. Davis racked up astronomical numbers on the black east side of the ward. Kellam pulled numbers even more lopsided on the white west side.

Faced with a serious challenge for the first time in his political life, Kellam campaigned aggressively during the 1987 runoff. The result showed Kellam with 55 percent, a number greater than the nonblack voting age population.

There was also a 1986 committeeman election in the 18th Ward—or at least the semblance of one. Crosby and Marble filed against incumbent John Daley. Both were knocked off the ballot, leaving Daley unopposed. Even had the challengers won their ballot fight, their chances against Daley likely would have been minimal. Eddings faced Daley in 1984 and lost 16,181 to 6,436.

John Daley, a onetime attorney and cousin of the late mayor, is a barely visible committeeman who nonetheless runs a strong ward organization. A former state representative, he gained unwanted exposure in the early 1970s. Daley testified in 1975 that he paid Charles Bonk, chairman of the county board's Zoning Committee, $46,500 to influence a number of zoning decisions. Daley was offered blanket immunity, including a provision that his testimony could not be used against him in possible disbarment proceedings. The U.S. Court of Appeals later overturned that immunity. Daley quit his law practice rather than face disbarment proceedings.

As a committeeman Daley is best remembered, if that is the term, for a single word he uttered in 1982. Mayor Jane Byrne had named one of Daley's aides her patronage chief. In turn, she counted on his vote for Ed Vrdolyak as party chairman. Daley had straddled the fence on the issue, but when asked to ratify Vrdolyak instead bellowed "No!"

Neither Kellam nor Daley can feel safe here. The aging of the youthful black population, and its gradual westward expansion (Ashland Avenue was the western dividing line in the 1960s) almost ensure black elected officials in years to come. The Voting Rights Act of 1965 would seem to ensure that the ward could not be redrawn to create a white majority. However, the city council could easily restructure the 18th to ensure a black alderman and committeeman.

REDISTRICTING: The 18th Ward gained three black precincts on the east end which formerly belonged to the 17th and 21st Wards. Lost were three white northern tier precincts, one to the 13th Ward and two to the 15th.

MAYORAL: Only three wards (the Lakefront 42nd, 46th, and 48th) had a closer three-way split in the 1983 Democratic primary than the 18th, which produced a difference of only 18 percent between first-and third-place candidates. Richard Daley won the ward with 41 percent of the vote to 36 percent for Harold Washington and 23 for Mayor Jane Byrne. As expected Washington dominated in the black areas while the other candidates garnered the vote in the white west side. Daley outpolled Byrne in every white precinct, although she gained 100 or more votes in all but one white precinct.

Although he won a plurality, Daley "lost" the 18th Ward, For his candidacy to be successful, he needed overwhelming majorities in his Southwest Side base—majorities which did not materialize.

Bernard Epton beat out Washington in the general election, with 56 percent of the vote. Voting in the ward followed strict racial lines.

The redrawn ward map gave Harold Washington gains in 1987. He polled 49 percent in both the primary and general elections—with strength, as expected, coming from the black eastern precincts.

CENSUS DATA: Population (1980): 60,705. 48.32 percent white, 50.03 percent black, 1.26 percent Hispanic, .42 percent Asian and other. Voting age population: 51.44 percent white, 46.60 percent black, .99 percent Hispanic, .97 Asian and other.

CENSUS TRACTS: See ward map.

COMMUNITY NEWSPAPERS:
  Chicago Independent Bulletin, 2037 W. 95th St. (783–1040)
  Chicago Metro News, 2600 S. Michigan (842–5950)
  Southtown Economist, 5959 S. Harlem (586–8800)
  Southwest News-Herald, 6225 S. Kedzie (476–4800)

ALDERMAN: Robert T. Kellam. Elected 1977. Born 1922. Career: assistant to Ald. James T. Murray; assistant to Cong. William T. Murphy.
Committees: Budget and Government Operations; Claims and Liabilities; Capital Development; Ports, Wharves, and Bridges.
City hall telephone: 744–6856, 744–3087.
Ward office: 8024 S. Western (776–9000).
1986 special election:

Robert T. Kellam	12,666 (64%)	Doris J. Nogaj	385	(2%)
Monica Faith Stewart	4,720 (24%)	Charles E. Marble	369	(2%)
Eldora Davis	787 (4%)	Chester Marks	253	(1%)
George H. Eddings	415 (2%)	Bruce Crosby	252	(1%)

1987 election:

Robert T. Kellam	14,447	(48%)	Richard J. Jones	955	(3%)
Eldora Davis	12,011	(40%)	Raymond J. Carroll	405	(1%)
James N. McCann	2,278	(8%)			

1987 runoff:

Robert T. Kellam	17,571	(56%)
Eldora Davis	14,073	(44%)

DEMOCRATIC COMMITTEEMAN: John Daley. Appointed 1967. Born May 10, 1923. Career: B.A., St. Mary's College; J.D., DePaul University; U.S. Navy, World War II; attorney; assistant state's attorney; special deputy to Illinois Director of Insurance; state representative, 1961–63.

Ward office: 8024 S. Western (776–9000).

1984 election:

John M. Daley	16,181	(72%)
George H. Eddings	6,436	(28%)

1986 special election:

John M. Daley, unopposed.

MAYORAL ELECTIONS:

1983 Democratic primary:

Richard Daley	12,480	(41%)
Harold Washington	11,181	(36%)
Jane Byrne	7,125	(23%)

1987 Democratic primary

Jane Byrne	16,076	(51%)
Harold Washington	15,298	(49%)

1983 general:

Bernard Epton	19,096	(56%)
Harold Washington	14,894	(44%)

1987 general:

Edward Vrdolyak	16,146	(50%)
Harold Washington	15,810	(49%)
Donald Haider	568	(1%)

19th Ward

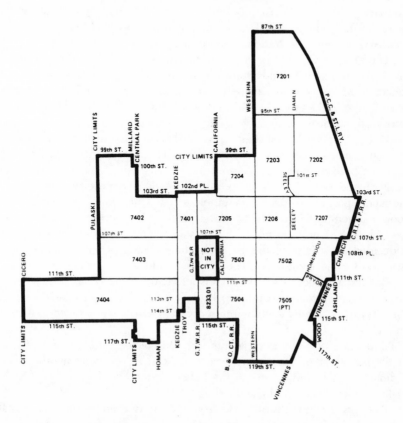

WHEN AFFLUENT IRISH workers left Bridgeport and Back of the Yards for the Far Southwest Side, they often were met with derision by friends and relatives they left behind. In fact, those in the old neighborhoods gave them a derogatory nickname—the "lace curtain" Irish.

The cultural rivalry has led to political feuds. Irish pols from the Far Southwest Side 19th Ward, which covers the Morgan Park and Beverly areas, fought their Bridgeport kin for mastery of the Democratic party. They always lost.

On at least one occasion this rivalry became a family feud. Thomas Nash, nephew of onetime chairman Patrick Nash, ruled the 19th Ward with alderman and Finance Committee chairman John Duffy in the forties. Jacob Arvey, later party chairman himself, disdainfully referred to Duffy and Tom Nash as "the Irish turkeys of Beverly."

Tom Nash, committeeman from 1932 to 1956, was a criminal lawyer whose clients included Al Capone. Such a background all but precluded him from public office, and he knew it. Duffy served as his front man.

Duffy was 19th Ward alderman beginning in 1935, and from the start an adversary to West Side party boss Arvey and the Bridgeport Irish who put Mayor Ed Kelly in power. He became chairman of the Finance Committee when Arvey joined the National Guard in 1941.

The Finance Committee chairman traditionally is the most powerful member of the city council, and Duffy was no exception. When independent but ineffective Mayor Martin Kennelly took office in 1947, Duffy took charge as the real ruler of the city. He told Kennelly what "we" are going to do, and the figurehead mayor went along with him.

Duffy, Tom Nash, and their 14th Ward allies nonetheless sought both the party chairmanship and the mayor's office. Their reluctance to act promptly cost them both positions.

Nash and Duffy had a large power base—those opposed to Arvey and the Bridgeport politicians. Duffy nonetheless bided his time and waited for the proper moment to take over party power. Even after Democrats suffered major losses in 1946, Duffy did not seek Arvey's ouster as party chairman. Instead, he decided to wait until the 1948 election—which promised to be equally disastrous for the Democrats. Then Duffy would strike.

But the Democrats scored surprising victories that year, from President Harry Truman to Senate candidate Paul Douglas and gubernatorial candidate Adlai Stevenson. Duffy could not oust a party chairman perceived as a miracle worker.

Two years later the miracles ran out. One of the victims was Duffy, who ran for president of the county board. A scandal involving another county candidate brought down most of the ticket. A notable exception was Richard J. Daley, who was elected county clerk.

The 1950 election disaster cost Arvey his party chairmanship. A caretaker chairman held the job while opposing factions fought behind the scenes for control.

That battle came to a head in 1953. The Bridgeport faction, with the blessing of interim chairman Joseph Gill, was ready to boost Daley to the chairmanship. The opposing side, backed by Duffy and fronted by 14th Ward committeeman Clarence Wagner, postponed a final vote in an attempt to group its forces.

Days later, Wagner died in a car crash, and Duffy's dreams of power died with him. Daley took over as party chairman, the final step on his way to becoming mayor. Duffy finally became county board president in 1961 but died the following year.

A generation later, hostilities have ceased between the 11th and 19th wards. In fact, 19th Ward committeeman Thomas Hynes engineered the second-largest vote total for Richard M. Daley in the 1983 Democratic primary.

Hynes, a state senator, became committeeman when aging party leader Thomas Fitzpatrick unexpectedly resigned in 1975. He outmaneuvered a crowded field which included Fitzpatrick's aldermanic successor, Jeremiah Joyce; Thomas Ryan, the party regulars' choice in the special aldermanic election to replace Fitzpatrick; Congressman Morgan Murphy; State Representative Daniel Houlihan; and "young Turk" precinct captain George Cullen.

Not long afterward, Mayor Richard Daley inadvertently did Hynes a favor. Cecil Partee, the state senate president, ran for attorney general rather than seek reelection. Daley was believed to have urged Partee into the race so that his son Richard could be installed as senate president.

Clout does not extend beyond the grave, the younger Daley learned. The mayor died in late 1976, and Richard M. Daley's support vanished immediately. After a protracted struggle (young State Senator Harold Washington fought for improved black representation among senate leadership), Hynes won the battle for the senate presidency. It was the first time, but not the last, that Washington and Hynes would be at odds.

Hynes did not stay in that office long. County Assessor Thomas Tully surprised party regulars by announcing that he would not seek another term in 1978. Hynes sought and received party backing for the position and has been elected three times without difficulty. In 1982 and 1986 he was the county's leading vote-getter.

He has not escaped controversy. When the Hilton Hotels sought a windfall property tax break to anchor North Loop redevelopment in 1981, Hynes sought an assessment compromise. Hilton rejected the proposal, thus scuttling the project.

Yet Hynes has remained free from scandal. In previous years the county assessor's office often was considered a license to steal. Assessors, by virtue of their power to fix real estate taxes, were able to extract favors for themselves and the Democratic party. No such charges have been leveled against Hynes.

He has received high marks for promoting legislation to increase property-tax exemptions for senior citizens and for home improvement; providing a taxpayers' advocate to review rulings; and offering tax incentives for job growth.

Hynes ally Joyce threatened to run for mayor as a Republican in 1987, and expected the support of the Daley wing of the party. Joyce, it was theorized, would draw enough primary votes to deprive Daley foe Jane Byrne of the Democratic nomination. But Joyce was considered too conservative to win Lakefront votes needed by a Daleyite in a general election.

Thus Tom Hynes, with his "Mr. Clean" image, entered the race only weeks after he vowed he would stay away. His campaign fell little short of disaster. Hynes's only real hope was to force fellow Harold Washington antagonist Ed Vrdolyak out of the race. Vrdolyak didn't budge, and Hynes withdrew two days before the election.

The ill-conceived run for mayor might have cost Hynes his political career. A campaign against Washington was a longshot at best, but for Hynes a high-level campaign could have given him visibility for a future candidacy—say, against U.S. Senator Paul Simon in 1990. Instead, his speeches made him look dull. His nebulous statements concerning Vrdolyak's alleged meeting with a mobster made him look wishy-washy. And his withdrawal, with its definite racial overtones, all but assures enmity from the black community.

Joyce left the city council for the state senate post when Hynes first ran for assessor. Michael Sheahan succeeded Joyce as alderman in 1979 and still serves there. Sheahan easily triumphed in the 1987 aldermanic election; his only opponent was Maurice Johnson, a follower of political cult leader Lyndon LaRouche. Since most of Johnson's votes came from black precincts, they may be seen as anti-Sheahan (-Hynes,-Daley,-Vrdolyak) protests rather than votes in favor of mandatory AIDS testing or censure of Britain's Queen Elizabeth. Johnson won a precinct, the only precinct won by a LaRouche follower in the city.

Sheahan, who was a reliable anti-Washington bloc vote, is best known as the only Big Ten referee on the city council. He served as chairman of the council's Police, Fire, and Municipal Institutions Committee. That committee chairmanship was an appropriate one. The 19th is home to a disproportionate number of policemen and firefighters, who are forced by law to live within the city yet seek homes as far from the inner city as possible.

Yet this ward is considerably more than a "cop ghetto." Morgan Park and Beverly Hills communities, the self-proclaimed "Village in the City," form the eastern part of the ward. These communities served as affluent suburbs before their annexation to the city in the late 1890s and early 1900s.

The Ridge District, in the heart of the communities, received historic district status in 1976. Here gracious mansions (many designed by Frank Lloyd Wright disciple Walter Burley Griffin) are fronted by huge, tree-lined lawns and broad, winding streets. Elaborate Protestant, not Catholic, churches predominate.

Nearby 95th Street, the main commercial street, offers baby furniture, Oriental rug, and waterbed stores, plus an art gallery. Commuter trains, not the elevated, whisk residents to the Loop. Beverly Hills and Morgan Park project more an air of Winnetka than the Southwest Side.

"Beverly Hills" is no misnomer. The community contains the highest point in Chicago—at 103rd and Oakley.

The 19th also includes Mount Greenwood, the southwesternmost community in Chicago. Housing is not as inspiring as in Beverly or Morgan Park, but is by no means shabby.

Mount Greenwood contains a number of unusual features. St. Xavier College at 103rd and Pulaski occupies the northeast corner of the community along with Mother McAuley High School, a statewide volleyball power.

The community also serves as Chicago's cemetery capital. Mount Olivet (111th and California) and St. Casimir's Lithuanian Catholic (111th and Kostner) are both located here. Mount Greenwood Cemetery (107th to 111th, California to Sacramento) is situated entirely within the Mount Greenwood community, yet is not part of the city.

At the southwest end of the ward lies Chicago's most unusual high school—

the Chicago High School for Agricultural Sciences, featuring the only remaining farm in the city.

The 19th Ward for years housed another unique Chicago institution: Lar "America First" Daly, who for years ran for office clad in an Uncle Sam suit. Daly ran in more than 40 elections, for every position from president to clerk of the circuit court—and lost every one of them.

REDISTRICTING: The 19th was unaltered by the 1986 ward remap.

MAYORAL: Only one other ward, his own 11th, performed better for Richard Daley in the 1983 mayoral primary than did the 19th. He received 63 percent of the vote—and only 500 votes fewer than he got in the 11th. Jane Byrne finished second with 25 percent of the vote. Harold Washington received 12 percent of the vote, mainly in the integrated Morgan Park community.

Bernard Epton won 80 percent of the vote in the general election. Washington's support, as in the primary, was concentrated in integrated Morgan Park precincts.

Jane Byrne captured the ward in the 1987 Democratic primary, with 78 percent of the vote. Ed Vrdolyak garnered roughly the same number of votes in the general election, but earned a smaller percentage. Donald Haider did comparatively well here with 1,992 votes. Most likely, they came from die-hard Hynes supporters who opposed Washington yet would not vote for recent foe Vrdolyak.

CENSUS DATA: Population (1980): 59,786. 83.81 percent white, 14.66 percent black, 1.04 percent Hispanic, .41 percent Asian and other. Voting age population: 85.10 percent white, 12.50 percent black, .90 percent Hispanic, 1.50 percent Asian and other.

CENSUS TRACTS: See ward map.

COMMUNITY NEWSPAPERS:
Beverly Review, 9925 S. Wood (238–3366)
Chicago Independent Bulletin, 2037 W. 95th St. (783–1040)
Southtown Economist, 5959 S. Harlem (586–8800)
Southwest Sentinel, 10424 S. Kedzie (239–7400)

ALDERMAN: Michael F. Sheahan. Elected 1979. Born December 18, 1944. Career: Chicago State University; teacher and coach, Chicago public schools; officer, Chicago Police Dept., 1971–79.

Committees: Buildings; Human Rights and Consumer Protection; Land Acquisition, Disposition and Leases; License; Local Transportation.
City hall telephone: 744–3072, 744–5682.
Ward office: 10321 S. Western Ave. (238–8766).
1987 election:
Michael F. Sheahan   26,936   (91%)
Maurice E. Johnson   2,746   (9%)

COMMITTEEMAN: Thomas C. Hynes. Elected 1976. Born November 5, 1938. Career: J.D., Loyola University, 1962; attorney, 1962–; law professor, John Marshall Law School, 1967–9; first assistant to general attorney, Chicago Park District, 1969–71; state senator, 1971–78; Cook County assessor, 1978–.
Ward office: 10321 S. Western Ave. (238–8766).
1984 election:
Thomas C. Hynes, unopposed.

MAYORAL ELECTIONS:

1983 Democratic primary:
Richard Daley   20,687   (63%)
Jane Byrne   8,110   (25%)
Harold Washington   4,029   (12%)

1983 general:
Bernard Epton   28,095   (80%)
Harold Washington   7,086   (20%)

1987 Democratic primary:
Jane Byrne   23,825   (78%)
Harold Washington   6,590   (22%)

1987 general:
Edward Vrdolyak   23,634   (74%)
Harold Washington   6,248   (20%)
Donald Haider   1,992   (6%)

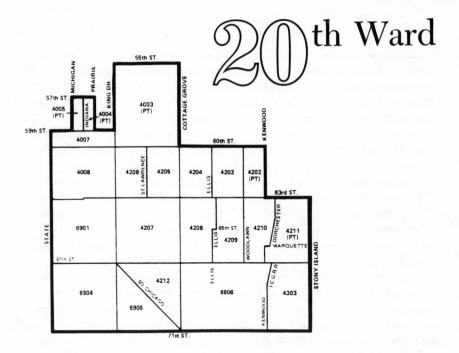

20th Ward

DEATHBED WISHES ABOUND in romantic novels. A dying king designates his successor or requests that his daughter wed a baron. Such requests are not common in real life—or even in the surrealistic world that is Chicago politics.

In recent years, the closest thing to a dying request took place in the South Side's 20th Ward. Kenneth Campbell, high-living alderman known for his fine suits and pink Cadillac, was about to depart for the Great Council Meeting in the Sky. It appeared doubtful that he would live until the 1971 aldermanic election.

Campbell arranged for his successor. He saw to it that his precinct captains circulated petitions for both himself and Clifford Kelley, an attorney and delegate to the recent constitutional convention. It turned out to be an astute move. Campbell passed away shortly before the election. Kelley, who would have merely filled a ballot space had Campbell lived, succeeded to the local throne.

His "realm" was the area known as Washington Park. It includes the park itself, with the nationally famous DuSable Museum of Afro-American History, a riggers' shop, and a peace sculpture, at the northernmost portion of the ward. Otherwise, the ward is roughly bounded by 60th Street, State Street, 71st, and Stony Island Avenue.

This truly was a magical kingdom in earlier times. The original Washington Park racetrack at 61st and Cottage Grove played host to the American Derby, one of the most important horseraces in the country. But it faced problems after betting was outlawed in 1896. Eventually it was razed. Now the area is residential.

White City, at 63rd and Calumet, was another amusement palace which graced the Washington Park area. This "City of a million electric lights" featured a roller rink, a penny arcade, and a ballroom. It also featured a blimp hangar which indirectly led to one of Chicago's many unusual tragedies. The blimp Wingfoot Air Express was making its initial flight, a sightseeing cruise of Grant Park, on July 21, 1919, when it caught fire and fell through the skylight of a downtown bank. Eleven persons were killed.

The 20th Ward, which also includes parts of the Woodlawn and Greater Grand Crossing communities, is anything but a pleasure palace today. Instead, it is one of the poorest wards in Chicago.

In some parts, the 20th Ward is one of the most crowded in the city. Two CHA projects, Midway Gardens (60th and Cottage Grove) and an extension of Washington Park Homes (62nd and Wabash), house hundreds of people. Two other huge projects, not part of the Chicago Housing Authority, are the Woodlawn Gardens at 61st and Cottage Grove and the Parkway Gardens at 64th and King Drive.

The main business thoroughfare, 63rd Street, is not the prosperous strip one finds further west. East of Cottage Grove are shells of former businesses, a poverty reflected by the dormant Jackson Park elevated tracks which hang overhead. West of Cottage Grove the street perks up, due in part to the traffic from the Englewood elevated line. Many of these businesses are fast food outlets, including one called Ms. Piggies at 63rd and Eberhart which pictures an orange and black pig in a bikini.

Oakwood Cemetery at 71st and Cottage Grove forms much of the southeast corner of the ward (a cemetery that serves, ironically, as a resting place for both Harold Washington and Bernard Epton). A company at the opposite end (60th and State) provides the auxiliary service. Elmo's Tombstone Service advertises "B 4 you go, see Elmo."

This ward was the scene of massive black immigration during and shortly after World War II (it was a "newly created" ward because of the rapidly changing demographics). Campbell, a loyal follower of Congressman William Dawson, was its first Democratic committeeman in 1947. He would have been the likely Dawson successor after the congressman's death, but his own poor health precluded his taking the office.

Kelley was more than slightly a maverick. A product of the Regular Democratic Organization, he nonetheless showed some independence. His pro-Washington votes kept him from the council's Vrdolyak bloc, yet he was distrusted by the mayor's inner circle.

The articulate Kelley, a regular panelist on a radio political talk show, was that city council rarity: an alderman with a well-developed sense of humor. During a debate over Mayor Jane Byrne's proposal for a hefty pay raise for her bodyguards, Kelley agreed, saying the raises might be appropriate ("because bodyguards should be paid in inverse proportion to the popularity of the person they are guarding"). In one early heated Council Wars debate, an alderman suggested that bulletproof glass be placed between the council floor and the gallery. Kelley supported the proposal by commenting, "It's a good idea. It might protect them from us."

Kelley was more than a humorist. He led the fight for a variety of legislation. He proposed, with success, a residency requirement for teachers. Other Kelley proposals met with less success. His work to break a ceiling on cab licenses thus far has been unsuccessful. A drive for an elected school board met with opposition from many of his fellow Washington-bloc aldermen. His proposed gay rights ordinance split both the Washington and Vrdolyak factions of the city council and failed to pass.

Kelley also received less than favorable publicity. A 1983 investigation showed Kelley owed more than $4,000 in fines on more than 200 parking tickets. Kelley claimed that most of those tickets were issued when he was at city hall on official business. But the investigation showed that half the tickets were issued near Rush Street—an area close to neither city hall nor the 20th Ward.

More recently, Kelly was the target of a probe in which he was accused of taking money from a firm under investigation for allegedly giving payoffs to aldermen and other city officials. Kelley admitted accepting money from FBI undercover operative Michael Raymond, but said that he considered it a campaign donation and recorded it as such on his ethics statement. At first he said he received $1,000; later he admitted to receiving $7,500. He was indicted in November 1986 on charges of extortion, mail fraud, and racketeering. He later admitted to accepting payoffs and gifts in excess of $30,000.

Operation Incubator no doubt took its electoral toll on Kelley, but foes argued that his lack of attentiveness to ward affairs would have sealed his doom anyway. "The perception (was) that he cared more about what was going on in Beirut and Damascus than what was happening at 67th Street and Stony Island Avenue," according to a local reporter. Six challengers ran against him in 1987.

Kelley received 42 percent to 18 percent for Ernest Jones, who was running against him for the third time. The ensuing runoff proved two axioms of Chicago aldermanic politics: that an incumbent alderman forced into a runoff, no matter what his February percentage, is in trouble; and that an alderman running against an incumbent committeeman or a protégé of that committeeman usually loses. Jones, a Chicago police investigator whose two sons were killed on the streets, once served as bodyguard for Committeeman Cecil Partee. Kelley gained votes in the runoff, but his foes rallied successfully behind Jones. Soon after the election, Kelley pleaded guilty to four counts of mail fraud and one count of failing to file a federal tax return.

Jones ranked among the finalists in any Most Obscure Alderman sweepstakes until November 1987. Then he suggested at a city council budget hearing that the city is paying too much in medical benefits because of lost workdays by female Chicago police officers due to "minister (sic) periods," although admitting that he had no statistics to back up his allegation. When his statement drew outrage from women and many men, he charged that "white newspaper writers" and "white radio stations" were distorting his thoughts. Jones's remarks took place shortly before Thanksgiving, thus allowing a newscaster at one radio station to present him with a "turkey of the year" award.

Democratic Committeeman Partee has had a career as colorful as that of

Kelley. First elected to the state house of representatives in 1956, Partee spent ten years there before serving another ten years in the state senate. The last two years were served as state senate president, making him the highest-ranking black state legislative official in the country at the time. He even served as acting governor on occasion, when both Governor Dan Walker and Lieutenant Governor Neil Hartigan were out of state.

Partee wished to run for lieutenant governor in 1976 but was dissuaded from doing so by Mayor Richard Daley. Instead he was slated for attorney general and made a suicide run against popular Republican incumbent William Scott. Despite the loss, Partee landed on his feet. He was appointed to head the Department of Human Services in 1977 and won election as city treasurer two years later.

He lost one election of note early in 1986. When state Democratic Committee chairman Calvin Sutker was defeated in the March primary, Partee was considered a frontrunner for the job. He even received the endorsements of Cook County chairman Edward Vrdolyak and City Clerk Walter Kozubowski, an ally of Alderman Edward Burke. But two black Chicago committeemen deserted him, and he lost to downstate senator Vince Demuzio.

Partee and Harold Washington were not close. When Partee supported incumbent Michael Bilandic for mayor in 1977, challenger Washington called him "the biggest Uncle Tom on God's green earth." During the 1987 campaign, talk existed of replacing Partee on the Harold Washington "ticket" with a white Lakefront liberal.

Yet Partee helped Washington's career on two different occasions. It was he who persuaded Mayor Daley to slate Washington as his state senate replacement, in spite of the mayor's reservations. And Partee's 20th Ward organization gave Washington the votes he needed to overcome a James Taylor ally in the 1978 state senate primary.

Few have accused Partee of activism, yet this seeming passivity may have helped his stature among whites. When Washington sought the mayor's office in 1983, many whites were heard to say that they could not abide Washington but could support the "right" black man, one such as Partee.

That argument was totally academic, as Partee has never shown any signs of bucking the Democratic establishment in a quest for higher office—nor have the regular Democrats ever shown any inclination to slate him for a policy-making office.

REDISTRICTING: The 20th Ward was not altered by the 1986 remap.

MAYORAL: Harold Washington scored a resounding victory here in the 1983 mayoral primary. He won every precinct and carried 84 percent of the vote. Jane Byrne took 13 percent and Richard Daley, 3 percent.

Byrne received 135 votes in the 31st precinct—60 more than she received in any other precinct. As there is little difference between the 31st and other precincts, the anomaly may be explained by a zealous Byrne precinct worker there.

Washington, as expected, scored a massive victory in the general election—99.2 percent of the vote. Bernard Epton got 220 votes out of the 25,933 total votes cast, reaching double figures in only four precincts. Washington exceeded Epton's vote total for the entire ward in every precinct but two.

That dominance continued in 1987. Jane Byrne and LaRouchie Sheila Jones received only 244 out of 21,208 votes cast in the Democratic primary. Edward Vrdolyak and Donald Haider got 261 votes in the general election to 21,748 for Harold Washington.

CENSUS DATA: Population (1980): 59,981. 1.83 percent white, 97.50 percent black, .65 percent Hispanic, .02 percent Asian and other. Voting age population: 2.27 percent white, 96.44 percent black, .50 percent Hispanic, .89 percent Asian and other.

CENSUS TRACTS: See ward map.

COMMUNITY NEWSPAPERS:
  Chatham Citizen, 412 E. 87th St. (487–7700)
  Chicago Independent Bulletin, 2037 W. 95th St. (783–1040)
  Chicago Metro, 2600 S. Michigan (842–5950)
  Hyde Park Herald, 5420 S. Harper (643–8533)

ALDERMAN: Ernest Jones, Elected 1987. Born July 6, 1926. Career: Arkansas A & M College; U.S. Marine Corps; Chicago Police Department.
Committees: Economic Development (vice-chairman); Aging and Disabled; Beautification and Recreation; Budget and Government Operations; Education; Finance; License; Police, Fire, and Municipal Institutions; Ports, Wharves, and Bridges; Traffic Control and Safety.
City hall telephone: 744–6840, 744–5688.
Ward office: 610 E. 61st St. (667–6300).
1987 election:

Clifford P. Kelley	7,281	(42%)	Dino F. McNeal	1,447	(8%)
Ernest "Ernie" Jones	3,175	(18%)	Beverly Thomas	1,131	(6%)
Malinda C. Keys	2,080	(12%)	Donald L. Birden	577	(3%)
Inez M. Gardner	1,791	(10%)			

1987 runoff:

Ernest "Ernie" Jones	9,288	(53%)
Clifford P. Kelley	8,197	(47%)

DEMOCRATIC COMMITTEEMAN: Cecil Partee. Appointed 1971. Born April 10, 1921. Career: B.S., Tennessee State University; J.D., Northwestern University;

attorney, 1947–48; assistant state's attorney, 1948–56; Illinois House of Representatives, 1957–67; Illinois Senate, 1967–77; Commissioner, Department of Human Services, 1977–79; City Treasurer, 1979-.
Ward office: 610 E. 61st St. (667–6300).
1984 election:
Cecil Partee, unopposed.

MAYORAL ELECTIONS:

1983 Democratic primary:

Harold Washington	18,313	(84%)
Jane Byrne	2,687	(12%)
Richard Daley	721	(3%)

1983 general:

Harold Washington	25,713	(99%)
Bernard Epton	220	(1%)

1987 Democratic primary:

Harold Washington	20,964	(99%)
Jane Byrne	226	(1%)

1987 general:

Harold Washington	21,748	(99%)
Edward Vrdolyak	146	(1%)
Donald Haider	115	(1%)

②1st Ward

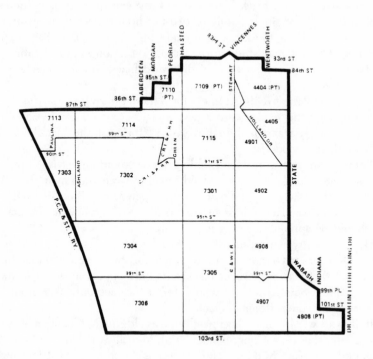

PERHAPS NO OTHER WARD is less known to most Chicagoans than the Far South Side's 21st. It is a place that is out of the way unless one happens to live or work there.

The Dan Ryan Expressway forms most of the eastern boundary of the 21st Ward, then snakes through the southern section. Downtown skyscrapers—Sears Tower, the Hancock and Standard Oil buildings—are visible from here. But they appear at a great distance, like the sun from the planet Neptune.

Distance from the Loop (and poor transportation to there) explains why the 21st is one of the "youngest" wards in the city in terms of settlement. Although development took place as early as the 1860s (the Washington Heights railroad station at 103rd and Loomis that gave the ward's community its name) and most of the area was annexed to Chicago in 1890, much of the land belonging to the 21st ward remained vacant until after World War II.

Construction of new housing after the war preceded by only a few years another major development—an influx of blacks into the eastern portion of the ward and the subsequent flight of the Germans, Irish, and Swedes who were the descendents of the earliest settlers.

Freed from housing restrictions which limited their mobility, blacks moved at first into the area east of Halsted and eventually into the entire ward. Now the 21st is virtually all black.

For the most part this is a middle-class ward, full of pleasant residential tree-lined streets with brick houses and occasional ma-and-pa corner stores. Children from these single-family or two-flat homes may spend winter afternoons sledding down the large man-made hill at Robichaux Park (93rd and Eggleston). Or they may study in the Carter Woodson Regional Library (95th and Halsted), which contains one of the finest black studies collections in the United States.

The Penn Central Railroad tracks form the western boundary of the ward. For many years the tracks were a psychological as well as physical dividing line. To the west was all-white Beverly, to the east the black Washington Heights neighborhood.

Bennett Stewart, a former Building Department supervisor fired in the midst of a 1968 scandal, was elected alderman in 1971 when incumbent Wilson Frost ran in the newly mapped 34th Ward. When Mayor Richard J. Daley died in late 1976, other black aldermen argued that Frost, who was the mayor pro tem, should be appointed acting mayor. Stewart remained silent.

His popularity appeared to hit a low by March 1978. Stewart was the Regular Democratic Organization's candidate for state committeeman that year in a district that was 80 percent black. His only opponent was a white independent named Sam Ackerman who entered the race only as a protest. Ackerman won the committeeman election.

If Stewart was living on borrowed time as alderman, he got an unexpected reprieve later that year. Congressman Ralph Metcalfe died in October. Stewart was tapped to replace him in a secret meeting closed to the district's independent committeemen.

He barely won that election. Last-minute Republican substitution A. A. "Sammy" Rayner polled 40 percent of the vote. Harold Washington thrashed Stewart with 83 percent of the vote in the 1980 Democratic primary.

Stewart, who was elected committeeman in 1972, slated Krista Ligon, a Cook County jury commissioner, to succeed him in the city council. Five others entered the race, including former DuSable High School basketball star "Sweet Charlie" Brown.

Niles Sherman, a former policeman and president of the Brainard Community Action Coalition, was the major challenger. He attacked both Stewart and Ligon as "Uncle Toms." "The people want leadership," he was quoted as saying, "All Uncle Bennie did was to give the 21st a handkerchief-waving, foot-shuffling image and now the regulars have replaced him with Auntie Krista, and she's got a rag on her head, too." Sherman won that 1979 election and defeated Stewart the following year for committeeman.

No one has accused Sherman of being an Uncle Tom. On the other hand, many associate him with a statement he made after Edward Vrdolyak wrested the Cook County Democratic party chairmanship from George Dunne in 1982. "This isn't a dumping process," Sherman said of the Dunne ouster. "This is a coming together process to broaden the horizons for everybody so all can get to the rainbow and stick our hand into that pot of gold."

Some claimed that Sherman's remarks represented an open admission of what humorists called Chicago's unofficial motto: "Ubi est mea?" (Where's mine?). Sherman answered that critics misunderstood the interpretation of the rainbow and wrote a newspaper commentary describing it as racial equality, equal opportunity, and good schools, parks, and churches for all.

But a comment made after Harold Washington's 1983 victory (and his own reelection) left little doubt on interpretation. Sherman reportedly was upset because his son was laid off from his sewer department job. He suggested that minority aldermen might abandon the mayor if not given "the spoils."

Washington confronted Sherman's criticism by saying "He's a potent politician. I'm almost certain he could carry a bucket of water across the ward. He couldn't carry much else."

The mayor's response did not mark the end of Sherman's campaign for better treatment for aldermen. When an Hispanic group "called roll" on city aldermen to determine their stance on the proposed ward remap, Sherman told them, in effect, that they should be ready to give him favors if they wanted to receive any. When advised that the Hispanics expressed outrage at his comments, he said "They can kiss my turkey."

Late in 1986 Sherman proposed an ordinance which would allow aldermen to park in no-parking zones while on official business—thus legalizing a practice which many had followed illegally for years. Sherman attempted to make his proposal part of the omnibus—uncontroversial bills passed without argument at the end of a council session. Alderman David Orr (49th) objected to that procedure, and the matter was brought to a full vote. Sherman's proposal passed but Washington vetoed it.

Despite Sherman's crusades for aldermen's rights, he was a consistent pro-Washington vote on the city council. Such votes might have been less out of philosophical agreement than out of self-preservation. Any significant disagreement would be tantamount to political suicide in the 21st, one of the strongest Washington wards in the city.

Washington endorsed Sherman for reelection early in the campaign. Yet even that vote of confidence was not enough to reelect the acerbic two-term alderman. Sherman outpolled his closest opponent, postal union official Jesse Evans, nearly five-to-one in the February election. Yet those who did not favor the incumbent in the February election clearly were against him. Evans won the runoff by a fourteen-vote margin, which held up after a Sherman-ordered recount. Sherman still serves as Democratic committeeman, but a challenge from Evans (and perhaps others) is inevitable.

REDISTRICTING: The 21st Ward lost one northern precinct to the 18th Ward in the 1986 remap.

MAYORAL: No ward gave Harold Washington a higher percentage of the 1983 Democratic primary vote. He won 88 percent, with 9 percent going to Jane Byrne and 3 percent to Richard Daley.

Likewise, Washington rolled to an astounding 120-to-1 victory in the general election. His plurality over Bernard Epton—32,687—was larger here than in any other ward in the city.

Washington took every precinct in 1987, winning both primary and general elections with totals just short of 99 percent.

CENSUS DATA: Population (1980): 59,836. 1.25 percent white, 98.35 percent black, .53 percent Hispanic, .67 percent Asian and other. Voting age population: .84 percent white, 97.90 percent black, .41 percent Hispanic, .85 percent Asian and other.

CENSUS TRACTS: See ward map.

COMMUNITY NEWSPAPERS:
Chicago Independent Bulletin, 2037 W. 95th St. (783–1040)
Southeast Citizen, 412 E. 87th (487–7700)

ALDERMAN: Jesse J. Evans. Elected 1987. Born May, 27, 1937. Career: City Colleges of Chicago, 1955–58; U.S. Postal Service, 1958–87; union representative, American Postal Union, 1980–87.
Committees: Intergovernmental Relations (vice-chairman); Beautification and Recreation; Budget and Government Operations; Historical Landmark Preservation; Finance; Housing; Land Acquisition, Disposition, and Leases; License; Local Transportation; Municipal Code Revision.
City hall telephone: 744–4810, 744–4811.
Ward office: 9107 S. Ashland Ave. (445–2404).
1987 election:

Niles Sherman	12,186	(45%)	Roosevelt Ely III	996	(4%)
Jesse J. Evans	2,532	(9%)	Thomas E. Coleman	908	(3%)
Stanley Johnson	2,279	(8%)	Emma J. Brandon	717	(3%)
Arthur Jones	2,158	(8%)	Myles R. Reed	529	(2%)
Leonard DeVille	1,537	(6%)	La Dara Jones	517	(2%)
Martin A. Henderson	1,316	(5%)	Lula Mae Clay	447	(2%)
Paul Grant	1,109	(4%)			

1987 runoff:

Jesse J. Evans	13,716	(50%)
Niles Sherman	13,702	(50%)

DEMOCRATIC COMMITTEEMAN: Niles Sherman. Elected 1980. Born 1929. Career: officer, Chicago Police Department; alderman, 1979–87.
Ward office: 1234 W. 95th St. (881–7405)

1984 election:

Niles Sherman	10,779	(57%)
Martin A. Henderson	8,282	(43%)

MAYORAL ELECTIONS:

1983 Democratic primary:

Harold Washington	25,550	(88%)
Jane Byrne	2,687	(9%)
Richard Daley	865	(3%)

1983 general:

Harold Washington	32,962	(99%)
Bernard Epton	275	(1%)

1987 Democratic primary:

Harold Washington	29,625	(99%)
Jane Byrne	306	(1%)

1987 general:

Harold Washington	30,370	(99%)
Edward Vrdolyak	206	(1%)
Donald Haider	138	(0%)

22nd Ward

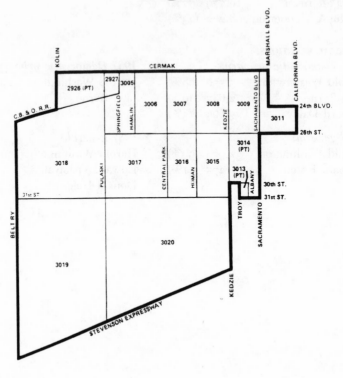

HISPANICS, ESPECIALLY MEXICAN-AMERICANS, are the city's fastest-growing ethnic group. Nowhere is the new political power among Mexican-Americans more evident than in the Near Southwest Side's 22nd Ward.

The 22nd coincides almost exactly with the community officially designated South Lawndale but known locally as Little Village; no other ward matches up more closely with a particular community. It runs from Ogden Avenue and Cermak Road on the north to Marshall Boulevard, California, and Kedzie on the east, the Stevenson Expressway on the south, and the city limits on the west.

Largely a residential area of single-family homes and two-flats, the 22nd Ward also includes a hodgepodge of sights: 31st Street, also named Home Run Inn along one stretch, after a nearby pizzeria which distributes frozen pizzas throughout the city; the Toman Branch Library at 27th and Pulaski, home of a local historical society; McCormick School at 27th and Sawyer, which despite transfers of seventh and eighth graders remains one of the most overcrowded schools in the city; and Millard Congregational Church at 23rd and Central

Park, which houses both a branch of North Park College and the only J. W. Steere pipe organ in the Midwest.

Washburne Trade School, where apprentices have built one of the city's few solar-powered homes, can be found at 31st and Kedzie. The nationally regarded trade school, operated by the board of education with the help of trade unions, has been the subject of controversy in recent years. Various unions have threatened to withdraw their apprenticeship programs rather than conform to the racial and sexual quotas established by the board.

One thing you won't find in the 22nd Ward is 29th Street. Numbers of Little Village streets jump from 28 to 30, for reasons lost to antiquity.

Heart of the ward is 26th Street, a colorful strip of *carnicerias, taquerias, panaderias*, Mexican nightclubs, Spanish-language book and record stores, and bars with huge satellite dishes pointed southwest—to pick up soccer and boxing matches aired from Mexico City. Neatly maintained and with renovated building facades, 26th Street is the most prosperous Hispanic shopping area in the city.

Brightly hued murals adorn several 26th Street walls—at a bank, a fast food restaurant, an industrial park. These murals, unlike those in nearby Pilsen, are sponsored by local businesses and avoid political themes. They are a part of the establishment, not a rebellion against it.

Community groups have proposed renaming 26th Street after favorite sons, and their choice of heroes reflects the ideological split in the local Mexican community. Older, more established Mexicans (who view themselves as merely another ethnic group) promote Manuel Perez, Jr., a local World War II hero. Younger, more liberal Mexicans (who see themselves as a disadvantaged minority) want it named after civil rights leader Rudy Lozano.

Anton "Pushcart Tony" Cermak formed his political base here in the early 1900s, creating a multiethnic coalition which swept him into the mayor's office in 1931. Local Poles and Bohemians were part of this coalition. For the most part, their descendants have fled to the suburbs. Mexican-Americans have taken their place.

The 22nd now hosts the largest percentage of Hispanics in the city—78 percent, nearly all of them Mexicans. This concentration is no accident. Many Mexicans first settled in neighboring Pilsen in the 1950s and, following traditional migration patterns, moved toward the outskirts of the city. For years neighboring Cicero and Berwyn opposed their immigration to those suburbs. Thus Little Village was as far west as most Mexicans could go; it became, in effect, a suburb within the city. Mexicans are free to move to the suburbs now. Still, many choose to remain in Little Village.

Demographics explains why the 22nd perennially casts fewer votes than any other ward in the city. Mexicans, with large families of young children, have fewer voting age residents than other groups. And despite the success of recent citizenship drives, many of the ward's residents are not U.S. citizens, including an undetermined number of illegal aliens.

Of course, not all of the 22nd Ward's residents are Hispanics. Blacks living in the northern tier of precincts constitute about 5 percent of the population. Whites living mainly in the southwest precincts are another 17 percent. The two groups, although greatly outnumbered by Hispanics, traditionally cast half the ward's votes. But Hispanics gradually are taking over. Local newspapers' new citizens lists show people with Spanish surnames, while people with Eastern European names dominate the obituaries.

Recent elections have seen a 180-degree turn in ward politics. At one time a machine bastion, the 22nd now hosts perhaps the most efficient independent political organization in the city. That organization helped elect Washington ally Jesus Garcia as alderman and committeeman in 1986.

For years the alderman was Frank Stemberk, one of the council's quieter members and a reliable Vrdolyak-bloc vote. Perhaps his most memorable act took place in 1977, when he offered a $1 per head bounty on all rats captured in the ward. He also inadvertently made headlines in 1985 when the *Sun-Times* charged that he maintained his principal residence in a western suburb.

Stemberk won a spirited aldermanic election in 1983 against four Hispanic challengers. Most important of those was labor organizer Rudy Lozano, an early backer of Harold Washington. Lozano missed a runoff by seventeen votes; his followers charged that systematic purging of Spanish-surname voters from poll sheets shortly before the election denied Lozano the votes he needed to force a runoff.

Lozano, a rising political star, was shot to death in his home that June. A reputed gang member was convicted of the murder, but Lozano's allies still contend that his labor and political activities formed the motive for the killing.

Backers of Lozano rallied behind his campaign manager, Jesus Garcia. They took to the 1984 Democratic committeeman race with a religious fervor. It turned out to be a classic Washington (represented by Garcia) versus Vrdolyak (Stemberk) race. Washington campaigned extensively for Garcia, including an important visit to a CHA project (then in the ward) two days before the election. The result: a fifty-nine-vote Garcia triumph.

It was the second time in recent years that the otherwise socially conservative 22nd Ward made history. Lillian Piotrowski in 1969 became the first woman on the Democratic Central Committee. Garcia was the first independent Hispanic to be elected committeeman.

Garcia was an exception among committeemen. He used his office to provide constituent services that are usually the realm of the alderman alone— and maintained a high profile in the process.

Washington wished to support Garcia in his upcoming aldermanic run but could not make a direct contribution, lest he be approached by any number of (black) hopefuls also seeking funds. Instead, he gave Garcia (and fellow Hispanic allies Juan Velazquez and Luis Gutierrez) high-paying city jobs from which they could help finance their campaigns.

Stemberk declined to seek reelection when special elections were announced in 1986; instead he sought, unsuccessfully, a post on the county board.

JESUS GARCIA

Stemberk and party regulars slated supermarket owner Guadalupe Martinez for alderman. Former labor union leader August Sallas, a two-time loser for committeeman, was the regulars' choice for that post. Billed as "the team that works," the Martinez-Sallas ticket was an unlikely match in at least one respect. Martinez spoke halting English and Sallas spoke little Spanish.

State Representative Juan Soliz, a former Garcia ally, also backed two candidates: beauty supply store owner Fred Yanez for alderman and Boy Scout leader Ed Rodriguez for committeeman. Anita Villarreal, a Little Village businesswoman, was the fourth committeeman candidate.

Serious issues (housing, schools, gangs) were generally ignored during the campaign. Instead, up popped such "issues" as garbage cans (Martinez gave them away while attacking Garcia for selling them at cost) and patriotism (Martinez was quoted as calling Garcia "100 percent communist"; Yanez one-upped Martinez by peppering his campaign literature with a sixteen-year-old photograph of himself in army fatigues).

While not exactly landslides, the elections were hardly close. Garcia carried twenty-six of twenty-seven precincts in the alderman race and lost only three precincts for committeeman. He won 54 to 55 percent of the vote despite losing two of his strongest precincts in the remap.

Six candidates opposed Garcia in the 1987 election. He again carried every precinct and 54 percent of the vote. His failure to increase this percentage hints that a single strong candidate could give Garcia a battle. But the disorganized state of the regular Democrats here indicates such a challenge is not forthcoming.

REDISTRICTING: Even though the 22nd Ward was the source of special aldermanic elections, it suffered only minor changes from the remap. Two northern precincts, both almost entirely black, were transferred to the 24th Ward. They were replaced by two Hispanic precincts, one previously belonging to the 12th and the other formerly a part of the 25th.

MAYORAL: Traditional party loyalties played a major role in the 1983 mayoral races here. State's Attorney Richard M. Daley, backed by Stemberk, captured the ward in the primary with 3,907 votes to 3,067 for Mayor Jane Byrne. Washington trailed badly with only 1,780 votes.

Despite Stemberk's covert backing of Bernard Epton in the general election, voters stuck with the Democrat. Washington squeezed to a narrow victory, 4,674 to 4,279. The 22nd was the only ward won by Washington in which he failed to garner at least 60 percent of the vote.

The 22nd was the city's closest ward (indeed, one of the few close ones) in the 1987 Democratic primary, so close that the 36 votes received by Lyndon LaRouche follower Sheila Jones prevented either Harold Washington or Jane Byrne from claiming a majority. Two black-majority precincts gave Harold Washington the overwhelming margins he needed to claim a thirty-vote victory in this ward.

Washington captured the general election with a more comfortable 56 percent of the vote, the difference coming from Hispanics who traditionally support the Democratic nomimee.

CENSUS DATA: Population (1980): 59,803. 16.57 percent white, 4.55 percent black, 79.11 percent Hispanic. Voting age population: 22.56 percent white, 4.75 percent black, 71.77 percent Hispanic.

CENSUS TRACTS: See ward map.

COMMUNITY NEWSPAPERS:
El Dia 2648 S. Kolin (277–7676) (Spanish)
El Heraldo 3740 W. 26th St. (521–8300) (Spanish)
El Imparcial, 3610 W. 26th St. (376–9888) (Spanish)
El Informador, 1821 S. Loomis (942–1295) (Spanish)
El Norte, 2714 W. 23rd Pl. (254–1623) (Spanish)
Impacto, 3507 W. North Ave. (486–2547) (Spanish)
La Opinion, 2501 S. East Ave., Berwyn (795–1383) (Spanish)

La Voz de Chicago, 8624 S. Houston (221–9416) (Spanish)
La Raza, 53 W. Jackson (427–6100) (Spanish)
Lawndale News, 2711 W. Cermak (247–8500)
Momento, 3934 W. 26th St. (522–0288) (Spanish)

ALDERMAN: Jesus Garcia. Elected 1986. Born April 12, 1956. Career: B.A., University of Illinois at Chicago, 1980; paralegal, Legal Assistance Foundation, 1977–80; assistant director, Little Village Neighborhood Housing Service, 1980–84, deputy commissioner, Department of Water, 1984–86.

Committees: Aviation (chairman); Budget and Government Operations; Committees, Rules, Municipal Code Revision, and Ethics; Economic Development; Education; Finance; License; Ports, Wharves, and Bridges; Streets and Alleys; Traffic Control and Safety.

City hall telephone: 744–9491, 744–9492.
Ward office: 2500 S. Millard (762–1771).

1986 special election:

Jesus Garcia	3,293	(55%)
Guadalupe Martinez	2,013	(33%)
Fred Yanez	727	(12%)

1987 election:

Jesus Garcia	3,998	(55%)	Jessie R. Ramos	519	(7%)
Peter Sandoval	989	(13%)	Ed Campos	167	(2%)
August Sallas	952	(13%)	Rogelio Pena	126	(2%)
Dante H. Plata	710	(10%)			

DEMOCRATIC COMMITTEEMAN: Jesus Garcia. Elected 1984.

1984 election:

Jesus Garcia	2,811	(41%)
Frank Stemberk	2,752	(40%)
August Sallas	1,357	(19%)

1986 special election:

Jesus Garcia	2,772	(54%)
August Sallas	1,571	(31%)
Anita Villarreal	633	(12%)
Ed Rodriguez	159	(3%)

MAYORAL ELECTIONS:

1983 Democratic primary:

Richard Daley	3,907	(45%)
Jane Byrne	3,067	(35%)
Harold Washington	1,780	(20%)

1987 Democratic primary:

Harold Washington	3,831	(50%)
Jane Byrne	3,801	(50%)

1983 general:

Harold Washington	4,674	(52%)
Bernard Epton	4,279	(48%)

1987 general:

Harold Washington	4,006	(56%)
Edward Vrdolyak	2,963	(41%)
Donald Haider	183	(2%)

23rd Ward

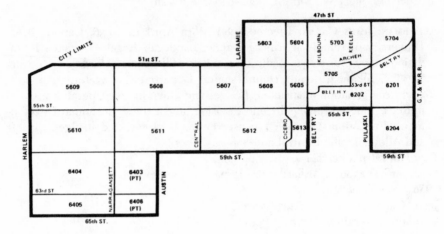

AN OUTLINE OF THE MAP of Chicago reveals a figure that roughly resembles a man's profile. O'Hare International Airport, for example, is a shock of hair. The Southeast Side's 23rd Ward is the man's nose.

This is a ward as far away from downtown (and mainstream) Chicago as any other in the city. Residents of 64th and Harlem, at the southwest corner of the ward, have more in common with their neighbors in Summit than the rest of the South Side.

The community known as Garfield Ridge constitutes most of the ward. Street after street of single-family homes make up this community. The northern half of Midway Airport, a few light industrial areas, and a few scattered commercial strips (Harlem Avenue, the city's western limit; 63rd Street west of Midway; Pulaski Road; and Cicero Avenue) break up the residential pattern.

Archer Avenue bisects the 23rd Ward from northeast to southwest from 46th to 55th Street and runs due west from there. A prosperous thoroughfare containing a variety of department and specialty stores, offices and fast food outlets, Archer Avenue is the main commercial strip on the Southwest Side.

Many taverns and banquet halls also may be found on Archer Avenue. One of these might have played host to Resurrection Mary. Chicago legend has it that every Halloween Mary hitchhikes home from a dance hall. Well-meaning motorists pick her up but she suddenly disappears as the motorists pass in front of Resurrection Cemetery, in suburban Justice.

Another yearly spectacle takes place at the 5200 block of South Keating. Every July 7 reporters gather outside the John Matar house to view the gag birthday gift from his brother Sam. The results of this yearly one-upmanship have included a 2 1/2 carat diamond lodged inside a nine-ton block of concrete, 100 skunks, an elephant, a disassembled Volkswagen, and 3,000 golf balls.

If the 23rd Ward is far from the rest of Chicago geographically, it is equally distant politically. This is a very conservative area, one that gave Ronald Reagan 60 percent of the presidential vote in 1984. Only a strong local Democratic organization keeps the ward from falling completely into the Republican column.

Not that many years ago the 23rd was Republican. In fact, the local committeeman ran for mayor. John Waner (born Jan Ludwig Wojanarski) challenged Richard Daley in 1967. Waner failed to carry a single ward.

Another Republican, Joseph Potempa, bested Democrat Frank Kuta in the 1971 aldermanic runoff. He failed to last long. Potempa was indicted in March 1973 for accepting bribes to fix zoning changes. He pleaded guilty to extortion, mail fraud, and tax evasion in October of that year and resigned as alderman.

Kuta preceded Potempa as alderman from 1967 to 1971. He encountered a fate similar to that of his successor. Kuta was found guilty of extortion and income tax evasion from a zoning change shakedown and was convicted in November 1974.

The 23rd Ward finally found an honest alderman in 1975. He was William Lipinski, a park district supervisor, the choice of the local Democratic organization and founder of the local Patriots Weekend, Freedom Club, and Southwest Liberty Society. He defeated seven opponents in the aldermanic election and also assumed the committeeman position from Kuta that year.

Lipinski served as alderman until 1982, when he ran for Congress against aging incumbent John Fary. The Democratic primary turned out to be an early Jane Byrne-Richard Daley battle. Lipinski at first embraced Byrne and then turned away from the mayor; he got Daley's endorsement. Byrne backed Fary. The Daley influence was stronger, and Lipinski won an easy (61 to 36 percent) victory.

During his city council years, Lipinski perhaps was best known for his bright orange corduroy suit, which won him at least one worst-dressed alderman award. But he has grown in stature since abandoning city hall for the Capitol. The national Democratic party named him to head a committee on ethnic American affairs.

Despite representing a constituency which gave Harold Washington few votes in 1983, Lipinski cooperated with the mayor. He and Washington helped steer through a $169.5 million bond issue in 1985. They also worked together for a southwest rapid transit line. Washington offered to name Lipinski park superintendent if the congressman would help oust then-superintendent Ed Kelly. Lipinski declined the offer.

Lipinski nonetheless led what many saw as an anti-Washington move in mid-1986. He emerged as the most visible spokesman for a nonpartisan mayoral election in 1987. Such a change was seen as a possible benefit to Lipinski's ally

Daley. Washington forces saw the proposed change as an attempt by party regulars to hurt the mayor's chances by forcing him to run one-on-one against a white foe. When a court refused to order a rules change referendum on the November 1986 ballot, Lipinski quietly abandoned the issue.

After that election, Lipinski endorsed Jane Byrne, Washington's 1987 Democratic primary opponent. This endorsement of Byrne, a longtime Daley foe, may have come from a reading of election results. Lipinski's ward gave Harold Washington only 3 percent of the vote in the 1983 general election. And the defeat of Lipinski's state senate choice in the November 1986 election indicated that Lipinski's organization is not invulnerable here.

William Krystyniak, Lipinski's aldermanic secretary, succeeded his former boss in 1983. Thus far his swearing in has generated more publicity than any subsequent action. As he was filling a vacant seat (Lipinski resigned before entering Congress in January 1983), Krystyniak was allowed to be sworn in immediately after the February election instead of waiting until after the April runoffs.

His 1983 election was doubly easy. Krystyniak has an identical twin brother, and the two of them campaigned together. The real candidate would greet parishioners leaving one door of a church, and the brother would welcome those coming out the other door.

Krystyniak may be the most obscure alderman to the public at large. Yet his colleagues rank him among the best when it comes to providing ward services. He sponsored legislation requiring television and video repair shops to provide written estimates of their work and led a campaign against realistic toy guns and paint-splattering pistols. His ward's zoning advisory council is considered one of the finest in the city.

He faced only one challenger in 1987: a cop named Wayne Starza. The campaign featured at least one dirty trick. A Starza aide circulated a photo which featured Krystyniak with Pope John Paul II (obviously a favorite in this Polish ward). The pope was removed and replaced in the photo by Harold Washington and former Israeli prime minister Shimon Peres, an appeal to antiblack and anti-Jewish prejudices.

The ruse failed. Krystyniak won every precinct, and 68 percent of the vote.

He may not last out the term. Krystyniak in late 1987 announced his candidacy for the state senate post now occupied by Republican Robert Raica. As Raica defeated an unusually weak incumbent in 1986, Krystyniak is given a good chance to return the seat to the Democratic column.

REDISTRICTING: The 23rd Ward was unaffected by the 1986 remap.

MAYORAL: This was a solid ward for Richard Daley in the 1983 Democratic primary, although not as solid as Daley needed for the nomination. He got 63 percent of the vote (his best percentage outside the 11th Ward) and Jane

Byrne received 36 percent. Harold Washington received only 199 votes, his lowest total in the city, and .5 percent of the vote, likewise his lowest.

Washington did not fare much better in the general election. His 4 percent total here matched the 13th Ward for his lowest ward total. The 1,373 votes he received was his lowest total anywhere.

As in 1983, the 23rd Ward was Harold Washington's worst in the city in 1987. He received fewer votes (1,127) and a lower percentage (3.71) than anywhere else in the primary against Jane Byrne.

In the general election, Washington did even worse—only 961 votes and 3.14 percent. The 23rd was one of only four wards (the 38th, 41st, and 45th being the others) in which Republican candidate Don Haider outpolled Democrat Washington.

CENSUS DATA: Population (1980): 58,596. 95.37 percent white, .09 percent black, 3.66 percent Hispanic, .88 percent Asian and other. Voting age population: 95.84 percent white, .03 percent black, 3.15 percent Hispanic, .98 percent Asian and other.

CENSUS TRACTS: See ward map.

COMMUNITY NEWSPAPERS:
   Brighton Park & McKinley Park Life, 2949 W. 43rd St. (523–3663)
   Clear-Ridge Reporter, 6221 S. Kedzie (476–4800)
   Southtown Economist, 5959 S. Harlem (586–8800)
   Southwest News-Herald, 6225 S. Kedzie (476–4800)

ALDERMAN: William Krystyniak. Appointed and elected 1983. Born October 28, 1952. Career: Daley College; assistant to Ald. Joseph Potempa; ward secretary, 1975–83.
Committees: Capital Development (vice-chairman); Aging and Disabled; Aviation; Claims and Liabilities; Human Rights and Consumer Protection; Local Transportation.
City hall telephone: 744–6828, 744–5683.
Ward office: 5838 S. Archer Ave. (582–7323).
1987 election:
William F. Krystyniak 20,561 (68%)
Wayne M. Starza   9,648 (32%)

DEMOCRATIC COMMITTEEMAN: William Lipinski. Appointed 1975. Born December 22, 1937. Career: Loras College, 1956–57; alderman, 23rd Ward, 1975–83.
Ward office: 5838 S. Archer Ave. (582–7323).
1984 election:
William Lipinski, unopposed.

MAYORAL ELECTIONS:

1983 Democratic primary:

Richard Daley	19,598	(63%)
Jane Byrne	11,159	(36%)
Harold Washington	199	(1%)

1983 general:

Bernard Epton	32,404	(96%)
Harold Washington	1,373	(4%)

1987 Democratic primary:

Jane Byrne	29,170	(96%)
Harold Washington	1,127	(4%)

1987 general:

Edward Vrdolyak	28,567	(94%)
Donald Haider	994	(3%)
Harold Washington	961	(3%)

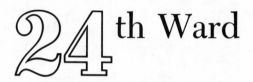

24th Ward

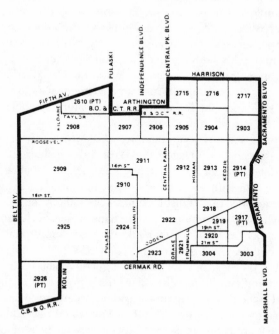

To UNSUSPECTING OUTSIDERS, the name "Lawndale" may evoke a pleasant image of rural or at least suburban charm. When applied to Chicago, the reality is completely different. The West Side community designated North Lawndale (locally known simply as Lawndale) is the embodiment of the urban black ghetto.

Lawndale at one time lived up to its gracious name. A system of boulevards flowed through the West Side, connecting large parks, such as Douglas Park at Lawndale's eastern border. Houses on Douglas Boulevard (an extension of 14th Street) or Independence Boulevard (an extension of Hamlin) were a status symbol at the turn of the century.

Russian Jews dominated Lawndale then. "This was a ward where everyone knew what *bar mitzvah* meant," wrote Len O'Connor in *Clout*. Even today Hebrew writing on buildings throughout the ward indicates the longtime Jewish presence. But the closest resemblance to Jewish culture active in the ward is "Righteous Branch of Afrikan Hebrews," a colorful black storefront church at Cermak and Troy.

Lawndale was a starting point for Chicago Jews; once they became prosperous, they moved northward. The migration process was quickened in the 1950s. Blacks moved into the northern fringes in the late 1940s and early 1950s. Unscrupulous real estate dealers hastened "panic peddling" which all but evacuated the white population during the fifties. White population in the North

Lawndale community was 87,000 in 1950, only 11,000 in 1960. Today it is virtually zero.

The economic and social base of a once-thriving community left after the Jews. Large employers in or near the community—Sears Roebuck, International Harvester, Western Electric—either closed their doors or cut down their staffs. Smaller businesses were driven away by redlining, either making insurance rates intolerably high or canceling policies altogether.

Slum conditions provided an apt backdrop for Dr. Martin Luther King's Chicago campaigns. He rented a third-floor apartment at 1550 S. Kolin in 1966. Although his "residence" at the apartment was more symbolic than real, he worked out of the flat when in Chicago.

Any economic stability that remained disappeared after 1968. Riots following King's assassination ravaged the West Side, including Lawndale. The scars of those riots have not healed. If anything, those scars magnify the area's poverty. A huge sign with a rocket advertises the former Lawndale Motors at Ogden and Drake, once the largest local business and now boarded up. Another major establishment, the Community State Bank at Roosevelt and Central Park, is now the Rainbow Disco. The only bank, the Community Bank of Lawndale, is housed in a building best described as a fortress.

Vacant lots ("prairies" in local terminology) dominate entire blocks. Those buildings remaining are often substandard (only 8 percent of the buildings in one section of Lawndale are structurally sound, according to one study). Those businesses remaining are liquor and lottery stores and fast food outlets, which offer immediate gratification in a community where chances of long-term gratification are remote.

A depressing physical appearance is mirrored in the human condition of the ward. The 24th Ward is fraught with unemployment, illegitimacy, alcoholism, drugs, and crime. West of Pulaski and south of Roosevelt is the area known as "K-town," one of the city's major gang crime centers. The Area 4 police headquarters at Harrison and Kedzie handles more murders, robberies, and aggravated assaults than any other in the city. Lawndale's evils and misfortunes are detailed in *The American Millstone*, a twenty-nine-part 1985 *Tribune* series that earned the newspaper a Pulitzer prize.

Critics charged, not without justification, that the *Tribune* series focused on negative aspects to the exclusion of anything positive. City, church, and community groups are working hard to improve Lawndale. Residents themselves have taken action to improve the quality of life. A group called Slumbusters cleans up vacant lots and replaces them with community gardens. Many blocks have formed block clubs and post strictly enforced rules at the end of their streets. The 3300 block of Flournoy, for example, issues twelve commandments "Speed limit 15 MPH; No ball playing on front; no 5 or 10 speed bike riding on the sidewalk; No dogs or cats allowed on the front without leashes; No washing or repairing cars on streets; No littering streets, gangways or backyards; Observe curfew 17 and under; No peddling; Ice cream truck no music or bells; No double parking; No loud music after 9 p.m.; Please keep off grass." Despite such efforts, life remains grim in Lawndale. This remains an area where most of those who can, leave.

One internationally famous movie star got his start here. The former Kraml Dairy (Ogden and Kostner) was a frequent advertiser in the early days of television. A younger Kermit the Frog pointed a lit cannon at viewers and asked "What do *you* think about Kraml milk?"

Franklin D. Roosevelt knew of the 24th Ward; he called it "The best Democratic ward in the country." Small wonder—it carried for him 24,000 to 700 in the 1936 election.

Over the years the 24th has lived up to the reputation bestowed by FDR. Led by party boss Jake Arvey, it became the strongest of the "automatic eleven"wards which provided resounding support for the Democratic machine. Mayor Richard J. Daley faced his stiffest challenge from Republican Ben Adamowski in 1963. But the 24th carried for Daley by an eighteen-to-one margin.

Arvey's religion stopped him, the city's leading Jewish politician, from entertaining mayoral dreams for himself. Arvey instead played kingmaker and wielded clout for a generation. He became alderman in 1923, when brothers Moe and Ike Rosenberg ran the ward. Eleven years later he succeeded Moe as Democratic committeeman. Arvey rose to the chairmanship of the Finance Committee but resigned to enter the army in World War II.

Arvey returned to city politics after the war and assumed party chairmanship from Mayor Ed Kelly in 1946. The following year he arranged Kelly's ouster in favor of a mild-mannered businessman named Martin Kennelly. During his time he helped engineer the rise of a politician named Richard Daley. His protégé became mayor in 1955. By that time, Arvey was reduced to the role of elder statesman, and was no longer an active power.

Arthur X. Elrod, father of the recent sheriff, served as county board member and 24th Ward committeeman in the 1950s. He was succeeded in both posts by Sidney Deutsch after he died in 1960. Deutsch passed away in late 1961. The ward, by then nearly all black, finally got its first black committeeman at this time. He was Benjamin Lewis, a longtime ward organization member who became the ward's first black alderman in 1958. Lewis was party boss in name only; a real estate magnate named Irwin "Izzy" Horowitz ran the ward from his Gold Coast condominium.

Lewis epitomized the high-living Chicago politician. He had extensive real estate holdings, vacationed in Acapulco, and kept a string of girlfriends—all on an $8,000 annual salary. But even hardened Chicagoans were shocked on February 26, 1963, when Lewis was found handcuffed to a chair and shot to death in his headquarters. The murder was never solved. Police speculated street gang revenge, business failures, personal jealousies, a possible Lewis attempt to take over the local policy racket. The investigation's director claimed the main problem police faced was "too many motives."

George Collins took over as committeeman and alderman, serving in the latter position until his election to Congress in 1970. Collins is best remembered for his death. He perished in the late 1972 plane crash which also claimed Dorothy Hunt, wife of Watergate conspirator Howard Hunt.

David Rhodes, a building department supervisor succeeded Collins as alderman. He served as a typical, silent machine alderman until 1977, when he backed Harold Washington for mayor against incumbent Michael Bilandic. This effrontery cost him the support of the regular organization in 1979. Two-term state legislator Walter Shumpert, committeeman since Collins's death, faced Rhodes. Shumpert had defeated him for committeeman in 1976. He triumphed once again in 1979.

Shumpert died in late 1982. William Henry, who replaced Shumpert in the legislature, also replaced him as committeeman. Henry defeated teacher and activist Bobbie Steele and two others for alderman in 1983. Henry looks the part of a stereotypical alderman, down to his thin cigars and pinky ring. So far he has made most of his headlines outside city hall. In late 1983 he was kidnaped at gunpoint outside a bar his wife owned; an off-duty policeman rescued him. The only soft drink magnate on the council, he introduced Soul Cola in early 1986. A resolution praised Henry and wished his new enterprise well, that resolution introduced by Henry himself.

William Henry was a faithful Harold Washington vote, although his alliance spread not from love of the mayor as much as fear of voter reprisal (he complained about an ethics ordinance that was one of the mayor's proudest achievements; Washington threatened to run an aldermanic candidate against him unless he silenced his protests). Henry wasted no time after hearing of Washington's heart attack in lining up black aldermen to support Eugene Sawyer for acting mayor rather than the Washington administration's choice, Timothy Evans. By the time Evans forces got around to them, Henry had enlisted twelve black aldermen for Sawyer. Even though six later defected, the black aldermen Henry managed to round up proved the difference in electing Eugene Sawyer acting mayor.

REDISTRICTING: One southwest corner and one southeast corner precinct were added from the 22nd Ward, and four northeast corner precincts from the 27th Ward were transferred to the 24th as a result of the 1986 remap. The 24th also transferred four northwest corner precincts to the 28th Ward and received one northeast corner precinct from that ward.

MAYORAL: Harold Washington carried the ward by a wide margin in the 1983 Democratic primary, 79 percent to 18 percent for slated candidate Jane Byrne and 3 percent for Richard M. Daley.

The ward lived up to its Democratic reputation in the general election. Washington won 99.5 percent of the vote against Bernard Epton—his best percentage in the city.

Washington tallied more than 22,000 votes, just short of 99 percent, in both the Democratic primary and the general election in 1987.

CENSUS DATA: Population (1980): 63,808. .98 percent white, 97.31 percent black, 2.16 percent Hispanic, .44 percent Asians and others. Voting age population:

.85 percent white, 96.47 percent black, 1.95 percent Hispanic, .73 percent Asian and other.

CENSUS TRACTS: See ward map.

COMMUNITY NEWSPAPERS:
Chicago Metro News, 2600 S. Michigan (842–5950)
Westside Journal, 16618 S. Hermitage, Markham (333–2210)

ALDERMAN: William C. Henry. Elected 1983. Born 1936. Career: Herzel Junior College, Malcolm X Junior College; U.S. Army; vice-president of security, Commercial Security Enforcers; deputy chief, Cook County Sheriff's Department; Illinois House of Representatives, 1979–83.
Committees: License (chairman); Aviation; Budget and Government Operations; Buildings; Committees, Rules, Municipal Code Revision, and Ethics; Historical Landmark Preservation; Economic Development; Finance, Municipal Code Revision; Ports, Wharves, and Bridges.
City hall telephone: 744–6839, 744–6849.
Ward office: 3851 W. Roosevelt Rd. (522–2444).
1987 election:

William C. "Bill" Henry	15,120	(75%)
Moses Walker, Jr.	3,058	(15%)
Melvin Gray	1,058	(5%)
Edward Washington II	997	(5%)

DEMOCRATIC COMMITTEEMAN: William C. Henry. Elected 1982.
1984 election:

William C. "Bill" Henry	9,822	(78%)
Albert D. Chesser, Jr.	2,838	(22%)

MAYORAL ELECTIONS:

1983 Democratic primary:

Harold Washington	16,296	(79%)
Jane Byrne	3,598	(18%)
Richard Daley	633	(3%)

1983 general:

Harold Washington	24,265	(99%)
Bernard Epton	129	(1%)

1987 Democratic primary:

Harold Washington	22,200	(99%)
Jane Byrne	227	(1%)

1987 general:

Harold Washington	22,241	(99%)
Edward Vrdolyak	125	(1%)
Donald Haider	107	(0%)

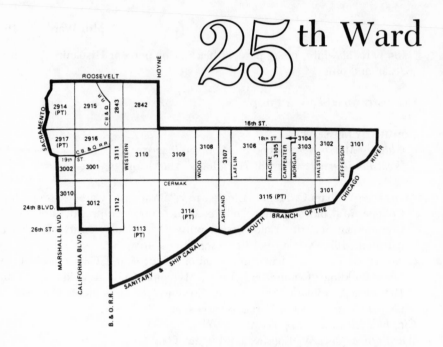

25th Ward

"PORT OF ENTRY"—this is the term used for years to describe the Near West Side community of Pilsen. It refers to Pilsen being an initial living spot for recently arrived immigrants. They usually started here, saved their money, then moved elsewhere.

Just as other ethnic groups have in the past, Mexicans now use Pilsen as a stopping-off point. Yet there are differences between Mexicans and earlier groups that have arrived here. The Europeans, almost all properly documented, got to Chicago by rail after a boat trip across the Atlantic Ocean. Mexicans, many of them illegal aliens, arrive by bus or automobile.

More important, central and eastern Europeans found a thriving industrial base along the Chicago River. Mexicans entering the same area likely as not find beat-up carcasses of factories that provided jobs to their predecessors. They find work in the Chicago area. But for most new immigrants Pilsen is a place to sleep, not to live and work.

Originally this was a truck farming area outside city limits. But Irish and German immigrants built the nearby Illinois-Michigan canal in the 1840s and thus opened the region for industry. Soon lumberyards, brickyards, and a limestone quarry appeared along the banks of the south branch of the Chicago River. The McCormick Reaper Company built a huge plant at 27th and Western in 1873.

The Great Chicago Fire of 1871 did not strike the area. Yet its effects were felt here. Displaced workers, mainly Bohemians, moved into a neighborhood already overcrowded with the Irish and Germans. The Bohemians called the neighborhood Pilsen, after the second-largest city of their homeland.

Pilsen was a battleground in the closest thing the country has ever had to a proletarian revolution. Workers in 1877, fed up with wage cuts in the face of increased company profits, protested *en masse* throughout Pilsen and the Near West Side. These demonstrations often were met with force. The animosity came to a head at 16th and Halsted, in a July 26 confrontation that became known as the Battle of the Viaduct. When the fighting was over, no policemen were dead, although more than fifty were wounded. At least thirty workers lay dead and hundreds more wounded.

Today Halsted and 16th Street is a quiet intersection. A tavern on one corner may have been the old Viaduct Hotel, living quarters of many of the workers.

In the late 1800s, workers poured into Pilsen from all around Europe—not just Bohemia but also Lithuania, Poland, Slovenia, Croatia, and Italy. Once they established themselves their first priority was the building of a church. Pilsen remains home to some of the most awe-inspiring churches in the city, monuments to the different ethnic groups.

Bohemians constructed St. Procopius Church at 18th St. and Allport in 1883 and added the handsome green copper spire nine years later. Poles built the alabaster-columned St. Adalbert Church at 17th and Paulina. Irish were served by St. Pius at 19th and Ashland. Germans erected St. Paul at 22nd Place and Hoyne, a huge Gothic church whose red twin towers are visible for miles along the Dan Ryan Expressway. Lithuanians built Providence of God at 18th and Union, a site now within auto fumes of the Dan Ryan. Pope John Paul II visited the church in 1979 and gave an open air mass.

The above parishes offer further evidence to Pilsen as a port of entry. The ethnic groups who built these houses of worship for the most part have left the neighborhood. Mexicans replaced them.

Beginning in the 1950s, Mexicans (mainly from the central highlands) moved here. Pilsen is not the first Mexican settlement in Chicago (communities thrived in both South Chicago and the Maxwell Street area). But now it is the most visible and colorful one.

Few if any other ethnic neighborhoods in Chicago so completely capture the feel of their nationality as does Pilsen with the Mexican community. Any visitor can walk along 18th Street, the heart of the community, and order tacos from a walk-up window at a *taqueria*, munch on a yeasty pastry at one of the many bakeries, or eat corn on the cob spiced with lemon and hot pepper purchased from a street vendor. He or she can hear lively music which jumps out from many of the Spanish record stores on the street.

That same visitor is likely to view evidence of Mexican pride and heritage. One example is a barber shop at 18th and Bishop, its windows lined with old photographs of Pancho Villa, Emiliano Zapata, and other Mexican Revolution heroes.

More imposing are the murals, often both major works of art and major political statements. Perhaps the most elaborate of those is the exterior of Casa Aztlan at 18th and Racine. Portraits of Chicago, Mexican, and Latin American heroes adorn the entrance to the social service center.

Other community centers, although not as brightly decorated, also perform unique services for the Hispanic community. These include Mujeres Latinas en Accion (17th and Wood), a women's counseling service; El Valor (21st and Wolcott), a training center for mentally handicapped Hispanic adults; and El Hogar del Niño (19th and Racine), a child care center.

The Mexican influence is pervasive in Pilsen and the neighboring Heart of Chicago area. It can be seen in Decima Musa (19th and Loomis), a restaurant that also serves as intellectual center; Juarez High School at Cermak and Laflin, a new high school built in response to community activism; the Mexican Fine Arts Center Museum at 19th and Damen; or a Greyhound bus depot at Cermak and California that specializes in trips to the border town of Laredo, Texas.

Despite the Mexican predominance, other groups have maintained their identities. Holy Trinity Church (19th and Throop) holds mass in Croatian. St. Stephen's (22nd Place and Wolcott) is a midwestern center for Slovenians, although most of that nationality have left Heart of Chicago. One neighborhood that has remained largely intact is an Italian enclave centered at 23rd and Oakley. Immaculate flower boxes line the sidewalks. So do a number of small Italian restaurants, many of which were started during Prohibition.

A surprise inhabits almost every corner of Pilsen. It may be the Garden of Eden, a community garden announced by a brightly colored sign at 19th and Morgan; the Inner City Sports Hall of Fame, a small museum of sports memorabilia located in a playground at Cermak and Oakley; or the David Lee Animal Care Center, a state-of-the-art animal treatment facility at 27th and Western.

History comes alive here. The former public bathhouse at Cullerton and Wolcott reminds passersby of the days when private baths were uncommon; horse-head sculptures identify a former stable at 21st and Paulina; intricate cornices and imaginative roofs of buildings throughout Pilsen attest to the talents of Bohemian artisans.

The former Schoenhofen Brewery at 18th and Canalport provided employment in the early 1900s to eastern European workers; it has been placed on the National Historic Register. But it failed to provide housing in the 1970s. Community groups, fearing gentrification, blocked a developer's plan to convert nearby units into an artists' colony.

Pilsen nonetheless is an active art center. Many Hispanic artists live and work throughout the area. The most organized colony, consisting mainly of non-Hispanics, resides in a hidden compound near 18th and Halsted; they open their studios each fall at an art fair.

Until recently another example of living history represented Pilsen in city hall: Vito Marzullo, who served more than thirty years as alderman of the 25th Ward. Marzullo as a state representative spearheaded legislation which created the Near West Side Medical District. He assumed the alderman's seat in 1953 when longtime incumbent William Bowler was elected to Congress at age seventy-eight.

The machine stalwart served for years as head of the patronage-rich Local

Transportation Committee. But he is best remembered for his colorful (sometimes purple) commentaries which amused both constituents and Harvard professors:

—On liberals and "good government" types: "You give them ten dollars and they couldn't get your dog out of the pound."

—When asked by a student if the Haymarket statue (site of annual bombings by radicals in the late 1960s) should be watched by police: "Sure it should, because it gets dirty."

—When asked if he would cooperate with Democrat Harold Washington after supporting his mayoral opponent in the 1983 election: "I play cards with my wife, and I try to win. But if I lose, she's still my wife."

It would be foolish, however, to dismiss Marzullo as a buffoon. He ran one of the most effective cogs in the Democratic machine. Even after his retirement, it remains one of the few potent old-line ward organizations left in Chicago.

The 25th Ward Regular Democratic Organization's strength frightened away challengers for a generation. Only once before 1983 (John Nahtigal in 1967) did Marzullo have an aldermanic opponent, and he won that election by a fifteen-to-one margin.

But the ward changed in the 1980s. Hispanics such as attorney Juan Soliz and community activist Juan Velazquez came out in open opposition to Marzullo and the Democratic regulars. Velazquez ran against Marzullo in 1983 and did surprisingly well; he captured 41 percent of the vote against the veteran alderman. But it was not a measure of Hispanic solidarity. Most Hispanics went with Marzullo. Velazquez, a Harold Washington ally, found his strength in the black precincts.

A year later Velazquez tried again. Marzullo retired as committeeman in 1984 but endorsed State Representative Marco Domico for the post. Domico failed in his legislative reelection bid (losing to Soliz) but defeated Velazquez for committeeman with 58 percent of the vote.

Soliz, the most influential of the ward's independents, made his peace with party regulars before the 1984 general election. He joined the fold after party chairman Edward Vrdolyak agreed to help retire his campaign debt. Branded a traitor by many of his erstwhile allies, Soliz argued that it was only fair that the regulars help him retire the debt since they forced him to accrue it in the first place.

Afterward, Soliz kept silent on the issue of a ward remap, a redistricting to correct discrimination against black and Hispanic voters. Despite protests and lawsuits from Vrdolyak-bloc aldermen (including Marzullo), the remap and special elections were ordered. Ward boundaries were altered to increase the Hispanic percentage.

Marzullo suffered a direct effect of the remap; his residence was transferred to a different ward. Rather than move, the eighty-eight-year-old council patriarch retired. He claimed (perhaps correctly) that moving him out of the ward was the only way his foes could defeat him.

JUAN SOLIZ

Soliz was Vrdolyak's man, not Committeeman Domico's, yet he received the 25th Ward Regular Democratic Organization's backing. In return for Domico not opposing Soliz, Vrdolyak arranged the committeeman's 1986 slating for the county board.

The major issue of the special election was Juan Soliz's dual candidacy. Soliz had already announced plans for reelection as state representative, where even enemies admitted that he made an impressive record. When the special elections were announced, Soliz declared his candidacy for alderman *and* state representative and said that he would resign the latter post if also elected alderman. His foes went to court to knock Soliz off one or both ballots. A judge ruled that he could not run for state representative. However, the board of elections upheld Soliz's dual bid, claiming that Chicago alderman is a part-time job.

Three opponents faced Soliz: Velazquez, a deputy commissioner in the Department of Streets and Sanitation, who ran as the Washington-endorsed candidate; Virginia Martinez, a Pilsen attorney supported by local religious groups; and Phil Coronado, director of a Pilsen athletic association.

Although most observers expected Soliz to take a plurality of the votes, many expected a Soliz-Velazquez runoff. However, Soliz captured a majority of the vote—55 percent to 23 percent for Velazquez, 13 percent for Martinez, and 9 percent for Coronado.

The Soliz victory sent mixed signals, despite the huge victory margin. He received less than the normal machine vote, even though Velazquez's strongest precincts were transferred out of the ward. Soliz, Velazquez, and Martinez more or less split the Hispanic vote. Huge margins in the predominantly white precincts gave Soliz his victory.

After the election Soliz called for unity among his fellow Hispanic aldermen, a plea which they ignored. There was so little unity that both Soliz and new 22nd Ward alderman Jesus Garcia celebrated their inauguration by hiring different mariachi bands to serenade outside council chambers—surely the first Battle of the Mariachi Bands in city hall history.

Domico won reelection as committeeman in a little-publicized special election that coincided with the aldermanic one. Domico won 2,997 votes (56 percent) to 1,985 for Velazquez and 361 for two other Hispanics planted on the ballot by the Domico organization, one of those a professional wrestler known as Blacky Rodriguez.

Although claiming neutrality in Council Wars, Juan Soliz was a solid anti-Washington vote and an outspoken Washington critic. Some of his charges bordered on the irrational. When Washington allies threatened to replace him as chairman of the Aviation Committee with fellow Mexican-American Garcia, he called it a racist move. Before the 1986 gay rights vote, he blasted gays in Spanish as "social scum." On another occasion, he defended the petition drive for a nonpartisan mayoral election and called Mayor Harold Washington's charges of petition fraud an attack on voters' rights. This accusation backfired when Washington allies showed that Soliz signed nonpartisan petitions not once, but three times.

Soliz's anti-Washington votes and rhetoric were not enough to prevent a rift between himself and Domico. The committeeman withdrew his support from Soliz and backed Ambrosio Medrano, a bowling alley manager, in the 1987 aldermanic race. Velazquez and Martinez also filed.

Medrano captured the Italian enclave vote, while Soliz won most of the Mexican vote. Velazquez (losing his fifth election in four years) carried the black precincts.

Administration foe Soliz met Domico-backed Medrano in the runoff, a choice that hardly met with favor among Washington allies. Those Washington backers who did take sides favored Medrano. The runoff provided a three-vote Soliz win, a victory that survived Medrano challenges.

Soliz has expressed ambitions of becoming the city's first Hispanic mayor, and he came within a vote of that dream after Harold Washington's death. When Eugene Sawyer wavered on accepting the position, Soliz was one of those considered as an alternative. Soliz, a member (if not necessarily an enthusiastic one) of the Hispanic bloc which supported Timothy Evans, would have been the deciding vote with his crossover to the white ethnic bloc. But one of the white bloc refused to support him, thus scuttling Soliz's candidacy.

That may be as close as Soliz gets to the office of mayor. Over the years he has moved from Washington ally to Vrdolyak ally to Jane Byrne ally to Tom Hynes ally, back to Washington ally (he voted with the pro-Washington majority on council reorganization after the 1987 election), to Tim Evans ally—political leapfrogging which tends to win few long-term friends.

Back in the 25th Ward, Soliz and Domico will face off for Democratic committeeman in 1988. It should be an interesting contest—one of the last old-line organizations against the only candidate ever to defeat it.

REDISTRICTING: Major changes were made in the geography of the 25th Ward in order to bring in enough Hispanics for a court-ordered "supermajority." All precincts north of Roosevelt Road were transferred away. Two white and Hispanic precincts east of Western Avenue were moved to the 1st Ward. Five black precincts west of Western became part of the 27th Ward. At the southwest corner of the ward, one precinct each was transferred to the 12th and 22nd Wards.

In exchange the 25th received one northern and six eastern precincts from the 1st Ward. Thus the 25th Ward is now bounded roughly by the 16th Street viaduct and Roosevelt Road on the north, Sacramento and Marshall Boulevard on the west, and the ship canal and south branch of the Chicago River on the south and east. These boundaries conform almost exactly to the Pilsen, Heart of Chicago, Marshall Square, and Douglas Park neighborhoods.

MAYORAL: Alderman Vito Marzullo, a strong Jane Byrne supporter, got out enough of the vote to give her a plurality in the 1983 Democratic primary. But it was hardly an overwhelming margin. Byrne received 45 percent to 31 percent for Richard Daley and 24 percent (mainly in black precincts) for Harold Washington.

Despite Marzullo's open support for Republican Bernard Epton, traditional Democratic sentiment among Hispanic voters made it a close race in the general election. Epton took 6,099 votes (51 percent) to 5,925 for Washington. The 174-vote difference made this by far the most evenly split ward in the city.

Jane Byrne, a popular figure here, took the Italian and Mexican precincts and 58 percent of the 1987 primary vote—a total similar to recent percentages by party regulars here.

Harold Washington squeaked to a victory in the general election, with only 51 percent of the vote. As in other Hispanic areas, the Democratic candidate, Washington, gained support in the general election.

CENSUS DATA: Population (1980): 60,075. 18.37 percent white, 7.79 percent black, 72.95 percent Hispanic, .89 percent Asian and other. Voting age population: 24.93 percent white, 7.18 percent black, 66.74 percent Hispanic, 1.15 percent Asian and other.

CENSUS TRACTS: See ward map.

COMMUNITY NEWSPAPERS:
 El Dia, 2648 S. Kolin (227–7676) (Spanish)
 El Heraldo, 3740 W. 21st St. (521–8300) (Spanish)
 El Informador, 1821 S. Loomis (942–1295) (Spanish)
 El Imparcial, 3610 W. 26th St. (376–9888) (Spanish)
 El Norte, 2714 W. 23rd Pl. (254–1623) (Spanish)
 Hispanic Times, 1656 W. 21st St. (666–9767)
 Impacto, 3507 W. North Ave. (486–2547) (Spanish)
 La Raza, 53 W. Jackson (427–6100) (Spanish)
 La Opinion, 2502 S. East Ave., Berwyn (795–1383) (Spanish)
 La Voz de Chicago, 8624 S. Houston (221–9416) (Spanish)
 Lawndale News, 2711 W. Cermak (247–8500)
 Momento, 3934 W. 26th St. (522–0388) (Spanish)
 West Side Times, 2711 W. Cermak (247–8500)

ALDERMAN: Juan M. Soliz. Elected 1986. Born 1950. Career: B.A., University of New Mexico, 1973; J.D., University of Washington, 1976; attorney, 1976–85; Illinois State Representative, 1985–86.
Committees: Historical Landmark Preservation (vice-chairman); Budget and Government Operations; Capital Development; Education; Intergovernmental Relations; Local Transportation; Ports, Wharves, and Bridges; Traffic Control and Safety.
City hall telephone: 744–6845, 744–6846.
Ward office 1718 S. Loomis (733–4440).
1986 special election:

Juan M. Soliz	3,798	(55%)	Virginia Martinez	904	(13%)
Juan A. Velazquez	1,616	(23%)	Philip Coronado	624	(9%)

1987 election:

Juan M. Soliz	3,724	(40%)	Juan A. Velazquez	1,632	(18%)
Ambrosio Medrano	2,708	(29%)	Virginia Martinez	1,197	(13%)

1987 runoff:

Juan M. Soliz	4,714	(50%)
Ambrosio Medrano	4,911	(50%)

DEMOCRATIC COMMITTEEMAN: Marco Domico. Elected 1984. Born 1919. Career: City of Chicago, Department of Streets and Sanitation; Illinois House of Representatives, 1975–85; city council, Transportation Committee, 1985–86; Cook County Board, 1986–.

Ward office: 2524 S. Blue Island (247–1200).

1984 election:

Marco Domico	4,798	(58%)
Juan A. Velazquez	3,500	(42%)

1986 special election:

Marco Domico	2,997	(56%)	Raul Rodriguez	205	(4%)
Juan A. Velazquez	1,985	(37%)	Jesse A. Negrete	156	(3%)

MAYORAL ELECTIONS:

1983 Democratic primary:

Jane Byrne	4,977	(45%)
Richard Daley	3,179	(31%)
Harold Washington	2,620	(24%)

1987 Democratic primary:

Jane Byrne	5,604	(58%)
Harold Washington	3,960	(41%)

1983 general:

Bernard Epton	6,099	(51%)
Harold Washington	5,925	(49%)

1987 general:

Harold Washington	4,940	(51%)
Edward Vrdolyak	4,528	(47%)
Donald Haider	249	(3%)

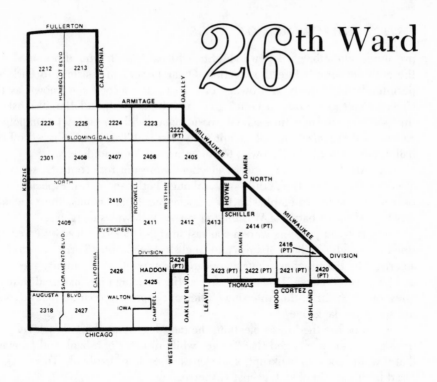

IT WAS AN ELECTION that could truly be called historic. Luis Gutierrez, an ally of Mayor Harold Washington, faced off against Manuel Torres, aligned with the faction of Alderman Edward Vrdolyak, in a runoff of the March special election in the Near Northwest Side's 26th Ward. At stake was not just the ward but the balance of power in the entire city council. When the polls closed, it was Gutierrez who held the victory party. His runoff win gave the council a twenty-five-to-twenty-five split along factional lines, which allowed the mayor to cast tie-breaking votes.

The celebration followed one of the most colorful, and at the time the most expensive, aldermanic election in Chicago history. It was a contest fraught with name-calling, lawsuits, death threats. It was a contest in which a part-time school crossing guard, surely one of the most unlikely footnotes in Chicago political history, played a pivotal role. It was a contest that might not have been decided until election eve, when one candidate made an unnecessary gaffe which probably cost him a victory. Here is what happened:

1. Federal judge Charles Norgle ruled in late 1985 that the existing city ward map discriminated against blacks and Hispanics and ordered a remap which would enable those groups to elect representatives in seven wards, including the 26th. He also ordered special elections in those wards to coincide with the March 1986 primary elections.

Immediately, candidates entered the long-anticipated special election. Five filed petitions in the 26th Ward: Luis Gutierrez, an assistant director in the Department of Streets and Sanitation, who ran as an independent for Democratic committeeman in the 32nd Ward in 1984 and moved to the 26th shortly after that election; Manuel Torres, a Cook County commissioner and former precinct captain for 33rd Ward alderman Richard Mell, who also moved into the 26th not long before the election; Omar Lopez, an assistant to Park Superintendent Ed Kelly and owner of a Hispanic soccer team known as the Chicago Vultures; Roberto Grau, a community activist; and Jim Blasinski, a thirty-six-year-old part-time school crossing guard with no experience in politics and no real organization. All except Gutierrez and Torres were ruled off the ballot, although Blasinski vowed to run as a write-in candidate.

2. Most of the other special elections were not real contests, so media attention focused on the 26th Ward. Although both candidates, especially Gutierrez, attempted to emphasize their backgrounds and issues, the race soon was turned into a battle of Washington versus Vrdolyak surrogates.

The two campaigners were a contrast in styles. Short, wiry Gutierrez was fluent, even glib, in both Spanish and English. Weightlifter Torres, often characterized by the press as "dour," appeared ill at ease in community meetings and press conferences. However, early in the campaign he answered difficult questions in Spanish, thus diffusing Gutierrez supporters' charges that he could not speak the language.

Even before the March election, the race degenerated into low-level politicking. Gutierrez charged that Torres, while director of a bank and knowing that it would soon go bankrupt, sold shares of stock in that bank. Torres countered by filing a libel suit against Gutierrez.

The weekend before the election, Torres supporters claimed that an unexploded bomb was found in front of the candidate's office, and that someone fired shots at him. As no explosion occurred and no bullets were found, few took the charges seriously.

3. Gutierrez workers claimed during the afternoon of the March primary that polling places were not opened on time in five precincts (coincidentally, those five precincts were considered Gutierrez strongholds). Judge Joseph Schneider ordered those five precincts to stay open until 9:00 P.M.

4. Torres cried foul and demanded that five of *his* best precincts be allowed to stay open. Schneider agreed to the Torres petition and ordered that all late ballots in the ten disputed precincts be kept separate from those cast beforehand. Yet in at least one of those precincts, the ballots were mixed.

5. With all votes apparently counted, Gutierrez held a twenty-vote lead. Blasinski was credited with eleven write-in votes—not enough to force a runoff.

6. Circuit court judge Eugene L. Wachowski on March 25 threw out Torres's lawyers' request for a new election, a request made on the grounds that the court order to keep the ten precincts open was improper. Wachowski, however, did not allow Gutierrez to be certified as alderman pending a Torres appeal.

7. Torres's lawyers claimed to have signed affidavits from thirty-one voters who cast ballots for Blasinski (One political reporter commented, "If they allow this challenge, why bother to hold elections at all? Just count the affidavits afterwards"). An appeals court refused the request to search for additional write-in votes, and the Illinois Supreme Court on April 15 refused to overturn that ruling.

8. Wachowski, following a different Torres petition, ordered a different vote search. The elections board on April 3 found ten new Blasinski write-in votes—enough to force a runoff. Gutierrez lawyers charged that these new ballots were invalid because they were transported from the election board's warehouse to the office outside the view of Gutierrez or Torres representatives.

Nonetheless, the board of elections voted to count the write-in ballots. This decision took place April 16—the same day that Gutierrez was scheduled to be sworn in as alderman.

The Municipal Canvassing Board certified the results early April 17, counting Blasinski's newly discovered write-in votes and disallowing ten Gutierrez votes which had been declared invalid by election judges. After a month's delay, seven lawsuits, hearings before three different circuit court judges, and appeals to the Illinois appellate and supreme courts, a new election was ordered for April 29.

Gutierrez workers, claiming that the March election had been stolen from them, issued campaign buttons and brochures with the slogan "Re-elect Gutierrez."

9. "The 26th Ward contest has resembled a gang rumble more than an election," the *Tribune* stated in an editorial. During the twelve-day campaign before the April 29 election, Gutierrez and Torres took turns hurling (often unsubstantiated) charges at each other.

Gutierrez charged that Torres workers were pressuring voters to sign absentee ballots to be filled out by Torres precinct captains. Torres countered that Washington twisted the arms of contractors doing business with the city to support Gutierrez. Torres accused Gutierrez of supporting the Puerto Rican nationalist group FALN and soliciting votes from Cook County Jail inmates, although he could not prove the latter charge. Gutierrez claimed that Torres had fallen behind in child support payments and was arrested in 1971 for possession of cocaine. He retracted the latter charge after discovering that the Manuel Torres implicated in police records he saw was not his opponent.

10. A Spanish-language television station made each candidate sign an affidavit promising to refrain from personal attacks during their election eve debate. Both lived up to that agreement. Gutierrez came out the clear winner in that debate. Torres spoke a few words in Spanish, then told viewers that he was more comfortable in English and finished the debate speaking English— a decision many observers cited as Torres's fatal flaw.

11. Election day brought a carnival atmosphere to the ward, the festive celebrations of democracy that elections can be. Precinct workers, cars with loudspeakers, impromptu bands, and politicians (Washington, Aldermen Jesus Garcia, Dorothy Tillman, and state senate nominee Miguel del Valle for Gutierrez; Vrdolyak, former mayor Jane Byrne, State's Attorney Richard Daley, and Aldermen Miguel Santiago and Juan Soliz for Torres) livened the streets outside the polling places. Inside, voters cast their ballots in rooms that often were filled with election judges, pollwatchers, Chicago policemen, federal marshals, assistant state's attorneys, and reporters.

Those voters gave Gutierrez 7,429 votes (53 percent) to 6,549 for Torres.

Luis Gutierrez (far right) with (from left) Ray Figueroa, Gloria Chevare, Harold Washington and Ronnie Jarabo, Speaker of the House in Puerto Rico.

The defeated candidate responded that he was not conceding "a damn thing" and added a thinly veiled racial slur against the mayor—surely one of the most graceless and tasteless concession speeches in local history.

Gutierrez did not slow down once in office. He became a major Washington spokesman and the unofficial leader of the council's Hispanics. Following the debate concerning a property tax increase, the sharp-tongued Gutierrez began reading property tax figures of Vrdolyak-bloc aldermen, at which point 50th Ward alderman Bernie Stone denounced him as "you little pipsqueak!"

No other alderman felt more heat over the 1986 gay rights vote than Gutierrez. His liberal base (plus gay supporters who threw large sums of money into his campaign) insisted he support the bill. Equally adamant were Pentecostal church congregations, who provided strong support in his 1986 win. Gutierrez pondered his dilemma openly (even threatening to resign) and conferred with everyone from political advisors to reporters before voting for the unsuccessful measure.

However, Gutierrez showed himself to be a workhorse as well as a show-horse. He has pressed hard for local economic development, plus construction of new housing.

Gutierrez's aldermanic win overshadowed Torres's victory in the simultaneous Democratic committeeman election. Gutierrez declined to seek that post, fearing (with good reason) that enough voters might be confused by a dual candidacy to cost him the coveted aldermanic victory. Torres easily defeated Norma Quintana, a community worker and Washington ally, and Oscar Martinez, a policeman and friend of Blasinski.

Torres decided not to run for alderman in 1987. Instead he slated his wife Brenda. Blasinski also entered the race. So did Felicita Claudio and Hector Franco, directors of local social service agencies.

This time, voters made no doubt of their decision. Gutierrez captured every precinct but one and almost two-thirds of the vote. He announced plans to run for committeeman in 1988, and must be considered the heavy favorite to win that position. The Torres family, first husband and wife combination to lose Chicago aldermanic elections, declined to seek reelection. Lopez was Gutierrez's only opponent. Gutierrez inherited a realm with a colorful past, an often dreary present, and a sometimes hopeful future. The past is evident here, an area once considered upper middle class. Beautiful Victorian houses characterize the Wicker Park neighborhood at the eastern edge of the ward. Germans and Scandinavians built these homes. Both groups left the area by the 1920s.

Poles and Russian Jews displaced the earlier residents. The latter group also departed the neighborhood, but left its mark in such structures as bathhouses on Division Street and North Avenue, and a former synagogue across from Humboldt Park (which now houses a Hispanic social service agency). At one time Poles were so dominant here that the corner of Milwaukee and Division became known as Polish Downtown. Many Poles followed Milwaukee Avenue northwest, but a sizable Polish community still lives here.

Puerto Ricans have replaced Poles as the main ethnic group. Signs of the culture are everywhere, from murals throughout the ward to Libreria Yuquiyu (a bookstore specializing in Puerto Rican culture) at Division and Rockwell to the Ruiz Belvis Cultural Center at North and Milwaukee.

The Puerto Rican barrio erupted in violence in 1966 and again in 1977, unleashing the pent-up frustration of a group which lived in some of the city's worst conditions. Rioting has ceased, but depressing living conditions continue. Despite efforts from many sources, Humboldt Park remains the worst gang crime center in the city. The Hispanic dropout rate at two local high schools is 50 percent according to board of education figures; an independent study placed the dropout rate at 70 percent. Division Street, the lively, gutsy topic of a Studs Terkel book, now stands as the most decayed business strip outside of certain streets in black neighborhoods.

Yet West Town and Humboldt Park have seen community victories in recent years. Josephinum High School, a much-acclaimed Catholic girls' school at Oakley and LeMoyne, was kept open by citywide support in 1985 after the governing religious order threatened to close it. Sabin School at Leavitt and Hirsch, which had been used as a garage, was reopened as a magnet school after a community-wide effort. Bickerdike Redevelopment Corporation has constructed low-cost housing on dozens of sites which formerly were vacant lots.

Luis Gutierrez is not the first Hispanic alderman from West Town. That honor goes to William Emilio Rodriguez, alderman from 1915 to 1918 in what was then the 15th Ward. Born in Naperville and raised in Wisconsin, he was part Mexican and part German and considered himself a German socialist. He ran unsuccessfully for mayor in 1911.

Since Rodriguez's time the area has not been known for colorful representatives. The last two 26th Ward aldermen before Gutierrez, Polish-American Stanley Zydlo (1963–79) and Italian-American Michael Nardulli (1979–86) were unswerving regular Democrat loyalists. Mathew Bieszczat, the Democratic committeeman from 1956 to 1986, was a long-term (1966-86) if not exceptional member of the Cook County Board. The 1986 remap pushed both Nardulli and Bieszczat out of the 26th Ward. Neither sought reelection, although Nardulli filed an unsuccessful lawsuit to strike down the remap.

Nardulli was one of three lame-duck aldermen (with Frank Stemberk of the 22nd and Frank Damato of the 37th) who decided to seek citywide county board seats rather than fight it out in their remapped wards. All three received party slating for the posts. Ironically, Nardulli's endorsement came at the expense of his mentor, the crusty eighty-six-year-old Bieszczat. Nardulli finished twelfth in the thirty-seven-person Democratic primary; the top ten finishers received nominations. Michael Nardulli is living proof that defeated aldermen never die; they end up in an administrative position. He now serves the city council as an assistant to 32nd Ward alderman Terry Gabinski in the redrawn ward he now calls home.

REDISTRICTING: It can be argued that the 26th Ward is the "newest" ward in the city. No other ward underwent such drastic changes as a result of the 1986 remap. Only a periscope-shaped corridor bordered by Western on the east, Chicago on the south, California on the west, and the Milwaukee Railroad on the north, a western extension to Kedzie between North and the railroad, plus a few eastern precincts, remain from the ward's previous incarnation. Half the precincts of the "old" 26th Ward are elsewhere now.

Before the remap, this was a heavily Italian ward, extending south to Kinzie Street and east to Racine. The remap took the southeast half of the ward. All or parts of sixteen precincts, mainly in the Ukrainian Village area, were shifted to the 32nd Ward. All or parts of five others went to the 27th Ward. Nine precincts at the southeastern edge of the former ward went to the 1st Ward.

The 26th received four Humboldt Park precincts, including the park itself, from the 31st Ward; nine northwest precincts from the 33rd Ward, and all or parts of eight eastern precincts from the 32nd Ward.

One precinct not obtained by the 26th Ward is the result of the weirdest bit of gerrymandering in the city—a tooth-shaped precinct in the heart of Wicker Park that contains a senior citizens high-rise building. Depending on what source one hears, it was kept in the 32nd either to prevent dilution of Hispanic percentage in the 26th Ward, or because 32nd Ward committeeman Dan Rostenkowski wanted to keep a dependable regular Democratic precinct in the ward.

MAYORAL: The 26th Ward secured a bare majority of the vote for Mayor Jane Byrne in the 1983 Democratic primary. She won 8,208 votes (50.3 percent) to 6,610 (41 percent) for Richard Daley and 1,488 (9 percent) for Harold Washington.

Republican Bernard Epton carried the general election with 54 percent of the vote. His relatively small majority, given Washington's poor showing in the primary, indicates the Democratic leanings of many of the ward's residents.

The remapped ward produced a dramatically different mayoral vote total in 1987. A number of factors contributed to Washington's 61 percent in the primary: reduction of the Italian population, addition of Hispanics, the presence of Puerto Rican Gloria Chevare as Washington's running mate, Jane Byrne's refusal to back the ward remap, the strength of Gutierrez's ward organization, and the virtual absence of a regular Democratic organization in the ward. In the general election Washington attracted many of those Hispanics who had voted for Byrne, although the decline in total votes hints that many Byrne supporters stayed home. The mayor won 69 percent of the vote.

CENSUS DATA: Population (1980): 60,612. 22.95 percent white, 10.59 percent black, 64.21 percent Hispanic, 2.25 percent Asian and other. Voting age population; 30.36 percent white, 9.16 percent black, 57.69 percent Hispanic, 2.79 percent Asian and other.

CENSUS TRACTS: See ward map.

COMMUNITY NEWSPAPERS:
El Dia, 2648 S. Kolin (277–7676) (Spanish)
El Imparcial, 3610 W. 26th St. (376–9888) (Spanish)
El Informador, 1821 S. Loomis (942–1295) (Spanish)
El Norte, 2714 W. 23rd Pl. (254–1623) (Spanish)
Free Press, 2608 N. California (342–5737)
Impacto, 3507 W. North Ave. (486–2547) (Spanish)
La Opinion, 2501 S East Ave. Berwyn (795–1383) (Spanish)
La Raza, 53 W. Jackson (427–6100) (Spanish)

Northwest Herald, 2711 W. Cermak
West Town Extra, 3918 W. North Ave. (252–3534) (Spanish)

ALDERMAN: Luis V. Gutierrez. Elected 1986. Born December 10, 1956. Career: B.A., Northeastern Illinois University, 1976; teacher, Chicago public schools: social worker, Illinois Department of Children and Family Services; administrative assistant, Mayor's Subcommittee on Infrastructure, 1984–85.
Committees: Special Events and Cultural Affairs (chairman); Buildings (vice-chairman); Beautification and Recreation; Budget and Government Operations; Historical Landmark Preservation; Economic Development; Finance; Health; Housing; Land Acquisition, Disposition and Leases.
City hall telephone: 744–6853, 744–4198.
Ward office: 2116 W. Division (486–1123).
1986 special election:

Luis V. Gutierrez	5,239	(50%)
Manuel A. Torres	5,214	(50%)

1986 special runoff:

Luis V. Gutierrez	7,429	(53%)
Manuel Torres	6,549	(47%)

1987 election:

Luis V. Gutierrez	9,010	(66%)	Felicita Claudio	952	(7%)
Brenda S. Torres	2,496	(18%)	Hector Franco	231	(2%)
Jim R. Blasinski	955	(7%)			

DEMOCRATIC COMMITTEEMAN: Manuel Torres. Elected 1986. Born 1951. Career: B.A., University of Illinois at Chicago; investigator, Office of Professional Standards; investigator, Department of Neighborhoods; commissioner, Cook County Board, 1984–86.
Ward office: 1020 N. Western (779–1799).
1984 election:
Mathew Bieszczat, unopposed.
1986 special election:

Manuel Torres	3,846	(57%)
Norma Quintana	2,339	(35%)
Oscar Martinez	586	(9%)

MAYORAL ELECTIONS:

1983 Democratic primary:

Jane Byrne	8,208	(50%)
Richard Daley	6,610	(41%)
Harold Washington	1,488	(9%)

1987 Democratic primary:

Harold Washington	8,927	(61%)
Jane Byrne	5,658	(39%)

1983 general:

Bernard Epton	8,823	(54%)
Harold Washington	7,449	(46%)

1987 general:

Harold Washington	9,027	(69%)
Edward Vrdolyak	3,543	(27%)
Donald Haider	432	(3%)

27th Ward

BLACKS FORM THE overwhelming majority on both the South and West sides of Chicago. But it is a mistake to consider both areas alike.

The South Side was the home of a long-established black community, the first such community of any northern city. If there was poverty (and there was), the South Side also contained a strong middle class which created its own economic, social, and cultural institutions.

West Side blacks lacked such potent institutions. Those who moved into the West Side (beginning in the 1940s) were often-uneducated working-class immigrants from the South, not the middle class. Black doctors and lawyers moved to Hyde Park and Avalon Park, not Garfield Park.

Most important, South Side blacks had a heritage of political representation that preceded even William Dawson. The West Side, on the other hand, contained "plantation" wards, lived in and represented by blacks but ruled by whites who usually lived far away from the ward. The stereotypical plantation ward was the Near West Side's 27th.

This was one of the first wards to attain plantation status, and one of the last to lose it. Whites made no secret of their unwillingness to share power with blacks. The current 27th Ward includes part of the former "Bloody 20th."

A black named Octavus Granady once ran against white Bill Pacelli for committeeman. He was gunned down in gangland fashion.

The most notorious ward boss in the 27th was Ed Quigley, whose name reporters universally prefaced with the description "sewer boss." Quigley rose from the ranks as secretary to former ward boss John Touhy. His qualifications to head a sewer department were, at best, questionable. When asked if he was ever a sewer worker, he replied, "No, but many's the time I lifted a lid to see if they were flowing."

He became committeeman in 1968. One of his first acts was to dump Harry Sain, alderman since 1933 and onetime city council powerhouse who made the ward one of the "automatic eleven" which always rolled huge majorities into the Democratic column. The seventy-six-year-old Sain was enraged by the ouster but unable to fight it.

Rioting which followed the 1968 assassination of Martin Luther King may have influenced Quigley's decision. He slated black precinct captain Eugene Ray in 1971 for alderman in a ward that by now was almost entirely black. Ray, formerly a supervisor of the linen room at Cook County Hospital, had a vocabulary during council meetings that was usually limited to "aye" or "no". It made no difference that the alderman had a black face; Quigley ruled the ward. Through his Sewer Department, he controlled thousands of patronage jobs which gave him sway over this and other West Side wards as well.

The 27th Ward at that time extended east to the Chicago River. It included West Madison Street's skid row, a ramshackle collection of flophouses, gin joints, cheap restaurants, and storefront churches. At one time it was a respectable, if forlorn, neighborhood, home to railroad workers and other pensioners (The Workingman's Hotel, one of the more notable flophouses, indeed once was a working man's hotel). But as the pensioners died or left, down-and-out alcoholics predominated.

Skid row nonetheless was a gold mine for Quigley, a harvest of cheap, docile votes. Occasionally there were problems. A Quigley precinct captain was convicted in 1970 of buying votes from bums for $1 per head.

Quigley faced controversy in other areas as well. Area businesses routinely were "asked" to buy $200 ads in ad books. Workers in 1973 claimed Quigley requested $300 for a favorable result on civil service tests. The *Tribune* in 1974 claimed massive inefficiency in the Sewer Department, that it wasted $9.6 million out of a $13.8 million budget. In 1977 he was accused of "protecting" skid row flophouses from "too careful" building and fire inspectors.

The veteran sewer boss was one of the first casualties of the Harold Washington administration in 1983. Quigley, like other department heads, submitted a *pro forma* resignation. The newly elected mayor accepted Quigley's. The resignation was announced immediately after Quigley's brother-in-law, James Monaco, was found guilty of illegally casting votes in a skid row hotel.

Soon afterward, Quigley surprised most Chicagoans by resigning as ward committeeman. His successor was, to put it mildly, an unexpected choice. Thomas Fuller, a sanitary district board member, lived in Evanston. He moved into a local Holiday Inn after ward precinct captains chose him to succeed Quigley, although he did not give up his Evanston home.

Local residents, encouraged by the progress made in other wards, were disgusted at Quigley's power play. They met with Fuller and urged him to resign. Fuller responded by telling them, "I don't need your ——" and challenged them to defeat him at the polls.

That is exactly what they did. They bypassed Fuller for Wallace Davis, Jr., who was elected alderman in 1983. Davis beat Fuller for Democratic committeeman in 1984.

Davis's entry into the political scene was an unusual one. He owned three small businesses on the West Side in 1976, when a policeman shot him in the back, reportedly mistaking him for a thief. The shooting became a *cause célèbre* in the black community, and Davis later received a huge out-of-court settlement from the city. He successfully exploited the fame from the shooting case, and defeated organization-backed Mattie Coleman in a 1983 aldermanic runoff.

Wallace Davis's most notable legislative accomplishment was an ordinance to outlaw cremations in the city, except for those performed in cemeteries. However, Davis was probably best known for his extracurricular adventures, a good many of which have involved the police:

—In May 1983 he helped two officers arrest a suspected gang member by running him down.

—Later that month he charged that Quigley made threats on his life and claimed that Quigley was spreading rumors of his using illegal drugs.

—In November 1983 he reported to police that his Cadillac Fleetwood had been stolen overnight in suburban Glenwood. Inside the car was $3,000 in $50 bills, which Davis claimed was to pay a contractor for work on his home. When asked what he was doing in the suburb, he said he was visiting a nurse friend who had hurt her foot and was going to help her to the hospital. When asked why he would leave so much cash in a car overnight, he replied that he thought the suburbs were safe.

—In January 1984 he caught two burglary suspects in his home.

—In March 1984, his car (which bore the painted message "I [heart] Wallace Davis") was repossessed.

—In June of that year, he announced to reporters that he would lead them to the scene of a double homicide in his ward. When he, the reporters, and police arrived at the "murder" scene, they encountered a rotten odor—which came from several packages of decaying meat left in an unplugged refrigerator.

—That August, Davis performed what he thought was a public service. He leaped from his car to aid a woman he said was being abducted by two men. The men in question turned out to be undercover policemen arresting a prostitute. Davis himself was arrested but charges later were dropped.

Davis managed to make the newspapers for other reasons as well. He incurred the wrath of his constituents in 1986 when, as committeeman, he cast his vote for party chairman Edward Vrdolyak instead of black challenger John Stroger. Davis later explained that his vote was cast by proxy, that the attorney casting the ballot was ordered to choose Vrdolyak if the vote was unanimous, and that he did not know of the plans of fellow black committeemen to back Stroger.

Most damaging, Davis was the subject of an FBI investigation involving alleged acceptance of money from "mole" Michael Raymond. Davis was indicted in late 1986 on a number of charges, including taking kickbacks from a niece who worked as his secretary. The above circumstances and others combined to oust Davis and provide what may have been one of the most accidental aldermanic victors in Chicago history.

No fewer than seventeen persons filed against Wallace Davis. Ten of those challengers survived on the ballot. They included three surrogates of well-known West Side pols: Consuela Williams, ally of former 24th Ward alderman David Rhodes; Cindi Sanders, friend of State Representative Douglas Huff; and Sheneather Butler, daughter of West Side minister (and perennial candidate) Jesse Butler.

Jane Byrne achieved little success campaigning on the West Side; none of the local ministers would let her speak from their pulpits. Finally, Jesse Butler let the former mayor address his congregation, although claiming that this move did not amount to a Byrne endorsement. Her father's action helped set library assistant Sheneather Butler apart from the others in the mind of some voters— enough to gain her fourteen percent of the vote and sneak into a runoff.

The 27th Ward had an important issue—possible location of a new Chicago Bears stadium, a move which might create economic benefits but dislodge several hundred residents. Yet that issue played little part in the runoff.

Soon after the February election, Davis was arrested and charged with pistol whipping the secretary, supposedly because she had planned to testify against him in federal court. He spent the rest of the campaign in jail.

Ward residents thus were saddled with a difficult choice—vote for an alleged woman beater, or a lady who appeared "soft" on Harold Washington. The mayor's backers urged a vote for Davis—reportedly with the idea that Davis might soon be forced out of office anyhow and could be replaced by a more desirable candidate.

Butler won the runoff, but her hundred-vote margin hardly amounted to a mandate. Since coming to office, she has not established herself as a knowledgeable leader. When asked on a television show if she talked with the Wirtz family (owners of the Chicago Stadium and the most influential businessmen in the ward) about a new Bears stadium, she responded, "I never heard of them."

Davis was acquitted of the charges brought by his secretary. But he was not so fortunate with the Operation Incubator charges. A jury convicted him of racketeering, extortion, attempted extortion, and lying to the FBI while in office in late 1987.

The conviction provided Democrats the opportunity to replace him on the Central Committee. The new committeeman is Ricky Hendon, an independent film producer who worked with the independent campaigns of Aldermen Ed Smith and Danny Davis and State Representative Art Turner.

The 27th Ward, an irregularly shaped turf bordered roughly by Ashland Avenue on the east, Roosevelt Road on the south, Kedzie on the west, and Chicago Avenue on the north, has its share of sites and history. Housing varies from graystone buildings with arched doorways on Warren Boulevard to run-down apartments on Fifth Avenue, described as "the kind of neighborhood where heat escapes from every apartment." Two of the larger Chicago Housing Authority projects, Henry Horner Homes (Washington and Wood) and Rockwell Gardens (Western and Jackson) also are located here.

Churches of all varieties abound. One of Chicago's landmark churches, the First Baptist Congregational Church, is located at Ashland and Washington. This limestone church, the joint effort on several congregations which had opposed slavery, was begun in 1869 and dedicated shortly after the 1871 fire. Precious Blood, a Catholic church, is located at Western and Congress. New Life Baptist Church at Maypole and California advertises itself as "where the Holy Spirit is boss."

Lake Street, underneath the Lake-Dan Ryan elevated tracks, is viewed by many outsiders as one of the toughest areas in the city. This is an area loaded with bars (many of which have first-class blues bands), factories, and motorcycle clubs. But black pride is evident, at least in the names of local institutions. Malcolm X College, a junior college at Wolcott and Van Buren, always flies the red, green, and black Afro flag as well as the American one. The Martin Luther King Boys Club at Washington and Sacramento is the largest such club in the city. A portion of Warren Boulevard is also named Nancy B. Jefferson Boulevard, after a widely respected community worker.

The 27th also has features of citywide importance. Chicago Stadium, once the largest such indoor arena in the country, towers over the neighborhood at Madison and Wood. Cook County Hospital and Rush-Presbyterian-St. Luke's are part of the medical district which also spills over into the 1st Ward.

The Chicago and North Western Railway viaduct, running roughly parallel to Kinzie Street, splits the ward. North of the viaduct is a white neighborhood known locally as "the Patch," home of Italians and Mexicans. These residents, plus a handful of Hispanics south of Polk and west of Western, are the only nonblacks in the ward and account for less than 20 percent of the population.

Much of the Patch is industrial, but it also contains working-class homes, taverns, small businesses, and a World War I tank at Grand and Western. One of the stores is the hundred-year-old Gonnella bakery at Damen and Erie. For years it advertised its wares over the radio with the slogan, "Have some Gonnella, it's sweller, fella!"

One of Chicago's shorter streets is located in this area—Anson Court. This was named after Adrian "Cap" Anson, Chicago White Stockings star of the late 1800s. Anson set back integration in baseball sixty years when he refused to take the field against a team that had black ballplayers. Ironically, his namesake street is now in a predominantly black ward.

This is a ward which breathes history. In the late nineteenth century, Ashland near Madison became known as "Union Row," because of the many unions located nearby. Many headquarters remain, including the Pipefitters,

Beef Boners and Sausage Makers, Clothing and Textile Workers, and Truck Drivers. Union Park, at Madison and Ashland, is appropriately named.

Not far from Union Park, at Ashland and Jackson, was the home of Carter Harrison, mayor during the early 1890s. Harrison presided over the 1893 Columbian Exposition. The city was celebrating the completion of the successful fair when suddenly thrown into mourning because Harrison was assassinated at his home. A Union Park statue honors him, the only such commemoration of any Chicago mayor.

Other famous (and infamous) persons have called the near West Side home. Edgar Rice Burroughs wrote the first Tarzan book in 1912 at 445 N. Damen. The Grand and Ogden area, once called "The Badlands," spawned the Panczko brothers, legendary Chicago burglars.

Two deaths in this ward proved to have citywide ramifications. Black Panther leaders Fred Hampton and Mark Clark were gunned down in their apartments by police in a predawn raid in December 1969. The police claimed self-defense, but evidence suggested otherwise.

Black anger at State's Attorney Edward Hanrahan manifested itself at the polls, as blacks were instrumental in ousting Hanrahan in his 1972 reelection bid. It was the start of a sustained drive for black independence throughout the city. Ironically, one of the last places to experience that independence was the site of the killings, the 27th Ward.

REDISTRICTING: The 27th underwent major changes as a result of the 1986 remap to accommodate nearby wards which were mandated for black or Hispanic "super-majorities." The ward lost all or parts of five eastern precincts to the 1st Ward, seven western precincts to the 28th, and four southwest precincts to the 24th ward. It gained two western precincts from the 28th Ward, plus five southern ones which had belonged to the 25th Ward and two other southern ones formerly part of the 1st Ward.

MAYORAL: Harold Washington carried the ward in the Democratic primary, with 72 percent of the vote. Jane Byrne received 23 percent, mostly in the northern precincts and in southern precincts no longer part of the ward. Richard Daley got 5 percent of the vote.

Washington won 93 percent of the vote in the general election, with the support of black voters plus Hispanics and whites who voted along traditional Democratic party lines.

The 1986 redistricting cut the black percentage slightly, and those newly infused white votes meant lower Harold Washington vote totals. Even so, the mayor took 86 percent of the vote in the Democratic primary and 89 percent in the general election. His strength, as expected, came from near-unanimous votes in black precincts.

CENSUS DATA: Population (1980): 60,891. 8.02 percent white, 81.16 percent black, 9.71 percent Hispanic, 1.11 percent Asian and other. Voting age population: 10.37 percent white, 77.50 percent black, 9.27 percent Hispanic, 2.86 percent Asian and other.

CENSUS TRACTS: See ward map.

COMMUNITY NEWSPAPERS:
Chicago Metro, 2600 S. Michigan (842–5950)
Northwest Herald, 2711 W. Cermak (247–8500)
Westside Journal, 16618 S. Hermitage, Markham (333–2210)

ALDERMAN: Sheneather Y. Butler. Elected 1987. Born November 13, 1960. Career: Wright Junior College; administrative assistant, Alternative Health Care, 1980–82; receptionist, Saxon Paint Co., 1982–85; secretary, Oak Park Public Library, 1985–87.
Committees: Ports, Wharves, and Bridges (vice-chairman); Aging and Disabled; Aviation; Budget and Government Operations; Claims and Liabilities; Education; Energy, Environmental Protection, and Public Utilities; Finance; Health; Intergovernmental Relations; Ports, Wharves, and Bridges; Traffic Control and Safety.
City hall telephone: 744–6124, 744–6125.
Ward office: 2043 W. Madison St. (421–3030).
1987 election:

Wallace Davis, Jr.	4,535	(32%)	Eddie Wallace, Jr.	868	(6%)
Sheneather Y. Butler	1,957	(14%)	Consuela Aida Williams	539	(4%)
Ben Franklin	1,736	(12%)	Marion E. Thomas	523	(4%)
Cindi E. Sanders	1,646	(12%)	Sylvia Y. Welch	507	(4%)
Eddie A. Rasul	1,093	(8%)	Verdell Trice	472	(3%)

1987 runoff:

Sheneather Y. Butler	7,179	(50%)
Wallace Davis, Jr.	7,079	(50%)

DEMOCRATIC COMMITTEEMAN: Ricky Hendon. Appointed 1987. Born December 8, 1953. Career: Omega School of Communications; engineer-producer, news announcer, and salesperson for WAIT, WBMX, and WLOO radio stations; independent film producer and teacher.
Ward office: 2905 W. Madison (734–7615).
1984 election

Wallace Davis, Jr.	6,628	(65%)
Thomas Fuller	2,206	(21%)
Douglas Huff, Jr.	1,438	(14%)

MAYORAL ELECTIONS:

1983 Democratic primary:

Harold Washington	13,811	(72%)
Jane Byrne	4,304	(23%)
Richard Daley	1,024	(5%)

1983 general:

Harold Washington	20,710	(93%)
Bernard Epton	1,577	(7%)

1987 Democratic primary:

Harold Washington	14,697	(86%)
Jane Byrne	2,299	(14%)

1987 general:

Harold Washington	15,282	(89%)
Edward Vrdolyak	1,775	(10%)
Donald Haider	168	(1%)

28th Ward

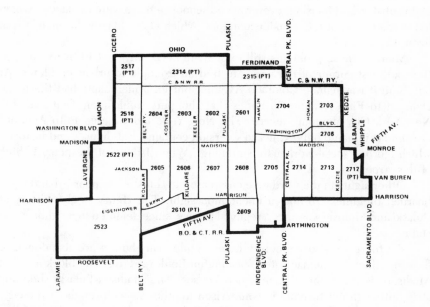

AN UNEASY CALM hung over Chicago's West Side immediately after the April 4, 1968, assassination of Rev. Martin Luther King. Then all hell broke loose. Rioters, arsonists, and looters ravaged the black ghetto in a spree of destruction and death. Mayor Richard J. Daley examined the fires and pillaging from a helicopter. "I never believed that this would happen here," he said. The "here" he referred to included areas like Garfield Park in the heart of the West Side. Twenty years later these areas have not fully recovered from the effects of the rioting.

Even before King's death (for that matter, even before the black migration into the area following World War II), the communities designated West Garfield Park and East Garfield Park were experiencing declines. At the turn of the century, Irish, Germans, Jews, and Italians flocked to what was being touted as "Chicago's nearest suburb." They were drawn by the huge park with its newly opened conservatory that was one of the largest in the world. Families spent Sunday afternoons strolling through the park or rowing boats available at its lagoon. During the week men worked at nearby factories that took advantage of the area's cheap rents.

By 1930, new housing construction had all but ceased. After the war, many of the single-family homes were being converted to multifamily units. The suburb was fast becoming a slum.

White residents started leaving Garfield Park, now the heart of the 28th Ward, in the 1950s. During the 1960s, the flight was all but complete. Many of the businesses followed suit. Lack of employment opportunities, aging and often substandard housing, overcrowded schools—these were the factors which led to the riots, not the "outside agitators" which Daley blamed for many racial ills in the 1960s.

Many of those problems still exist. One need only visit Fifth Avenue, in the southeast corner of the ward, to find an example of urban problems. At one time it was named Colorado Avenue, but local merchants had the name changed to Fifth Avenue, in hopes that shoppers would identify it with the New York City shopping mecca. The New York and Chicago Fifth Avenues are similar in name only. Chicago's version contains drab houses and factories which led one social worker to comment, "When I think of the poor, I think of this street."

Other sights in the ward give one reason to think of the poor. Abandoned, boarded buildings are not an uncommon sight. The Henry Legler library at Pulaski and Monroe was once a regional library, since demoted to neighborhood status.

Yet there are also symbols of hope. While many houses are abandoned or forlorn, others are immaculate. Washington Boulevard, just one block north of Madison, is the scene of many such houses. The Madison-Pulaski shopping strip, although not thriving in comparison to other strips throughout the city, is the busiest shopping area on the West Side. Arbor Plaza was a debris-filled vacant lot until April 1987 when the Department of Streets and Sanitation and Marshall High School students created a plaza with trees, flowers, drinking fountains, and a working antique light. Benches display "ads" proclaiming "Adopt-a-Flower Bed" and "Join the A-Team—a-broom, a-rake, a-shovel."

New housing, for the first time in decades, is making its way into the 28th Ward. Bethel New Life, Inc., has rehabilitated or built more than 300 units. The most publicized effort has been that of Habitat For Humanity, a private church-based group. Former president Jimmy Carter helped construct new houses at Kildare and Maypole in the summer of 1986.

Local institutions help anchor a neighborhood which may have been down but was never out. One such institution is Providence-St. Mel High School at Central Park and Monroe, a Catholic school which was abandoned by the archdiocese but rescued by private funders. Another is the Off the Street Club at Washington and Karlov, where a sign urges youngsters, "Don't wait to be a grownup to be great. Be a great kid now."

And the ward still has Garfield Park. This onetime jewel of the West Park Board had been allowed to deteriorate. It has since undergone improvements, thanks to a court decision which forced equal distribution of park funds throughout the city. A new gymnasium and a remodeled swimming pool are the immediate results of that decision. Even during the lean years, the spacious park contained objects of beauty. The golden-domed field house was (and is) one of the more inspiring buildings on the West Side. Garfield Park Conservatory, containing more than 5,000 varieties of plants, remains an undervisited treasure.

If new life is visible in the 28th Ward, credit must be extended to Ed Smith, alderman since 1983. Not a household name, Smith nonetheless is considered by his city hall colleagues to be a hardworking alderman who is successful at bringing money and services into his ward. He also has been able to keep existing businesses in the ward. After a fire damaged the Elgin-Honey Hill Dairy at Harrison and Lawndale in 1985, Smith worked with city economic developers to help the company rebuild and expand.

Smith, a former economic development specialist with the Peace Corps in India, had to wait quite awhile for his political opportunity. Before 1983 he ran three times for alderman, once for Democratic committeeman, and twice for Democratic convention delegate—losing each time. He became the first independent alderman in a ward that for many years had been dominated by absentee whites.

Joseph Jambrone was the last white alderman in the 28th. He was elected in 1967 but ordered by Daley not to seek reelection in 1971. Nevertheless, Jambrone made history. In 1973 he became the first present or former city council member to be convicted of bribery. He died in early 1974, while appealing the sentence.

Jimmy Washington replaced Jambrone and served throughout the 1970s. He died in 1980 much as he lived—barely known, even in his ward. Even Washington's mentor in the early 1970s, State Representative Isaac "Ike" Sims, had little clout. Sims, the ward committeeman, also was a sewer worker on Ed Quigley's payroll, and thus beholden to the (white) 27th Ward boss.

William Carothers replaced Sims (his father-in-law) as committeeman in 1976. A former state representative and ward superintendent, he took over as alderman upon Washington's death. Carothers's aldermanic career was short but colorful. During his tenure, he and assistant Ozie Hutchins threatened to block a $14.5 million hospital expansion unless they received $15,000 worth of remodeling in their ward office. Both were convicted in 1983.

By this time, Carothers was out of office. He led the field in the 1983 aldermanic election but failed to secure a majority. Smith, who backed Harold Washington from the outset, defeated Jane Byrne-supporter Carothers with 60 percent of the vote in the runoff. He likewise wrested the committeeman post from Carothers in 1984.

Smith was challenged by Wynell Parker, a social worker with the Department of Human Services, but captured 79 percent of the vote in the 1987 election.

REDISTRICTING: The 28th Ward was "moved" slightly southward and eastward by the 1986 remap. All or parts of nine northern precincts were transferred to the 37th Ward. In return the 28th received one precinct from the 37th, five southern precincts from the 24th, and seven eastern ones from the 27th Ward.

MAYORAL: Harold Washington dominated the vote in the 1983 Democratic primary. He received 81 percent to 15 percent for Jane Byrne and 4 percent for Richard Daley.

As was the case in other all-black wards, Washington took the general election over Republican Bernard Epton, with 99 percent of the vote.

Other wards gave him more votes, but no ward provided higher percentages for Harold Washington in 1987. The popular mayor got 99.11 percent of the primary vote, 99.18 in the general election. Republican Donald Haider received only seventy-five votes, his lowest total in the city.

CENSUS DATA: Population (1980): 58,626. .75 percent white, 98.62 percent black, .99 percent Hispanic, .26 percent Asians and others. Voting age population: .65 percent white, 97.77 percent black, .75 percent Hispanic, .83 percent Asian and other.

CENSUS TRACTS: See ward map.

COMMUNITY NEWSPAPERS:
Chicago Metro, 2600 S. Michigan (842–5950)
Westside Journal. 16618 S. Hermitage, Markham (333–2210)

ALDERMAN: Ed H. Smith. Elected 1983. Born 1945. Career: Alcorn State University; Northeastern Illinois University; teacher, Chicago public schools; Peace Corps; vice-president, Chicago Economic Development Corporation.
Committees: Capital Development (chairman); Aviation; Budget and Government Operations; Buildings; Energy, Environmental Protection, and Public Utilities; Finance; Health; Intergovernmental Relations; Ports, Wharves, and Bridges; Traffic Control and Safety.
City hall telephone: 744–3066, 744–3097.
Ward office: 10 N. Hamlin (533–0900).
1987 election:

Ed H. Smith	12,262	(79%)
Wynell Parker	2,144	(13%)
Ollie Simmons	1,294	(8%)

DEMOCRATIC COMMITTEEMAN: Ed H. Smith. Elected 1984.
1984 election:

Ed H. Smith	7,858	(72%)
Joseph Davis	2,272	(21%)
R.T. Tucker	777	(7%)

MAYORAL ELECTIONS:

1983 Democratic primary:

Harold Washington	13,811	(81%)
Jane Byrne	2,674	(15%)
Richard Daley	727	(4%)

1983 general:

Harold Washington	22,339	(99%)
Bernard Epton	224	(1%)

1987 Democratic primary:

Harold Washington	18,517	(99%)
Jane Byrne	152	(1%)

1987 general:

Harold Washington	19,141	(99%)
Edward Vrdolyak	82	(0%)
Donald Haider	75	(0%)

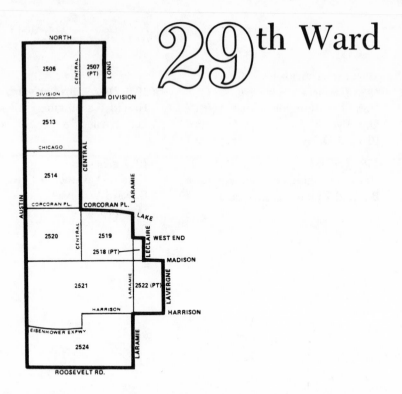

EVEN BY CHICAGO political standards, Iola McGowan's claims bordered on the absurd. The 1983 candidate for 29th Ward alderman stated that she lived in a house that was boarded up and without electricity, gas, and telephone service.

The 29th Ward hopeful told reporters that she had resided at a house at 5859 W. Midway Park since August 1982, despite the fact that the house had been boarded and padlocked by the Department of Housing and Urban Development as of October 5, the day she registered to vote from that address. McGowan admitted that she was receiving mail at an address outside the ward, but attested that she spent four or five nights a week in the house, and that she relied on portable lights and a kerosene stove. She claimed that she entered the house through a loosely boarded window.

Neighbors disputed that story, saying that they never saw her at the house in question and never saw lights there at night. Mayoral candidate Harold Washington seized a good visual opportunity and held a press conference in front of the house. The *Sun-Times* understated the case: "Any reasonable person would have been suspicious about McGowan's claim to have been living in a boarded-up house without any utility service."

Yet McGowan almost was allowed to stay on the 29th Ward aldermanic ballot. Elections board chairman Michael LaVelle at first claimed that it was only important that she resided in the house on December 27, 1982, the day she filed nominating petitions. The board later reversed itself and removed her from the ballot a week before the aldermanic election.

The McGowan flap served to show how committed party regulars were to the defeat of Alderman Danny K. Davis, the first independent alderman elected on the West Side. McGowan's candidacy backfired. Even though she resorted to a write-in campaign, Davis won the election with 83 percent of the vote.

For years the 29th was a solid machine ward, one of the "automatic eleven" wards which routinely delivered staggering pluralities for any Democratic machine candidate. Al Horan, committeeman since 1944, contributed three-to-one margins for Richard Daley in the 1955 Democratic primary and general elections. In 1963, when Daley faced his roughest electoral challenge from Democrat-turned-Republican Benjamin Adamowski, the 29th Ward carried for Daley by an eight-to-one margin.

Bernie Neistein ascended to the 29th Ward lordship upon Horan's 1960 death. He was the classic absentee ward boss. The violin-playing reputed Mafia front man claimed residency at 4123 W. Harrison, yet ruled the ward from his Gold Coast condominium.

Neistein "retired" as committeeman in 1972, but only briefly. At the time of the election, he was under indictment for his role in a racetrack scandal (he was later acquitted). The appearance of propriety demanded that someone under investigation not be slated for a party post. Yet, miraculously, no one else chose to run for 29th Ward commiteeman in 1972 (miracles were not uncommon during the Daley years). Neistein won reelection as a write-in.

The ward boss yielded to racial change in the ward in 1976 by designating Streets and Sanitation superintendent Willie Flowers his successor as committeeman. That move made little real difference in ward politics, as Neistein still directed the ward's patronage. Flowers defeated Iola McGowan by 500 votes.

Robert Biggs, an undertaker, preceded Flowers as the first black political official in the ward, although he had no more power than did Flowers. Biggs first ran for alderman as an independent in 1963 but joined the regulars and won two terms.

Le Roy Cross took over following Biggs's death in 1972. A real estate and insurance broker, he was Neistein's handpicked candidate. Cross won the 1973 special election to replace Biggs, although it took a runoff to do it. Even among proadministration aldermen, Cross stood out. The *Tribune* in 1974 described him as "undisputedly the quietest member of the City Council." Two years later he spoke up, proposing curbs on car rental agencies—only after he had been detained for driving a car mistakenly reported as stolen by a rental company.

Davis, a community worker and former teacher, defeated Cross in 1979 but lost the 1980 committeeman race. McGowan, appointed to the park board by Mayor Jane Byrne, won with 51 percent of the vote over Davis and Flowers.

"Thugs and hustlers were keepers of the process, and solid citizens were not in control of the voting apparatus," charged Davis after the election. "The most vile thing I saw was use of an army of hustlers masquerading as election

DANNY K. DAVIS and SHENEATHER BUTLER

judges and poll watchers. The people who supported me couldn't cope with these strong-arm niggers."

Four years later, incumbent alderman Davis rebounded and won the committeeman election with 69 percent of the vote. However, he lost another election the same day. Davis sought unsuccessfully the 7th District congressional seat held by Cardiss Collins. He carried the West Side portion of the polyglot district, but lost the upper-income Loop, Gold Coast, and suburban areas; Collins won 48 to 39 percent. In 1986 he tried again, with much the same results; Davis carried the West Side but lost the primary 60–40 to Collins.

The baritone-voiced Davis, one of the council's most effective speakers, has been one of its more visible figures. His most notable legislative accomplishment was an ordinance cosponsored by Alderman Joseph Kotlarz (35th) to ban the sale of leaded gasoline in the city—the only major legislation during Washington's first term to be cosponsored by members of the Washington and Vrdolyak blocs.

Margaret Parker, an interior decorator and ward secretary under Cross, challenged Davis in the 1987 aldermanic race. The mayor gave Davis a strong endorsement, and he carried all but the far southern precincts.

Davis, one of Harold Washington's most important council allies, gained control of the Zoning Committee after the election. He worked with Washington on a zoning ordinance revision which would strip individual aldermen of their prerogatives in arranging zoning changes and transfer those powers to the Zoning Committee. The future of these proposed changes under acting mayor Eugene Sawyer is not yet known.

The 29th Ward lies entirely within Austin, the largest designated community in the city. Yet it would be a mistake to consider this a homogeneous ward. Originally a comfortable suburb and part of the township of Cicero, Austin became part of Chicago in 1899—against Austinites' wishes. Austin residents favored extension of the Lake Street elevated line into their town, a move opposed by residents of neighboring Oak Park. Cicero and Oak Park residents secured revenge by voting for annexation of their neighbor suburb to the expanding city, although most Austin residents opposed the annexation. The introduction of the elevated line and subsequent annexation changed the nature of Austin. Originally a Protestant community of native Americans, it saw an influx of Swedes, Germans, Greeks, Jews, and Italians. These groups predominated until the 1960s.

After World War II, blacks moved into the Near West Side and moved steadily westward along a path roughly centered on Madison Street. In 1960, Austin was still almost entirely white. Ten years later, blacks accounted for 32 percent of the population, in 1980, 73.8 percent.

An ever-changing brigade of community groups worked to prevent the panic peddling and block busting that had hurt both blacks and whites in South Side and West Side communities. To some extent, they succeeded. The 29th Ward today consists of four sharply contrasting sections. A portion north of Augusta Boulevard is still white, a "bungalow belt" neighborhood. Italians are the dominant ethnic group.

Division and Monitor is the location of a theater with a colorful history— the Rockne. Originally a theater serving the Irish and Scandinavian communities, the Rockne became an "adult" theater in the 1960s. When neighborhood groups protested the change, the theater's owner agreed to try a change and offered special family rates. But the families stayed home, and the Rockne reverted to adult films.

Central Austin, also known locally as Austin Village, is the most integrated part of the ward. This is the showplace section of Austin, a collection of Queen Anne houses and elegant Protestant churches that reminds an observer more of neighboring Oak Park than the West Side of Chicago. Heart of this area (which runs from Augusta south to West End) is Midway Park, a parkway-bounded street that extends from Austin to Waller. This area, designated Old Austin, has been named a historic district.

Two blocks east is the "capitol" of Austin, the Austin Town Hall, modeled after Philadelphia's Independence Hall. Constructed on the site of the building which served as the seat of the township of Cicero, it is now a park district facility.

South Austin is virtually 100 percent black, with a different history than the neighborhood to the north. This area was settled later than the rest of the community, after Austin became part of Chicago. Multiunit buildings, not allowed in the then-suburb, proliferated here. Younger blacks displaced an aging white population, with overcrowded schools and buildings as a result.

If central Austin appears a continuation of suburban Oak Park, South Austin appears a continuation of the impoverished West Side. One does not have to travel far here to find an abandoned or boarded-up building. Madison Street is the main thoroughfare of the South Austin. Some of its buildings offer soul food, others salvation. One place which offers both is St. Rest #2 Dining Room at Laramie, a restaurant owned and operated by a pastor. South Austin offers religion in other forms, too. Jackson and Laramie is the location of Friendship Baptist Church, Chicago's first black church built from the ground up. The church, designed in an African motif, was dedicated in 1983. The far southwest section of South Austin is Columbus Park, the last major park built on the West Side. It contains a small golf course.

Eisenhower Expressway separates a small southern section from the rest of the ward. The eastern sector here is industrial. The western part is a white enclave known as "The Island." Geographically a part of the mainly black 29th Ward, the Island is in every other sense more a part of neighboring Cicero. Ronald Reagan posters and stickers, virtually unseen elsewhere in the ward, were visible here years after Reagan's 1984 election victory.

When a black family tried to move into an apartment on Roosevelt Road in late 1984, several whites barraged them with bricks and bottles. The blacks soon moved away, and the Island remains completely (and determinedly) white.

REDISTRICTING: The 29th Ward underwent minor changes from the remap, swapping a few precincts with the 37th Ward. The 29th gained four northeastern and part of one eastern precinct. It lost all or parts of four precincts to the 37th.

MAYORAL: Harold Washington swept to a solid majority in the 1983 mayoral primary, with 76 percent of the vote, especially in the South Austin area. Jane Byrne managed 18 percent of the vote and Richard Daley, 6 percent.

Washington took 93 percent of the vote in the general election against Bernard Epton. The Republican's strongest showing came, not surprisingly, in the Island.

Jane Byrne also carried the Island and showed strong votes in northern precincts in the 1987 Democratic primary. Washington swept elsewhere and took 94 percent.

Similar totals showed themselves in the general election. Washington received 95 percent of the votes. Edward Vrdolyak captured the Island but did poorly elsewhere.

CENSUS DATA: 9.99 percent white, 84.38 percent black, 3.70 percent Hispanic, 1.93 percent Asian and other. Voting age population: 12.47 percent white, 81.71 percent black, 3.47 percent Hispanic, 2.35 percent Asian and other.

CENSUS TRACTS: See ward map.

COMMUNITY NEWSPAPERS:
Chicago Metro, 2600 S. Michigan (842–5950)
Westside Journal, 16618 S. Hermitage, Markham (333–2210)

ALDERMAN: Danny K. Davis. Elected 1979. Born September 6, 1941. Career: B.A., Arkansas A.M.&N. College, 1961; M.S., Chicago State University, 1968; Ph.D., Union Graduate School, 1977; teacher and counselor, Chicago public schools; executive director, Greater Lawndale Conservation Commission; training director, Martin Luther King Community Health Center; executive director; Westside Health Planning Organization; special assistant to the president, Miles Square Health Planning Organization.

Committees: President Pro Tempore; Zoning (chairman); Committees, Rules, Municipal Code Revision, and Ethics (vice chairman); Budget and Government Operations; Claims and Liabilities; Finance; Health, Human Rights, and Consumer Protection; License; Local Transportation; Police, Fire, and Municipal Institutions; Streets and Alleys.

City hall telephone: 744–3070, 744–8805.
Ward office: 5637 W. Chicago Ave. (626–2700).
1987 election:

Danny K. Davis	14,754	(85%)
Margaret K. Parker	2,567	(15%)

DEMOCRATIC COMMITTEEMAN: Danny K. Davis. Elected 1984.
1984 election:

Danny K. Davis	7,128	(69%)
Iola McGowan	3,235	(31%)

MAYORAL ELECTIONS:

1983 Democratic primary:

Harold Washington	13,592	(76%)
Jane Byrne	3,112	(18%)
Richard Daley	1,110	(6%)

1983 general:

Harold Washington	19,884	(93%)
Bernard Epton	1,531	(7%)

1987 Democratic primary:

Harold Washington	18,883	(94%)
Jane Byrne	1,117	(6%)

1987 general:

Harold Washington	19,389	(95%)
Edward Vrdolyak	927	(5%)
Donald Haider	153	(1%)

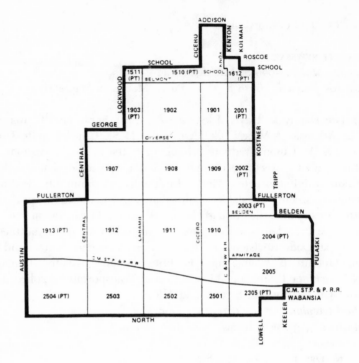

SOME WARDS HAVE TAKEN on distinct personalities over the years, so much that the mere mention of their number evokes a definite image. The 5th Ward is the home of Hyde Park liberals, as every student of Chicago politics knows. The 11th Ward is Bridgeport and Mayor Daley, the 43rd is Lakefront independents, and so on.

Then again, there are those like the 30th. Even the most dedicated of political junkies may have trouble drawing a bead on this Northwest Side ward.

The 30th Ward is roughly bordered by Belmont, Kostner, Austin, and North avenues. It serves the community known as Belmont Cragin. This is a part of the city which seldom makes the guidebooks. The great architects built their houses and churches elsewhere. Restaurant critics seldom visit. Drama critics never do.

It's an area with a lot of industry and has been ever since the Cragin brothers introduced a metals manufacturing company here in 1883. The Helene Curtis cosmetics plant dominates the corner of North and Kostner. An Archer Daniels Midland grain elevator at Laramie and Cortland symbolizes the megacompanies which also do business here. Small factories pockmark lots near the several railroad tracks which crisscross the ward.

The industry emphasis may not last forever. The former W. F. Hall printing plant at Diversey and Kenton symbolizes Chicago's modern industrial dilemma. Hall left the city in the mid-1980s. Developers have offered to buy the former plant and convert it into a shopping mall. Local groups, seeking high-paying factory jobs instead of the low-paying service jobs offered by retailers, have sought to block the proposed shopping center and seek other manufacturers. Others argue that any jobs are better than none at all, and that an active center provides more tax revenue than a vacant plant.

Mainly, the area is residential, with the sort of unpretentious housing that pops up near a factory town. Factory owners go home to higher-rent areas; the proletarians live here.

Nonetheless, the 30th Ward is not completely devoid of interest to a Chicago explorer in search of the offbeat or unusual. Here one can find Hanson Stadium (Fullerton and Central), the largest Chicago stadium not used by a professional or major college sports team; Area 5 police headquarters at Grand and Central; St. Stanislaus Bishop and Martyr Church with its statue-laden courtyard at Belden and Long; and WXRT (Belmont and Lavergne) an eclectic radio station that advertises itself as "Chicago's Finest Rock," and one of the few major Chicago radio stations not located downtown.

Grand Avenue runs along the southern portion of the ward, joining Armitage near Leclaire. Long ago this area was known as Whiskey Point, because the earliest settlers bought the existing trading post and saloon from the Indians for a bottle of whiskey. Other pubs exist in the neighborhood now, the type that paste shamrocks in the windows in honor of St. Patrick's Day.

Although not as visibly "ethnic" a neighborhood as some, signs of prevailing groups exist. Puerto Rican stores, bars, and fast food restaurants can be seen along Armitage Avenue. Fullerton is Polish, with restaurants, grocery stores, and a travel agency serving that nationality. Casa Del Regalo, at Central and Drummond, displays Italian ceramic statues and clocks. Shamrock Imports at Laramie and Belmont sells Irish goods.

People do take their roots seriously here, in the old country as well as Chicago. Demonstrators carrying Solidarity banners picketed the Cardinal Club (Laramie and Belmont) after that Polish nightclub presented an entertainer with alleged Communist sympathies.

Armenian culture is not apparent in the 30th Ward. Yet the alderman is George J. Hagopian, the first (and so far, only) Armenian-American in the city council. First elected in 1975, Hagopian is one of the less vocal city council members. But when he speaks others cannot help but listen. Hagopian's voice once was measured at 95 decibels, a "record" according to *Sun-Times* reporter Ray Hanania.

He made himself well known in the early Council Wars days of 1983 when good government often took a back seat to bad theater. Frank Brady, then chairman of the Committee on Employment, had been assigned an office which Washington administration officials decided to appropriate for use as a press room for TV cameramen. This news prompted a sit-in of Brady and Hagopian, two aldermen who could (physically at least) be called city council heavyweights. "I won't move unless they kill or cripple me," Hagopian asserted. Brady emerged triumphant in "Cubbyholegate." And Hagopian went home, without being killed or crippled.

No one has ever accused George Hagopian of being a flaming liberal. He is one of the few anti-Washington aldermen whose stance is based on ideological considerations as much as political expediency. He once claimed that his greatest legislative triumph was opposition to the proposed gay rights ordinance. He berated a representative from the National Organization of Women who proposed that the police department establish a sexual assault unit.

It would be unfair, however, to dismiss George Hagopian as an urban redneck. By most accounts, he is a hardworking public official. If not a legislative leader, he is adept at the nuts-and-bolts job of constituency service. "He is so decent, so industrially conscientious about serving the people that he comes off as a hopeless square," according to the *Jefferson Park Leader*. Hagopian takes particular pride in the jobs he helped create in the ward and the effort made to keep factories (and jobs) from moving elsewhere.

Only days before the 1987 election, Hagopian predicted victory by a fifteen-to-one margin over Burt Sillins, an assistant district attorney. He fell short of that lofty prophecy but still won with 62 percent. Sillins carried southern precincts recently redistricted into the ward.

Hagopian is one of a line of 30th Ward aldermen who have given ward operations priority over citywide headlines. Daniel Ronan served as alderman for many years, until his election to Congress in 1964. He served as chairman of the Buildings and Zoning Committee during the Daley years, gaining a reputation as a hardworking public servant. His 1969 funeral attracted thousands of mourners.

Edwin McMahon, chief clerk of the civil division of the state's attorney's office, succeeded Ronan as alderman in 1965. He took over as Democratic committeeman upon Ronan's death. McMahon did not stay long at either position. He retired as committeeman in 1970 and declined to seek reelection as alderman in 1971. Elmer Filippini won the election that year.

Elmer Filippini was a political oddity, a Streets and Sanitation ward superintendent who interrupted his career with a term in city hall. Formerly the acting ward superintendent, he vowed to stay in office only one term. He did not last that long, quitting on the last day of 1974 to return as ward superintendent. Hagopian, then an assistant director of the Illinois Housing Development Authority, immediately was slated to replace him.

The man who slated Hagopian was Thaddeus "Ted" Lechowicz, Democratic committeeman since 1970. Lechowicz heads one of the lesser-known yet more effective ward organizations in the city. A state senator, he has shown signs of ambition for higher office, having thrown out feelers in 1981 for the Illinois secretary of state nomination. Black leaders in late 1983 made overtures to him, hoping for a black-Polish alliance which would secure the clerk of the circuit court position. He declined the offer.

One opportunity he may not refuse is a congressional vacancy. Congressman Daniel Rostenkowski has hinted that he may retire in the near future. If so, Lechowicz should be considered as one of the ambitious Northwest Side politicians in the running to succeed the longtime congressman. Even if he loses that bid, he appears comfortable at home. Lechowicz was unopposed for committeeman in 1984, and no strong upcoming challenge is likely.

REDISTRICTING: The neighboring 37th Ward was one of those mandated to become a black "super-majority" ward under the terms of the 1986 ward remap. As a result, some of the ward's predominantly white precincts had to be shifted elsewhere. The logical dumping ground was the 30th Ward.

The 30th got fourteen precincts (mainly between North Avenue and the Milwaukee Railroad tracks) from the 37th Ward. Two northwest precincts were gained from the 38th, one from the 36th Ward, and one southeast precinct from the 31st Ward.

In return, the 30th lost fourteen northeast precincts to the 35th Ward.

MAYORAL: The 30th Ward, with only a handful of blacks, gave Harold Washington 2 percent of the vote in the 1983 Democratic primary. Only five wards in the city gave him a lower total. Jane Byrne and Richard Daley roughly split the ward, with Byrne getting 45 percent of the vote and Daley, 38 percent.

Washington, as the Democratic nominee in a ward where party affiliation still holds meaning, got some of that lost primary vote back in the general election. He won 13 percent of the vote, compared with 87 percent for Republican Bernard Epton.

The mayor gained in the 1987 primary, due mainly to support from southern Puerto Rican precincts. Jane Byrne took the rest of the ward and 75 percent of the vote.

Washington showed only slight gains in the general election, again showing strength in the Hispanic areas. Edward Vrdolyak won 68 percent of the vote, Don Haider taking 5 percent.

CENSUS DATA: Population (1980): 60,108. 78.56 percent white, .30 percent black, 17.91 percent Hispanic, 3.23 percent Asian and other. Voting age population: 83.02 percent white, .29 percent black, 14.19 percent Hispanic, 2.50 percent Asian and other.

CENSUS TRACTS: See ward map.

COMMUNITY NEWSPAPERS:
Belmont/Central Leader, 6008 W. Belmont (283–7900)
Chicago Post, 2810 W. Fullerton (772–3300)

Chicago's Northwest Side Press, 4941 N. Milwaukee (286–6100)
Cragin Leader, 6008 W. Belmont (283–7900)
Free Press, 2608 N. California (342–5737)
Northwest Extra, 3918 W. North Ave. (252–3534)
Northwest Leader, 6008 W. Belmont (283–7900)
Northwest Times, 4600 N. Harlem, Harwood Heights (867–7700)

ALDERMAN: George J. Hagopian. Elected 1975. Born November 1, 1920. Career: Wright Junior College; U.S. Air Force; court clerk; assistant commissioner, Department of Streets and Sanitation, 1961–73; assistant director, Illinois Housing Development Authority, 1973–75.

Committees: Veterans Affairs (chairman); Local Transportation (vice-chairman); Aviation; Budget and Government Operations; Historical Landmark Preservation; Health; Police, Fire, and Municipal Institutions.

City hall telephone: 744–6851, 744–6842.
Ward office: 4908 W. Cicero (637–8700).
1987 election:

George J. Hagopian	11,541	(62%)
Burt Sillins	7,140	(38%)

DEMOCRATIC COMMITTEEMAN: Thaddeus "Ted" Lechowicz. Elected 1972. Born December 20, 1938. Career: A.A., Wright Junior College; B.A., North Park College; U.S. Army, 1960; Illinois House of Representatives, 1969–83; Illinois Senate, 1983– .

Ward office: 4908 W. Cicero (637–8700).
1984 election:
Thaddeus "Ted" Lechowicz, unopposed.

MAYORAL ELECTIONS:

1983 Democratic primary:

Jane Byrne	12,571	(58%)
Richard Daley	8,250	(40%)
Harold Washington	516	(2%)

1983 general:

Bernard Epton	20,853	(87%)
Harold Washington	3,034	(13%)

1987 Democratic primary:

Jane Byrne	15,018	(75%)
Harold Washington	4,851	(24%)

1987 general:

Edward Vrdolyak	13,319	(68%)
Harold Washington	5,160	(26%)
Donald Haider	1,011	(5%)

31 st Ward

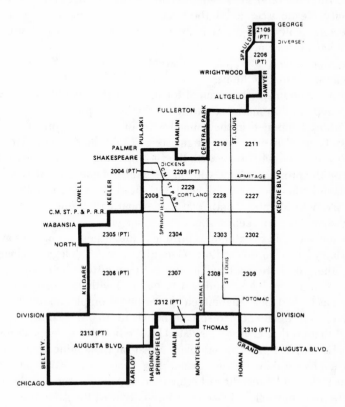

"DALEY WANTED POWER, and I wanted to make money, and we both succeeded." These were the words of Thomas Earl Keane, 31st Ward alderman and city council Finance Committee chairman during the Daley years.

Keane got money, but he also had power. Through his absolute control over the city purse strings, he ruled not only the Finance Committee but all others as well. Foes described him as an iron-fisted czar, both of the council and his ward organization.

Thomas E. Keane inherited what his sister once described as "the family business." The dynasty had controlled the Humboldt Park area's ward since the turn of the century. Keane's maternal grandfather and an uncle served as alderman. His father, Thomas P. Keane, served from 1931 until his death in 1945.

The younger Keane, then a state senator, took over upon his father's death and immediately became one of the city's more influential politicians. He and fellow committeemen Jacob Arvey (24th), Al Horan (29th), Joseph Gill (46th), and William Dawson (2nd) combined to oust Martin Kennelly and slate Richard Daley as mayor in 1955.

These kingmakers might have thought they were going to control the new mayor. They were mistaken; Daley refused to allow himself to be ruled by anyone. But he soon made Keane his council floor leader and number two man in the city. Keane ascended to the Finance chairmanship when P. J. Cullerton was elected county assessor in 1958, and became the most powerful alderman the city has ever seen.

Former *Daily News* reporter Jay McMullen described Keane as an example of how far one can go if he has "a little tin in the pot to start with; an I.Q. that goes into the stratosphere; a talent for mischief that would excite the envy of Boss Tweed; and no more scruples than the law requires."

Nothing happened in the council without Keane's approval. "Keane runs the City Council like a circus ringmaster," McMullen wrote. "He designates who is to speak on what issue with the flick of a finger." Keane gave Fred Roti signals on the proper machine vote on the issue at hand, the 1st Ward alderman obeyed, and other aldermen followed Roti's lead. He also controlled who would not speak. Vito Marzullo, 25th Ward alderman with a questionable command of English syntax, was kept out of debates for years.

Keane was able to extend his influence into other committees as well. His crony Harry Sain chaired the Rules Committee, which delegated chairmanships to the other committees. Thus no one got committee chairmanships (and resultant extra money, clout, and patronage jobs) without Keane's approval.

Just as he had had "guaranteed" government employment when his father was alive, Tom Keane helped spread the wealth to other family members. He saw to it that brother George was slated for the board of tax appeals for eighteen years. His son, Thomas P., was given a seat on the zoning board of appeals.

When foes tried to debate Keane, they always lost. "Keane knows the City Council Rules and Procedures better than anyone for the simple reason that he wrote them himself," McMullen commented. At the same time, Keane was not entirely disrespectful of the independents and Republicans who formed the minority bloc. When an antiadministration alderman introduced a bill Mayor Daley liked, that bill would be killed. Keane would make minor alterations in the bill, reintroduce it as an administration measure, and it would pass.

Busy though he was as a city council leader, legislation was the tip of Keane's iceberg. He operated lucrative insurance and real estate businesses, which were aided by his political muscle. "You can't view him principally as an alderman. He's in the business of making a living off politics," charged archfoe Leon Despres, the 5th Ward alderman.

Some of Keane's extracurricular dealings caught up with him in the 1970s. He used his influence to obtain insider information on 1,878 parcels of land available through a scavenger sale, which he purchased and resold to other government agencies at enormous profits. He was convicted in 1974, a major triumph for then-U.S. Attorney James Thompson. The conviction resulted in his removal from office.

Even away from the city council, Keane exerted power. He slated his wife Adeline to replace him as alderman in 1975. She ran a nearly invisible campaign, but still won an easy victory. Mrs. Keane did not show "even the modest qualifications expected of a Chicago alderman," the *Tribune* editorialized. She once showed her misunderstanding of the ward's growing Latino community by saying that she supported the teaching of Latin in public schools.

Keane went to prison (a minimum security facility in Lexington, Ky.) in 1976. He still ran the ward from there, aided by Adeline and former ward secretary Edward Nedza, whom he picked to replace him as committeeman in 1976. Keane called the office (collect) after Monday night ward meetings and kept appraised of the political situation there.

Adeline Keane declined to seek reelection in 1979. Polish-American Chester Kuta, a probation officer and precinct captain, was picked to replace her. For the first time, the ward saw an election rather than a ratification, as Puerto Rican school principal Aracelis Figueroa put up a strong challenge.

Kuta, described as a "sluggish" alderman, fell victim to a power play involving Byrne and Keane. The newly elected mayor kept an eye toward the ward's growing Hispanic vote and engineered a city council change.

Chester Kuta surprised the city by resigning in late 1981. Minutes after the Kuta resignation, the city council received notice of Byrne's nomination for a replacement (even though the mayor was vacationing in Arizona at the time). That replacement was one Joseph Martinez, an attorney in Alderman Edward Burke's law firm, who also had ties to Keane's brother. "Call me Jose," the red-haired lawyer asked reporters, and perhaps some were able to do so without smirking.

The Martinez appointment enraged local activists, who claimed that he had no record of community involvement. They also noted that his home, while located within the boundaries of the current 31st Ward, was four blocks outside of the soon-to-be implemented remapped version of the ward. Two residents (represented by Aracelis's husband, attorney Raymond Figueroa) attempted to block the Martinez appointment for the latter reason without success.

Martinez irritated the 31st Ward Regular Democratic Organization as well. Nedza, by now independent of Keane (he won the 1980 committeeman election over 6'7", 300-pound John Kardzionak, a Keane bodyguard), did not mind a Hispanic as alderman—as long as it was *his* Hispanic. He earlier leaked word that he would get Kuta to resign and replace him with ward secretary Joseph Berrios. Keane outmaneuvered him.

Needless to say, Kuta landed on his feet—at least temporarily. Within days he found work as a deputy Streets and Sanitation commissioner at double his aldermanic salary. But since the post was not exempt by the Shakman antipatronage decree, Harold Washington wasted little time in firing him after the 1983 election.

Keane, a minister without portfolio for Byrne, made one other major contribution to her administration. He drew up the 1981 ward map, one that in 1982 was ruled by the court to discriminate against blacks and Hispanics. Even though the city's black population increased (and white population decreased) during the 1970s, the revised map did not show that black increase. Hispanics, although representing more than 10 percent of the population, were given only two wards. Keane asserted that he was under no obligation to maximize black or Hispanic voting strength.

In some respects, the map was a cartographic masterpiece for Keane, and he handled its presentation with the same smoothness he displayed as Finance chairman. Alderman Joseph Bertrand, 7th Ward foe of Byrne ally Edward Vrdolyak, was redistricted out of his ward by one block. Byrne herself was transferred from the 42nd into the 43rd Ward, to enable her to run for committeeman and thus gain a foothold in the Democratic Central Committee (this alteration was later repealed).

Had the aldermen seen the entire new ward map, they might have registered complaints and worked among themselves to make changes. But Keane gave each alderman a map only of his or her ward, assuring that the council members would have to appeal to a central authority in order to cut redrawing deals.

Keane "lost" Joseph Martinez in 1983. The alderman announced that he would not seek reelection and accepted a position with the city's cable commission. Nedza seized the opportunity to slate Miguel Santiago, a schoolteacher and precinct captain. Santiago won the 1983 election without difficulty.

Mere days after Harold Washington won the general election, Santiago called his first press conference. An ally of the newly elected mayor, he proclaimed, had threatened to set his feet on fire. Peter Earle, the West Town activist in question, responded thusly to the charges: "I simply asked him how he was going to vote, and he told me it was none of my business. I said, 'In that case, you need to know that we'll be watching you under a microscope. You are accountable. We will hold your feet to the fire.' " Those remarks are generally interpreted to mean that citizens' groups will watch Santiago's legislative actions and complain if he fails to vote according to their wishes, not that said groups will hogtie Santiago, hold him under an electron microscope, and give him a hotfoot.

As the only Hispanic alderman at that time, he might have been expected to be a leading anti-Washington spokesman. But Santiago never entirely escaped the ridicule stemming from that first press conference. His other major moment in the sun (in which he reacted during a debate on gang program funding by tossing a sheaf of papers into the air) likewise did little for his image as a community leader.

Santiago, one of the original members of the "Vrdolyak 29," tried to walk a tightrope between loyalty to the Vrdolyak block and pressures from the ward's dominant Puerto Rican community. He declared himself in favor of the ward remap (although not an active spokesman in its behalf). Even though supporting the remap, he opposed special elections in the newly designated black and Hispanic "super-majority" wards.

Despite this opposition, he won the 1986 special election. Unlike the 22nd, 25th, and 26th Wards, which all had well-known Hispanic Harold Washington allies preparing for a possible race months in advance, the 31st lacked such a candidate. Two last-minute challengers emerged: Benjamin Rosado, a Streets and Sanitation supervisor, and Migdalia Collazo, a community activist.

Washington forces all but wrote off this ward from the onset. The mayor gave Collazo a last-minute endorsement, too late to prove effective. Santiago won reelection with 55 percent of the vote to 29 percent for Collazo and 16 percent for Rosado.

Those three candidates headed for a rematch in the 1987 election, joined by four others: attorney Figueroa; Francisco DuPrey, an official with the Department of Human Services, who had been urged by some Washington allies to run in the special election but declined (his use of turquoise and shocking pink as campaign colors got him dubbed the "Miami Vice" candidate); Noel Cristia, a policeman; and Carnell Adams, a job counselor and the only black candidate.

The candidates represented various shades of the political spectrum. Collazo, the most liberal, tied herself to Washington. Figueroa ran as a civil rights candidate. DuPrey stressed his experience as an administrator. Adams went after the black vote (opponents accused him of being planted by party regulars to lure black votes from more pro-Washington candidates). Rosado appealed to the many Hispanic Pentecostal churches in the ward. Cristia likewise went after the conservative vote.

The mayor declined to make an endorsement, despite pressures from both DuPrey and Collazo forces. Likewise, two other influential figures, 26th Ward alderman Luis Gutierrez and State Senator Miguel del Valle, kept out of the fray (although del Valle endorsed longtime friend DuPrey in the final days after Collazo workers passed out literature that hinted Washington's endorsement). Both candidates' followers spent as much time attacking each other as incumbent Santiago. As a result, they split the diehard Washington vote and Figueroa faced Santiago in the runoff.

Even though Santiago finished first in the February election (with 40 percent), his runoff loss was a foregone conclusion. Although residual bitterness remained from February (and some Washington allies questioned Figueroa's dedication to the mayor), Santiago foes united to give Figueroa 53 percent of the runoff vote.

Lost in the shuffle of the 1986 aldermanic race was the special election for Democratic ward committeeman. Despite changing demographics, Nedza had been able to hold onto this position. He won 63 percent of the vote against youth worker Luis Velasquez in 1984 (a race where the challenger's police record became an issue). Nedza was successful in erasing all challengers from the ballot in 1986.

Nedza's luck ran out in 1987, when he was convicted on extortion charges involving a local flea market (former alderman Kuta pleaded guilty to the same charges). Nedza resigned as committeeman, and precinct captains voted Berrios (who in 1983 became the first Hispanic state representative) to replace him.

Faced with the likelihood of stiff opposition in a 1988 legislative race, Berrios instead accepted party slating for a board of (tax) appeals vacancy occurring from the November 1987 death of commissioner Harry Semrow. The Berrios choice was a logical one; he had served as an accountant for the board while also serving as state representative (such "double dipping" being a common prerogative among Illinois legislators). Former alderman Santiago replaced him on the legislative slate.

For once, independents fell behind one 31st Ward candidate—Figueroa— in the 1988 Democratic committeeman election. He ran against Berrios, a classic fight between the two factions which have split Chicago politics in recent years.

The 31st Ward includes the western Humboldt Park community, although not the park itself. Kedzie is the eastern boundary, including Palmer Square, Kedzie Boulevard (with the grandest houses in the ward), and Logan Square (the Illinois Centennial Monument, a fifty-foot column topped by an eagle, is here). Division Street forms a southern boundary, although the ward extends as far south as Chicago Avenue. The Belt Railway is as far west as it goes; the western boundary is an irregular stairstep extending north to George Street.

Germans and Scandinavians were among the first to settle in the inexpensive houses that were built west of the park, one block at a time (although the style of home varies from block to block, the homes within any given block are similar). Those first settlers emigrated years ago, but their influence may be seen by such institutions as Roeser's Bakery (German) at North and Kedzie, the oldest bakery in Chicago; ninety-plus-year-old Norwegian-American Hospital at Augusta and Francisco; and the red-brick Norwegian Lutheran Memorial Church at Logan Square, which still conducts services in that language.

Jews and Poles came after the original residents. The Jews have gone, although they left traces of their existence (the Logan Square Boys Club at Palmer and Sawyer is housed in a former synagogue). Some Poles remain, but fewer than in the areas directly north and east.

Today the southwest precincts (those south of Division Street) are predominantly black. Otherwise, the prevailing atmosphere is Latino. Puerto Ricans are the main ethnic group, although Cuban stores and restaurants near Logan Square show evidence of a group that is influential here far beyond its numbers.

Murals visible throughout the ward offer the best example of the local artistic heritage. One such mural, "Unity, a New Dream," at North and Springfield, briefly had the distinction of being the world's first holographic mural. Small holograms were designed as part of the mural but were stolen from it in a matter of days.

That action exemplifies the tough life here. Gang activity is at a higher level in the local police districts than in any other part of Chicago. The Hispanic dropout rate at local high schools has been estimated as high as 70 percent. Unemployment has been rampant, as plants such as Playskool (Augusta and Kolmar) and Schwinn (Lawndale and Cortland) have moved elsewhere without adequate replacement. Gangs, education, jobs—the problems besetting the 31st Ward are unlikely to be settled soon.

REDISTRICTING: As one of the seven wards scheduled for black or Hispanic "super-majority" in 1986, the 31st Ward underwent a major facelift. Humboldt Park and five surrounding precincts were moved to the 26th Ward. One southern precinct was transferred to the 27th Ward and four went to the 37th Ward. Two western precincts also went to the 27th Ward.

The 31st gained six northern precincts which had been part of the 33rd Ward and three others which previously belonged to the 35th. The latter addition gave the 31st a strange two-block wide "finger" which extended into the 33rd. This addition reportedly was made at the request of 33rd Ward alderman Richard Mell, so that he could avoid what he considered to be a particularly irritating constituent.

MAYORAL: Nedza-backed Jane Byrne carried the "old" 31st Ward with 53 percent of the vote, not a particularly strong showing for an incumbent with the support of the local ward organization. Richard Daley came in second, with 30 percent. Harold Washington trailed with 17 percent of the vote.

This heavily Puerto Rican ward (it was the only one in the city which numbered Hispanics as the majority of registered voters in 1983) kept traditional Hispanic ties to the Democratic party in the general election. Harold Washington won 61 percent of the vote here, despite covert support from Nedza's organization for Republican challenger Bernard Epton.

Byrne kept some of her power in the Nedza strongholds in the southwest part of the ward. Elsewhere, Washington dominated the polls in the 1987 Democratic primary with 56 percent of the vote.

That number skyrocketed in the general election, as many Hispanics who voted for the still-popular Byrne went to Democratic nominee Harold Washington in the general election. Washington polled 67 percent to 30 percent for Edward Vrdolyak and 3 percent for Donald Haider.

CENSUS DATA: Population (1980): 59,293. 32.02 percent white, 5.65 percent black, 59.48 percent Hispanic, 2.85 percent Asian and other. Voting age population: 39.91 white, 4.94 percent black, 52.21 percent Hispanic, 2.94 percent Asian and other.

CENSUS TRACTS: See ward map.

COMMUNITY NEWSPAPERS:
Chicago Post, 2810 W. Fullerton (772–3300)
El Dia, 2648 S. Kolin (277–7676) (Spanish)
El Imparcial, 3610 W. 26th St. (376–9888) (Spanish)
El Informador, 1821 S. Loomis (942–1295) (Spanish)
El Norte, 2714 W. 23rd Pl. (254–1623) (Spanish)
Free Press, 2608 N. California (342–5737)
Impacto, 3507 W. North Ave. (486–2547) (Spanish)
La Opinion, 2501 S. East St., Berwyn (795–1383) (Spanish)

La Raza, 53 W. Jackson (427–6100) (Spanish)
La Voz de Chicago, 8624 S. Houston (221–9416) (Spanish)
Northwest Extra, 3918 W. North Ave. (252–3534) (Spanish)

ALDERMAN: Raymond A. Figueroa. Elected 1987. Born July 10, 1947. Career: B.A., Roosevelt University, 1973; J.D., DePaul University, 1975; attorney, 1975– .
Committees: Education (vice-chairman); Beautification and Recreation; Buildings; Claims and Liabilities; Capital Development; Finance; Health; Local Transportation; Police, Fire, and Municipal Institutions; Traffic Control and Safety.
City hall telephone: 744–6102, 744–6123.
Ward office: 1234 N. Pulaski (342–1100).
1986 special election:

Miguel A. Santiago	4,479	(56%)
Migdalia Collazo	2,226	(28%)
Benjamin Rosado	1,302	(16%)

1987 election:

Miguel A. Santiago	5,157	(40%)	Benjamin Rosado	804	(6%)
Raymond A. Figueroa	2,764	(21%)	Esmagde Noel Cristia	516	(4%)
Migdalia Collazo	2,099	(16%)	Carnell Adams	223	(2%)
Francisco DuPrey	1,472	(11%)			

1987 runoff:

Raymond A. Figueroa	7,106	(53%)
Miguel A. Santiago	6,304	(47%)

DEMOCRATIC COMMITTEEMAN: Joseph Berrios. Appointed 1987. Born February 14, 1952. Career: B.A., University of Illinois; chief clerk, Cook County Board of Appeals; Illinois House of Representatives, 1983– .
Ward office: 1314 N. Pulaski (486–6488).
1984 election:

Edward Nedza	6,211	(64%)
Luis Velasquez	3,579	(36%)

1986 special election:
Edward Nedza, unopposed.

MAYORAL ELECTIONS:

1983 Democratic primary:

Jane Byrne	8,357	(53%)
Richard Daley	4,791	(30%)
Harold Washington	2,709	(17%)

1987 Democratic primary:

Harold Washington	7,899	(56%)
Jane Byrne	6,177	(44%)

1983 general:

Harold Washington	9,857	(61%)
Bernard Epton	6,399	(39%)

1987 general:

Harold Washington	9,332	(67%)
Edward Vrdolyak	4,123	(30%)
Donald Haider	479	(3%)

32nd Ward

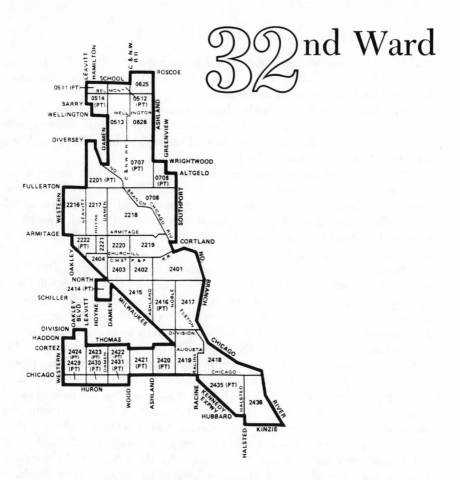

A 1986 COURT-ORDERED ward remap mandated the transfer of Hispanic pre-cincts to create a Hispanic "super-majority" 26th Ward. Those precincts had to come from somewhere; many came from the neighboring 32nd Ward. As a result the "new" 32nd is the most strangely shaped ward in the city.

At one time this was an unquestionably Polish ward. Poles still abound. But the 32nd Ward now also is the home to Ukrainians, yuppies, artists, punks, Latinos, street people, blacks, Italians—and sometimes combinations of the above.

The southeasternmost point of the 32nd is a stone's throw from the Loop; the northernmost spot is a stone's throw from the former Riverview amusement park. In addition, a southwest arm branches off all the way to Western Avenue.

That latter section is known as Ukrainian Village, one of Chicago's ethnic delights. This is a self-contained neighborhood, so strongly ethnic that children come here from the suburbs to attend Ukrainian school on Saturdays. Ukrainian Village teems with restaurants, real estate agencies, insurance companies, bak-eries, a credit union, funeral homes, bookstores, a museum—and churches.

Louis Sullivan-designed Holy Trinity Orthodox Cathedral, built wih funds donated by Czar Nicholas II, is one such place of worship. The cathedral at

Haddon and Leavitt attained landmark status in 1979. Nearby is St. Vladimir's Ukrainian Orthodox Cathedral at Oakley and Cortez, the first religious structure built by Ukrainians in the neighborhood.

Two huge churches on Oakley bear witness to a major religious schism. St. Nicholas Ukrainian Catholic Cathedral, a neo-Byzantine structure with many green copper domes, was the first of these churches. This church was built by people who followed the Julian calendar.

The majority of the parishioners voted in 1968 to change to the Gregorian calendar. As a result, more than 1,000 families split from St. Nicholas and formed their own congregation which would continue following the Julian calendar. Their place of worship is SS. Volodymyr and Olha Church, two blocks away on Rice Street, a golden-domed church with an elaborate front mural of the Ukrainian patron saints.

Polish influence remains strong throughout the ward. It contains the intersection of Milwaukee, Division, and Ashland, once known as "The Polish Times Square." A sign reveals the former office of the Polish *Daily Zgoda*, the largest Polish newspaper in the city (since moved further northwest). Not far away (at Augusta and Milwaukee) is the Polish Roman Catholic Union, one of the largest fraternal insurance companies in the nation. The building also houses the Polish National Museum, the largest museum in America devoted to an ethnic group.

Perhaps the typical Polish neighborhood here is Bucktown, bounded by Armitage, Fullerton, Western, and Damen. It is a cozy neighborhood of small, neat homes, corner drugstores, taverns, and churches. Poles coexist with yuppies who have moved westward to escape the higher rents of Lincoln Park.

Polish churches dot the ward: St. Helen's at Augusta and Oakley; St. Boniface at Noble and Chestnut; St. Stanislaus Kostka at Noble and Evergreen, a parish that was endangered when hundreds of parishioners were displaced by the construction of the Kennedy Expressway. The most frequently viewed church is St. Mary of the Angels (Cortland and Wood), an elaborate church with a huge green dome, seen by thousands of commuters as they pass by on the Kennedy or the Chicago and North Western Railway.

Signs of other nationalities can be seen. Luxor Baths at North and Damen advertises Russian and Turkish baths. Como Inn, an Italian restaurant at Ohio and Milwaukee, has long been a favorite for political fundraisers. El Criollo, at Fullerton and Ashland, is a restaurant and Monday night gathering place for Chicago's Argentine population.

The 32nd also includes three of Chicago's major diagonal streets: the north side of Milwaukee Avenue, a busy hodgepodge of Polish and Puerto Rican stores; Elston, an industrial street that is the only one in Chicago that both begins and ends at the same street (Milwaukee Avenue); and Clybourn, another industrial street interrupted by fast food outlets or corner taverns. Just off Clybourn is Terra Cotta Place, a one-block long street and the only one in Chicago named after a type of clay.

Art is in evidence. The 32nd Ward includes the Randolph Street Gallery

(Milwaukee and Chicago), home of avant garde exhibits; Facets Multimedia Theatre at Fullerton and Greenview, which shows what in other years might have been called "art" movies; the Chicago Gallery and Say Goodbye Gallery, murals of animals along the Chicago and North Western viaduct; and a four-block long stretch of Belmont between Damen and Western, site of many antique stores.

The 32nd Ward even houses some of the more unusual bars in Chicago. Many display their ethnicity by *cerveza fria* or *zimne piwo* signs. Others cater to yuppies. Then again, there are spots such as O'Sullivan's (Halsted and Milwaukee), a would-be dwarf-tossing site (proposed dwarf tosses were canceled after public protests, but the bar had marked distances on its outside wall in preparation for the event, including the reputed world record toss); Music's Corner (Southport and Webster), a cozy country and western bar; and the Artful Dodger (Hermitage and Wabansia), a punk bar in which local residents may sign up to be a disc jockey for an evening.

Two of the largest companies in the city are located here: the *Chicago Tribune* Freedom Center printing plant at Halsted and Chicago, where a lonely band of strikers have picketed the giant newspaper since 1985, and the Montgomery Ward headquarters across the street. But the company that has caused the most controversy here in recent years is Stewart-Warner at Diversey and Wolcott, which has threatened to leave the area despite the efforts of community groups.

Not far away from Stewart-Warner was the site of the A. L. Luetgert Sausage works, located at Diversey and Hermitage. This was the scene of one of Chicago's most sensational murders. Adolph Luetgert, the owner, killed his wife here in 1897 by throwing her into a pit of potash and arsenic. This "boiling cauldron murder case" made nationwide headlines. Children sang "Old man Luetgert made sausage out of his wife." And Chicago sausage sales took a preciptous decline.

One family name has dominated 32nd Ward politics for two generations. Joseph Rostenkowski ran the ward both as alderman and committeeman from the 1930s until the 1950s. His son Daniel has been committeeman since the 1960s. In one respect, the dominance is no surprise, since the family has been part of the neighborhood for decades (Dan Rostenkowski claims his grandmother watched the Chicago Fire from the St. Stanislaus Kostka church tower).

Without a doubt, this unassuming working-class area houses the most powerful ward committeeman in the United States. Daniel Rostenkowski, congressman since 1958 and now chairman of the House Ways and Means Committee, takes his committeeman role seriously. He keeps a vow which he reportedly made to Mayor Richard J. Daley and returns to his district nearly every weekend. His family maintains no Washington residence.

The 1987 mayoral race passed, as have all since Daley's death, without "Rosty" as a contestant. He was urged to seek the office during the Washington

THERIS "TERRY" GABINSKI

term. Would-be allies (and Harold Washington foes) viewed him as the candidate who could best unite business, labor, and Democratic regulars—the old Daley coalition.

"I've always said I'd like to be mayor. The question is whether I'd want to run first," Rostenkowski once said. That statement may explain his reluctance to seek the highest Chicago office. Rostenkowski has never attracted any more than token opposition during his congressional elections. Many question whether he has the stomach for what would undoubtedly be a fierce mayoral election campaign.

One reason he may have skipped the 1987 election race was his aspiration for the House speakership. He lost that struggle in 1986 to Texan Jim Wright. Although Rostenkowski appears to be next in line for the speakership, that prize most likely is years away.

Rostenkowski publicly contemplated retiring from Congress in 1986, claiming that he could make more money in the private sector. A year later he announced he would not seek reelection as committeeman. The heir apparent to the latter post is local alderman Theris "Terry" Gabinski.

A former high school chemistry teacher, Gabinski replaced Robert Sulski as alderman in 1969 when the latter became a circuit court judge. For many years, Gabinski liked to be known as "the stop sign alderman," for the many such signs he installed in his ward.

The 32nd Ward Regular Democratic Organization received little or no opposition until 1984. Luis Gutierrez, a former social worker, challenged Rostenkowski for committeeman that year and waged a spirited campaign. The Gutierrez candidacy put Washington in a bind. On one hand, Gutierrez was an unabashed Washington ally and emerging leader of the city's growing Hispanic community. On the other hand, the mayor had no desire to rile Rostenkowski, a force in Congress who had not been a major Washington critic. The mayor finally gave Gutierrez a lukewarm endorsement during the last few days of the campaign. Rostenkowski won that election with 77 percent of the vote. Yet Gutierrez used the lessons he learned from that election, plus the worker base he attained, in his successful 1986 aldermanic election in the 26th Ward.

Likewise, Gabinski faced a Hispanic challenge in 1987: Emma Lozano Rico, community activist and sister of slain Little Village labor leader Rudy Lozano. Washington made no question of his support of Lozano, although not campaigning strongly in her behalf. None but the most devoted Lozano supporters expected a close race. And the result showed a Gabinski landslide—75 percent, although the challenger did well in southern black and Hispanic precincts. Gabinski received a surprising committeeman challenger in 1988—Walter "Slim" Coleman, an unsalaried yet influential Harold Washington advisor who lost his clout when the mayor died.

Gabinski paid the price for Rostenkowski's endorsement of Washington foe Tom Hynes. After council reorganization, he lost the chairmanship of the influential Zoning Committee. He was the senior alderman among those without either a committee chairmanship or vice-chairmanship. But the council shakeup resulting from Washington's death left a committee chairmanship opening. Gabinski now chairs the committee on Streets and Alleys—not as powerful as Zoning but better than nothing.

The Gutierrez and Lozano candidacies show the ultimate path of this ward. Even after the removal of Hispanics to the 26th Ward, the 32nd still has a population 45 percent Hispanic (and a voting age population 37 percent Hispanic). Those percentages, most likely, will grow in the future. A city council remap following the 1990 census could convert this into a Hispanic-majority ward.

REDISTRICTING: To understand the remapped status of the 32nd Ward, one needs the eye of a draftsman, the calculating skills of a demographer, and the mind of a politician.

The 32nd lost all or parts of seven northwest precincts to the 33rd Ward, part of one southern precinct to the 1st Ward, and all or parts of eight southwest precincts to the 26th Ward. It received sixteen precincts in the southern part of the ward from the 26th Ward.

One precinct retained was the 8th, near Wicker Park, although barely contiguous to the rest of the ward. This precinct stayed because it contains a senior citizens' housing project (which brings in strong totals for party regulars at election time).

MAYORAL: Daniel Rostenkowski, a Daley family supporter since the late mayor's time, endorsed Richard M. Daley for mayor in 1983. That endorsement helped the state's attorney carry the ward in the Democratic primary, but not by much. Daley won 46 percent of the vote. Jane Byrne took 39 percent (carrying the Hispanic precincts). Harold Washington finished third with 8 percent of the vote.

Once again, the Democratic leanings of the voters showed themselves in the general election. Washington scored 44 percent of the vote (including large pluralities in the Hispanic precincts) to 56 percent for Bernard Epton, who was covertly supported by 32nd Ward precinct captains.

Jane Byrne, backed by Rostenkowski's organization, swept the 32nd Ward with nearly 70 percent of the vote in the 1987 Democratic primary. Harold Washington's strength lay in the southern black and Hispanic precincts.

Washington's main general election foe, Vrdolyak, carried the ward in the general election, although not nearly as well (62 percent) as Byrne. Washington gained 3 percentage points, and Donald Haider won 4 percent of the vote.

CENSUS DATA: Population (1980): 61,459. 48.48 percent white, 5.23 percent black, 44.74 percent Hispanic, 1.55 percent Asian and other. Voting age population: 54.64 percent white, 5.03 percent black, 36.59 percent Hispanic, 1.74 percent Asian and other.

CENSUS TRACTS: See ward map.

COMMUNITY NEWSPAPERS:
  El Dia, 2648 S. Kolin (277–7676) (Spanish)
  El Imparcial, 3610 W. 26th St. (376–9888) (Spanish)
  El Informador, 1821 S. Loomis (942–1295) (Spanish)
  El Norte, 2714 W. 23rd Pl. (254–1623) (Spanish)
  Free Press, 2608 N. California (342–5737)
  Impacto, 3507 W. North Ave. (486–2547) (Spanish)
  La Opinion, 2501 S. East Ave., Berwyn (795–1383) (Spanish)
  La Raza, 53 W. Jackson (427–6100) (Spanish)
  La Voz de Chicago, 8624 S. Houston (221–9416) (Spanish)
  Lincoln/Belmont Booster, 1647 W. Belmont (281–7500)
  Northwest Herald, 2711 W. Cermak (247–8500)
  West Town Extra, 3918 W. North Ave. (252–3534) (Spanish)

ALDERMAN: Theris "Terry" M. Gabinski. Elected 1969. Born November 30, 1938. Career: B.A., M.A., Northern Illinois University; high school teacher,

1962–64; coordinator, Kettering Foundation, 1964–66; special education instructor, 1966–68; aide, U.S. Rep. Daniel Rostenkowski, 1968–71.

Committees: Streets and Alleys (chairman); Beautification and Recreation; Buildings; Finance; Zoning.

City hall telephone: 744–6567, 744–6574.

Ward office: 2150 N. Damen (227–1100).

1987 election:

Theris M. Gabinski	11,437	(75%)
Emma Lozano Rico	3,775	(25%)

DEMOCRATIC COMMITTEEMAN: Daniel Rostenkowski. Elected 1964. Born January 2, 1928. Career: Loyola University, 1948–51; U.S. Army; Illinois House of Representatives, 1953–55; Illinois Senate, 1955–59; U.S. House of Representatives, 1959–.

Ward office: 2150 N. Damen (227–1100).

1984 election:

Daniel Rostenkowski	9,094	(77%)
Luis V. Gutierrez	2,661	(23%)

MAYORAL ELECTIONS:

1983 Democratic primary:

Richard Daley	8,452	(46%)
Jane Byrne	7,303	(39%)
Harold Washington	2,698	(15%)

1987 Democratic primary:

Jane Byrne	11,164	(69%)
Harold Washington	4,831	(31%)

1983 general:

Bernard Epton	10,526	(56%)
Harold Washington	8,268	(44%)

1987 general:

Edward Vrdolyak	9,067	(63%)
Harold Washington	4,832	(33%)
Donald Haider	605	(4%)

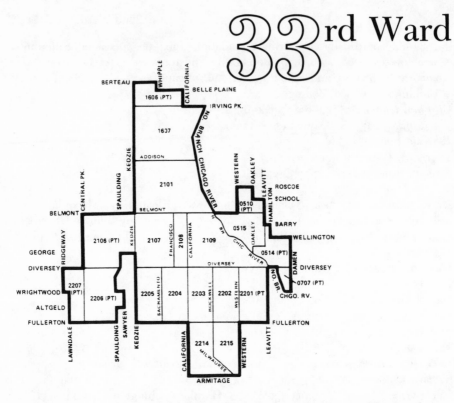

CHICAGO IS A DREAM TOWN for real estate speculators. Neighborhoods rise and fall in value, seemingly on a whim. Some neighborhoods may show property appreciation and depreciation simultaneously. One neighborhood in such a state of flux is the Near Northwest Side's Logan Square.

Young affluent professionals have grabbed up the Victorian houses along Logan Boulevard, making this area perhaps the "hottest" real estate in the city outside the Lakefront. But a block or two away from the boulevard in any direction lie frame houses that can hardly be classified as distinguished. These are inhabited by blue-collar workers often in fear of losing their manufacturing jobs, many of which have already fled the city for the suburbs or the Sun Belt.

If yuppies live in the Logan Square area, street gangs are not far away. A graphic example of the conflict of cultures occurred in the summer of 1986. When the Kennedy Expressway was built in the late 1950s, a tunnel was constructed as a shortcut for parishioners at the boulevard's St. John Berchmans Church. Eventually the tunnel became a gang haven, and residents fought (successfully) to have the tunnel sealed.

The Logan Boulevard doctors and lawyers are a part of the 33rd Ward. So are the neighboring Poles and Hispanics. The 33rd is an irregularly shaped ward, reaching as far north as Berteau, as far south as Armitage, east to Damen (including the Lathrop Homes Chicago Housing Authority project, the only significant black concentration in the ward), and west as far as Ridgeway.

Many Hispanic ethnic groups are in evidence, be they Colombian (a restaurant at Sacramento and Diversey), Ecuadorian (a restaurant at Richmond and Diversey), Cuban (many small grocery stores and restaurants throughout the ward), or Puerto Rican. The ward also contains Quenchers, a bar at Western and Fullerton that serves as a gathering place for Puerto Rican yuppies.

White ethnics, however, are the prevailing group in this ward. North of the Illinois Centennial statue at Logan Square, Milwaukee Avenue becomes decidedly Polish, a busy commercial strip of colorful stores and street signs depicting Polish provinces. A cocktail lounge at Wellington and Elston bears an appropriate name—Europe at Night.

Other ward attractions are not "ethnic." The northern end of the 33rd Ward contains California Park, an extension of nearby Horner Park. This is the site of the McFetridge Sports Center, the only indoor sports arena and ice skating rink in the Chicago Park District. Gordon Technical High School, a football powerhouse, is located nearby, at California and Addison.

The arts flourish here, albeit in unusual forms. This ward houses both the Animart Puppet Theatre (Byron and Kedzie) and the Chicago School of Violin Making (Elston and Troy).

Ghosts of past enterprises haunt this ward. A sign on a bar at Central Park and Wolfram boasts of Encore beer on tap, although Encore was discontinued long ago. A factory on Diversey near Rockwell once housed the Bally Manufacturing Company, the world's largest supplier of pinball games during the Daley years (when, ironically, pinball machines were outlawed in Chicago).

One manufacturer very much alive is the R. F. Mell Spring and Manufacturing Company at California and Roscoe. Not far away, at Albany and School, is the Richard F. Mell Social Athletic Club. These are enterprises, needless to say, of Richard F. Mell, the ward's alderman and Democratic committeeman.

A bizarre set of circumstances paved the way for Mell's entry into the political picture. The opportunity began in 1970. Rapid population growth on the Far South Side necessitated creation of a new ward there. As a result, the old 34th Ward (which had been located on the Northwest Side) was merged into the 33rd.

Mayor Richard J. Daley engineered a political compromise between the two wards. Elderly John Brandt, the longtime ward committeeman, was allowed to continue in that position. Rex Sande, the 34th Ward alderman (and last Norwegian-born alderman, by the way) was slated for alderman over the incumbent, Brandt's nephew Robert.

Not surprisingly, it was a compromise that satisfied neither party. Brandt won reelection as committeeman in 1972. One of his challengers was young businessman Mell, who as a precinct captain once carried a precinct for Brandt 408 to 5.

Brandt dumped Sande in 1975, instead slating ward secretary Joseph Gavin. Mell, with Sande's backing, entered the race. He attacked Gavin as "an errand boy who mows John Brandt's lawn" and won the election. He bumped Brandt as committeeman a year later.

Mell took a moribund ward organization and consolidated it into a Chicago power. He has worked closely with State Representative Alfred Ronan (D-12), a young but patronage-rich legislator, to form one of the few ward organizations still capable of a healthy, unified turnout. Twelve wards gave Jane Byrne more votes in the 1983 Democratic primary (because of the relatively small number of eligible voters in his ward). But none gave her a better percentage than the 61 percent amassed in the 33rd.

When Harold Washington won the 1983 election, Mell immediately emerged as one of the leaders of the anti-Washington bloc. At times his posturings were comical, as when he vowed to go to jail rather than vote for a (Washington-backed) school bond issue.

One offhand remark backfired on him. Mell and the "Vrdolyak 29" worked in 1985 to block a general obligation bond issue for street repairs because of fears that Washington would use the public works program in his 1987 reelection campaign. He told a reporter, "I will sacrifice a vote that probably won't be popular in my community for the good of the (anti-Washington) coalition."

He met with an energetic challenger in 1987. Rev. Donald Benedict was a retired minister, former director of the Community Renewal Society, and chairman of a committee to develop a city ethics ordinance—in short, a classic "good government" candidate. He quickly received the endorsement of Mayor Washington, the Independent Voters of Illinois-Independent Precinct Organization, and other progressive groups.

Benedict leveled sharp attacks at the incumbent, citing his anti-Washington voting record. He gave a press conference on Point Street, at the extreme southern end of the ward, to show how Mell neglected that part of the ward in favor of the northern sector. Benedict claimed that Mell used the general obligation bond money to pave streets in front of his house, his spring manufacturing company, the social athletic club, and the homes of two of his top assistants.

Yet Benedict's campaign never quite caught on in the ward. It lacked the early punch needed to put the incumbent on the defensive. The alderman tied one Lathrop Homes precinct and won all others, gaining 77 percent of the vote. Mell was able to concentrate his energies on the Jane Byrne campaign and think about the city council leadership (perhaps even party chairmanship) that might be his if Byrne was reelected.

A bigger prize appeared within Mell's grasp in late 1987. After Mayor Harold Washington's death, Mell wasted little time in declaring that he was the front runner to succeed the late mayor, claiming twenty aldermen's votes. He had support from white ethnics but needed votes from blacks committed to 6th Ward alderman Eugene Sawyer. Both tried to talk each other out of the race. Mell finally yielded, conceding that a black mayor would be more acceptable to white aldermen under the circumstances than vice versa.

Mell may have won the 33rd Ward battle for Jane Byrne, but another battle he fought put his name in the nation's newspapers. Among his enterprises

RICHARD MELL

is a community newspaper, the *Chicago Post*. When a TV show starring Mary Tyler Moore depicted her working for a mythical *Chicago Post* scandal-sheet newspaper, Mell sued CBS—and won. The newspaper name was changed to the *Chicago Eagle* for the remainder of the short-lived series.

Richard F. Mell, in addition to his other duties, was also vice-mayor of Chicago. This position, created after Mayor Daley's death (and at the time considered reserved for Polish aldermen), ensures an orderly transfer of power. The vice-mayor takes authority as acting mayor until a special election can be held. In truth, the position is largely ceremonial, although it allows funds for a staff. Mell used part of that "bonus" money to supply bagels and sweet rolls for city council meetings.

REDISTRICTING: The remap proved a blessing of sorts for incumbent Richard Mell, as it enabled him to rid the ward of a potentially pesky Hispanic vote. The 33rd lost seventeen southern precincts altogether, nine to the 26th Ward, all or parts of six to the 31st, and all or parts of four to the 35th.

It gained nineteen precincts altogether. Nine were western precincts which had belonged to the 35th Ward. Three northern precincts came from the 35th and one from the 40th Ward. Six eastern precincts, including five east of the Chicago River, were added from the 32nd Ward.

MAYORAL: Mayor Jane Byrne, as mentioned, carried the 33rd Ward in the 1983 Democratic primary with 61 percent to 31 percent for Richard Daley and 8 percent for Washington. It was the only ward in which the incumbent gained at least 60 percent of the vote.

Almost the exact same number which voted for Byrne (62 percent) cast their general election ballots for Bernard Epton in the general election. The Byrne-Epton voters were not a one-to-one correspondence, however. An exit poll conducted by the Midwest Voter Registration and Education Project inferred that more than half the Hispanic voters in the 33rd Ward voted for Jane Byrne in the primary, yet Harold Washington (because of his Democratic party status) took most of the Hispanic vote there in the general election. Thus the Washington gains among Hispanics were offset by the Richard Daley primary vote which went to the Republican candidate.

Mell did his part for Byrne in 1987; she won 77 percent of the primary vote, strongest in the northern white precincts.

Although Mell never made a formal endorsement in the general election, Tom Hynes posters (presumably put up by 33rd Ward workers) peppered the ward before the general election. Such enthusiasm must not have been shared for chief Washington foe Ed Vrdolyak. He won the ward, but Washington gained eight percentage points over the primary (23 to 31), and Don Haider polled an above-average showing of 6 percent here.

CENSUS DATA: Population (1980): 58,693. 58.49 percent white, 1.77 percent black, 35.90 percent Hispanic, 3.84 percent Asian and other. Voting age population: 65.31 percent white, 1.38 percent black, 30.04 percent Hispanic, 3.23 percent Asian and other.

CENSUS TRACTS: See ward map.

COMMUNITY NEWSPAPERS:
Chicago Post, 2810 W. Fullerton (772–3300)
Community News, 2958 N. Milwaukee (235–6397)
El Dia, 2648 S. Kolin (277–7676) (Spanish)
El Imparcial, 3610 W. 26th St. (376–9888) (Spanish)
El Informador, 1821 S. Loomis (942–1295) (Spanish)
El Norte, 2714 W. 23rd Pl. (254–1623) (Spanish)
Free Press, 2608 N. California (342–5737)
Impacto, 3507 W. North Ave. (486–2547) (Spanish)
La Opinion, 2501 S. East Ave., Berwyn (795–1383) (Spanish)
La Raza, 53 W. Jackson (427–6100) (Spanish)
La Voz de Chicago, 8624 S. Houston (221–9416) (Spanish)
Lincoln/Belmont Booster, 1647 W. Belmont (281–7500)
Logan Square Extra, 3918 W. North Ave. (252–3534) (Spanish)
Logan Square Times, 4600 N. Harlem, Harwood Heights (867–7700)

ALDERMAN: Richard F. Mell. Elected 1975. Born May 5, 1939. Career: University of Michigan; owner, R. F. Mell Spring and Manufacturing Co., 1967– .

Committees: Municipal Code Revision (chairman); Economic Development; Finance; Housing; Ports, Wharves, and Bridges; Streets and Alleys.

City hall telephone: 744–6825, 744–6826.

Ward office: 2810 W. Fullerton (772–5424).

1987 election:

Richard F. Mell	13,796	(77%)
Donald L. Benedict	3,905	(22%)
V. Steven Vetter	303	(2%)

DEMOCRATIC COMMITTEEMAN: Richard F. Mell. Elected 1976.

1984 election:

Richard F. Mell, unopposed.

MAYORAL ELECTIONS:

1983 Democratic primary:

Jane Byrne	11,171	(61%)
Richard Daley	5,658	(31%)
Harold Washington	1,508	(8%)

1987 Democratic primary:

Jane Byrne	14,186	(77%)
Harold Washington	4,248	(23%)

1983 general:

Bernard Epton	11,298	(62%)
Harold Washington	6,909	(38%)

1987 general:

Edward Vrdolyak	9,837	(63%)
Harold Washington	4,737	(31%)
Donald Haider	1,003	(6%)

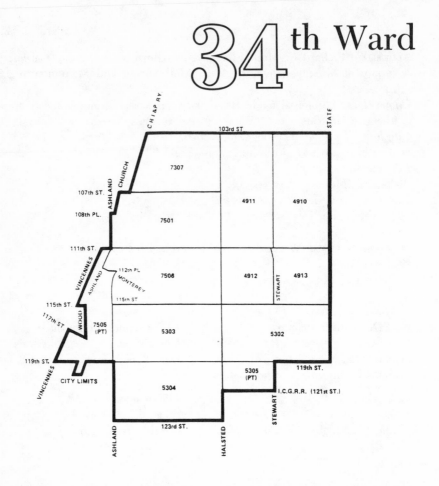

FOR THE MOST PART, the numbering system of Chicago's wards follows an orderly pattern. Beginning with the Loop's 1st Ward, the wards follow a clockwise pattern, taking the South, Southwest, West, Northwest, and North sides, ending up near the Lakefront.

If the city were to take an entirely orderly pattern, it would renumber every ward after every redistricting to provide a logical geographical sequence. But Chicagoans form emotional attachments to their ward numbers; people identify with the 11th Ward or the "Fighting 47th." With the possible exception of Catholic parishes, the wards are the easiest source of instant geographical identification for Chicago residents.

However, the one-person one-vote rule decrees changes, at times major ones, during redistrictings. Sometimes, rather than make changes that would cause major disruptions to many neighboring wards (and ward political organizations), it is easier to "create" a new ward. This creation is what happened in the Far South Side during the 1960s, and it explains what the 34th Ward, the biggest numbering anomaly in the city, is doing there.

The Far South Side was the last area of the city to experience major housing construction. Although people lived in the region since the 1860s, rapid growth took place only in the 1940s. This growth could be ignored until the 1960s, when federal law required that districts be apportioned only by population. Thus a "new" 34th ward came about, encompassing parts of the West Pullman, Washington Heights, Morgan Park, Beverly, and Roseland communities. It replaced a ward on the Northwest Side.

A black-majority ward when first formed, the 34th is almost entirely black now. Business areas exist (most notably, a shopping plaza at 115th and Halsted), but for the most part the ward is residential.

Frame houses exist, remnants from the time before this area was annexed to the city and thus exempt from its building code. But for the most part, these are brick houses, middle class, comfortable but not presuming. The rich live elsewhere—in integrated north Lakeshore or Hyde Park neighborhoods, or black neighborhoods such as Chatham. Yet the standard of living here is visibly above the average for black Chicago.

The blocks here have a distinct Middle America look about them. One block in a northeast corner precinct has a street lamp enclosed by a plastic globe in front of every house. Another (108th Street at Normal) has blue signs in every window warning "We call police." Judging by the immaculate state of the block, one has to believe that the signs are no idle threat.

Private schools, one sign of a middle-class neighborhood, can be seen here. The 34th has Mt. Calvary Christian Academy (111th and Throop) and Tabernacle Christian Academy (109th and Throop). St. Catherine of Genoa School (118th and Lowe) is located near a church of the same name which has a new Spanish-style addition.

The 34th Ward also contains Christ Universal Temple at 119th and Ashland, the largest church on the South Side. The church's minister, Rev. Johnnie Coleman, claimed she would not hold funerals in the church. But she made and exception—for Mayor Harold Washington.

Industry, both present and departed, has made its impact on the ward. A Libby's plant at the southwest corner of the ward is one of the major employers. But a long-abandoned factory may have had a greater influence on local residents. A Dutch Boy paint factory at 120th and Peoria, closed since 1976, changed hands several times after its closing. It burned in 1985, a fire of suspicious origin. The following year, tests revealed that more than 300 persons living near the plant suffered from varying degrees of lead poisoning, and workers had to remove what Environmental Protection Agency officials described as "very hazardous levels of lead and asbestos."

The first (and, until recently, only) alderman of this 34th Ward was Wilson Frost, at one time one of the more powerful council members and perhaps even the first black mayor.

Frost was elected from the 21st Ward in 1967, one of three blacks who tried to oust white Republican incumbent Samuel Yaksik (the other two challengers, Gus Savage and James Montgomery, also were to play important roles in Chicago politics in later years), and switched to the 34th in 1971 (he was named acting ward committeeman by Mayor Richard J. Daley in 1970 and was first elected committeeman in 1972). Even though one of the members of the "coffee rebellion," he rose rapidly to the position of president pro tempore of the council. In the later Daley years, because of the mayor's illness, Frost presided over the council often as not.

When Daley died in late 1976, Frost declared himself acting mayor on the grounds that the president pro tempore was the successor to the mayor. But when the "Mayor for a Minute" came to work the following day, he found the mayor's office padlocked. White aldermen, it seems, were of no mind to allow a black man to serve as mayor, no matter for how temporary a period.

Some of the more strident black community members urged Frost to fight to keep the temporary mayor status. But the pragmatic Frost knew how to count votes. Realizing that he lacked the necessary support to be named even temporary mayor, he settled for a compromise—chairman of the finance committee, while former chairman Michael Bilandic assumed the mayoral powers.

Frost worked with the Bilandic administration but played a role in his 1979 defeat. The snubbing of Frost played a role in the large black vote which turned out for Jane Byrne and proved pivotal in the 1979 Democratic primary. After Byrne was elected, Frost worked with Edward Vrdolyak and Edward Burke as the controllers of the city council.

His vote-counting powers atrophied four years later. After Harold Washington won the 1983 mayoral election, Frost declared that the pro-Washington forces had won council control. But when preliminary votes were counted, the Washington forces had only twenty-one persons to twenty-eight for the anti-administration faction headed by Vrdolyak. Frost was offered the chairmanship of any committee except finance if he sided with the Vrdolyak forces, but he declined.

Few black politicians have risen further in Chicago than Wilson Frost. Few have made less of an attempt to hide their ambitions. He courted Vrdolyak in late 1983 for county recorder of deeds slating, but failed to receive it. In 1985 he sought, and got, party endorsement for a seat on the board of tax appeals. Although some Northwest Side committeemen did not endorse him in the 1986 primary, he won it and the November election with ease.

Even though election to the board of appeals (generally considered a sinecure) was a boon to Frost, it caused problems to Harold Washington. The mayor's faction picked up four city council seats from the 1986 special elections, giving each side twenty-five votes (and Washington a tie-breaking vote). With Frost out of the council, Washington's forces would have only twenty-four votes, and the mayor would lose his tie-breaking power.

Washington and his council allies tried to avoid this dilemma by appointing a Frost successor, Annette Bitoy, an assistant superintendent of Streets and Sanitation. They counted on Frost, who had submitted a postdated letter of resignation, to cast a deciding vote if necessary.

Mayoral foes argued, not without logic, that the Bitoy appointment was illegal. It became a Catch-22 situation. If Frost were still an alderman, there was no vacancy and thus no need to cast a vote. But if his resignation was considered to take effect, he no longer would be eligible to cast a vote. The ploy created the expected amount of furor from opposition aldermen. Bernard Stone (50th) shouted at civic reformer and corporation counsel Judson Miner that this was "the day you lost your virginity."

Washington ally Martin Oberman (43rd) shouted back to Stone, "I think it's risky, particularly in your case, to start throwing charges of public officials prostituting themselves. Your remarks would be unbecoming in any legislative body excepting perhaps this one."

A Washington foe, Terry Gabinski, asked Oberman, "Where would you have been four years ago if another administration had tried to do the same thing? You'd be screaming your lungs off."

The council vote took place, with Frost abstaining until all others had made their decision. Since no opposition bloc alderman switched sides to support the mayor, Frost cast the deciding vote for Bitoy. The opposition bloc appealed the decision, but a court upheld the vote.

Procedural battles notwithstanding, the other council members still honored the colleague they affectionately called "Squints." Frost noted his departure by commenting on his happiness that it was not prefaced by "The Lord in his infinite mercy . . . ," the usual farewell for a deceased alderman.

Some political observers thought his departure might have come none too soon for the veteran alderman. Frost supported Jane Byrne until the final days of the 1983 campaign, switching sides only when a Washington victory appeared likely. His less-than-firm stance cost him a clear-cut win, and he beat Tommy Savage (son of Congressman Gus Savage) by only 2,381 votes in a runoff. Despite his tenure, Frost did not play a large role in the Washington administration.

With Frost retired and Bitoy declining to seek another term, the field became open in the 1987 aldermanic race. Frost promoted the candidacy of his ward superintendent, Lemuel Austin, Jr. Austin, however, did not tie himself too closely to his former mentor. "I'm running on the record of Lemuel Austin, not Wilson Frost," he commented.

Austin was joined by nine other pretenders: Tommy Briscoe, head of a postal workers union local and third place finisher in 1983; Gary Harper, a high school teacher; Henry Hudson, a contractor and onetime Frost precinct captain; Mercedes Mallette, a Department of Human Services director; Ronald Phelps, a Streets and Sanitation driver; Savage, director of minority vendors for the Metropolitan Sanitary District; Rochelle Simmons-Watson, a natural gas analyst for Amoco Corporation who took a drug test and challenged other candidates to do so also; Howard Snipe, a follower of political cult leader Lyndon LaRouche; and Ernie Terrell, former heavyweight boxing champion and leader of a band called "Ernie Terrell and the Heavyweights." Mayor Washington declined to make an endorsement in the election, but Mallette, who organized his election campaign in the ward in 1983, was believed to benefit most by association with him.

The campaign produced the usual amount of mayhem associated with an aldermanic election. Two men arrested for spray-painting Austin ad benches claimed they were working for Briscoe, although he denied the allegation. Terrell said that two of his campaign office's windows were shot out.

Austin finished first in the February election, but with only 33 percent of the vote. Terrell, runner-up with 16 percent, was his runoff opponent. Terrell tried to link Austin with Frost. But Austin received an important endorsement—that of Harold Washington—and won the runoff handily.

REDISTRICTING: No changes were made in the 34th Ward from the 1986 ward remap.

MAYORAL: Frost's all but total endorsement of Jane Byrne in the 1983 primary did her little good. The incumbent mayor gained 10 percent of the vote in the 34th Ward. Only three other wards, the black middle-class 8th and 21st wards, and Richard M. Daley's home 11th Ward, gave her a lower percentage. Daley received only 3 percent of the vote, a tie for his lowest citywide vote total.

As was the case in other all-black wards, Harold Washington crushed Republican Bernard Epton in the general election with 99 percent of the vote.

Washington continued the landslide pattern in 1987 with 99 percent totals in both primary and general elections.

CENSUS DATA: Population (1980): 60,082. 2.04 percent white, 96.86 percent black, 1.31 percent Hispanic, .25 percent Asian and other. Voting age population: 1.67 percent white, 96.84 percent black, 1.10 percent Hispanic, .39 Asian and other.

CENSUS TRACTS: See ward map.

COMMUNITY NEWSPAPERS:
  Chicago Independent Bulletin, 2037 W. 95th St. (783–1040)
  Chicago Metro, 2600 S. Michigan (842–5950)
  Southend Citizen, 412 E. 87th (487–7700)

ALDERMAN: Lemuel Austin, Jr. Elected 1987. Born 1945. Career: Richard J. Daley College; United States Post Office, 1965–69; Chicago Transit Authority, 1969–75; legislative aide to State Rep. Emil Jones, Jr., 1971–73; inspector, Cook County Sheriff's Department, 1973–75; administrative aide to Ald. Wilson Frost, 1975–77; legislative fiscal analyst to Chicago City Council, Committee on Finance, 1975–77; ward superintendent, 1981–87.
Committees: Traffic Control and Safety (vice-chairman); Beautification and Recreation; Budget and Government Operations; Historical Landmark Preservation; Energy, Environmental Protection, and Public Utilities; Finance;

Health; Human Rights and Consumer Protection; Minicipal Code Revision; Zoning.

City hall telephone: 744–6820, 744–6829.

Ward office: 507 W. 111th St. (928–6961).

1987 election:

Lemuel Austin, Jr.	8,182	(33%)	Henry L. Hudson	742	(3%)
Ernest Terrell	3,865	(16%)	Gary William Harper	447	(2%)
Tommy Savage	3,418	(14%)	Rochelle Simmons-		
Ronald Larry Phelps	2,766	(11%)	Watson	282	(1%)
Mercedes Mallette	2,635	(11%)	Howard Snipe	120	(0%)
Tommy Briscoe	2,181	(9%)			

1987 runoff:

Lemuel Austin, Jr.	14,649	(59%)
Ernest Terrell	10,030	(41%)

DEMOCRATIC COMMITTEEMAN: Wilson Frost. Appointed 1971, elected 1972. Born 1926. Career: B.A., DePaul University, 1951; J.D., Kent College of Law, 1958; attorney, 1958–67; alderman, 21st Ward, 1967–71; 34th Ward, 1971–86; Cook County Board of (Tax) Appeals, 1986– .

Ward office: 507 W. 111th St. (928–6961).

1984 election:

Wilson Frost, unopposed.

MAYORAL ELECTIONS:

1983 Democratic primary:

Harold Washington	22,601	(87%)
Jane Byrne	2,676	(10%)
Richard Daley	659	(3%)

1983 general:

Harold Washington	29,372	(99%)
Bernard Epton	336	(1%)

1987 Democratic primary:

Harold Washington	26,537	(99%)
Jane Byrne	328	(1%)

1987 general:

Harold Washington	27,407	(99%)
Edward Vrdolyak	231	(1%)
Donald Haider	94	(0%)

35th Ward

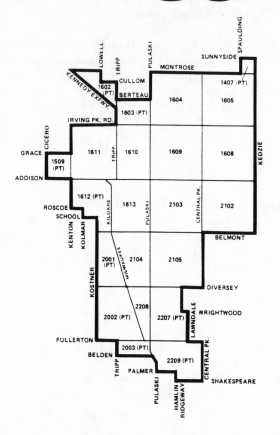

IN YEARS PAST, Polish immigrants to Chicago first settled in the Milwaukee-Division-Ashland area. As they became more affluent, they gradually moved northwest along the Milwaukee Avenue corridor.

That pattern of immigration has changed somewhat. Hispanics now predominate in the Milwaukee-Division-Ashland West Town area. When Poles enter the city now, they most likely settle in the Avondale neighborhood that makes up much of the 35th Ward.

This is the most visibly Polish ward in the city. The *Daily Zgoda* is the preferred newspaper for many over the *Sun-Times* or *Tribune*. Radio listeners may tune in WPNA, the first predominantly Polish radio station in the city. Wise is the local travel agent who keeps a "*Mowimy po polsku*" sign in his or her window.

"Welcome to Jackowo" announces a sign on Milwaukee Avenue, still the major Polish thoroughfare. Colorful signs indicate Polish provinces, delis and restaurants offer the food of those provinces. Homesick Poles may visit night-clubs such as Warsaw at Night (Newport and Pulaski).

The Polish heritage is visible in other ways. A plaque honors the 499 American Citizens of St. Hyacinth parish who fought in World War I. It is located in front of a huge church at George and Central park, featuring Corinthian columns with cherubs, the Holy Grail, and bas relief figures, one of the largest Polish parishes in the city. A vivid abstract mural at Belmont and Karlov honors the Polish Solidarity movement. Poles are honored, at least in name, at Kosciuszko Park (Avers and Diversey), although the park's field house has a definite German decor.

In addition to symbolic honors, Poles receive real assistance here as well. Institutions such as the Vistula Employment Assistance Bureau (Hamlin and Diversey) and the Copernicus Center for the Disabled and Elderly (Milwaukee and Devlin) offer services to members of Chicago's largest ethnic group.

The 35th Ward offers attractions to people other than homesick Poles. The House of German Songs at Montrose and Ridgeway attests to the onetime powerful influence of that ethnic group. The Sulo Restaurant at Irving Park and St. Louis advertises the unusual combination of Oriental, Hungarian, and American cooking.

Not all the residents are of European ancestry. Blacks make up less than .2 percent of the population, but Hispanics are a growing segment of the community; many have followed the Poles' path, outward from West Town. Asians, mainly Filipinos, are also scattered throughout the ward.

Most of the ward is residential, often homes with swings on the front porches. One area deserves particular note: the Villa Historic District, bordered roughly by Avondale, Addison, Pulaski, and Hamlin.

It also contains the occasional place of interest. One such spot is Bernie Hoffman's Animal Kingdom, the world's largest pet store, at Drake and Milwaukee.

A K-Mart store located at Addison and St. Louis is not notable except that the store, instead of a Greyhound bus depot, lies there. The bus company was prepared to move its downtown headquarters to this Northwest side locale, but the company altered its plans after community complaints.

Poles have never been as influential in Chicago politics as their numbers would seem to warrant. Nonetheless they have long held the office of city clerk, traditionally viewed by slatemakers as a "Polish" office. The holder of this office (rich in patronage, poor in power) for many years was John Marcin, also the 35th Ward Democratic committeeman.

Marcin originally was slated by Richard J. Daley for city treasurer, although Poles demanded his slating for clerk. He won the 1955 Democratic nomination for treasurer, while Alderman Benjamin Becker won the city clerk primary over Morris B. Sachs, a department store owner and host of the popular Morris B. Sachs Amateur Hour.

During the primary campaign it was disclosed that Becker had been involved in illegal zoning deals. Daley booted him from the ticket by playing a game of political musical chairs. Marcin, the city treasurer nominee, was "promoted" to city clerk candidate. Sachs, the recent loser for the city clerk nomination, was inserted onto the ticket for city treasurer. The revised team beat their Republican rivals.

Marcin served as city clerk without distinction for Daley's entire term. "I'm the most colorless man in city hall," he once said.

The ward's alderman served equally quietly during that time. Casimir "Casey" Laskowski, one of the last funeral director-aldermen, held office starting in 1955. He was notable as the only alderman elected in 1955 who supported Democratic primary candidate Benjamin Adamowski.

Laskowski made history of sorts in 1977. He was the first alderman to be given the largely honorary title of vice-mayor, which meant that he would preside during a vacancy in the office of mayor until a special election could be held. The 35th Ward alderman was given this position for both his seniority and his acknowledged lack of ambition for higher office.

Ward politics took a dramatic turn in 1979. Marcin learned that even though friendship may extend beyond the grave, clout does not. He was dumped from the party slate in favor of Walter Kozubowski, a Southwest Sider. Marcin then decided to run for alderman, taking the 35th Ward Regular Democratic Organization with him. The move caught Laskowski, who had never needed an organization before, off guard. "It seems like Mother and Father have left and you're on your own two feet," said the "All of a Sudden Independent."

Laskowski, however, had a potent weapon. He disclosed that Marcin lived not at a modest apartment on Diversey, but at a mansion in suburban Antioch—"a veritable Mt. Vernon," he called it. Marcin admitted that he owned the Lake County residence, but claimed that he used it as a farm and weekend retreat and barely visited it. Laskowski scoffed, "When you compare where he says he lives to where he lives, only an idiot would believe him."

The Marcin residence was well known within city hall circles for years. When asked why he did not disclose it beforehand, Laskowski responded, "because he's running against me now." Nonetheless, Marcin won the election.

Marcin, who supported Jane Byrne over Michael Bilandic, turned out to be one of her more rabid foes. The onetime ally charged the mayor with running a "government of chaos" and rapped Byrne's cabinet as "arrogant and incompetent." Byrne went out of her way to ignore Marcin's outbursts, either leaving the podium or conversing with others while he talked. She also made concrete attempts to eliminate the bothersome Marcin, including remapping him out of the ward. Her cartographic wizard, Thomas Keane, drew a new ward map which would have ensured his obliteration by placing him in the 33rd Ward with Richard Mell. But Mell objected that the proposed map removed his (Mell's) best precincts while moving half of Marcin's old territory into the 33rd. Keane's revised map allowed Marcin to remain in the 35th Ward.

The seventyish Marcin was considered vulnerable in his 1983 reelection campaign and attracted five challengers. One of them was a law student named

Joseph Kotlarz, a toddler when Marcin first became city clerk. Kotlarz, backed by well-known local independents Michael Holewinski and Judith Gregory, benefited from Marcin's tactical mistakes. The incumbent sent out two fliers mentioning Kotlarz by name, thus shooting up the young challenger's name recognition immediately.

Kotlarz finished runner-up to Marcin in the 1983 election with 24 percent of the vote to the incumbent's 34 percent. Four weeks later, Marcin made his most important mistake. Kotlarz workers put up eight ad benches throughout the ward. The following day two were gone.

Afterward, Kotlarz workers were assigned to guard the benches. One was able to photograph city workers destroying Kotlarz benches while leaving Marcin ones unharmed. The controversy obviously helped the challenger, as he took 74 percent of the vote against Marcin in the runoff.

A rematch was scheduled for the 1984 Democratic committeeman race, as Kotlarz attempted to capture the post Marcin had held since 1952. Marcin died only days before the election.

For three years, Joseph Kotlarz was alderman number 29. When factions emerged immediately after the Harold Washington election, the original head count was 28–21; Kotlarz stayed on the fence. Eventually he moved over to the Edward Vrdolyak faction. With few exceptions, he remained there throughout the Council Wars years.

One of those exceptions involved an ordinance to prohibit the sale of leaded gasoline in the city. Kotlarz cosponsored the bill with 29th Ward alderman Danny Davis—the only major "bipartisan" legislation during Harold Washington's first term.

The rookie alderman was no city council wallflower. In addition to the leaded gas ban, he also cosponsored a linked development bill, which would tax downtown development and return monies to the outlying communities. He succeeded in keeping Greyhound out of the ward (although foes insisted he did not move against the bus company until pressured to do so). Kotlarz also engineered a petition drive (which collected 40,000 signatures) to repeal a record 1986 property tax hike.

One of the youngest aldermen, Kotlarz is one of the more ambitious. He sent up trial balloons for the Illinois secretary of state nomination in late 1985, but later yielded to fellow Pole Aurelia Pucinski. Considering Pucinski's Democratic primary loss to a follower of political cult leader Lyndon LaRouche, the retreat might have been a blessing for Kotlarz.

Despite his visibility, Kotlarz attracted six challengers in the 1987 aldermanic election: Chester Hornowski, a policeman and the ward's Republican committeeman, who also was on the Republican ballot for mayor (he said that he filed for mayor only so that voters could have an alternative to Democrat-turned-Republican Don Haider; when 39th Ward Republican committeeman Ken Hurst announced his candidacy, Hornowski halted his mayoral campaign and concentrated on the aldermanic race); Warren Sikorski, a city employee who ran for state representative in the 12th District as a Republican in 1986 (but who supported Jane Byrne in 1987); Paul Gall, director of the police crime lab and the only Harold Washington supporter in the race; Joseph Jurek, a businessman who supported six-year terms for mayors and reduction in size of the city council; Therese Samulski, a teaching assistant and former ward secretary to Alderman Roman Pucinski (41st); and Terry Allen, a LaRouche backer.

Kotlarz had no problem disposing of the challengers. Since then, he has shown himself to be a pragmatist. Although making no recommendations in the general election, he supported the Washington-led council reorganization. He chairs Claims and Liabilities, a low-profile yet high-volume committee.

REDISTRICTING: The 35th Ward "moved" south and west (becoming more Hispanic) as a result of the 1986 redistricting. Gone were all or parts of thirteen eastern and southeastern precincts to the 33rd Ward and two to the 31st Ward. The 35th received two northwest precincts which had belonged to the 45th Ward, four southern ones from the 33rd, and eleven southwest precincts from the 30th Ward.

MAYORAL: Harold Washington received only four percent of the vote here in the Democratic primary, one of sixteen Northwest and Southwest Side wards in which he failed to reach double figures. Richard Daley, backed by Marcin, obtained 44 percent. Jane Byrne won the ward, but her 52 percent of the vote was less than a knockout victory.

Washington quadrupled his percentage in the general election, but nonetheless fell behind Epton. As with other Near Northwest Side wards, part of the gains came from Hispanics who traditionally vote Democratic in general elections, even for candidates they might have opposed in the primary.

Jane Byrne in 1987 once more captured the majority of the vote—84 percent, including near-unanimous totals in some Polish areas. Washington's percentage (15) and vote totals remained similar in primary (2,690) and general (2,628) elections. Republican Don Haider did better than his citywide average here (with 8 percent), even though Committeeman Hornowski backed Illinois Solidarity party candidate Edward Vrdolyak.

CENSUS DATA: Population (1980): 58,780. 83.71 percent white, .17 percent black, 11.84 percent Hispanic, 4.28 percent Asian and other. Voting age population: 87.53 percent white, .14 percent black, 9.56 Hispanic, 2.77 percent Asian and other.

CENSUS TRACTS: See ward map.

COMMUNITY NEWSPAPERS:
Chicago Post, 2810 W. Fullerton (772–3300)
Chicago's Northwest Side Press, 4941 N. Milwaukee (286–6100)

Community News, 2958 N. Milwaukee (235–6397)
Free Press, 2608 N. California (342–5737)
Logan Square Extra, 3918 W. North Ave. (252–3534)
Logan Square Times, 4600 N. Harlem, Harwood Heights (867–7700)

ALDERMAN: Joseph Kotlarz. Elected 1983. Born October 29, 1956. Career: B.A., Loyola University; J.D., John Marshall Law School; attorney.
Committees: Claims and Liabilities (chairman); License (vice-chairman); Aging and Disabled; Housing; Human Rights and Consumer Protection; Land Acquisition, Disposition, and Leases; Special Events and Cultural Affairs.
City hall telephone: 744–6835, 744–3109
Ward office: 3455 N. Pulaski (463–3505).
1987 election:

Joseph S. Kotlarz, Jr.	10,188	(56%)	Warren W. Sikorski	901	(5%)
Chester R. Hornowski	2,644	(15%)	Joseph A. Jurek	807	(4%)
Therese Samulski	2,480	(14%)	Terry E. Allen	228	(1%)
Paul S. Gall	985	(5%)			

DEMOCRATIC COMMITTEEMAN: Joseph S. Kotlarz, Jr. Elected 1984.
1984 election:

Joseph S. Kotlarz, Jr.	9,165	(74%)
John C. Marcin	3,288	(26%)

MAYORAL ELECTIONS:

1983 Democratic primary:

Jane Byrne	10,404	(52%)
Richard Daley	8,841	(44%)
Harold Washington	744	(4%)

1987 Democratic primary:

Jane Byrne	15,561	(85%)
Harold Washington	2,690	(15%)

1983 general:

Bernard Epton	18,661	(84%)
Harold Washington	3,414	(16%)

1987 general:

Edward Vrdolyak	13,871	(77%)
Harold Washington	2,628	(15%)
Donald Haider	1,454	(8%)

36th Ward

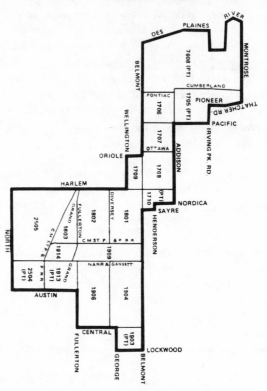

"MY SUBURB IN THE CITY"—that is how former alderman John Aiello described the sprawling Northwest Side 36th Ward. In many ways, the alderman was correct.

True, the 36th Ward (covering the Dunning, Montclair, and parts of the Belmont-Cragin and Austin communities) is largely residential. And much of the shopping that takes place occurs in shopping malls rather than shopping strips. There is even a commuter train stop (the Milwaukee Road's Dunning stop) and a county forest preserve, which borders the Des Plaines River at the ward's (and the city's) western boundary.

Yet the atmosphere is much different here than in, say, Palatine or Park Ridge. People may have moved to this outlying area in an attempt to escape the problems of the inner city, but they did not leave their ethnicity behind.

European cultures, mainly southern and eastern, have left their mark on this ward. Ethnic pride is still strong. It can be seen at the Socrates School (Greek culture) at McVicker and Diversey, the Alliance of Polish Clubs at

Diversey and Monitor, St. Gregory the Illuminator Armenian Church at Normandy and Diversey, Norwegian Lutheran Bethesda Home at Nordica and George, and any number of Irish restaurants, specialty stores, and bars throughout the ward.

St. Nicholas Albanian Orthodox Church (Schubert and Narragansett) gained worldwide fame in late 1986. A "weeping" icon of the Virgin Mary drew thousands of worshipers and other visitors. Orthodox officials called the icon a "miraculous sign."

Italians are the dominant ethnic group. Many were "exiled" here from the Taylor Street area when the Chicago Circle campus (now University of Illinois at Chicago) was constructed in the 1960s. Because of that upheaval, the 36th is now the most Italian ward in Chicago. Harlem Avenue is the most visible site of Italian-American culture, with imported Italian food stores, Italian bakeries, and gelato stores. Churches nearby offer services in Italian, including Leyden Baptist (Oriole and Roscoe).

Homes, especially single-family ones in the western precincts, resemble those in neighboring River Forest or Elmwood Park more than those of most other Chicago wards. They have large front yards, often decorated; this ward is the stone statuary capital of Chicago. Buildings in the southern and eastern precincts are most likely two-flats and bungalows.

Although shopping is available everywhere, the commercial capital of the ward is the Brickyard Mall, located at Diversey and Narragansett. Built in 1978, the Brickyard (which was once a brickyard) is the largest shopping center located within the Northwest Side of the city.

Much of the credit for the Brickyard goes to Aiello, one of the most active ward boosters of any alderman. "This is the utopia of Chicago," he said of the 36th. "We have the best of schools, the shopping, everything." Aiello claimed at the time that the Brickyard was the only major shopping center in the nation to be built within the city limits of a major city.

A former policeman, Aiello was appointed alderman in 1965 when his predecessor, Robert Massey, received a judgeship. During the 1970s, he was one of the "coffee rebellion" aldermen who sought to obtain a greater say in council affairs.

Aiello died unexpectedly in 1980. He was replaced by an alderman who in less than one full term became a Chicago political legend. This was Louis Farina, variously described as "the Lou Costello of city hall" and "the last alderman who fit the description of a pinky-ringed, chalk-striped double-breasted suited, cigar-chomping, back-slapping politician." *Tribune* columnist Bob Wiedrich wrote, "In the annals of the Chicago City Council, many have become fools by accident. But few have worked so hard at it."

His reputation preceded Farina to city hall. Once he called the Chicago newspapers with the earth-shattering news that he had found a pearl in his clam pizza. During the 1960s, while supervising the city's meter maids, he designed green-and-yellow uniforms for them. He also designed himself a special braided uniform. Mayor Richard Daley saw the costume and asked, "What's he trying to be, some South American dictator?" The uniform soon disappeared, but the nickname "El Supremo" followed him for years afterward.

Farina won a special election to succeed Aiello. He defeated Richard Pope, chief deputy clerk of the juvenile court; Edward Hanrahan, making his fifth consecutive unsuccessful bid for office after the 1969 Black Panther raid which stained his career as state's attorney; and Frank Ranallo, a retired train engineer and perennial candidate.

Pope's candidacy was significant. He was the first aldermanic candidate to receive the endorsement of the firefighters' union. The union gave Pope its backing as a protest against Jane Byrne's handling of a firefighters' strike. Farina (like Aiello, a protégé of longtime committeeman Louis Garippo) won despite such opposition.

Once in office, Farina continued his colorful ways. Because he once was nearly hit by a bicyclist wearing headphones, he proposed an ordinance banning headphones from bikers. Another required boxers to wear protective headgear. He originated a resolution banning nuclear war.

Farina thought the songs "Chicago, Chicago, That Toddlin' Town" and "My Kind of Town" lacked the proper dignity for state occasions, so he proposed a city song. Mayor Byrne went along with the idea. The contest was not settled until 1983, when Harold Washington took office. The new mayor heard the winning entry, declared "It doesn't move me," and shelved the song.

Louis Farina might have been eccentric, but not all of his ideas were ignored. While heading the parking department, he urged soft drink manufacturers to change the shape of their flip top rings to prevent their use as slugs—a move that saved the city thousands of dollars. As alderman, he successfully proposed an ordinance to ban the sale of spray paint to minors.

He declined to seek reelection in 1983, reportedly because of "family pressures." In truth, the pressure came from Byrne, because of Farina's imminent indictment on extortion charges. That indictment came in early 1983. Then, in Chicago political tradition, the ward organization held a fundraising party to help defray the alderman's legal fees. Farina and 48th Ward committeeman Marty Tuchow were convicted in early 1984.

The man who succeeded Farina was William J. P. Banks, a former corporation counsel who took over as committeeman when Garippo died in 1981. Pope again challenged in the 1983 election. Despite Pope's attempts to pin Banks as a tool of the 1st Ward Democratic organization, Banks won the aldermanic election with 56 percent of the vote. He also won reelection as committeeman in 1984 without opposition.

William Banks (who is of Italian ancestry, despite his name) is one of the less visible city council members. Nonetheless, he gets things done. Banks helped save some sewer department jobs when Mayor Harold Washington attempted to cut the city payroll in the early days of his administration. More recently, he cosponsored a linked development ordinance which would funnel monies from downtown construction into each of Chicago's neighborhoods. A

1987 Banks proposal would have limited the size of "for sale" signs, an attempt to circumvent a court ruling which struck down bans on such signs in residential areas.

Banks faced no opposition in his 1987 reelection bid. One city hall reporter theorized that his lack of opponents was due to intimidation; Banks's supporters shouted down all opposition during a 1983 debate.

Banks sought Democratic slating for clerk of the circuit court in late 1987. He appeared to have enough committeemen's backing for the slating, yet withdrew to avoid a primary fight against former mayor Jane Byrne. His withdrawal did not prevent a primary squabble. Metropolitan Sanitary District commissioner Aurelia Pucinski, not Byrne, got party backing.

REDISTRICTING: The 36th lost one eastern precinct to the 30th Ward in the 1986 remap.

MAYORAL: This ward, one of the "whitest" in Chicago, gave Harold Washington some of his lowest percentages in the 1983 mayoral elections. Washington received only 1 percent of the vote in the Democratic primary (a tie for his lowest percentage in the city). Jane Byrne won 55 percent of the primary vote, to 44 percent for Richard Daley.

Likewise, Republican Bernard Epton scored well against the (black) Democratic nominee. Epton got 95 percent of the vote in the general election; only the Southwest Side 13th and 23rd wards gave him higher percentages.

Washington's gains were only slight ones in 1987—up to 7 percent in both primary and general elections. Ed Vrdolyak won 89 percent of the vote in carrying the ward in the April election.

CENSUS DATA: Population (1980): 58,942. 95.87 percent white, .08 percent black, 2.66 percent Hispanic, 1.39 percent Asian and other. Voting age population: 96.43 percent white, .07 percent black, 2.32 percent Hispanic, 1.18 percent Asian and other.

CENSUS TRACTS: See ward map.

COMMUNITY NEWSPAPERS:
Belmont Park Leader, 6008 W. Belmont (283–7900)
Belmont-Central Leader, 6008 W. Belmont (283–7900)
Chicago Post, 2810 W. Fullerton (772–3300)
Harlem-Irving Leader, 6008 W. Belmont (283–7900)
Harlem-Irving Times, 4600 N. Harlem, Harwood Heights (867–7700)
Montclaire Post, 6008 W. Belmont (283–7900)
Northwest Times, 4600 N. Harlem, Harwood Heights (867–7700)
West Belmont Leader, 6008 W. Belmont (283–7900)

ALDERMAN: William J. P. Banks. Elected 1983. Born July 28, 1949. Career: B.A., De Paul University, 1971; J.D., De Paul University, 1975; attorney; administrative aide to Congressman Morgan Murphy, 1976–78; assistant corporation counsel, 1978–83.

Committees: Land Acquisition, Disposition, and Leases (chairman); Aging and Disabled; Budget and Government Operations; Capital Development; Health; Housing; Local Transportation.

City hall telephone: 744–6857, 744–7947.

Ward office: 6839 W. Belmont (622–3232).

1987 election:
William J. P. Banks, unopposed.

DEMOCRATIC COMMITTEEMAN: William J. P. Banks. Appointed 1981.

1984 election:
William J. P. Banks, unopposed.

MAYORAL ELECTIONS:

1983 Democratic primary:

Jane Byrne	16,486	(55%)
Richard Daley	12,940	(44%)
Harold Washington	343	(1%)

1983 general:

Bernard Epton	31,968	(95%)
Harold Washington	1,651	(5%)

1987 Democratic primary:

Jane Byrne	26,248	(93%)
Harold Washington	1,958	(7%)

1987 general:

Edward Vrdolyak	25,096	(89%)
Harold Washington	1,886	(7%)
Donald Haider	1,372	(5%)

3̶7̶th Ward

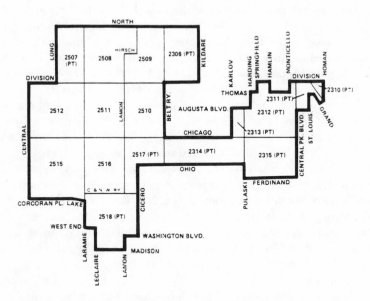

CHICAGO'S WEST SIDE was Italian in earlier years. Now it is black. Those statements explain the 37th Ward, a dumbbell-shaped piece of real estate that extends as far north as North Avenue, as far south as Madison Street, westward to Central Avenue, and east to Homan Avenue, within a chip shot of Humboldt Park.

This is a ward designed for political purposes rather than geographical, social, or economic continuity. It was drawn in late 1985 to create a black "super-majority" ward. The 37th Ward is 81 percent black by 1980 census figures, and the black percentage has increased since then. Geographically, it is two mini-wards in one. The eastern thirteen precincts represent the western part of the Humboldt Park community. These are the precincts that are home to the Hispanics (mainly Puerto Ricans) who make up 9 percent of the ward's population. This is mainly a residential area, with houses older than in the western part of the ward. Housing deterioration and gang violence are the two major problems here.

Orr High School, located at Chicago and Pulaski, has aroused community controversy with its proposal to make contraceptive devices available to students. A nearby grammar school, Our Lady of Angels (Iowa and Hamlin), was the scene of one of the greatest tragedies in Chicago history. A December 1, 1958, fire took the lives of ninety-two children and three nuns. The fire broke out only minutes before the students would have been dismissed for the day.

A two-block-wide corridor (between Chicago and Ohio) connects the eastern precincts with the thirty-six western ones, which are part of the Austin community. The corridor is occupied by the Northwest Waste to Energy Facility, a city waste disposal plant.

The western precincts, especially near LaFollette Park in the northwest corner, are more prosperous than the eastern ones. Central Avenue particularly contains some of the fancier rehabbed old homes of the Austin area. Other Austin homes are in varying states of repair and renovation. This section also contains an institution of note. St. Anne's Hospital, at Division and Lavergne, is the city's leading center for treatment of sickle cell anemia.

In one respect, the 37th Ward makes sense. Blacks moved north from the Austin and Garfield Park neighborhoods during the 1960s and 1970s; whites (mainly Italians, Irish, Poles, and Germans) left as blacks entered the neighborhoods. The 37th Ward as it existed in the 1970s almost certainly would have elected a black alderman sometime in the 1980s. That possibility was foreseen, and temporarily forestalled by 1981 remapper Tom Keane. Mainly white precincts north of North Avenue were added, and black-majority precincts deleted, thus allowing the predominantly white ward organization to retain power.

Thomas Casey was the beneficiary of this redistricting. Casey, former ward secretary for Paul Corcoran, took office after a 1965 special election following Corcoran's 1964 death. He became ward committeeman in 1972.

Casey was a typical Daley-era alderman, an amiable sort who made no waves and backed no losers. Although he chaired the Rules Committee, members Keane and Michael Bilandic assumed most of the committee's power. Nonetheless, Casey was respected. His ward organization for many years was one of the more powerful in the city. Philip Rock, now Illinois Senate president, was an alumnus of Casey's organization.

Casey suffered a fatal heart attack in 1982 while making a ward street inspection. His untimely passing evoked the usual hyperbole. Mayor Jane Byrne declared, "He died with his boots on." A close friend, Alderman Fred Roti, declared, "Like the late mayor Richard J. Daley, he loved his work so much it cost him his life."

The man who replaced Casey as both alderman and committeeman was Frank Damato, a former member of Vito Marzullo's organization who worked his way up through the Department of Consumer Services to become deputy commissioner. Damato won both the 1983 aldermanic and 1984 committeeman elections by capturing almost all of the ward's white vote while a number of candidates split the black vote.

He needed the favorable remap. Even with virtually unanimous support among whites, he received only 52 percent of the vote in the aldermanic election and 46 percent of the committeeman vote. Despite the ward's black majority, Damato sided early with the Edward Vrdolyak council bloc. He remained opposed to Mayor Harold Washington to the end.

When a court-ordered ward remap appeared imminent, Damato declined to seek reelection. Instead he sought (and received) party slating for a county board seat. Unlike other "lame duck" aldermen similarly slated (Frank Stemberk of the 22nd and Michael Nardulli of the 26th), Damato actively campaigned for the post. His attractive billboards showing a three-dimensional flag against a black background appeared throughout the city. Unlike Stemberk and Nardulli, he polled well enough to win election to one of the at-large seats.

Damato crowed, "Mayor Washington is not going to pick the black alderman who will serve the 37th Ward. My Regular Democratic Organization will. The next alderman will be one of my thirty-eight precinct captains who is black." He was proven wrong.

Washington endorsed Percy Giles, a West Side business leader who chaired a mayoral committee which oversaw distribution of Community Development Block Grant funds. Damato covertly backed Ray Myles, an attorney and precinct captain. Myles ran out of Damato's office, which had been redistricted out of the ward. Seven others also entered the race.

Giles moved into the ward shortly before the election, and opponents tried to make his "carpetbagging" an issue. But Washington's endorsement obviously made the difference. Giles received 56 percent of the vote and carried all but two precincts. Myles finished a distant second with 12 percent of the vote.

Another Washington ally won the Democratic committeeman election. High school teacher Johnny Johnson, runner-up in the 1984 committeeman election, was unopposed after forcing Damato ally Thomas Simmons off the ballot. Johnson (who later assumed an administrative post with the Department of Aviation) did not seek reelection. Instead, Giles ran for committeeman in 1988.

Percy Giles has not been one of the more vocal council members. Yet in at least one respect he has proven himself effective. Giles's 37th Ward organization was among the leaders in new voter registration prior to the February 1987 primary.

Only one challenger faced Giles in the 1987 aldermanic election: attorney James Hammonds, a former aide to Congresswoman Cardiss Collins and Washington's 1983 endorsed choice. Giles, again with the mayor's support, gained a landslide win with 86 percent of the vote.

REDISTRICTING: Major alterations were made in the ward map to change the black percentage from 60 percent of the 1981 map to the 80 percent population of the 1986 remap. Fifteen northern precincts were removed, one going to the 31st Ward and the rest to the 30th. All or parts of five western and southwestern precincts were shifted to the 29th Ward, and one southern one to the 28th Ward.

The eastern Humboldt Park area precincts were the main addition to the 37th Ward map. Four northeast precincts were gained from the 31st Ward, one from the 27th, and eight from the 28th Ward. Also, one southern precinct was added from the 28th Ward and a southern one from the 29th.

MAYORAL: Harold Washington carried the ward in the 1983 Democratic primary. He won 58 percent of the vote—a number that coincided almost precisely with the black voting age percentage in the ward. Jane Byrne (27 percent) and Richard Daley (15 percent) split the white vote.

Washington took 77 percent of the vote in the general election, retaining his black base and adding white ethnics and Hispanics who maintained traditional Democratic loyalties.

Black population (and voting age percentage) increased in the areas now included in the 37th Ward since the 1980 census. Those increases showed themselves in the mayor's 1987 vote total. Washington carried 96 percent of the vote in both primary and general elections, dominating every precinct.

CENSUS DATA: Population (1980): 60,723. 8.53 percent white, 80.69 percent black, 9.25 percent Hispanic, 1.53 percent Asian and other. Voting age population: 11.10 percent white, 77.81 percent black, 8.66 percent Hispanic, 1.43 percent Asian and other.

CENSUS TRACTS: See ward map.

COMMUNITY NEWSPAPERS:
Chicago Metro, 2600 S. Michigan (842–5950)
Northwest Extra, 3918 W. North Ave. (252–3534)
Westside Journal, 16618 S. Hermitage, Markham (333–2210)

ALDERMAN: Percy Giles. Elected 1987. Born January 17, 1952. Career: University of Arkansas; assistant store manager, Walgreens, 1974–79; executive director, Westside Business Improvement Association, 1980–86.
Committees: Human Rights and Consumer Protection (chairman); Energy, Environmental Protection, and Public Utilities (vice-chairman); Aging and Disabled; Budget and Government Operations; Capital Development; Finance; Local Transportation; Ports, Wharves, and Bridges; Special Events and Cultural Affairs; Streets and Alleys.
City hall telephone: 744–8019, 744–5686.
Ward office: 740 N. Cicero Ave. (287–8500).
1986 special election:

Percy Giles	4,562	(56%)	Patrick Keen	422	(5%)
Ray Myles	941	(12%)	Larry G. McCullum	406	(5%)
Andre A. Foster	475	(6%)	James Pruitt	208	(3%)
John W. Davis	455	(6%)	William A. Marshall	171	(2%)
Carter Jones	454	(6%)			

1987 election:

Percy Giles	14,483	(86%)
James S. Hammonds	2,295	(14%)

DEMOCRATIC COMMITTEEMAN: Johnny Johnson. Elected 1986. Born April 23, 1948. Career: B.A., Arkansas A & M (University of Arkansas at Pine Bluff), 1971; M.A., Southern Illinois University, 1972; teacher, Chicago Public Schools, 1972–75; lounge owner, 1975–78; substitute teacher, 1979–82; M.A., Northwestern University, 1982; teacher, Chicago Public Schools, 1982–87; assistant to commissioner, Department of Aviation, 1987– .

Ward office: 740 N. Cicero Ave. (287-8500).

1984 election:

Frank Damato	5,872	(46%)	Bruce Washington	950	(7%)
Johnny Johnson	4,259	(33%)	William A. Marshall	453	(4%)
Herman A. Tucker	1,308	(10%)			

1986 special election:

Johnny Johnson, unopposed.

MAYORAL ELECTIONS:

1983 Democratic primary:

Harold Washington	11,673	(58%)
Jane Byrne	5,482	(27%)
Richard Daley	2,947	(15%)

1983 general:

Harold Washington	17,555	(77%)
Bernard Epton	5,254	(23%)

1987 Democratic primary:

Harold Washington	19,808	(96%)
Jane Byrne	817	(4%)

1987 general:

Harold Washington	20,552	(96%)
Edward Vrdolyak	551	(3%)
Donald Haider	130	(1%)

38th Ward

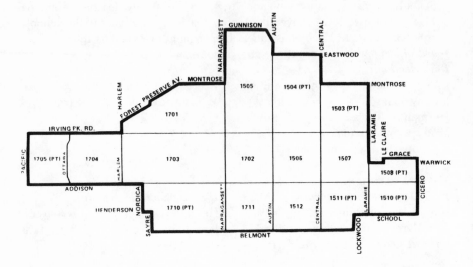

THERE ARE THE DALEYS and the Keanes, the Burkes and the Vrdolyaks, and the Rotis and the Rostenkowskis. But no political dynasty in Chicago has been longer lasting than the Cullerton family, now of the 38th Ward. That dynasty gained a reprieve, if not a mandate to continue, in 1987.

A Cullerton has been on the city council for most of the time since the Great Chicago Fire of 1871. The first of the clan, Edward, was elected a few months before the fire. He represented South Side wards (20th Street was renamed in his honor) for forty-eight years—a city council record. A knowledgeable parliamentarian, Edward also ran a profitable "tax-adjusting" company on the side.

Despite his longevity, Edward was not the most famous member of the clan. That honor goes to P(atrick) J(oseph) Cullerton, alderman and county assessor during the Richard Daley years. "Parky" Cullerton, first elected alderman in 1935, ultimately became Finance Committee chairman and boasted of never having missed a city council meeting in twenty-three years. He left only after being elected assessor in 1958.

Of all the county offices, none is valued more highly by political parties than county assessor. It is the assessor who sets value on city properties. In theory, there are standardized criteria for determining property tax assessments. In practice, the property tax break has often been proportional to the size of the real estate owner's contribution to the party's campaign fund. It's a small wonder that the assessor has often been called "the party's banker."

Cullerton in that respect was the quintessential county assessor. *Sun-Times* reporter Charles Nicodemus once wrote, "The party holding the (assessor) job is able to help its friends, tweak its enemies, or, more important, make people believe that it's willing to do one or the other." In any case, telephone calls from Cullerton to Chicago real estate magnates were found to be remarkably effective.

P. J. Cullerton never denied his wealth, most of which came from a lucrative insurance business. Nonetheless, he spent much of his political life as the subject of various legal investigations, including allegations that he received $1,500 per month from a parking company after issuing it two no-bid contracts for garages in 1954. No charges against him were ever issued.

Cullerton "developed a reputation for never losing an election or making a statement in public," according to the *Chicago Free Press*. His billboards— the Cullerton name in letters appearing as pillars supporting the Supreme Court building—became an election institution.

A scandal rocked the assessor's office in 1973, one which saw eighteen employees convicted of bribery. Cullerton was not implicated in the proceedings, but nonetheless declined to seek reelection in 1974.

Cullerton anointed his successor—Tom Tully, a deputy assessor and member of Cullerton's ward organization. Tully was hired by Cullerton during the assessor's last term. He gained a "Mr. Clean" reputation by replacing patronage workers with professionally trained persons.

Tully beat Edward Vrdolyak in the 1974 Democratic primary and won an easy general election victory. This win fired speculation after Richard Daley's death that Tully might be the North Side candidate to take on the 11th Ward Democrats in the 1979 mayoral election.

Such a battle never took place. Tully surprised most observers by announcing that he would not seek reelection in 1978. Later a probe examined whether Tully got huge breaks for real estate deals with property developers while assessor. No charges were issued from the probe, but the adverse publicity might have cost Tully a promising political career.

The Cullerton clan proliferated in local government during P. J.'s time, including a fire commissioner, a sanitary district board member, and a particularly well-heeled electrical contractor. All were as verbose as Parky. It was said, "If it talks, it ain't a Cullerton."

Another family member who kept that tradition was William Cullerton, P. J.'s brother and replacement as 38th Ward alderman. William Cullerton served until his death in 1973, one of the least memorable souls ever to hold a city council seat.

Thomas Cullerton, nephew of P. J. and William, assumed the aldermanic post shortly afterward and holds it to this day. He took office after serving as an administrative assistant to William and supervising electrical inspectors for the building department (many in the family have been electricians). He assumed the Democratic committeeman position upon P. J.'s 1981 death.

The craggy-faced Thomas also has inherited the family verbosity. When

THOMAS CULLERTON

asked during one reelection campaign about his city hall accomplishments, he answered only, "We'll let the people decide."

In his last two campaigns, the people have decided in his favor—just barely. Cullerton eked out a 50.2 percent election win over policeman Walter Dudycz and one other candidate in 1983, avoiding a runoff by 258 votes. That margin might have been closer had it not been for State Representative Roger McAuliffe, the ward's Republican committeeman. McAuliffe and Cullerton have developed a nonaggression pact over the years. Cullerton has not slated strong opponents against McAuliffe, Chicago's only Republican state representative. In turn, McAuliffe has not opposed Cullerton.

Dudycz appeared ready to challenge Cullerton for Democratic committeeman in 1984, but McAuliffe instead talked him into the G.O.P. fold. With McAuliffe's help, Dudycz was elected state senator in 1984.

Cullerton appeared to have strong opposition in 1987, this time in the form of Republican businessman Martin Serwinski. However, a filing error left Serwinski off the ballot, despite numerous appeals.

Serwinski's departure left four Cullerton opponents: Victor Cacciatorre, who ran as "the only candidate who's an attorney"; Albert Opitz, a water department engineer who sought Republican backing; James Simpson, an engineering supervisor with the Metra Railroad; and Dennis Boyle, publicity chairman for a group which represented striking *Chicago Tribune* employees.

Cacciatorre received Serwinski's support, and Cullerton spent most of his time attacking the now obvious front running opponent. Cacciatorre was labeled as a carpetbagger (he moved to the ward from River Forest) and son of "one of the biggest slum operators."

Once again, the race was close. Cullerton escaped a runoff but gained less than 52 percent of the vote. Cacciatorre fared well in Portage Park and garnered 39 percent; none of the others received more than 4 percent.

Local Republican officeholders once more boycotted the ward's aldermanic race. McAuliffe made no endorsement; Dudycz worked for 41st Ward candidate Richard Kunicki rather than Opitz or Cacciatorre.

Cullerton claimed two major accomplishments during the last term: cosponsorship of a city linked development ordinance, which is intended to spur neighborhood development by taxing downtown construction, and acquisition of surplus land at Montrose and Narragansett (known as the Dunning property), which was proposed for everything from an industrial park to a shopping center and residential development to an addition to Wright College.

That tract belonged to the largest single block of land in the ward. Chicago-Read Mental Health Center (originally called the Cook County Infirmary and Insane Asylum) has been located at Irving Park and Narragansett since 1868.

Wright College (which gained citywide attention in the 1960s because of the administration's attempt at banning a James Baldwin book) is the major educational institution of the 38th Ward. Otherwise, this is an area of homes, a ward with more large cemeteries than large factories. A number of parks also dot this ward, most notably Portage Park (Irving Park and Central) in the northeastern section.

The 38th (bordered on the south by Belmont, east by Cicero, west by Pacific, northwest by suburban Norridge, and north by Gunnison) has one of the oldest populations of any ward. Local political leaders claim that it has more retired persons than any other.

It also has ethnic flavor. One may buy Italian records in a store at Irving Park and Marmora, worship at St. Mary's Rumanian Orthodox Church (Central and Berteau), play soccer with the Argentine Soccer Club (headquartered at Irving Park and Lockwood), or quaff an ale at McEnroe's Irish Pub (Addison and Cicero).

Poles are the most important ethnic group (Cacciatorre stressed his Polish grandfather rather than his Italian heritage during candidate forums), but Germans and Italians are also found in considerable numbers. The ward is all but lily-white; only the Far Northwest Side 41st Ward has a larger percentage of white residents, according to 1980 census figures.

The 38th is an appropriate setting for Europe Travel, an agency at Long and Belmont highlighted by a large sculpture of a radio tower sending out "signals." Another business decoration of note is the Fort Dearborn Federal Bank (Belmont and Newcastle), rebuilt to look like a log fort with a lookout tower.

REDISTRICTING: The 38th Ward lost parts of three southeast precincts to the 30th Ward and gained a northeast precinct from the 45th Ward.

MAYORAL: Harold Washington received only one percent of the vote in the 1983 Democratic primary (Jane Byrne won it with 53 percent to 46 percent for Richard Daley). He gained only 6 percent of the vote in the general election against Republican Bernard Epton. But Washington's vote totals were not the major 38th Ward mayoral story in 1983.

The ward contains St. Pascal's Church (Irving Park and Malvina), scene of one of the most controversial moments of the campaign. Washington and former vice-president Walter Mondale attended a Palm Sunday service there. Afterward, they were met by more than 150 protesters. The demonstration received worldwide coverage, only adding to the theme of racial polarization which almost all outside media used to describe the election.

Washington forces turned the St. Pascal's affair to their advantage with a campaign ad depicting the assassinations of John and Robert Kennedy and Martin Luther King and the 1968 Democratic convention riots. The ad ended with the demonstrators shouting "Epton! Epton!" It was an attempt (generally believed successful) to identify Epton with reactionary forces and thus win over white liberal voters.

Peace broke out in the 38th during the 1987 election, but Washington saw no gains. Jane Byrne took the ward in the primary with 94 percent of the vote.

In the general election, Harold Washington lost ground, making this one of the few wards where he fared worse than in the primary. Edward Vrdolyak won with 89 percent. Donald Haider finished second with six percent, and Washington took the remaining five percent.

CENSUS DATA: Population (1980): 59,784. 96.45 percent white, .37 percent black, 1.98 percent Hispanic, .20 percent Asian and other. Voting age population: 96.95 percent white, .29 percent black, 1.73 percent Hispanic, 1.03 percent Asian and other.

CENSUS TRACTS: See ward map.

COMMUNITY NEWSPAPERS:
Belmont/Central Leader, 6008 W. Belmont (283–7900)
Chicago Post, 2810 W. Fullerton (772–3300)
Chicago's Northwest Side Press, 4941 N. Milwaukee (286–6100)
Edgebrook Times-Review, 1000 Executive Way, Des Plaines (824–1111)
Harlem-Irving Leader, 6008 W. Belmont (283–7900)
Harlem-Irving Times, 4600 N. Harlem, Harwood Heights (867–7700)
Portage Park Times, 4600 N. Harlem, Harwood Heights (867–7700)

ALDERMAN: Thomas Cullerton. Elected 1973. Born 1924. Career: Washburne Trade School; administrative asst. to Ald. William J. Cullerton; supervising electrical inspector, Chicago Building Department.

Committees: Zoning (vice-chairman); Aviation; Buildings; Committees, Rules, Municipal Code Revision, and Ethics; Historical Landmark Preservation; Finance; Municipal Code Revision; Ports, Wharves, and Bridges.

City hall telephone: 744–6811, 744–6812.

Ward office: 5815 W. Irving Park Rd. (237–0900).

1987 election:

Thomas W. Cullerton	14,684 (52%)	Albert F. Opitz	842 (3%)
Victor J. Cacciatorre	11,040 (39%)	James A. Simpson	751 (3%)
Dennis M. Boyle, Jr.	1,073 (4%)		

DEMOCRATIC COMMITTEEMAN: Thomas Cullerton. Appointed 1981.

1984 election:

Thomas W. Cullerton, unopposed.

MAYORAL ELECTIONS:

1983 Democratic primary:

Jane Byrne	15,180 (53%)
Richard Daley	13,275 (46%)
Harold Washington	385 (1%)

1983 general:

Bernard Epton	30,942 (94%)
Harold Washington	1,883 (6%)

1987 Democratic primary:

Jane Byrne	26,615 (94%)
Harold Washington	1,536 (6%)

1987 general:

Edward Vrdolyak	25,024 (89%)
Donald Haider	1,659 (6%)
Harold Washington	1,292 (5%)

3**9**th Ward

QUEEN OF ALL SAINTS BASILICA towers over the blocks around Sauganash and Keane. A large park fronts the church. This Gothic-style parish church is one of the largest, in physical size, of any church in the city.

The name and size are appropriate. Queen of All Saints serves an area that may be queen of all neighborhoods in the city—Sauganash. The Sauganash and adjoining Edgebrook neighborhoods combine to form the Forest Glen community, which has the highest per capita income ($31,000) of any community in Chicago.

"Sauganash" is an Indian word meaning "English-speaking." It referred to Billy Caldwell, a half-Irish, half-Mohawk Indian agent. Caldwell negotiated the Treaty of Chicago, a September 26, 1833, deal under which the Potawatomi Indians gave up their Illinois and Wisconsin lands—the greatest steal this side of Manhattan. The treaty took place near the present Queen of All Saints grounds, and a stained glass window in the church depicts the treaty.

This affluent and pleasant area makes up part of the Northwest Side's 39th Ward. In every sense except geographic, it is suburban, not urban. Sprawling homes cover spacious lots. A forest preserve and golf course form the western boundary, with the placid north branch of the Chicago River winding through both. Business is confined to a small but prosperous-looking shopping strip near the Edgebrook train station (Devon and Central).

Sauganash is Jane Byrne country. Young Jane Burke grew up here and married Marine Corps pilot William Byrne, who later died in an airplane accident. Byrne lived here while director of consumer affairs during the Richard Daley administration but had moved to the Gold Coast by the time she became mayor.

Byrne might have left, but others stayed. Since city employees (even top administration officials) are required to reside within city limits, the affluent Sauganash and Edgebrook neighborhoods are the home of many professional municipal workers. They are as "suburban" (in terms of home quality and rural ambience) as one can obtain and still be within the city.

The 39th Ward is not entirely well-to-do. It may be roughly divided into four different parts. Edgebrook and Sauganash neighborhoods, bordered roughly by Devon, Ionia, the Milwaukee Railroad, the river, and the Chicago and Northwestern Railroad, form the northwest quarter.

Sauganash is not particularly "ethnic" per se, but it is the site of a major ethnic institution. The Polish National Alliance, the largest Polish fraternal association in Chicago, is located at Cicero and Lemont. Chicago's most influential Polish newspaper, the *Daily Zgoda*, is published here.

A slightly less affluent, although still comfortable, area lies to the east. This is the North Park community, positioned roughly from Devon on the north, Kedzie on the east, and the river on the south. Large brick homes may be found here, as well as the Lincoln Village shopping center in the northeast corner of the ward.

North Park College at Kedzie and Foster, a small-college basketball power, is the main landmark of this sector. With its small, cozy, immaculate campus and nearby football field, North Park College would appear more at home in a small town in Iowa or Minnesota than in Chicago. North Park was founded by the Swedish Evangelical Covenant Church. The conservative surroundings (Covenant Press across the street, ice cream parlors rather than bars near the campus) show the church influence.

The center of the 39th Ward contains a hodgepodge of features that are neither industrial, commercial, nor (with one exception) residential. Land between Bryn Mawr and Peterson, Central Park and the North Western tracks housed the Municipal Tuberculosis Sanatorium between 1905 and 1974. Senior citizens' housing at Bryn Mawr and Pulaski now occupies the former headquarters of the sanatorium; the rest of the land is a nature preserve.

Three large cemeteries—Montrose, St. Lucas, and Bohemian National—lie directly south of the former sanatorium, extending south to Foster. Directly to the east of Bohemian National is Northeastern Illinois University, which has been a spawning ground for much of the city's Puerto Rican political leadership. WTTW, Chicago's public television station, has its studios located nearby at Catalpa and St. Louis.

The 39th also encompasses the inner city, an area decidedly less prosperous than Sauganash or Edgebrook. This area is Albany Park, which makes up the southern quarter of the ward. No other part of the city displays such marked ethnic variety in so little distance. A drive of only a few blocks along Lawrence Avenue yields at least five *alphabets*: Roman, Greek, Hebrew, Arabic, and Korean.

At one time this was a heavily Jewish area, home of first- or second-generation immigrants who moved northward from the older Jewish neighborhoods of West Town and Lawndale. Jews formed a prospering business area on Lawrence but gradually migrated north to Rogers Park. With their departure came a gradual decline in the Albany Park business community.

Thanks to help from small business loan programs, Albany Park is again on the upswing. This time Asians are the entrepreneurs. Altogether, the 39th Ward has the third-highest percentage of Asians (12.29 percent) of any city ward.

Koreans are the most numerous group; Albany Park has more Koreans than any other community in the city. The most visible sign of community progression is the Lakeside Evangelical Church at Lawndale and Wilson. At one time the building housed a synagogue; now it gives services in Korean.

Residents of the 39th Ward may give visiting friends eclectic tours. One could begin with bread at the Holy Land (Middle Eastern) bakery at Kedzie and Lawrence, or coffee at the P.S. Oriental coffee and snack shop (Bryn Mawr and Kimball), shop for Spanish-style tiles at Hispanic Designe (Cicero and Glenlake), play golf at the Billy Caldwell Golf Course (Caldwell and Leoha), have sore muscles examined at Sports Medicine Ltd. (Central and Tahoma), and finish the day with country music at Moose's Lounge (Wilson and Pulaski).

For years this relatively wealthy ward was represented by the wealthiest of aldermen. Patrick Shapiro inherited an $8 million fortune from his uncle. He served as alderman from 1950 (and Democratic committeeman from 1948) until 1964, when he was elected circuit court judge.

Anthony Laurino, Shapiro's ward secretary, replaced him in 1965. A former amateur boxer and city license inspector, Laurino has been both alderman and committeeman ever since. With the 1986 retirement of his mentor (and former 25th Ward alderman) Vito Marzullo, Laurino is now dean of the city council.

He serves as the last surviving link to "Hinky Dink" Kenna and "Bathhouse John" Coughlin. Laurino worked under those colorful 1st Ward legends as an assistant precinct captain.

Laurino has never been one of the major city council powers. A 1986 *Sun-Times* article described him as "somewhere below the movers and shakers and somewhere above the lumps of clay." He is considered strong on constituent services ("an alley alderman," he likes to describe himself). And when there is a particular cause, he has proven effective. Laurino saved a local landmark (at the time located in the ward) in 1973. When a gasoline company pressured the Buffalo Ice Cream Parlor to move so that it could build a gas station on a corner that already had three others, Laurino sponsored legislation to prevent gas stations at more than three corners of any intersection.

More important for the Democratic machine, Laurino roused a moribund ward organization here. At one time the ward was solidly Republican, reflecting in part its upper-class Protestant population. "When I took over the ward, you could put all the Democrats in Sauganash in one pocket," Laurino claimed. Laurino and Shapiro's efforts (plus changing demographics which saw Protestants leave while Catholic/Democratic Irish, Poles, and Italians moved in) changed that state of affairs. Now the 39th is one of the most reliable wards for the Democratic organization.

Only once—in opposition to the proposed Crosstown Expressway which would have caused some displacement in his ward—has Laurino opposed the party regulars. He backed Daley, then Bilandic in 1979 against Byrne. Once Byrne won, however, he became one of her staunchest supporters.

Laurino—rather, his family and friends—have profited by the association with the party. Son William "Billy" Laurino is a state representative and a division superintendent with the Department of Streets and Sanitation. Daughter Margie is a state central committeeman. Son-in-law John D'Amico (believed the heir apparent to Laurino's aldermanic position) has a high-level position with the Bureau of Forestry. A close friend, Michael Damato, is ward superintendent.

If voters are upset with the Laurino family connection, they have not shown their displeasure at the polls. Laurino was unopposed in 1983. Four years later he scored 79 percent against three opponents. The closest rival, self-employed building contractor Richard Fattore, received 13 percent of the vote. Leif Johnson, a Lyndon LaRouche disciple, got 4 percent.

The other opponent deserves special mention. He was Kenneth Hurst, 39th Ward Republican committeeman and perennial candidate who also received 4 percent of the vote. Hurst (either personally or through daughter Fawn) has waged war against the Laurino political family in every local election of recent years. The House of Hurst has come out second best (or in 1987, third best) every time. Hurst ran and lost against Billy Laurino for state representative in 1984. Fawn Hurst likewise was swamped by the younger Laurino in the 1986 election, while her father lost a bid for the board of tax appeals.

Ken Hurst also ran for mayor in 1987. Previously his most notable moment in mayoral politics occurred in 1983, when he was among those protesting candidate Harold Washington's appearance at St. Pascal's church. Four years later he was a serious candidate for the Republican nomination.

Despite a low-budget campaign (his major piece of campaign literature was a photocopied piece of paper depicting himself shaking hands with that great Chicago favorite, New York congressman Jack Kemp), Hurst threw fear into Republican party leaders. When Thomas Hynes entered the mayoral race, many Republican leaders feared that the Hynes entry might distract enough attention from slated candidate Donald Haider to allow the eccentric Hurst to win. It was a groundless fear. Hurst gained only 20 percent of the citywide vote to Haider's 70 percent, even losing his home ward by 200 votes.

REDISTRICTING: Boundary lines remained unchanged in the 39th Ward after the 1986 ward remap.

MAYORAL: Despite having grown up in Sauganash, Jane Byrne did not particularly enjoy "favorite daughter" status in the 1983 Democratic primary. Even though she captured all but a handful of precincts, she won only 55 percent of the vote. Richard Daley finished second with 42 percent. Harold Washington at 3 percent finished a distant last.

Nor did Washington fare appreciably better in the general election against Bernard Epton. The Republican captured the ward with 84 percent; Washington showing strength only in Albany Park.

Byrne won the 39th in the 1987 Democratic primary, this time with 85 percent of the vote. Washington, as earlier, performed best in Albany Park precincts.

Edward Vrdolyak won the ward in the general election, but his 79 percent total represents a dropoff from Byrne's. Washington received 13 percent. Donald Haider got 8 percent of the vote in a ward where many voters still go Republican out of party conviction rather than out of protest at Democratic choices.

CENSUS DATA: Population (1980): 60,669. 76.02 percent white, .55 percent black, 11.14 percent Hispanic, 12.19 percent Asian and other. Voting age population: 80.01 percent white, .52 percent black, 9.57 percent Hispanic, 9.90 percent Asian and other.

CENSUS TRACTS: See ward map.

COMMUNITY NEWSPAPERS:
   Albany Park News, 7519 N. Ashland (761–7200)
   Chicago's Northwest Side Press, 4941 N. Milwaukee (286–6100)
   Edgebrook Times/Review, 1000 Executive Way, Des Plaines (824–1111)
   Jefferson-Mayfair Times, 4600 N. Harlem, Harwood Heights (867–7700)

ALDERMAN: Anthony C. Laurino. Elected 1965. Born July 17, 1910. Career: DePaul University; ward secretary to Ald. Philip Shapiro; license inspector, Bureau of Water.
Committees: Traffic Control and Safety (chairman); Committees, Rules, Municipal Code Revision, and Ethics; Historical Landmark Preservation; Finance; Municipal Code Revision; Ports, Wharves, and Bridges.

City hall telephone: 744–6813, 744–6814.
Ward office: 4346 W. Lawrence (736–5594.)
1987 election:

Anthony C. Laurino	16,043 (79%)		Kenneth R. Hurst	885 (4%)
Richard Fattore	2,588 (13%)		Leif O. Johnson	790 (4%)

DEMOCRATIC COMMITTEEMAN: Anthony C. Laurino. Elected 1965.
1984 election:
Anthony C. Laurino, unopposed.

MAYORAL ELECTIONS:

1983 Democratic primary:

Jane Byrne	12,169 (55%)
Richard Daley	9,493 (42%)
Harold Washington	780 (3%)

1987 Democratic primary:

Jane Byrne	17,434 (85%)
Harold Washington	2,960 (14%)

1983 general:

Bernard Epton	22,161 (88%)
Harold Washington	3,127 (12%)

1987 general:

Edward Vrdolyak	16,308 (79%)
Harold Washington	2,731 (13%)
Donald Haider	1,632 (8%)

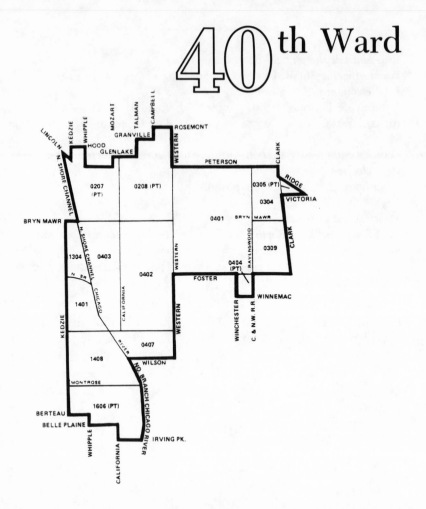

40th Ward

SOME WARDS ARE EASY TO CATEGORIZE. Others appear to be patched together from leftovers that didn't quite fit elsewhere. One of the latter is the 40th Ward, a crazy quilt of miscellaneous North Side neighborhoods.

The 40th is a ward in search of an identity. It is easier to say what the ward is *not*. It is not Ravenswood; south and east precincts are a continuation of the 47th Ward. It is not Andersonville; eastern precincts are a continuation of the 48th Ward. It is not North Town; northern precincts are a continuation of the 50th Ward. It is not Albany Park; southern and western precincts are a continuation of the 39th Ward. Instead, it is a combination of the above—and more.

Just as the North Side as a whole is not a monolithic unit, neither is the 40th Ward, a microcosm of the North Side, a homogeneous community. Housing, for example, varies greatly. The 40th contains classic Chicago bungalows, stucco houses, and multiunit buildings in Albany Park; two-flats and large single-family houses in the Ravenswood Manor and Ravenswood Gardens neighborhoods which flank the Chicago River; one-and-a-half-story homes along

Olive Street in Andersonville; even a few suburban-type ranch houses in the California and Catalpa area in the north end of the ward.

Two ethnic neighborhoods of citywide renown can be found here, although both are less prominent than in earlier years. Western and Lawrence is the heart of the "new" Greek Town, an area containing Greek restaurants, bakeries, food stores, and specialty stores. However, the neighborhood has seen in recent years the closure of a number of Lawrence Avenue Greek restaurants, and the razing of the Athens, formerly a Greek-owned nightclub on Western.

Andersonville forms the eastern end of the ward. At one time this was a heavily Swedish neighborhood. The Swedish influence (carefully nurtured by the local business community) remains obvious. A log cabin facade (the Swedes introduced the log cabin to America) marks the Swedish American museum at Clark and Berwyn. Other Swedish sights in this blue-and-yellow bedecked neighborhood include a gift shop, a knitting shop, a card shop, and a fish market. Not far away, Ebenezer Lutheran Church (at Foster and Paulina) still serves as Chicago's "Swedish cathedral."

West of Andersonville stands the most prominent Swedish institution: Swedish Covenant Hospital, which recently celebrated its hundredth anniversary. The hospital was founded by the Swedish Covenant Church, which also founded nearby North Park College.

Swedes along Andersonville now have company from other continents. The Andersonville stretch of Clark Street includes Chinese, Filipino, Lebanese, Peruvian, and Italian stores and restaurants.

Other parts of the ward showcase reminders of other diverse ethnic groups: Korean stores and social service agencies near Montrose and Kedzie; an Arabic-language video rental store on Lawrence Avenue; a Cambodian craft center at Lawrence and Washtenaw; Rios, a Portuguese and Brazilian restaurant at Kedzie and Wilson; Moscow at Night, a Russian Jewish night club at Albany and Peterson; the Carl and Bertha Miller Hebrew School at Campbell and Granville. Students from these diverse groups congregate at Mather High School (California and Ardmore), depicted in a 1985 WMAQ-TV special as an example of a multiethnic school.

Even though not a particularly old area by Chicago standards, the 40th Ward contains many footnotes of Chicago history. First is the police station once known as Summerdale (now Foster Avenue) at Foster and Wolcott. A petty crook named Richard Morrison ("the Babbling Burglar") shocked Chicago and the world in 1960 when he testified that Summerdale police not only knew of local burglaries but also took part in them. The resultant scandal produced a massive shakeup in the police department.

A National Guard armory at Foster and the river also made headlines. Four members of the Puerto Rican radical group FALN were arrested in 1984 on charges of attempting to blow up the armory.

The Bowmanville Cafe at Foster and Lincoln recalls (by name) simpler times. Nearby was the former home of the Bowman Dairy, one of the largest in an era when the city was dotted by a number of small dairies. The dairy formed the heart of the small community known as Bowmanville, established by a developer named Jesse Bowman, in the area now bordered by Foster, Lawrence, Western, and California. It was later discovered that Bowman's title to the land was not legal and thus buyers were forced to repurchase the land. Bowman, meanwhile, had skipped town.

Recent political history, with nationwide implications, took place in a small building at Kedzie and Sunnyside. Lyndon LaRouche candidates Mark Fairchild and Janice Hart worked out of this headquarters when they surprised nearly everyone by capturing the Democratic nominations for lieutenant governor and secretary of state in 1986—victories that instantly spelled doom for the Democratic nominee for governor, Adlai Stevenson.

Open space marks much of this ward. It may take the form of Horner Park at California and Montrose, a spacious park that hosted the 1986 Special Winter Olympics; Buffalo Park at Sunnyside and the river, one of the city's smallest; or Legion Park, a stringbean-shaped swath of land east of the river extending from Ainslie to Peterson. Nearby, at Albany and Carmen, one can find the city's only waterfall.

A different sort of open land covers much of the northeast quadrant of the ward. Rosehill Cemetery (Ravenswood and Thorndale), is the largest cemetery in metropolitan Chicago. Mayors, Civil War soldiers, industrialists, and thousands of lesser-known individuals are buried in the 350-acre grounds. Across the street, at Bryn Mawr and Western, is an appropriately named tavern— Rest n Pieces.

The diffused (and perhaps even apparently confused) nature of the ward for years reflected in its politics. That seeming anarchy may have passed, with young alderman and committeeman Patrick O'Connor apparently taking a firm grip on power.

Seymour Simon represented this ward during the 1950s. He was one of the more unusual Chicago politicians, one who jumped back and forth between siding with party regulars and showing independent tendencies. Simon became alderman in 1955, then quit to assume a county board seat in 1961. Richard Daley, needing an intelligent and articulate figure to serve as county board president in 1962, tapped Simon for the honor. He won the November election.

This honeymoon with the regulars did not last. Simon ran afoul of city council Finance Committee chairman Tom Keane over an issue involving land in suburban Techny. Such infidelity to a party lord and master cost Simon 1966 party slating for the board. Undaunted, he ran successfully for alderman as an independent in 1967, taking advantage of the empty seat in his ward when aldermanic successor Nathan Kaplan received a judgeship in 1966.

Simon won reelection in 1971 and voiced his criticisms of Daley on such issues as police brutality. Nevertheless, the mayor slated him in 1974 for a judgeship, thus putting the longtime alderman and committeeman (1959–74) out of Hizzoner's hair.

Years later he came back to haunt the Democrats. Simon, by now an Illinois

Supreme Court justice, had once been rebuffed by Adlai Stevenson in a bid
for appointment to the U.S. district court. In 1982 he cast a key vote to deny
Adlai Stevenson a recount following the closest gubernatorial race in Illinois
history.

Solomon Gutstein followed Simon on the council. He was an attorney
specializing in real estate law (and later author of a two-volume book on Illinois
real estate), director of two community groups, and the council's only Orthodox
Jewish rabbi.

Religion became an issue in this once-Jewish ward during the 1975 election.
Gutstein's major opponent, Virginia Boyd, married a man who converted to
Judaism. Democratic regulars passed out literature to Jewish precincts claiming
that Boyd was not Jewish and literature claiming that she was Jewish in Gentile
precincts.

Mayor Richard Daley installed (Greek-American) John Geocaris as committeeman in 1974, with the understanding that (Jewish) Gutstein would be
slated for alderman. Geocaris could tolerate Gutstein, but Daley could not force
Geocaris to like him.

The mayor's 1976 death freed Geocaris to act against his unwanted ward
partner. Geocaris claimed that Gutstein worked for his own personal good, not
for the citizens or the party. He briefly evicted Gutstein from the party headquarters on the grounds that he had not paid his rent. He refused to reslate
the alderman in 1978.

Gutstein charged that Geocaris resented the alderman's attempts at independent action. Gutstein held monthly town meetings and zoning sessions,
despite the committeeman's disapproval. He refused Geocaris's order to fire
an aldermanic aide and replace him with Geocaris's son, as well as his demands
that Gutstein not see residents unless they were brought in by a precinct
captain.

Ivan Rittenberg, an attorney and former cop, was Geocaris's choice against
Gutstein. He won and served a term largely without distinction. Rittenberg's
most notable contribution was a motel licensing ordinance designed to deter
prostitution, which had been rampant in some of the ward's motels.

Patrick O'Connor, a twenty-eight-year-old lawyer, challenged Rittenberg
in 1983. He charged (with success) that the incumbent had neglected the eastern
and southwestern sectors of the ward. O'Connor fell twenty-eight votes short
of avoiding a runoff.

Rittenberg did himself no favors during the runoff by distributing literature
claiming that O'Connor was a Harold Washington ally. Although Washington
did not carry the ward, voters saw through the blatant untruth. O'Connor won
an easy victory. The following year he likewise ousted Geocaris as committeeman.

Patrick O'Connor has been a major city council disappointment, in part
because so many of his peers acknowledged his intelligence and professed high
hopes for him. At first, those hopes might have seemed fulfilled. O'Connor,

as chairman of the council's education committee, was seen as instrumental in negotiating an end to a 1983 teachers' strike.

Events during the following year altered public perception of him. O'Connor was found to have used leftover funds from his committee to provide year-end jobs for fifteen persons, including his mother-in-law, his brother-in-law, his sister-in-law, wives of two former members of his law firm, and the wife of a former staff aide. Some of those hired admitted that they did not realize they were on the city payroll.

"All in the Family" was a popular name for O'Connor's hiring practices, and O'Connor became known as the "City Hall Santa." The alderman did little to help his cause when he compared his hiring practices to those of Britain's royal family. The nepotism charges erased O'Connor's "fair-haired boy" image, and may have destroyed any chances he might have had for higher office. But they did not hurt him in the 1987 aldermanic election.

Three persons who reflected the ethnic diversity of the ward challenged O'Connor. James Chronis, a Greek-American sporting goods store owner, received the endorsement of the *Tribune* and the Illinois Committee for Honest Government. John Bingham, a businessman of Korean and European ancestry, received the endorsement of the Independent Voters of Illinois-Independent Precinct Organization. Also in the race was Mary O'Connor Garay, an Irish-born former precinct captain.

O'Connor had the endorsement of the 40th Ward Regular Democratic Organization and its precinct captains. That turned out to be enough. The incumbent won 55 percent of the vote, 21 percent more than runner-up Chronis.

REDISTRICTING: The 40th Ward lost parts of two southern precincts to the 33rd Ward from the 1986 redistricting.

MAYORAL: This North Side ward split almost evenly between (Geocaris-backed) Jane Byrne and (O'Connor-backed) Richard Daley in the 1983 Democratic primary. Byrne won it 48 percent to 47 percent for Daley. Harold Washington finished with only 5 percent of the vote.

Regular Democratic forces buried the hatchet following the primary and worked for Bernard Epton. The Republican carried the ward with 83 percent.

Washington achieved similar percentages in the 1987 elections as in the 1983 general contest. He amassed 20 percent of the vote against Byrne, 19 percent against Edward Vrdolyak and Donald Haider.

CENSUS DATA: Population (1980): 58,685. 73.02 percent white, .71 percent black, 13.34 percent Hispanic, 12.93 percent Asian and other. Voting age population: 77.46 percent white, .59 percent black, 11.57 percent Hispanic, 10.38 percent Asian and other.

CENSUS TRACTS: See ward map.

COMMUNITY NEWSPAPERS:
Albany Park News, 7519 N. Ashland (761–7200)
Good News Weekly, 4710 N. Lincoln (878–7334)

ALDERMAN: Patrick J. O'Connor. Elected 1983. Born 1954. Career; J.D., Loyola University, 1979; attorney.
Committees: Education (chairman); Budget and Government Operations; Energy, Environmental Protection, and Public Utilities; Health; Police, Fire, and Municipal Institutions; Streets and Alleys.
City hall telephone: 744–6858, 744–7248.
Ward office: 5034 N. Western Ave. (769–1140).
1987 election:

| Patrick J. O'Connor | 9,536 | (55%) | Mary O'Connor Garay | 1,190 | (7%) |
| James Chronis | 5,802 | (34%) | John W. Bingham | 696 | (4%) |

DEMOCRATIC COMMITTEEMAN: Patrick J. O'Connor. Elected 1984.
1984 election:

| Patrick O'Connor | 7,612 | (60%) |
| John C. Geocaris | 5,456 | (40%) |

MAYORAL ELECTIONS:

1983 Democratic primary:

Jane Byrne	9,417	(48%)
Richard Daley	9,226	(47%)
Harold Washington	1,005	(5%)

1983 general:

| Bernard Epton | 18,217 | (83%) |
| Harold Washington | 3,772 | (17%) |

1987 Democratic primary:

| Jane Byrne | 13,350 | (79%) |
| Harold Washington | 3,395 | (21%) |

1987 general:

Edward Vrdolyak	11,518	(71%)
Harold Washington	3,050	(19%)
Donald Haider	1,724	(11%)

41st Ward

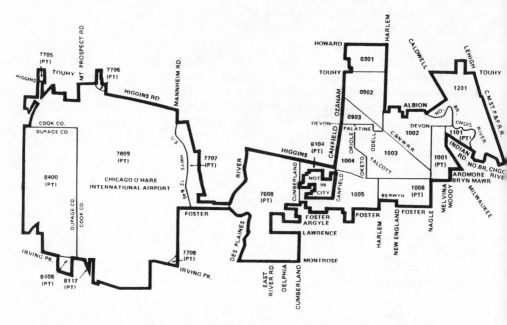

BELIEVE IT OR NOT, Republicans do exist in Chicago. For the most part, they are not found in the posh Gold Coast high rises. Instead, they live in the comfortable suburban-like homes of the neighborhoods at the fringes of the city—outlying areas such as the Far Northwest Side's 41st Ward.

No city ward has been so consistently Republican in the last generation as the 41st. Since 1956 the ward has backed a Republican for president in every election. Policemen living in its many "cop ghetto" neighborhoods were instrumental in electing Republican James O'Grady sheriff in 1986. The ward even carried for Richard Daley's Republican opponent during three of Daley's six mayoral elections, including 41st Ward Republican committeeman (and former congressman) Timothy Sheehan in 1959.

Yet even the 41st Ward has not been able to elect a Republican alderman in recent years. Despite a concerted effort by the Republican party, it stayed with its longtime favorite son, Roman Pucinski, in 1987.

Pucinski's predecessor, Edward T. Scholl, was a Republican. Scholl, a "boy wonder" (he wrote a neighborhood history of Edison Park, Norwood Park, and Oriole Park when he was 19) local newspaper editor, was elected alderman in 1963. At twenty-five, he was the youngest member of the council when elected.

The burly Scholl was considered something of a gadfly while in office. He uncovered city overpaying of asphalt inspectors and charged that a city anti-poverty official had Communist ties (the official was later fired). He criticized zoning amendments (usually considered sacred cows) in other wards. He even accompanied sheriff's police who made vice raids in 1st and 29th ward hotels.

Scholl left the city council after being elected to the state senate in 1972 and was defeated for reelection two years later. His future still appeared bright. Shortly after the losing effort, he got himself a position on Illinois attorney general William Scott's staff. He stayed with Scott only two weeks, forced out by breath of scandal. Scholl later was sentenced to eighteen months in prison for tax cheating in connection with a zoning scheme.

Scholl swamped sixty-year-old incumbent Harry Bell in his first aldermanic win. Republican mayoral candidate Ben Adamowski also carried that ward in 1963 by a three-to-one margin. Those totals were unacceptable to Daley; Bell agreed to step down as Democratic committeeman after the election "for personal reasons."

Bell's replacement was Roman Pucinski, a former newspaper reporter who already was familiar with the ward as its congressman. Pucinski was a 35th Ward resident at the time but accepted Daley's nod and moved into the 41st Ward.

Pucinski first ran for Congress in 1956, with Daley's blessing. He lost that election but defeated Sheehan (Chicago's last Republican congressman) two years later.

During his time in Congress, Pucinski became known as a watchdog of Northwest Side concerns ("He worked hard on areas of particular interest and benefit solely to his district" was the charge of a 1972 Ralph Nader report). He specialized in vocational education and ethnic studies issues. Pucinski took a sharp turn to the right in his later House years. Early in his career, he boasted a 100 percent support of civil rights programs and the War on Poverty. He received a shock in 1966. Republican candidate (and 47th Ward alderman) John Hoellen finished within 4,000 votes of Pucinski after attacking "Pooch" for his support of a bill designed to prevent discrimination in sale or rental of houses. Thereafter, he became markedly more conservative. The onetime civil rights supporter became a leading opponent of school busing and open housing. A man who once had a 100 percent rating from the liberal Americans for Democratic Action saw that rating plummet to 48 percent by the time he left Congress.

That exit came after the 1972 election. Pucinski likely could have remained in Congress indefinitely. Instead, he made an ill-advised run for the Senate against Charles Percy. Pucinski carried his district, of course, but won less than 40 percent of the vote statewide—including poor totals in Chicago's black wards.

Scholl's state senate victory created a fortuitous aldermanic vacancy (not that Pucinski might not have run even had Scholl remained in office). Pucinski won a 1973 special election over gift shop owner Emil Kolasa with 84 percent of the vote and has won reelection every time since then.

Pucinski in his early years became known as a publicity hound who never met a microphone, TV camera, or newspaper headline he didn't like. His thirst for higher office was evident, as showed in his 1977 run for mayor.

The special election following Richard Daley's death was a bizarre one, to say the least. Acting mayor Michael Bilandic, former 11th Ward alderman, was the choice of party regulars. A true-blue liberal, black State Senator Harold Washington, also was a candidate. Yet many of the Lakefront wine and cheese set backed Pucinski (who was anything but liberal), in part because of the perception that Washington could not possibly win.

Pucinski carried the Northwest Side 30th, 38th, 40th, 45th, and 50th wards and came close in four others. He swept 75 percent of the vote in his home 41st. Altogether, he took 33 percent of the vote. "(The election) establishes me as a respectable political force in the city, and I intend to be a voice in the (party's) affairs," he crowed on election night.

That prediction night have been a trifle premature. In fact, Pucinski had a difficult time maintaining control over his own ward. A vindictive Bilandic supported a rump organization headed by state legislator Ralph Capparelli, County Clerk Stanley Kusper, and board of tax appeals member Harry Semrow. This Northwest Democratic Organization, not Pucinski's 41st Ward Regular Democratic Organization, distributed ward patronage in Bilandic's time.

Pucinski got even by supporting Jane Byrne in 1979. He also defeated the Northwest Democratic Organization challenger, T. Ronald Herbert. The rebel group disbanded soon afterward.

The onetime party rebel quickly became one of Byrne's strongest supporters. Even so, his name constantly popped up as a 1983 mayoral challenger. One frequently mentioned scenario pictured Pucinski jumping parties to run as a Republican. Given the success of unknown Bernard Epton against Harold Washington in that year's general election, it is not inconceivable that a Pucinski Republican candidacy might have been successful.

Pucinski (unopposed for alderman in 1983) joined the anti-Harold Washington faction and remained there—a consistent but not particularly ardent foe. His name sprung up from time to time as a possible 1987 Washington opponent, but it appears his mayoral candidate days are over.

Part of the reason for the Pucinski decline might have to do with his daughter. Aurelia Pucinski (married to a man named Keithley) got party slating for a Metropolitan Sanitary District seat in 1984, possibly as part of a deal in exchange for his agreement not to oppose Byrne in 1983. The younger Pucinski led all vote-getters on the MSD ballot.

A year later she became part of a party slating fight. Feminists complained that no woman had received party slating for a statewide office, pointing especially to lieutenant governor and secretary of state. They sought Grace Mary Stern, Adlai Stevenson's 1982 running mate, for one of the posts.

Party regulars agreed to a woman, as long as it was *their* woman. Thus Aurelia Pucinski, a choice unacceptable to many feminists, was slated for secretary of state. It was expected to be a suicide run anyway, as most Democrats conceded they had little chance against popular Republican incumbent Jim Edgar.

Nonetheless, the move became a disaster for Democrats. Pucinski lost the Democratic nomination to Janice Hart, an acerbic follower of political cult leader Lyndon LaRouche. Pucinski did poorly in black wards (it was foolish for party leaders to think that black voters would support the daughter of an alderman who unfailingly opposed Harold Washington), Hispanic wards, and along the liberal Lakefront. She also did poorly downstate, where voters reportedly chose the candidate with the more "pleasant-sounding" (i.e., WASPish) name. The Hart victory, and that of Mark Fairchild over party-backed George Sangmeister, became the major contributing factor to the defeat of gubernatorial candidate Adlai Stevenson.

Yet the younger Pucinski did not curl up and die. She received party slating in late 1987 for clerk of the circuit court and is a favorite to move into her father's old congressional seat when incumbent Frank Annunzio retires.

Roman Pucinski was visibly distraught over his daughter's earlier loss, perhaps seeing it as a rejection of his own career. Opponents also saw what they perceived as a chance to knock off the venerable alderman. Republicans especially licked their chops. They slated Richard Kunicki, a community relations police officer. Kunicki received active support from his party (one of few Republican-leaning aldermanic candidates to get such backing) and such political notables as (Republican) Cook County Sheriff O'Grady and (Democratic) State's Attorney Richard M. Daley. Three other candidates—former board of health employee Salvotore Terranova, fire department paramedic Thomas Kolk, and former Pucinski precinct captain Sheila O'Connell—were expected to force the election into a runoff.

Pucinski, however, held off all foes. Despite Kunicki's police background, it was Pucinski who secured the endorsement of the Fraternal Order of Police. He captured a surprising 54 percent of the vote. Kunicki, the second place finisher, got only 33 percent—a sign that Chicago's Republican party may exist, but still has a way to go to match up with its Democratic counterpart.

More than just an alderman, Roman Pucinski is generally acknowledged as the political leader of Chicago's Polish community. His roots go deep. Lydia Pucinska, Roman's mother, was a Polish fixture well into her eighties as host of "The Sunshine Hour," a daily radio variety show. The program appeared on WEDC, a family-owned radio station (which Pucinski's late wife managed). Pucinski for years has been the president of the Illinois division of the Polish-American Congress.

Pucinski's activism aside, the 41st is not as obviously "ethnic" as many other Northwest Side wards. Granted, signs of eastern European culture exist here. Two of the most obvious are elegant churches not far from the Kennedy Expressway. St. Joseph's Ukrainian Catholic Church (Cumberland and Argyle) is adorned with fifteen gold domes supported by glass towers with an inside decorated with gold leaf. Holy Resurrection Serbian Orthodox Cathedral (on Serbian Road, just south of the expressway and across the street from an un-

ROMAN PUCINSKI

incorporated area) is another landmark for both locals and commuters, with its four corner domes surrounding a larger central one.

But most of the ward is suburban in character, not ethnic. In fact, the 41st is a collection of disparate and geographically separated "suburbs." To the northeast is the western section of Edgebrook, a well-to-do neighborhood that is found mostly in the 39th Ward. The Billy Caldwell Forest Preserve separates it from the rest of the 41st.

Norwood Park forms the center of the ward. Its curving avenues (including the appropriately named Circle Avenue) and distinctive railroad depot lend an air that is anything but urban. Norwood Park was the site of the Henry W. Rincker House, an 1851 farmhouse at Devon and Milwaukee that was declared a city landmark in 1980 despite protests from its owner. A midnight fire the following year made the Rincker House the first Chicago landmark to be illegally destroyed. The corner of Milwaukee, Nagle, and Devon may lack a city landmark, but it nonetheless has a point of interest. Superdawg is located at the southeast corner, the only hot dog stand in the city that still employs car hops.

Further north, extending to Howard Street, is Edison Park, the farthest northwest neighborhood in the city. Property values are high in Edison Park, due in part to demand from police and other city workers forced to live within city limits yet wanting to escape inner city woes.

The John F. Kennedy (originally Northwest) Expressway splits the ward into northern and southern sections. South of the expressway is a neighborhood known as Oriole Park, comfortable but more blue-collar than the northern half.

West of Cumberland Avenue is the most recently developed of the city's officially designated communities, O'Hare. This area, bordered by Higgins Road, Cumberland, the Des Plaines River, and Belmont (the 41st Ward extends south only to Montrose), originally was home for those working on O'Hare construction. Now it houses both single-family homes and multiunit apartment complexes.

The 41st Ward also includes the airport itself. At one time it was connected to the city only by a narrow ribbon of Higgins Road (which the city later traded to the Village of Rosemont for a wider strip along Foster Avenue). O'Hare, which vies with airports in Atlanta and Dallas for the title of world's busiest, has one full-time resident—a caretaker.

Finally, one can stroll down Memory Lane in the 41st Ward. The Chicago version is a block-long street just south of Foster and west of Canfield. Be careful; Memory Lane in Chicago is a dead-end street.

REDISTRICTING: The 41st Ward was unaffected by the 1986 ward remap.

MAYORAL: Even though the 41st is the "whitest" (97.04 percent) of Chicago wards, Harold Washington eked out a few votes here in the 1983 Democratic primary. Washington got 2 percent of the vote. Jane Byrne received only 52 percent of the vote, despite Pucinski's backing. Richard Daley captured 46 percent.

Washington made gains, although not overwhelming ones, in the general election. He scored 7 percent of the vote against Republican Bernard Epton, the largest concentration of those votes coming from a precinct near O'Hare.

Byrne captured this ward in 1987 with 93 percent of the vote. The 41st provided her best total anywhere except for the Southwest Side.

Edward Vrdolyak's 87 percent carried the ward in the general. Don Haider won only 8 percent, but his 879-vote differential over Harold Washington provided the Republican's largest second-place margin in the city.

CENSUS DATA: Population (1980): 60,579. 97.04 percent white, .28 percent black, 1.27 percent Hispanic, 1.41 percent Asian and other. Voting age population: 96.95 percent white, .32 percent black, 1.22 percent Hispanic, 1.51 percent Asian and other.

CENSUS TRACTS: See ward map.

COMMUNITY NEWSPAPERS:
Chicago Post, 2810 W. Fullerton (772–3300)
Chicago's Northwest Side Press, 4941 N. Milwaukee (286–6100)

Edgebrook Times-Review, 1000 Executive Way, Des Plaines (824–1111)
Edison-Norwood Times-Review, 1000 Executive Way, Des Plaines (824–1111)
Harlem-Foster Times, 4600 N. Harlem, Harwood Heights (867–7700)

ALDERMAN: Roman Pucinski. Elected 1973. Born May 13, 1919. Career: B.A., 1940, Northwestern University; J.D., 1949, John Marshall Law School; reporter, 1939–59, *Chicago Sun-Times*; U.S. Representative, 1959–73.
Committees: Intergovernmental Relations (chairman); Aviation; Claims and Liabilities; Finance; Housing; Municipal Code Revision.
City hall telephone: 744–3208, 744–3942.
Ward office: 6204 N. Milwaukee Ave. (763–4141)
1987 election:

Roman C. Pucinski	16,756	(54%)	Sheila B. O'Connell	698	(2%)
Richard R. Kunicki	10,095	(33%)	Thomas James Kolk	284	(1%)
Salvatore G. Terranova	3,147	(10%)		

DEMOCRATIC COMMITTEEMAN: Roman Pucincki. Elected 1964.
1984 election:
Roman C. Pucinski, unopposed.

MAYORAL ELECTIONS:

1983 Democratic primary:

Jane Byrne	15,964	(52%)
Richard Daley	14,243	(46%)
Harold Washington	543	2%)

1987 Democratic primary:

Jane Byrne	28,280	(93%)
Harold Washington	2,005	(7%)

1983 general:

Bernard Epton	32,733	(93%)
Harold Washington	2,380	(7%)

1987 general:

Edward Vrdolyak	26,530	(87%)
Donald Haider	2,461	(8%)
Harold Washington	1,582	(5%)

42nd Ward

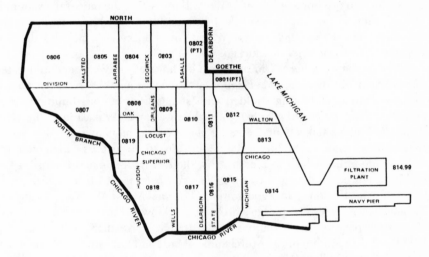

FIFTY YEARS AGO, a panel of University of Chicago social scientists divided the city into seventy-five communities (two have since been added). These communities represented areas that had similar social, economic, and cultural identities at the time.

Half a century later, the city has changed. So have the officially designated communities. Some have changed so much that describing the areas within them as a community is a meaningless exercise. The best example of such a community is the one known as Near North Side, which coincides almost precisely with the Lakefront 42nd Ward.

Any mention of median per capita income would be misleading, but other sets of figures show the Near North Side (and 42nd Ward) with a greater disparity between rich and poor than any other area. Only two other Chicago communities (Lincoln Park and Lakeview) have even half as many families as the Near North Side with incomes of $50,000 or more. Yet only eleven communities have more families with incomes of $5,000 or less.

The eastern half of the ward is the side that the Chicago Association of Commerce and Industry loves to show off; it has been a business hub ever since Chicago's first permanent settler, Jean Baptiste Pont du Sable, established a trading post on the north bank of the Chicago River 200 years ago. Here is the Michigan Avenue "Magnificent Mile," a glamorous shopping district which compares favorably with any other such strip in the world. Here amongst the Beautiful People and the smart boutiques which sell expensive clothing and paintings are a number of Chicago's most famous sights.

The north end of the "Magnificent Mile" contains the strangest but most familiar symbol of all—the odd-looking Water Tower, considered an architectural marvel at the time of its 1869 construction. The Water Tower, the only major edifice to survive the Great Chicago Fire, stands as a monument to the city's efforts to overcome adversity. Across the street is the namesake shopping plaza, Water Tower Place, one of the tallest buildings in Chicago and certainly the most elegant shopping center. Water Tower Place also includes the Ritz Carlton, *the* luxury hotel in Chicago.

The media work here. Chicago's two leading daily newspapers are located on the Near North Side: the *Tribune* at Michigan and the river (in Gothic Tribune Tower, a building studded with stones from famous buildings from around the world) and the *Sun-Times* a block away at Wabash and the river (journalists often talk about "crossing the street," moving from one paper to the other; it is almost a literal statement). Two other papers which often exert citywide influence are located nearby: the *Reader* (State and Illinois), a liberal-leaning free weekly; and *Crain's Chicago Business*, at Rush and Superior. Chicago's most-listened-to radio station, *Tribune*-owned WGN, is located at Tribune Tower. Two of Chicago's three network-owned television stations and their corresponding radio stations are in the Near North Side: NBC-owned WMAQ (TV and radio) in the Merchandise Mart, and CBS-owned WBBM (TV and radio) at McClurg Court (McClurg and Erie). Michigan Avenue also is home to the city's major advertising agencies.

Chicago's high and mighty work here. They labor at the Merchandise Mart, the wholesale home-furnishing center at Wells and Kinzie. Busts of eight nineteenth century business giants stand opposite the front of the huge (at one time the world's largest by acreage) building, which once was owned by Joseph P. Kennedy. Or perhaps they work at the Apparel Center, which is to clothing what the Merchandise Mart is to furniture.

The high and mighty play here. They work out at the East Bank, an exclusive athletic club at Kingsbury and Illinois. They seek the elusive mate at bars along Rush Street or Division Street. They buy art and antiques from the many stores and auctioneers of the SuHu (Superior and Huron) area. They go to be seen at the Limelight, a club at Ontario and Dearborn located in a former Historical Society building. They (or their suburban cousins) visit Old Town along Wells Street, a countercultural mecca in the 1960s but now a more mainstream strip of restaurants and boutiques.

The high and mighty live here. Present and future yuppies share or own condominiums at Sandburg Village, a high-rise complex along Clark and LaSalle streets. Others live at Lakepoint Tower, a high-rise located at the eastern end of Grand Avenue, or Marina City, a two-building complex at State Street and the river. The well-off also may reside at the John Hancock Center, the fifth-tallest building in the world and the world's tallest residential building. If they *really* have it made, they live on Lake Shore Drive, the Gold Coast's most exclusive street.

The high and mighty (as well as anyone else who wishes) even worship here. Holy Name Cathedral, seat of the nation's second-largest Catholic archdiocese, is located at State and Chicago. St. James Episcopal Cathedral at Wabash and Superior likewise serves the Episcopal community.

Another Near North church attracts affluent worshippers and attracted citywide attention in 1986. Fourth Presbyterian Church at Michigan and Chestnut was proposed for landmark status. This would-be designation came over the protests of its governing board, which wished to keep the option (available only with great difficulty in the case of landmark buildings) of making changes in the building.

The Near North Side contains other attractions of citywide note: onion-topped Medinah Temple (Ohio and Wabash); the Museum of Contemporary Art (Ontario and Fairbanks); the Peace Museum (Erie and Sedgwick); the Newberry Library (Clark and Walton), known for its genealogical studies; the Wrigley Building (Michigan Avenue and the river), a white terra cotta building illuminated at night; the James Jardine Filtration Plant and nearby Milton Olive Park, named after a Vietnam War hero; and Navy Pier, site of Chicagofest during the Michael Bilandic and Jane Byrne years.

Education is a major industry on the Near North Side, which includes both the board of education administrative offices (Wendell and Wells) and the national PTA headquarters (Rush and Huron). Both Northwestern University and Loyola University have downtown campuses here (Northwestern also operates a large hospital complex). Also located here are such varied centers of learning as the Rehabilitation Institute of Chicago (Superior and Fairbanks) and the American College of Surgeons and accompanying surgery museum (State and Erie), Moody Bible Institute (Chicago and LaSalle), and the Latin School (Clark and North), the city's most prestigious private high school. One "institution" city fathers do not brag about is located at Michigan Avenue and the river in the Mandel Building—two floors of which have been the "temporary" home of the Chicago Public Library for more than ten years.

Disasters, both natural and man-made, have visited the area now known as the 42nd Ward. One of Chicago's most famous involved the tour ship *Eastland*, which capsized in 1915, killing hundreds of people (one who was spared was a young man whose tardiness caused him to miss the boat—George Halas). Two of Chicago's premier early years gangsters also met their ends: Dion O'Banion, killed in his flower shop across the street from Holy Name Cathedral in 1924, and O'Banion lieutenant Hymie Weiss, shot to death in front of Holy Name Cathedral in 1926.

Much of the land now known as the "Magnificent Mile" is there thanks to an unlikely developer—George Wellington "Cap" Streeter, one of Chicago's more colorful characters. Streeter's boat ran aground on a sandbar north of the Chicago River's mouth in 1886 (near the site of the present Hancock Building). He set up headquarters there, formed a landfill, and welcomed other squatters to "Streeterville." The captain and his wife proclaimed the "District of Lake Michigan" and refused to obey Chicago liquor and gambling laws. Streeter ultimately was forced off the (now-valuable) land, but "Streeterville" lives on as the nickname of the eastern extremity of the ward.

Cap Streeter may be gone but funkiness survives. The Near North Side contains Washington Square Park, across the street from the Newberry Library. Nobody calls it Washington Square Park; it is universally known as "Bughouse Square." In years past "homos, pinkos, nature lovers, and nuts" used to congregate and espouse (often unpopular) views. Looking for Chicago's shortest street? It is Armstrong Street, located a block south of Chicago Avenue at Michigan—all 82 feet of it. A Japanese nightclub? There is the Cafe Shino at St. Clair and Ontario. An autograph museum? Try Signatures at Chicago and Wabash. The 42nd Ward also contains the 1944 St. Louis Browns (Illinois and Rush), the only bar in Chicago with decor of the worst pennant-winning team in history.

One other bar in the 42nd Ward deserves note. Brehon's Pub (Superior and Wells) is a neighborhood Irish pub, jammed on St. Patrick's Day with revelers and marching bands. But it gained footnote status in Chicago history under its former name—the Mirage. A *Sun-Times* investigative team ran the bar and used it to describe payoffs routinely "asked" of small businessmen by city inspectors.

The westernmost section of the ward is Goose Island, a man-made island now entirely industrial. Various politicians suggested Goose Island as an alternative site for the proposed Chicago World's Fair, suggestions not taken seriously by many people.

Much of the northwest quadrant of the ward is territory which does not appear in the tourist brochures. This is Cabrini-Green (Cabrini extention apartments are red high-rise ones south of Division Street; the Green apartments, white ones north of Division; the original Cabrini apartments are rowhouses built there in 1942). The 1955 groundbreaking of the Cabrini high-rise project was one of Richard Daley's first acts as mayor.

This area never was affluent (it displaced a grimy Italian neighborhood known as "Little Hell"). In some ways it is a nightmare. Rival gangs exchange shots from buildings 500 and 502 at 2:30 P.M. as children leave school—surely one of the grimmest rituals anywhere in America.

Cabrini-Green's years as a high-rise ghetto may be numbered. The rest of the Near North Side is booming, and seeking additional space. The housing project (considered by many a failure at providing quality low-cost living) is located in the path of expansion. When the rich and poor have collided over housing sites in Chicago, the former invariably have triumphed.

Occasionally (as when a policeman is shot to death) Cabrini-Green explodes into the evening news. One such event occurred in 1981. Local violence led to a temporary "resident"—Mayor Jane Byrne, who lived there briefly in order to draw attention to its problems. Byrne then returned to her regular 42nd Ward home on fashionable Chestnut Street.

The ward also contains Atrium Village, one of the few integration success stories anywhere in Chicago. Carefully regulated racial quotas assure that the development does not become either "Carl Sandburg West" or "Cabrini East."

GEORGE W. DUNNE

Whites currently have a shorter waiting list than blacks. As a result, an unlikely coalition of black activists (charging discrimination) and the Reagan administration (seeking to dismantle quotas) have opposed the Atrium admission system.

Mayor Jane Byrne might have been the most prominent 42nd Ward resident during her term in office, but she was never the most powerful political official in the 42nd Ward. That designation went (and goes) to George Dunne, Democratic committeeman for more than a quarter-century.

Dunne, a former majority leader of the Illinois House of Representatives, assumed a vacant county board seat in 1962 and became the board's president in 1969. Meanwhile, he became 42nd Ward committeeman in 1961. Dunne built one of the strongest ward organizations in the city, despite a ward with a highly transient population.

Already an elder statesman in 1974, Dunne was paid the ultimate compliment by Richard J. Daley. The venerable mayor, who had been in ill health for most of the year, asked Dunne to consider replacing him on the ticket in the 1975 election. Dunne immediately deferred and asked Daley to seek reelection—a response Dunne feels was the one the mayor wanted to hear.

He took a consolation prize after Daley's death. Dunne was elected county (and city) party chairman. However, other party leaders (fearing a Daley-style power consolidation) refused to grant him the control Daley had. Ed Kelly, not Dunne, was placed at the head of the party slating committee. An 11th

Ward triumvirate of acting mayor Michael Bilandic, State Senator Richard M. Daley, and patronage director Tom Donovan took control of patronage.

If Daley was dictatorial and secretive as county chairman, Dunne was open and easygoing. His presumed laxness was given as a reason for the 1982 Vrdolyak-led coup which displaced him. Dunne got the votes of Southwest Side and most suburban committeemen. But only one black committeeman (county board ally John Stroger) stayed with him.

The real reason for the Dunne removal had little to do with his style as party leader. Dunne was a supporter of State's Attorney Richard M. Daley, whom Byrne perceived to be her most formidable 1983 reelection foe. Byrne and ally Vrdolyak wanted party machinery out of a potential rival's hands.

Dunne supported Daley in the 1983 Democratic primary. But after that election, he became the only major white party official to back Democratic nominee Harold Washington.

His stance, in retrospect, was not a surprising one. Certainly it might have been a response to the covert backing of Republican Bernard Epton by Vrdolyak. But Dunne also long advocated giving blacks an increased voice in party affairs. He warned in 1981 that failure to amend reduced black representation stemming from Thomas Keane's remap plan would have serious repercussions. Dunne was proven correct when special elections resulting from a lawsuit over the map gave Harold Washington's faction a majority in the city council. Most important, George Dunne has always been the ultimate party man. Harold Washington won the Democratic nomination, and therefore as the Democratic nominee he deserved to be supported.

Dunne, a constant Washington backer, was approached by the mayor to mount a campaign to regain the chairmanship in 1984. He declined because of obvious lack of support. Two years later he might have had the votes had he wished to regain his former position. Once again he declined. But in 1987, after Vrdolyak's resignation, Dunne won unanimous reelection to the party leadership.

In 1987 Dunne once again played an important role in a mayoral election, through his alderman, Burton Natarus. After Harold Washington died, white aldermen looked for alternatives to Timothy Evans, choice of hard-core Harold Washington allies. Dunne did not back Evans. But when the white aldermen considered one of their own (such as Richard Mell or Terry Gabinski) Dunne threatened to withdraw his support unless black alderman Eugene Sawyer was the candidate. His threat convinced the other aldermen to stick with Sawyer.

Dorsey Crowe served as alderman of this ward longer than anyone else. He was first elected by accident—literally. Crowe (who first ran in 1915) was serving as an army aviator in 1919. While flying over the city dropping circulars urging Chicagoans to buy war bonds, his plane crashed in Lincoln Park. Crowe, campaigning on crutches, won a sympathy vote.

He remained in the council more than forty years, becoming the last survivor of the days when two aldermen were elected from a ward. He was dean of the city council at the time of his death in 1962.

Always interested in aviation (his work led to his title, "Father of Midway Airport"), Crowe remained to the end one of the council's more colorful members. When a 1959 opponent claimed he won because his workers paid residents fifty cents per vote, he told her, "Madame, you can't get that done for fifty cents. It costs five dollars."

Every 42nd Ward alderman since Crowe has been a solid Dunne ally. The first was Mayer Goldberg, who left the council to become a judge in 1968. Goldberg put his role as alderman in a realistic perspective. When an after-dinner speaker lauded him as "the leading light of Chicago's City Council," Goldberg answered "Big deal!"

Raymond Fried replaced Goldberg, only briefly. He was diagnosed as having cancer shortly after his name was locked on the ballot, and died not long after the special election to replace Goldberg.

Burton Natarus, an attorney and Dunne precinct captain, won election in 1971. For years, his reelection was a virtual certainty. In 1983, when Byrne backed an apparently strong challenger (Edward Howlett, son of a popular former Illinois attorney general), Natarus won by 7,000 votes.

For the most part, Natarus has tended to bills of particular importance to his Gold Coast and Sandburg Village constituents. He introduced the "pooper scooper" ordinance, which made pet owners responsible for cleaning up after their animals. He has worked to regulate the horse-drawn carriages that travel mainly in his ward. He moved to limit street musicians in the Rush Street area. In late 1986 he sought to eliminate 4:00 A.M. liquor licenses.

Natarus's often gloomy countenance has made him known in some political circles as "the Sad Sack alderman." He has had reason for a lack of cheer. Natarus had been known as a regular party man, not a reformer. Yet when city council alignments jelled in 1983, Natarus (because of Dunne's antipathy to Vrdolyak) found himself stuck in the Washington bloc. As a result, he was deprived of committee chairmanships that anti-Washington leader Vrdolyak doled out to his opposition bloc allies.

Nor was he glad in September 1986, when his stance on a property tax increase put the eyes of the city on him. Natarus at first favored a record $79.9 million property tax increase, then surprised most of the council by voting "nay" on the motion. That vote meant that the increase fell one vote short of the twenty-five votes needed for Mayor Washington to break a tie and pass the increase. For days afterward, he was the most highly wooed alderman in the city, by both pro- and anti-Washington factions.

Some observers professed not to know whether Natarus was going to change his vote. "Anyone who's ever dealt with Burt Natarus has no idea what goes on in his mind," said opposition-bloc leader Edward Vrdolyak. Others insisted that Natarus would vote for the tax increase because of Dunne. "Although Dunne insists he doesn't tell Natarus how to vote, about nobody believes him," claimed *Tribune* columnist Steve Neal.

Natarus finally voted for the increase, after giving a long, passionate speech about the city's financial troubles. Even though the vote cost him death threats, he could claim a victory for his ward. Natarus forced a compromise, under which $27 million (about one-third) of the property tax increase would be eliminated in exchange for a jet fuel tax and an increase in the gasoline tax. The latter tax was a minor coup; it would have minimal effect in a ward where, as one wag put it, "half the residents don't own cars and the other half send their chauffeurs out to refill their limousines."

The tax increase brought out a raft of opponents in the 1987 aldermanic election: Denise Barnes, the ward's Republican committeeman, endorsed by Governor James Thompson, Sheriff James O'Grady, and other prominent GOP members; Maxine Brown, an insurance broker; Robert Copia, marketing agent for an insurance company; Barbara Pressman, a real estate developer and former schoolteacher; Ray Smith, an attorney in practice with Jane Byrne's brother, Edward Burke; and James Wright, a chemist.

Natarus finished ahead of his nearest opponent, Pressman, by nearly a three-to-one margin, including resounding Cabrini-Green margins. Yet he placed just short of a majority with 47 percent.

The runoff proved vicious. Pressman continually attacked the property tax increase. Natarus's campaign accused Pressman of being a front for her husband, a lobbyist for the wholesale liquor industry. Natarus won (thanks to expected strong black support), but his 54 percent proved less than a resounding vote of confidence.

REDISTRICTING: The 42nd remained unchanged by the 1986 redistricting.

MAYORAL: All three candidates had strong bases and active support in this ward during the 1983 Democratic primary, and the 42nd showed a closer three-way split than any other ward. Harold Washington, thanks to near-unanimous support in Cabrini-Green, took 28 percent of the vote. Richard Daley, backed by Dunne, captured 34 percent. Jane Byrne, with 38 percent, won her home ward.

George Dunne's support, plus the already solid Cabrini-Green total, helped give Washington 46 percent of the vote in the general election against Bernard Epton. Of the six Lakefront wards, only the 46th (with 47 percent) gave Washington a higher percentage.

Washington nearly carried the ward in the 1987 primary, with 47 percent of the vote. He swept Cabrini-Green, and avoided huge losses elsewhere. Byrne's 53 percent came mostly from eastern precincts.

The 42nd proved to be the closest ward in the city during the general election. Edward Vrdolyak carried the eastern, predominantly white, precincts and 44 percent of the vote. Washington won 42 percent, with landslide returns from Cabrini-Green. Donald Haider won 14 percent, his second-best total in the city.

CENSUS DATA: Population (1980): 60,173. 58.74 percent white, 36.42 percent black, 3.06 percent Hispanic, 1.78 percent Asian and other. Voting age population: 70.89 percent white, 24.54 percent black, 3.05 percent Hispanic, 4.52 percent Asian and other.

CENSUS TRACTS: See ward map.

COMMUNITY NEWSPAPERS:
Lake Shore News, 108 S. Michigan (346–6884)
Lincoln Park/Lakeview Booster, 1647 W. Belmont (281–7500)
Near North News, 26 E. Huron (787–2677)
North Loop News, 800 N. Clark, (787–5396)

ALDERMAN: Burton F. Natarus. Elected 1971. Born November 7, 1933. Career: B.A., University of Wisconsin, 1956; J.D., University of Wisconsin, 1960; attorney; political science instructor, Loyola University; consultant, Committee on Housing, City and Community Development; commissioner, Cook County Justice Commission.

Committees: Local Transportation (chairman); Beautification and Recreation; Budget and Government Operations; Committees, Rules, Municipal Code Revision, and Ethics; Finance; Land Acquisition, Disposition, and Leases; License; Municipal Code Revision; Streets and Alleys; Zoning.

City hall telephone: 744–3062, 744–3065.
Ward office: 100 W. Grand Ave. (527–5607).
1987 election:

Burton F. Natarus	10,076	(47%)	Ray J. Smith	1,922	(9%)
Barbara K. Pressman	3,771	(18%)	Maxine Brown	837	(4%)
Denise A. Barnes	2,350	(11%)	James Wright	268	(1%)
Robert A. Copia	2,061	(10%)			

1987 runoff:

Burton F. Natarus	11,856	(54%)
Barbara K. Pressman	9,970	(46%)

DEMOCRATIC COMMITTEEMAN: George W. Dunne. Appointed 1961. Born February 20, 1913. Career: B.A., Northwestern University; U.S. Army; director of Office Organization and Administration, Chicago Park District; Illinois House of Representatives, 1955–60; Cook County Board, 1960–; President, County Board, 1968–.

Ward office: 945 N. State St. (787–9037).
1984 Democratic committeeman:

George W. Dunne	10,591	(80%)
Irwin J. Solganick	1,551	(12%)
James A. Wright	1,173	(9%)

MAYORAL ELECTIONS:

1983 Democratic primary:

Jane Byrne	9,068	(38%)
Richard Daley	8,123	(34%)
Harold Washington	6,602	(28%)

1983 general:

Bernard Epton	14,894	(54%)
Harold Washington	12,496	(46%)

1987 Democratic primary:

Jane Byrne	11,109	(53%)
Harold Washington	9,987	(47%)

1987 general:

Edward Vrdolyak	10,215	(44%)
Harold Washington	9,680	(42%)
Donald Haider	3,100	(13%)

4**3**rd Ward

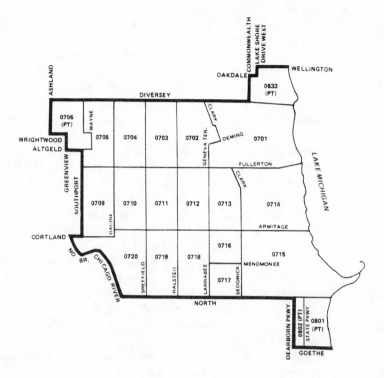

HOW TIMES HAVE CHANGED. Lincoln Park's 43rd Ward, once a German ethnic stronghold, is now the "silk stocking" ward of the city. Likewise, politics evolved over the years. From a German Democratic machine stronghold, the 43rd became the vanguard of the independent movement of the late 1960s and early 1970s.

Young liberals who grew up with the antiwar movement have mellowed or moved. The "yippies" of 1968 have been replaced by the "yuppies" of 1988, urban professionals stereotyped as being more interested in BMWs and CDs than social change. This changing philosophy is reflected in the aldermanic representation of the ward, although it is not certain which route that representation will take.

The 43rd Ward is roughly bordered by North Avenue, Southport, Diversey, and the lake, plus a southeast Gold Coast spur which includes some of the more luxurious real estate in Chicago. The three eras of the 43rd Ward—ethnic, liberal/countercultural, and yuppie—are all in evidence.

Other ethnic groups settled here; St. Vincent de Paul Church (Sheffield and Webster) represented an Irish parish, and St. Josaphat (Southport and Belden) was Polish. But the Lincoln Park area, especially around North Avenue, was German.

For the most part, Germans assimilated into American society and moved elsewhere. The Golden Ox, at North and Clybourn (across the street in the 42nd Ward), and Germania Inn (North and Clark) are the last surviving restaurants from the days when North Avenue was known as "German Broadway."

Further east, one reminder of German culture is seen daily by residents and thousands of Ravenswood elevated commuters. St. Michael's Church at Eugenie and Cleveland casts a benevolent shadow over Old Town. Every Christmas season red and green lights shine from the church's clock tower, a Chicago harbinger of the Yuletide season.

The 1960s brought the counterculture to Chicago, and its local capital was Wells Street in Old Town. Hippies and "weekend hippies" bought *The Seed* alternative newspaper while shopping in the many "head shops" that proliferated. The Old Town business strip has matured into a street of restaurants and boutiques. Hippie sightings in the 43rd Ward are rare these days, but the ward does contain a reminder of the free spirits of earlier times—Second City at North and Wells, proving ground for dozens of America's top comedians.

Further north is Lincoln Avenue, now one of Chicago's most popular entertainment strips. In the late 1960s and early 1970s music-rich clubs coexisted with laid-back neighborhood taverns. The only two of the latter remaining from that era are John Barleycorn's Pub (Lincoln and Belden), with piped-in classical music, and Sterch's (Lincoln and Webster), the only bar in Chicago with a carrot as its emblem.

Just off Lincoln Avenue at Webster is another counterculture monument— Oz Park. Chicago parks generally memorialize dead presidents or aldermen, but this one was named after a wizard. A local used-book dealer led the drive to honor Chicagoan L. Frank Baum, who wrote his Oz books from a home in Humboldt Park.

Between Old Town and Lincoln Avenue is the Tap Root Pub. This pub became a local cause célèbre in the 1970s when the owner refused to accommodate urban renewal by relocating from Sedgwick Avenue ("We shall not be moved" bumper stickers were a common feature on Old Town cars). The pub exists today—but at Willow and Howe, not Sedgwick.

Another major 1970s cause revolved around Lincoln Towing, a notorious towing company which had a concentration-camp-like pound at Fullerton and Lakewood. The late folksinger Steve Goodman satirized Lincoln Towing in his song "Lincoln Park Pirates."

Today, the 43rd Ward is the epitome of the good life in Chicago. If the 1960s had head shops in the ward, the 1980s bring a limousine service to Armitage and Clifton. Young urban professionals work out at clubs such as the Lakeshore Centre (Fullerton and Lakewood) or the Lehmann Sports Club (Lehmann and Drummond), dine at any of a hundred local upscale restaurants, shop at trendy stores on Clark Street, Fullerton, Halsted, or Armitage.

One measure of the Lincoln Park change is the subject of wine. For years

Sam's Wine Warehouse was located at a disreputable-looking building at the corner of North and Halsted (a sign outside billed it as "Sam's Cut-Rate Liquors"). Derelicts gathered outside the building for the 7:00 A.M. opening to buy cheap wine. More affluent customers shopped at the extensive wine cellar during evening hours.

Mayor Jane Byrne facilitated Sam's move to a new building two blocks west. Opponents (particularly State's Attorney Richard Daley) attacked her support of "Sam's Cut-Rate Liquors." The store now serves customers (the 7:00 P.M., not 7:00 A.M. ones) at North and Sheffield.

The North and Halsted neighborhood, seedy only ten years ago, has gentrified. Young (mainly white) professionals have largely replaced working-class blacks in the southwest corner of the ward—one of the city's few examples of whites "chasing" blacks out of a neighborhood. Nearby Clybourn Avenue exemplifies ward change. Developers have sought the street's empty factories for conversion to lofts. Remaining manufacturers, fearing they will be forced out of the area, seek to halt such conversions.

In a ward full of transient persons and businesses, a few institutions have survived the years. Two museums, the Chicago Historical Society and the Chicago Academy of Sciences, border Lincoln Park at North Avenue and Armitage respectively. Francis Parker School, at Clark and Webster, is one of the city's most prestigious private schools (as well as the only place in Chicago which regularly screens Japanese-language movies). Further west at Fullerton and Seminary is DePaul University, home of a law school which has graduated many of Chicago's civic leaders but now is more famous as a nationwide basketball power.

If producers of "Lifestyles of the Rich and Famous" took a road trip to Chicago, they most likely would stop at the 43rd Ward's Gold Coast boot heel. There they could see Astor Street, the quiet street which replaced Prairie Avenue as the home of Chicago's wealthy; the Pump Room of the Ambassador East Hotel (State and Goethe), where visiting celebrities have come to see and be seen; and the former Playboy Mansion (State and Banks), now a dormitory for students of the School of the Art Institute. A famous although not rich person lives at State and North Avenue—the archbishop of Chicago. The archbishop's residence is a Queen Anne mansion which boasts nineteen chimneys.

Some 43rd Ward sights defy categorization. Reebie Storage and Moving Company (Clark and Belden) draws attention by the colorful Egyptian statues and hieroglyphs on the building facade. Another building which captures one's attention is that of the Midwest Buddhist Temple (Menomonee and Hudson). One building deliberately unobtrusive is located on Webster and Lakewood— a "cop bar" which, to put it mildly, does not go out of its way to attract outsiders.

Cops and robbers have made their mark here, in two of the most famous incidents in the history of organized crime. The Biograph Theatre (Lincoln and Fullerton) now plays "art" films, but on July 22, 1934, it showed a movie called *Manhattan Melodrama*. Public Enemy Number One, John Dillinger, was shot down by federal agents as he was leaving the theater after watching the movie.

The SMC Cartage Company no longer stands at 2122 North Clark. "Police" showed up there February 14, 1929. Seven members of Bugs Moran's gang, plus an unfortunate bystander, were shot down by Al Capone allies dressed as cops, thus forever making Chicago one of the few places in the world which associates Valentine's Day with crime.

Most notable location in the ward is Lincoln Park itself. In the city's earliest years, it was the site of the municipal cemetery. The cemetery's remains (including those of many Confederate soldiers) were transferred elsewhere in the 1860s, when the living decided that the property was too valuable to be used for the dead.

Two monuments remain. One is the Ira Couch mausoleum, bearing the remains of one of the city's first hotelkeepers. The other is a stone commemorating David Kennison, last survivor of the Boston Tea Party, who died in Chicago in 1852 at age 115.

Lincoln Park hosts ponds, a lagoon, a large conservatory, a driving range, a theater, and statues of any number of famous people. But the most famous attraction is the free zoo which features a modern ape house, a rookery, and a children's zoo, among other attractions. The zoo is located in the ward's 69th Precinct; it would not be farfetched to assume that Mr. Lion or Mrs. Bear cast votes here in previous elections.

The person in charge of those votes most likely was Mathias "Paddy" Bauler, a Chicago political legend. His most famous moment came when Richard J. Daley won the 1955 mayoral election. Bauler uttered the words which are now a local political motto: "Chicago ain't ready for reform." It's not that Paddy was interested in reform—just the opposite. He held reformers in disdain, calling one "so dumb he probably thinks the forest preserve is some kind of jelly."

Bauler was the last of the saloonkeeper-aldermen. He ran a speakeasy at Willow and Howe during Prohibition and became the first person to obtain a liquor license in Chicago after its repeal. Afterward he ran a saloon (and a ward office) at 403 W. North Avenue. He controlled the Hudson Avenue police station and regulated gambling and vice in his ward.

He was also one of the freer spirits, dubbed the "clown prince" of the city council. For years an election night staple was Paddy Bauler, wearing a high silk hat, waving a stein of beer, and singing "Chicago, That Toddlin' Town." Bauler took ten or twelve trips a year, many with his boyhood friend and fellow saloonkeeper-alderman, Charlie Weber. Bauler occasionally went to Weber and said, "Charlie, there's nothing doing around here, so let's fly to Paris for a few beers."

No one accused Paddy Bauler of being an activist alderman. During his nearly thirty years on the council (1935–43 and 1947–67) he was virtually silent. What little interest he had in city government was lost after the 1960 death of Weber and the 1966 passing of his son (and heir apparent) Harry. His declining interest in the council also might have been due to election returns. The massive returns he rolled up in the western portion of the ward always made up for the more Republican high rises along the lake. But he won by only eighty votes in 1963.

Bauler pushed for ex-basketball star Frankie Cole as his successor in 1967. However, Cole withdrew when it was learned that he had a police record. A Republican, George Barr McCutcheon, scion of an old Chicago family, replaced Bauler. The retired alderman might have chuckled when it was revealed that McCutcheon had consorted with a prostitute. McCutcheon declined to seek reelection.

A new era opened in the 43rd Ward in 1971. William Singer, winner of a 1969 special election in the 44th Ward, was redistricted into the 43rd. Democratic regulars threw six candidates against him in the 1971 election, yet the popular liberal secured 70 percent of the vote.

Almost from the day of his 1971 reelection, Singer campaigned for mayor. He came up with an impressive list of accomplishments: a program for the licensing of auto towing companies; a resolution to prohibit construction of new "four plus one" apartment buildings; and a bill to allow the sale of meat after 6:00 P.M. (thus ending an irritating Butchers' Union perk). Singer led the (unsuccessful) fight to preserve the Chicago Stock Exchange as a landmark and the (successful) fight to minimize residential displacement during the construction of Truman College.

His most successful fight took place in Miami, not Chicago. He and a young black leader, Rev. Jesse Jackson, succeeded in seating a "reform slate" of delegates at the 1972 Democratic convention. National party leaders, still smarting from Daley's handling of the 1968 convention, gave approval to Singer's racially and sexually proportioned crew, even though many of those delegates had run (and lost) in the Democratic primary against Daley-backed delegates.

Singer ran an energetic campaign against Daley in 1975. He cited the recent convictions of seven top Daley officials as an example of pervasive corruption. He complained about white flight and school deterioration. He used the ailing seventy-two-year-old mayor's health as an issue. Singer even mounted a soapbox at the Civic Center Plaza and urged workers across the street at city hall to "shake off your bondage."

Influential congressman Ralph Metcalfe and many other black leaders backed Singer, despite the candidacy of black state senator Richard Newhouse, out of the belief that Newhouse could not possibly win. The Sun-Times also gave him its endorsement. That support did Singer little good. Daley won with 57.9 percent of the vote. Singer carried only three wards.

The failed Singer candidacy set the independent movement back several years. For awhile in the late 1970s, the independent bloc numbered only three alderman: Dick Simpson of the 44th, Ross Lathrop of the 5th, and Singer's successor, Martin Oberman.

Like Singer, Oberman proved to be a thorn in the side of the controlling regular Democrats. Like Singer, Oberman fought many battles and lost almost all of them. Some of his struggles produced victories, though. One of them was a proposal to curb police spying by the "red squads" which violated civil rights in the 1960s.

Oberman at first was one of the main supporters of maverick mayor Jane

Byrne. He extracted from her promises to give aldermen more time to review upcoming budgets, work for a Freedom of Information ordinance, and make the city council a real legislative body instead of a rubber stamp. When Byrne failed to act on any of those promises, Oberman became one of her harshest critics.

As early as 1982, Oberman had sights on higher office. He lobbied for Democratic slating for Illinois attorney general. When Richard Daley ally Neil Hartigan instead got the nod, Oberman withdrew from the race. Even so, he backed the younger Daley for mayor in 1983.

Oberman supported Harold Washington after the 1983 primary and was a constant Washington vote during the Council Wars years. Yet despite his seniority among council independents, he never became a major factor in the new administration. Fellow aldermen Timothy Evans (4th) and Larry Bloom (5th) became the mayor's major council advisors—not Oberman.

He tried once again for attorney general in 1986, this time staying in even though Hartigan decided to seek reelection. Although carrying his home ward by a two-to-one margin and winning in black wards, he gained only 38 percent of the statewide vote.

Oberman declined to seek reelection in 1987. Three factors might have influenced his decision. First was money. He amassed a $180,000 campaign debt from the attorney general attempt. Second, he saw many of his good-government programs come to fruition. Until 1983, Oberman was a lonely voice for an ethics law, an open budget process, and open public records. These reforms passed under Washington. Third, there was no guarantee that he would be reelected. Oberman barely (with 51 percent) avoided a runoff against Republican-backed college professor Barbara Wood in 1983. His lack of touch showed in the case of a proposed Old Town high rise, which he at first supported but later opposed after intense community pressure. His 1986 vote for a record property tax hike (in a ward where property tax freezes became a more important issue than nuclear test freezes) did little to endear him to an increasingly conservative constituency.

There was no shortage of aspirants to Oberman's seat. Even comedian Aaron Freeman briefly expressed interest. More serious contenders included Wood; schoolteacher Edwin Eisendrath, an ally of Committeeman Ann Stepan; Bob Perkins, president of the Chicago Council of Lawyers and one of the drafters of the ethics ordinance; businessman and activist Daniel Casey; attorney Brian Collins; and former DePaul basketball star Joe Ponsetto, also an attorney. Oberman at first endorsed Casey, but later backed Perkins when Casey withdrew.

Eisendrath (with 36 percent of the vote) and Perkins (32 percent) faced each other in a runoff, which helped make this the most expensive (costs estimated at above $500,000) aldermanic race in Chicago history. In some ways, they had more similarities than differences. Both were independently wealthy, the quintessential yuppies. A sour-grapes observer remarked, "A pox on both their townhouses."

Both appeared intelligent and qualified, but veteran political observers noted that something was missing from their respective campaigns. Both voiced concerns over issues like downzoning, control of unruly bars, and fiscal responsibility—important issues for the ward, but not the overriding human rights issues associated with past 43rd Ward aldermen. They reflected the changing philosophy of the 43rd, a ward now more identifiable with the outlying "economy bloc" wards of the 1950s than the liberal bastions of the 1970s.

Many expected the runoff outcome to be close. The results showed a different story. Perkins expanded little from the total he received in February. Eisendrath won by a 63-to-37 percent margin.

Eisendrath quickly established himself as one of the more intelligent aldermen, and one truly independent of any faction. His unpredictability showed itself after Harold Washington's death. While most other aldermen were clearly pegged as either Timothy Evans or Eugene Sawyer votes, Eisendrath made no commitment (Sawyer forces claimed he told them he would not be the deciding vote for their candidate, but would vote for Sawyer "to promote unity" if Sawyer already had the votes to win). Instead, he scurried back and forth between rival camps to ascertain their candidates' positions. Eisendrath broke the logjam at the marathon city council meeting which elected Sawyer with his motion to bring the issue to a vote (a motion which helped Sawyer, who had the votes to win). But he surprised even many of his fellow aldermen by supporting Evans.

Even though the 43rd has the reputation of a North Side liberal independent ward, that has never been entirely the case. Independents have held the aldermanic seat since 1971, but the Democratic committeeman post always has been occupied by party regulars.

Daniel O'Brien served in that capacity for a dozen years. He looked like a political "boy wonder" in 1969 when he became the youngest person (age twenty-four) ever elected to the state senate. That luster faded three years later when independent Dawn Clark Netsch captured the senate seat. Nonetheless, O'Brien won the committeeman race and repeated in 1976. He gained a solid majority in the west side of the ward when two challengers split the more independent Lakefront vote.

Independents never took to O'Brien, although he supported such issues as open primaries, gay rights, and legalization of marijuana. Nor did party regulars trust him much. O'Brien startled them in 1975 by suggesting himself for city clerk. He got one vote among committeemen—his own.

O'Brien especially irritated neighboring 42nd Ward committeeman George Dunne. Much of this animosity was due to the 1976 state representative primary. Under the election system then in effect, voters could cast a three-vote "bullet" for one candidate or give 1 1/2 votes to each of two candidates. O'Brien and Dunne agreed to push for split votes for both O'Brien and Dunne's candidate, Jesse White. Dunne kept his end of the bargain (although Cabrini-Green voters bulleted for White, the only black candidate). O'Brien went back on the deal and urged bullets in his ward. White lost the Democratic nomination to an independent.

Mayor Jane Byrne arranged for O'Brien's slating to the county board in

1981. Many saw this as a deal under which O'Brien would give up his committeeman title once a remap switched Byrne to the 43rd Ward. Once a member of the Democratic Central Committee, Byrne could then be in a position to take over as party chairman and assure her own reslating for mayor in 1983. However, she later changed her strategy. Instead of putting herself into the 43rd, she arranged a coup which allowed ally Ed Vrdolyak to oust George Dunne for the party chairmanship.

O'Brien, an outspoken Daley foe, faced two challengers in 1984. Attorney Jerry Meites, a local activist, was backed by Harold Washington. Ann Stepan was a Daleyite. Gender might have played a role in the outcome. Stepan took 39 percent of the vote (to 32 percent for O'Brien and 28 percent for Meites) in a ward with a higher-than-average female composition.

Stepan backed Daley ally Tom Hynes for mayor in 1987, providing one of the more absurd moments of an otherwise dull campaign. Shortly after the mayor appeared at a fundraiser at the Playboy mansion in Los Angeles, a group of pro-Washington women held a press conference to criticize Hynes for lack of women in assessor's office jobs. Stepan appeared in the back of the room during the press conference, passing out chocolate bunnies.

REDISTRICTING: The 43rd Ward remained unchanged by the 1986 remap.

MAYORAL: During the later Daley years, the 43rd Ward was in the forefront of opposition. In 1971 it was one of only two to give a majority to (ward resident) Richard Friedman. Bill Singer, another favorite son, carried the ward in 1975. Another antiadministration candidate, Jane Byrne, won here in 1979.

Yet Harold Washington, holder of strong liberal/independent credentials, has never done well here. Lakefront liberals in the 1970s sought coalitions with blacks as long as they, Lakefronters, remained in charge. When a black independent emerged as a viable contender, most did not return the favor.

This was the case in 1983. The mayoral primary split present and former Lakefront liberals in three different directions. Oberman and State Senator Dawn Clark Netsch backed Daley. Singer supported Byrne. Only Dick Simpson, retired 44th Ward alderman, lent his support to Washington.

A ward in which an IVI-IPO endorsement was once considered a divine mandate ignored that group's strong endorsement of Washington. Byrne won 48 percent of the vote, mainly in the more prosperous eastern precincts. Daley finished second with 37 percent, and Washington trailed with an unimpressive 15 percent of the vote.

Nor did Washington register impressive numbers in the general election. Bernard Epton won 74 percent of the vote.

Byrne rolled up 62 percent of the vote to take the ward in the 1987 primary. Washington did better than earlier elections (although losing ground in the 1st Precinct, Ranch Triangle area homes where whites replaced blacks).

Illinois Solidarity party candidate Ed Vrdolyak won the ward in the general election, although with a bare 52 percent majority. Washington finished second with 29 percent. Republican Donald Haider's 19 percent and 4,897 votes marked his best figures in the city.

CENSUS DATA: Population (1980): 60,156. 81.81 percent white, 7.72 percent black, 7.14 percent Hispanic, 3.33 percent Asian and other. Voting age population: 85.69 percent white, 6.46 percent black, 5.69 percent Hispanic, 2.16 percent Asian and other.

CENSUS TRACTS: See ward map.

COMMUNITY NEWSPAPERS:
Inside Lincoln Park, 4710 N. Lincoln (828–2277)
Lake Shore News, 108 S. Michigan (376–6884)
Lincoln Park/Lakeview Booster, 1647 W. Belmont (281–7500)
Near North News, 26 E. Huron (787–2677)
North Loop News, 800 N. Clark (787–5396)

ALDERMAN: Edwin Eisendrath. Elected 1987. Born February 3, 1958. Career: B.A., Harvard University, 1981; M.A., National College of Education, 1982; teacher, Chicago public schools, 1982–87.
Committees: Aging and Disabled (vice-chairman); Beautification and Recreation; Budget and Government Operations; Education; Health; Human Rights and Consumer Protection; Police, Fire, and Municipal Institutions.
City hall telephone: 744–3071, 744–5685.
Ward office: 735 W. Wrightwood (751–1133).
1987 election:

Edwin Eisendrath	8,838	(36%)
Robert Perkins	7,850	(31%)
Barbara Wood	6,549	(26%)
Joseph L. Ponsetto	783	(3%)
Brian M. Collins	721	(3%)

1987 runoff:

| Edwin Eisendrath | 16,384 | (63%) |
| Robert G. Perkins | 9,735 | (37%) |

DEMOCRATIC COMMITTEEMAN: Ann Stepan. Elected 1984. Born 1945. Career: secretary and director, Better Government Association.
Ward office: 732 W. Fullerton (525–4384).
1984 election:

Ann Stepan	6,741	(39%)
Daniel P. O'Brien	5,585	(32%)
Jerome B. Meites	4,889	(28%)

MAYORAL ELECTIONS:

1983 Democratic primary:

Jane Byrne	13,758	(48%)
Richard Daley	10,695	(37%)
Harold Washington	4,195	(15%)

1983 general:

Bernard Epton	19,620	(64%)
Harold Washington	11,008	(36%)

1987 Democratic primary:

Jane Byrne	14,566	(62%)
Harold Washington	8,715	(37%)

1987 general:

Edward Vrdolyak	13,707	(52%)
Harold Washington	7,723	(29%)
Donald Haider	4,897	(19%)

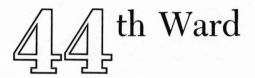

44th Ward

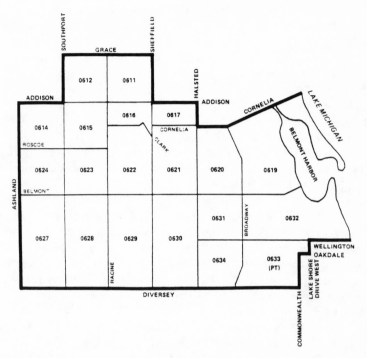

WHAT IS THE MOST diverse ward in the city? A good argument can be made for the 44th, which includes New Town and much of the community known as Lake View. Despite its relatively small size (boundaries are Diversey on the south, Ashland on the west, Addison on the north plus three precincts extending up to Grace which include Wrigley Field, and the lake on the east), the 44th Ward has a greater range of sights and activities than any other ward in the city.

It starts at the lake. The 44th includes a section of Lincoln Park, plus the Belmont yacht harbor. Fronting the park, between Lake Shore Drive and Broadway, are street after street of high rises, which give this part of the ward one of the highest population densities in the world. The area east of Broadway accounts for twenty-six precincts, nearly half of the ward's total.

Broadway, originally known as the Lake View Plank Road and later called Evanston Avenue, is one of the major streets of the ward. The strip between Diversey and Belmont, known as New Town, was at one time a straight singles center. Now it is the heart of the city's gay community.

Sex is a major commodity along this strip. Broadway houses such businesses as Victor/Victoria, a female impersonator bar; Pleasure Chest, a shop specializing in sadomasochistic gear; Broadway Mode, a unisex shop; the Second Story

All Male Emporium; and numerous shops selling cards and calendars of the type not found in Hallmark stores. Sex itself may be bought on occasion, although police run continuing crackdowns on prostitution.

Belmont, in the heart of the ward, is another offbeat entertainment strip, attracting the children of those suburbanites who spent Friday nights in Old Town during the 1960s. Punk bars abound here, as do nonalcoholic "juice bars." It also housed Crosscurrents (Belmont and Wilton), an alternative night club where comedian Aaron Freeman coined the phrase "Council Wars."

High point of the year locally is the Lakeview Festival, held near Labor Day. The openly gay, the openly punk, the openly yuppie, and the openly anything else congregate. In short, the festival provides the best three days of people watching anywhere in Chicago.

Broadway and Clark merge at Diversey Parkway. The Great Ace hardware store at the meeting point of the three streets serves as one of the more popular meeting points of Chicago singles.

Clark is also a popular entertainment street, although more subdued than Broadway. It has the standard yuppie fare of foreign restaurants (Ethiopian, Argentine, Mexican), plus the largest concentration of Japanese stores and restaurants to be found in the Chicago area. Clark Street also contains the Europa Book Store (Clark and Aldine), supplying French-, German-, and Spanish-language materials. Not far away, at Clark and Eddy, is The Wild Hare and Singing Armadillo Frog Sanctuary—A Tavern, perhaps the world's most unusual name for a reggae bar.

Of course, the most famous Clark Street landmark is Wrigley Field, at Addison and Sheffield. First built for the old Federal League's Chicago Whales in 1915, the park was taken by the Cubs the following season. It has not been a hotbed of October baseball activity in recent years; the Cubs have been World Series spectators since 1945. Nonetheless, the day games at Wrigley Field have made the Cubs media darlings. And the ballpark has helped make the surrounding Wrigleyville neighborhood some of the hottest real estate in Chicago.

The park also has unified neighborhood residents, to an extent not achieved by other areas. The former Cub owners, the Wrigley family, opposed night baseball in Wrigley Field. But the Tribune Company, after buying the club in 1981, expressed interest in putting in lights. A community group, Citizens United for Baseball in the Sunshine (C.U.B.S.) led a fight to prevent night baseball there.

Northern precincts offer more than Wrigley Field. The city's only revival movie theater, the Music Box, is at Southport and Waveland. Southport Lanes—the only Chicago bowling alley which still employs pinboys—can be found at Southport and Henderson.

The western part of the ward, more conservative and less affluent, contains more single-family homes and two-flats. The major shopping strip there is Lincoln Avenue, near Ashland and Belmont. This strip is aging yet busy, much more blue-collar than Clark Street or Broadway.

There is a serious side to life in the 44th Ward. Broadway north of Belmont houses two leading social service units: the Jane Addams Center Hull House Association (Broadway and Melrose) and the Salvation Army officer training school (Broadway and Brompton).

Just off Broadway, at Wellington, is another center of social activism: the Wellington Avenue United Church of Christ. The church, which has declared itself to be a nuclear free zone, made headlines for harboring Salvadoran refugees as a center of the sanctuary movement.

One minister at the Wellington Avenue church is no stranger to community movements in the 44th Ward. He is Dick Simpson, political science professor at the University of Illinois at Chicago and former alderman of the ward.

Bill Singer was the first independent alderman elected from the 44th. When incumbent Thomas Rosenberg obtained a judgeship in 1968, the young attorney entered the race to succeed him. Committeeman (and County Clerk) Edward Barrett slated a nondescript opponent. A Republican also ran.

It was a dirty campaign. Barrett charged that Singer workers were "long-nosed" (Jewish) and "porcupines" (hippies). Singer won in a runoff, thanks to the Lakefront high-rise vote.

Usually, it is a matter of form that ward redistricting protects incumbent aldermen. The Democratic machine felt no such need to aid maverick Singer after the 1970 remap. He was transferred into the 43rd and ran from that ward. Simpson then carried the Lakefront independents' banner against organization-backed Alan Karganon. Party regulars targeted this one more than any other aldermanic election.

Simpson came at a time when the local regular party organization was in disarray. In addition to Singer, independents had also elected a state representative and delegates to the 1970 constitutional convention. Barrett had retired as committeeman. While Joseph Gill, longtime committeeman of the 46th Ward, urged selection of protégé Thomas Henghan, precinct captains of the newly mapped ward named highly respected State Representative John Merlo to replace Barrett. He still serves in that position.

Simpson won in 1971 and was reelected in 1975. The Texas native claimed his first priority was "to develop services as a right and not as a favor." He succeeded in that respect. His second aim, "to establish a posture of aldermen as more than rubber stamps," met with less success. He also promised "a neighborhood government in which people would have a voice in what would occur." That promise was fulfilled when he created the 44th Ward Assembly. Simpson also organized a community zoning board and a traffic review committee. Simpson too led the fight for a 1974 ordinance to outlaw redlining. He downzoned much of the eastern end of the ward. He even found time to write a how-to book (*Winning Elections*) for independent candidates.

Dick Simpson also served as the conscience of city hall. He opposed the nomination of Tom Keane, Jr., who worked for real estate developer Arthur Rubloff, for a position on the zoning board of appeals. After that, Mayor Richard J. Daley attacked "college professors brainwashing children." When an insurance company employing two of the mayor's sons was found to be receiving large city contracts, Simpson rose in the council to protest. He remained standing—for six hours—even though Daley refused to recognize him.

Two terms in office were enough for Simpson, who believed that public officials ought to be citizen-statesmen instead of professional politicians. Simpson endorsed Bruce Young, president of the Lake View Citizens Council, who succeeded him.

The most memorable occurrence of Young's time in the council was the way he left it. Young abruptly quit in mid-1980, never giving any explanation. Some theorized that Young resigned because of aldermanic burnout. Yet the timing of his departure was unusual. He left the council shortly before a law went into effect which gave the mayor extended powers in the appointment of aldermen.

Jane Byrne had a replacement in mind—Gerald Shea, a Regional Transportation Authority board member, former Speaker of the Illinois House and her chief political troubleshooter. Shea had lived in a suburb but moved to the 44th shortly before the would-be appointment.

Community groups attacked Shea as a carpetbagger. A circuit court judge ruled that Byrne could appoint him alderman, but only until a special election could be held. Shea then withdrew his name from consideration.

Merlo, who had retired from the legislature in 1980, decided to seek the aldermanic post himself. Independents, still reeling from the Young fiasco, failed to put up a strong candidate. Merlo easily outdistanced his only real opponent, a black City News Bureau reporter named Michael Harrington, in the 1981 special election. He declined to seek reelection in 1983.

Merlo endorsed his ward superintendent, Bernard Hansen. Independents backed Jim Masini, former director of the Independent Voters of Illinois-Independent Precinct Organization. Hansen's residency became an issue; his family lived in the 47th Ward, although he maintained an apartment in the 44th. Had the liberal militancy of the Singer-Simpson era kept its momentum, Masini might have won. As it was, Hansen took 60 percent of the vote.

If someone ordered Central Casting to send over a Chicago alderman, the result most likely would be a clone of Bernie Hansen. He is a six-foot, two-inch, 275-pound, jovial, cigar-chomping pol, generally considered more interested in nuts-and-bolts ward issues than pursuing sweeping legislation or fiery oratory at the council chamber.

That ward dedication put him on the streets in the early days of his first term. He rode with district police on vice raids, and was known by local hookers as "the crazy alderman who locks up prostitutes."

Hansen repeatedly claimed neutrality in Council Wars. His protests of independence did not convince Harold Washington backers, who noted that he generally voted with the Edward Vrdolyak bloc.

Hansen bucked the Vrdolyak faction on one important issue. Both he and 46th Ward alderman Jerome Orbach, no doubt with an eye on the increasingly organized gay community, broke ranks and backed a gay rights ordinance favored by the mayor. The votes were not enough for the aldermen's foes, who pointed out that neither were able to persuade other Vrdolyak-bloc aldermen to support the issue.

The growing gay power in the ward was reflected in Hansen's 1987 opponent—Ron Sable, a physician at Cook County Hospital and the first openly gay candidate to run for alderman. Despite advice from some gay activists, Sable downplayed his sexual preference in his campaign. He campaigned for a gay rights ordinance and more money for AIDS research, but he also advocated greater tenants' rights, better health care, lower utility rates, and improved parking for the ward.

Sable had many of the ingredients of a successful campaign: a strong base, high visibility, an ample supply of money, plus workers who were not only fiercely loyal but also highly competent. But he lacked what is perhaps the most important factor for a challenger—massive dissatisfaction with the incumbent. As a result, Hansen won reelection with 54 percent of the vote.

Bernie Hansen endorsed Harold Washington in the 1987 general election when it appeared obvious that Washington was unbeatable—before Tom Hynes's withdrawal threatened to make the election a close race. His cooperation with the mayor allowed him to keep the chairmanship of the council's Committee on Economic Development.

Even though Hansen won reelection and Merlo appears a shoo-in for reelection as committeeman, the 44th Ward Regular Democratic Organization, as with other such groups along the Lakefront, is in a state of decline. Merlo moved his ward headquarters to Hansen's office in mid-1987, citing financial reasons.

Possible financial woes for a Lakefront political organization are not hard to imagine. Residents of this relatively affluent ward have little need for the type of city jobs the committeeman once provided. And those holding city jobs, freed from the worries of political firing, no longer feel obligated to put out extra effort on behalf of the party organization.

Such a decline would be good news for a strong independent political organization, if such a mechanism existed in the 44th Ward. But it doesn't. As a result, party regulars exert a less-than-strangling but stronger-than-tenuous hold on this ward.

REDISTRICTING: The boundaries of the 44th Ward were unaltered by the 1986 ward remap.

MAYORAL: As with the neighboring 43rd Ward, the 44th showed extreme independence of the Democratic organization in the late 1960s and early 1970s. Liberal Democrat-turned-Republican Richard Friedman nearly carried this ward against Richard Daley in 1971. Bill Singer won it in 1975.

Jane Byrne, running as a reformer, won the 44th Ward in 1979. Byrne, running as the establishment, repeated the victory four years later over Washington, the man generally perceived as the reform candidate.

Results from this ward showed that white independents might be willing to forge coalitions with blacks, but not if the blacks were controlling such coalitions. Washington received only 17 percent of the vote in the 1983 primary; Byrne won with 48 percent, and State's Attorney Richard Daley got 35 percent. Washington did slightly better in the general election with 39 percent against Republican Bernard Epton.

The mayor improved his total in the 1987 Democratic primary, to 42 percent, yet former mayor Jane Byrne again was able to carry the ward.

Republican Don Haider, as in most North Side wards, took votes from both Jane Byrne and Harold Washington primary supporters. His 13 percent here was Haider's third-best total.

Washington dropped in percentage from 42 to 38 in the general election. Ed Vrdolyak won the ward with 49 percent—one of four Lakefront wards in which none of the general election candidates received a majority of the vote.

CENSUS DATA: Population (1980): 60,163. 70.59 percent white, 5.95 percent black, 17.76 percent Hispanic; 5.70 percent Asian and other. Voting age population: 75.87 percent white, 5.53 percent black, 13.73 percent Hispanic, 4.87 percent Asian and other.

CENSUS TRACTS: See ward map.

COMMUNITY NEWSPAPERS:
  Inside Lincoln Park, 4710 N. Lincoln Ave. (828–2227)
  Lake Shore News, 108 S. Michigan (346–6884)
  Lincoln/Belmont Booster, 1647 W. Belmont (281–7500)
  Lincoln Park/Lakeview Booster, 1647 W. Belmont (281–7500)
  North Center/Irving Booster, 1647 W. Belmont (281–7500)
  Uptown News, 7519 N. Ashland (761–7200)

ALDERMAN: Bernard J. Hansen. Elected 1983. Born November 26, 1944. Career: Wright Junior College; process server; sheriff's deputy; ward superintendent, Department of Streets and Sanitation.
Committees: Economic Development (chairman); Budget and Government Operations; Capital Development; Education; Health; Housing; Intergovernmental Relations; Streets and Alleys; Traffic Control and Safety; Zoning.
City hall telephone: 744–3073, 744–3133.
Ward office: 3171 N. Halsted (525–6034).
1987 election:
Bernard J. Hansen   12,025 (54%)
Ron Sable   10,402 (46%)

DEMOCRATIC COMMITTEEMAN: John Merlo. Appointed 1969. Born 1912. Career: B.A., DePaul University; John Marshall Law School; Illinois House of Representatives, 1963–77; Illinois Senate, 1977–81; alderman, 1981–83.
Ward office: 3171 N. Halsted (348–3937).
1984 election:
John Merlo, unopposed.

MAYORAL ELECTIONS:

1983 Democratic primary:

Jane Byrne	12,225	(48%)
Richard Daley	8,771	(35%)
Harold Washington	4,315	(17%)

1983 general:

Bernard Epton	16,372	(61%)
Harold Washington	10,613	(39%)

1987 Democratic primary:

Jane Byrne	12,661	(58%)
Harold Washington	9,155	(42%)

1987 general:

Edward Vrdolyak	10,389	(49%)
Harold Washington	8,002	(38%)
Donald Haider	2,756	(13%)

45th Ward

CHICAGO'S BUNGALOW BELT is like the South's Bible Belt—as much a state of mind as of geography. The Bungalow Belt refers to Northwest Side and Southwest Side working-class residential neighborhoods with street after street of similar houses. The homes may not be elaborate, but they often are immaculate. If the lawns are tiny by suburban standards, they also are well tended by any standard.

For the most part, the homeowners are white ethnics of eastern or southern European background. If the homeowners themselves do not speak with an accent, their parents or grandparents most likely did. Hispanics, Asians, and Arabs may share the neighborhood, but very few blacks do. (Of course comparable black working-class neighborhoods exist, particularly on the South Side. But the term Bungalow Belt usually refers to the white, not black neighborhoods.)

Bungalow Belt residents generally are Catholic; tuition for parochial schools is a major expense for many families. If they are Protestant, most likely they belong to a conservative or even fundamentalist denomination. Baptists thrive here; Episcopalians and Unitarians do not.

Concerns here mirror those of Middle America. Crime is a major worry (if not the danger of violent crime, then the psychological menace of gang graffiti). Taxes are a sore point to those who feel the poor pay nothing and the rich escape through loopholes.

If many of the white residents welcome a new black neighbor with less than open arms, it should not come as a surprise. Some came from once-white neighborhoods which turned all-black in only a few years. A combination of redlining (insurance companies or lenders refusing to work within an area) and reduced city services made the old neighborhood much less livable.

It is small wonder that Bungalow Belt residents voted 90 percent in favor of a home equity plan in an April 1987 advisory referendum. Under this plan, taxing districts would be set up. Any homeowner participating in the voluntary plan would be assured that tax-backed insurance would make up the difference on his property should he be forced to sell it for a loss.

Pure racism exists, granted. But much of what outsiders see as racism is (often justified) fear of a changing neighborhood. And if Bungalow Belt residents resent blacks moving in and hastening a neighborhood change, they also resent economically insulated Lakefront liberals telling them that they are racist because of their fears.

The buckle of the Northwest Side Bungalow Belt is Jefferson Park, the Northwest Side's transportation hub. Jefferson Park and surrounding neighborhoods make up the Northwest Side 45th Ward. The many Polish delis, restaurants, and travel agencies nearby attest to Jefferson Park's predominant ethnic group. Heart of the community is the Copernicus Center at Lawrence and Lipps. This center, the largest such ethnic cultural center in the city, hosts an annual "Taste of Polonia."

Milwaukee Avenue is far and away the most important commercial street in the ward. Milwaukee, Cicero, and Irving Park converge at "Six Corners," one of the more prosperous shopping strips in the city.

Poles are not the only ethnic group in the 45th Ward. An Italian food store at Harlem and Carmen gives a clue to the prevailing nationality in the western end of the ward. The Scandinavian Fraternal Society (Lawrence and Long) serves a group no longer predominant here.

The 45th Ward has not always been located in this oddly shaped chunk of Northwest Side Chicago. For years it covered the western end of Lake View, streets now encompassed by the 32nd and 47th wards. Alderman and committeeman there for many years was saloonkeeper Charlie Weber, running partner of 43rd Ward alderman Paddy Bauler and a character in his own right. Weber had his fingers in many local businesses—gas stations, a milk business, neighborhood newspapers, taverns, even World's Fair concessions, plus gambling and vice operations.

If Weber was a sinner (and he was), in many ways he also was a saint. He was a fanatic on cleanliness who roared with anger if he saw anyone littering in his ward. Every Christmas he threw a large party for the ward's garbagemen, whom he dubbed the Knights of Cleanliness. He loved children, and organized them as his "deputy aldermen." An annual Chicago political highlight was his picnic for kids at Riverview amusement park—which included a goldfish bowl filled with 100,000 pennies for the future voters. More important, he started the state's first school lunch program.

Weber and his wife suffered tragic deaths in 1960. Both succumbed to carbon monoxide poisoning when he accidentally left his car's engine running and fumes from the garage leaked into their house. In a way, Weber's untimely death was a blessing for Mayor Richard J. Daley. The Northwest Side grew rapidly in the 1950s, and a new ward would have to be located there. With Charlie Weber gone, Daley could transfer the 45th to the Northwest Side without disrupting another elected official.

Edwin Fifielski defeated an organization-backed Democrat for alderman here in 1963. In some respects, he fit the ward well. A national AMVETS commander, Fifielski toured the nation in 1962, urging the construction of fallout shelters. Fifielski opposed Daley's 1963 Fair Housing ordinance and balked on some spending bills. But for the most part he made peace with the Democratic organization and kept appropriately silent once inside council chambers. He missed no tricks in his ward headquarters. The storefront office advertised "Fifielski's, your supermarket of service," and offered legal service, real estate, and insurance as well as aldermanic counsel.

Former state senator Thomas Lyons, who took over as committeeman in 1968, tolerated Fifielski while Daley was alive. But after the mayor's 1976 death, he replaced the alderman with his own man. He slated Richard Clewis, a docile precinct captain who held a number of patronage jobs.

Clewis won in 1979, but not without a struggle. Michael Holewinski (a liberal, of all things) forced him into a runoff. Internal conflict in the ward assured that Clewis would never gain full control of it.

Lyons quickly split from newly elected Mayor Jane Byrne and drifted into the camp of Richard Daley (Byrne was incensed in the 1980 general election when Lyons pushed for the straight Democratic ticket instead of a "Byrne ticket" which included Republican Bernard Carey for state's attorney instead of Daley). He was opposed by a major figure in the Byrne administration, Streets and Sanitation commissioner John Donovan.

Gerald McLaughlin, a policeman and former Byrne bodyguard, received Donovan's backing in 1983. Thanks in part to Donovan's organization, McLaughlin forced a runoff against Clewis in 1983. Clewis won 44 percent of the vote in the February election. But as is often the case, the incumbent failed to muster additional support in the runoff. McLaughlin took it with 54 percent of the vote.

A split between McLaughlin and Donovan enabled Lyons to win reelection as committeeman in 1984. Donovan was one of the first casualties of Harold Washington's administration. McLaughlin could have offered the deposed commissioner a job on his Cultural Development and Historical Landmarks Committee—but didn't. Donovan entered the 1984 committeeman race, and by doing so spoiled any chance McLaughlin might have had of beating Lyons. McLaughlin (33.2 percent) and Donovan (15.2 percent) together polled almost exactly the same vote as Lyons (48.8 percent).

By most accounts, McLaughlin was an effective alderman. He pushed strong antigraffiti laws, worked to remove billboards and ad benches from his ward, and toughened an ordinance designed to protect landmark buildings. He boasted of having led the fight to preserve the Chicago Theatre and the (ultimately unsuccessful) effort to keep the U.S.S. Silversides in Chicago. Yet he failed badly in his reelection effort.

Harold Washington never played well in this ward. Patrick Levar, a top

Lyons precinct captain and associate circuit court clerk, attacked McLaughlin as "soft" on Harold Washington. McLaughlin responded that he, like any other alderman, had to work with whoever was mayor.

McLaughlin grabbed Jane Byrne's coattails early in the campaign, but the Lyons organization's totals for Levar provided one of the major surprises of the 1987 aldermanic campaigns. Levar amassed 54 percent of the vote to 38 percent for McLaughlin. Donovan and conservative businessman Daniel Schmidt split the remainder of the vote.

Even though some aldermen in previously anti-Washington wards voted with the mayor in the city council reorganization, Levar was one of nine hard-core opponents. Thus far he has continued the recent tradition that, for the most part, 45th Ward aldermen are seen and not heard.

REDISTRICTING: Two southeast precincts were moved to the 35th Ward under the 1986 remap. Part of a southwest precinct was moved to the 38th Ward, in exchange for part of another precinct.

MAYORAL: Lyons's backing made the difference for Daley in the 1986 mayoral primary, giving the state's attorney his only victory in any Northwest Side ward. Daley received 52 percent of the vote (with his strongest showing in Jefferson Park) to 47 percent for Byrne, a native of the neighboring 39th Ward who did well in Edgebrook precincts. Harold Washington captured the remaining 1 percent.

Washington did little better in the general election, capturing only 7 percent of the vote. Bernard Epton won the remainder in a ward traditionally Democratic but increasingly Republican in recent years.

The 1987 Democratic primary produced nearly identical totals to the 1983 general election. Harold Washington's opponent, Jane Byrne, won 93 percent of the vote and showed strength everywhere.

Washington's foes, Ed Vrdolyak and Don Haider, both outpolled him in the April election. Vrdolyak received 88 percent to 7 percent for Haider and 5 for Washington.

CENSUS DATA: Population (1980): 58,818. 95.53 percent white, .03 percent black, 2.25 percent Hispanic, 2.19 percent Asian and other. Voting age population: 96.18 percent white, .03 percent black, 2.03 percent Hispanic, 1.76 percent Asian and other.

CENSUS TRACTS: See ward map.

COMMUNITY NEWSPAPERS:
Belmont/Central Leader, 6008 W. Belmont (283–7900)
Chicago Post, 2810 W. Fullerton (772–3300)
Chicago's Northwest Side Press, 4941 N. Milwaukee (286–6100)

Edison-Norwood Times-Review, 1000 Executive Way, Des Plaines (824–1111)
Edgebrook Times-Review, 1000 Executive Way, Des Plaines (824–1111)
Jefferson Park Leader, 6008 W. Belmont (283–7900)
Jefferson-Mayfair Times, 4600 N. Harlem, Harwood Heights (867–7700)
Portage Park Times, 4600 N. Harlem, Harwood Heights (867–7700)
Portage Park-Mayfair Leader, 6008 W. Belmont (283–7900)

ALDERMAN: Patrick J. Levar. Elected 1987. Born 1950. Career: B.A., Northeastern Illinois University; assistant to associate circuit court clerk, 1974–87.
Committees: Streets and Alleys (vice-chairman); Historical Landmark Preservation; Economic Development; Energy, Environmental Protection, and Public Utilities; Land Acquisition, Disposition, and Leases; Special Events and Cultural Affairs.
City hall telephone: 744–6841, 744–5864.
Ward office: 4405 N. Milwaukee Ave. (545–2545)
1987 election:

Patrick J. Levar	15,615 (54%)	John L. Donovan	1,434 (5%)
Gerald M. McLaughlin	10,950 (38%)	Daniel T. Schmitt	741 (3%)

DEMOCRATIC COMMITTEEMAN: Thomas G. Lyons. Elected 1968. Born May 24, 1931. B.A., J.D., Loyola University; U.S. Army, 1954–56; officer, Chicago Police Department, 1953–57; attorney; chief of Law Division, Cook County Assessor's Office; chief of Legislative, Revenue, and Public Utilities departments, Office of Illinois Attorney General; State Senator, 1965–67.
Ward office: 4405 N. Milwaukee Ave. (545–2545).
1984 election:

Thomas G. Lyons	10,609 (48%)	John L. Donovan	3,331 (15%)
Gerald M. McLaughlin	7,152 (33%)	Randy M. Ernst	831 (4%)

MAYORAL ELECTIONS:

1983 Democratic primary:		*1987 Democratic primary:*	
Richard Daley	15,920 (52%)	Jane Byrne	26,374 (93%)
Jane Byrne	14,309 (47%)	Harold Washington	1,965 (7%)
Harold Washington	483 (1%)		

1983 general:		*1987 general:*	
Bernard Epton	31,737 (93%)	Edward Vrdolyak	24,812 (87%)
Harold Washington	2,376 (7%)	Donald Haider	2,064 (7%)
		Harold Washington	1,562 (5%)

46th Ward

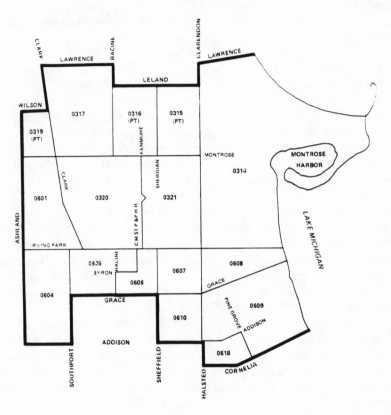

FEW, IF ANY, Chicago community names evoke a more distinct image than Uptown, the area bordered roughly by Irving Park on the south, Ashland on the west, Lawrence on the north, and the lake on the east. This community, plus the northern part of Lake View, coincides more or less with the 46th Ward.

Older Chicagoans may remember Uptown as the busiest shopping area north of the Loop, where residents lived in spacious Queen Anne houses near the Clarendon Street beach (then the largest in the city), listened to orchestras at the Bismarck beer garden, and spent Saturday nights at the elaborate, Spanish-inspired Riviera or Uptown theaters, or the Aragon Ballroom. Others may have different yet distinct memories of Uptown as an overcrowded community teeming with honky-tonk bars attracting soldiers and sailors. Real estate developers may picture Uptown as one of the city's coming neighborhoods, with rehabbed buildings attracting young urban professionals moving north from Lincoln Park and Lake View.

Most people have a different image—one of derelicts, flophouses, vacant lots, storefront day-labor agencies, resale shops, and taverns, with a social worker on every corner.

None of these images is entirely incorrect. Uptown over the years has seen both glamour and destitution, sometimes within blocks of each other. The rich and the poor live here, and it is uncertain which group will dominate the area over the next decade.

The rich—or at least upper middle class—have shown signs of prevailing. The eastern precincts, especially the area east of Sheridan Road between Irving Park and Montrose known as Buena Park—have long been upper class. Highlight of Buena Park is Hutchinson Street, whose attractive homes in varying architectural styles have given the street historic district status. Illinois governor James Thompson, never known for slumming it, lives here.

The upper class also inhabits the many high rises to be found along the Lakefront. One such high rise is the 4250 Marine Drive building which is the ward's 1st Precinct. With more than 1,000 registered voters, it is the largest precinct in the city.

Gentrification has been given a boost in the northwest corner of the ward. An area bounded by Montrose, Clark, Lawrence, and Broadway, generally known as Heart of Uptown, was designated the Sheridan Park Historic District in late 1985. Such designation facilitated tax credits for building renovation. Opponents of the designation claimed that the area was not architecturally significant. They also charged that historic district status was being used as a tool to force low-income people out of the area.

Poor people abound in Uptown. The area has been a port of entry and home for transients ever since the first apartment hotels appeared in the 1920s. Conversion of single-family homes to rooming houses during World War II furthered the low-income population. Southern whites and American Indians migrated here after the war. They have been joined by Mexicans, Puerto Ricans, *marielito* Cubans, blacks (from America, the Caribbean, and Africa), Koreans, Filipinos, Vietnamese, Cambodians, and Hmong from Laos, among others.

The poor here have not been without clout. The most visible 46th Ward political figure in recent times has been someone who until recently had never sought office. Walter "Slim" Coleman, Harvard-educated community organizer, led an umbrella community group known as the Heart of Uptown Coalition. An early supporter of Harold Washington, Coleman was a major force behind the massive 1982 voter registration which helped catapult Washington to the 1983 election victory. Supporters praise Coleman for his food giveaway and neighborhood help programs. Detractors call him an opportunist who demands dictatorial control of all programs he handles.

After the election, Coleman (who has since moved to the 32nd Ward) remained highly visible as a Washington advisor—and highly controversial. When the Uptown leader opened his headquarters for memorial services of a youth who had left a neo-Nazi gang, Alderman Edward Vrdolyak referred to Coleman during a city council meeting as "the funeral director of the Nazi party." An irate Coleman leaped over a railing onto the Council floor and advanced toward the alderman before being led away by security guards.

Traditionally, the 46th Ward has been the scene of the closest fights in the city between regulars and independents. That tradition was continued in the 1987 aldermanic race, considered by many a class struggle as much as an election. Helen Shiller, co-owner of a graphics company and a close Slim Coleman ally, won that election by less than 500 votes over incumbent Jerome Orbach. Shiller became the first independent alderman elected from the 46th Ward. Previous ones came from the Regular Democratic Organization, although they at times showed maverick tendencies.

One such alderman was Chris Cohen, handpicked choice of longtime (1922–72) committeeman Joseph Gill. Cohen, first elected in 1971, never officially broke off from the regulars. However Finance Committee chairman Tom Keane and other party leaders criticized him for leaving the council floor on several important roll calls.

He made his mark as a legislator, most notably in day-labor regulation. He also made a hobby of removing archaic ordinances from the municipal code. Thanks to Chris Cohen, Chicago no longer has laws outlawing kite flying, flagpole sitting, or marathon dancing; prohibiting women from tending bar or from wearing hatpins on public transportation; barring vehicles in tunnels which are under city streets; and banning ugly persons from walking the streets.

Cohen won reelection in 1975 over former street gang member "Cha Cha" Jimenez but retired in midterm for a federal administrative job. Ralph Axelrod, who had assumed the committeeman position after Gill's death, slated himself in the ensuing special election. One of his opponents was Shiller, who then edited a leftist magazine called *Keep Strong*. Axelrod beat her by 1,000 votes. The two met again along with others in 1979. This time, Shiller outpolled him, 46 to 40 percent. But Axelrod mustered enough support in the runoff to win by 247 votes.

Axelrod had a weak organization, and his ward secretary was willing to exploit that vulnerability. Jerome Orbach ran against his mentor for committeeman in 1980, losing by only four votes. Orbach never stopped running, and Mayor Jane Byrne gave him strong support. But Axelrod showed no signs of stepping down. Party regulars feared a split that would throw the aldermanic seat to an independent.

Party chairman Vrdolyak stepped in to quell the impasse. Axelrod quit the council to take a sheriff's office job just before the 1983 election. In turn, Orbach promised to respect Axelrod's position as committeeman.

Once again it was close. Community activist Charlotte Newfeld forced Orbach into a runoff, which he won by only sixty-six votes. The following year Orbach ran for committeeman despite any promises he might have made to Vrdolyak. He defeated Newfeld's campaign coordinator, former union official Paul Waterhouse.

Orbach's record as alderman in many ways was impressive. He cosponsored

Wrigley Field no-lights legislation, obtained a lighted schoolhouse program for Uptown, and successfully proposed a rebate of garbage fees for condominium owners. He backed the ward's influential gay population by assuring funding for AIDS research in the city budget and proposing vacated Henrotin Hospital for an AIDS research and care facility. Orbach and 44th Ward Alderman Bernard Hansen were the only two anti-Washington aldermen to vote for the gay rights measure.

Despite this record, Orbach's Council Wars stance assured him vehement opposition. No alderman tried harder than Jerry Orbach to portray himself on all sides of the political fence—to the point of passing out brochures of himself with Harold Washington in black precincts while vocally supporting Republican mayoral candidate Bernard Epton in white ones. Nevertheless, he sided with the council's Vrdolyak bloc on every significant issue. Washington made no secret of the fact that Orbach was the alderman he targeted for extinction more than any other.

Opposition to Orbach came from two sides in 1987: Shiller and attorney Nancy Kaszak, best known for her work in barring lights from Wrigley Field. A follower of political cult leader Lyndon LaRouche also entered the race.

Kaszak early on gained important endorsements: the IVI-IPO, National Organization of Women, AFSCME, Charlotte Newfeld, former aldermen Bill Singer and Dick Simpson. Shiller, however, gained two endorsements of greater value: those of Slim Coleman and Harold Washington. Orbach received not only the regular Democratic but also the regular Republican endorsement.

The intense dislike between Shiller and Kaszak became obvious during the campaign. Shiller accused Kaszak of being a last-minute intruder into ward politics. Kaszak charged that Shiller was a radical who could not obtain widespread ward support. After Kaszak was eliminated from the runoff, she eventually gave Shiller an endorsement, although many of her followers worked for Orbach.

Unlike many of the aldermanic runoffs, the 46th Ward race provided a true difference in philosophies. Orbach contended that every vacant building in his ward either was renovated or scheduled for rehabilitation. Shiller countered that Orbach was attempting to drive out low-income people and senior citizens and charged that most of his campaign donations were coming from large developers and regular Democrats from outside the ward. Orbach prided himself on his efforts to vote precincts "dry." Shiller argued that the bars affected were those that were social centers for poor people, and that troublesome bars could be regulated by other actions.

In the end, it might have been an unusual constituency which decided the election. Jesus People U.S.A., a religious group with many members living in the ward, supported Orbach throughout his career. They suddenly switched to Helen Shiller in the runoff. Orbach supporters charged that a city official had offered the Jesus People's construction firm city contracts if Shiller was elected—a charge the group denies.

Orbach retained his edge in the Lakefront and Jewish areas. Shiller captured the Uptown vote between Broadway and Clark, plus enough of the Kaszak vote to win 9,751 to 9,253.

Shiller, a rock-solid Harold Washington ally and firm supporter of Timothy Evans in the aldermanic election to succeed Washington, received a major setback in the first regular post-Washington city council meeting. Normally aldermen pass without question measures proposed by an alderman pertaining to his or her own ward. But the council rejected a measure proposed by Shiller which would have, in effect, increased the number of low-and moderate-income housing units in the 46th Ward.

Granted, that vote could be seen as a power demonstration on the part of former "Vrdolyak 29" aldermen and their newfound black allies (and it was). And most likely those aldermen welcomed a chance to embarrass one of their least popular colleagues and her ally Coleman. But a vote against additional low-income housing in Uptown could hold citywide implications. Low-income voters would be likely to support Shiller, and foes have no desire to help her shore up her fragile majority.

How important could a few Uptown votes be? Consider that Shiller defeated Orbach in 1987 by a handful of votes. Had Orbach won that election, he most likely would have sided with fellow Vrdolyak-bloc aldermen in determining Washington's successor. That additional aldermanic vote could have meant that Richard Mell, not Eugene Sawyer, would be mayor today.

Orbach declined to seek reelection as committeeman in 1988. State Senator William Marovitz at first appeared interested in the position. When he took a pass, regulars backed County Treasurer Ed Rosewell, who (what a coincidence!) moved into the ward just before the filing date. Shiller supported Chuck Kelly, an aide to the late mayor.

Shiller represents a ward that, despite its small size, is one of the most diverse in the city. Institutions in the ward range from the Center for Street People (Broadway and Wilson) to nearby Truman College, a much-needed school whose construction displaced dozens of residents, to the American Islamic College at Irving Park and Sheridan. The American Indian Center (on Wilson Avenue, a block west of the ward) serves many ward residents. Bars range from gay bars in the southeast corner to hillbilly bars in the Heart of Uptown to yuppie bars near Wrigley Field.

The diversity reflects itself in the ward's religious and spiritual organizations. The 46th is the home of the Paul Revere Masonic Temple (Wilson and Ashland). People worship at St. John's Assyrian-American Church (Lawrence and Dover); St. Mary of the Lake, a Roman basilica-style church with a freestanding bell tower; and Ahne Emmet Synagogue (Pine Grove and Grace), with its four huge Ionic columns.

Graceland Tabernacle (Grace and Halsted), a predominantly black church, stands on the site of the former Bismarck Gardens. Nearby is another entertainment spot of note. Marigold Bowling Alley occupies the site of the former Marigold Arena, a nationwide mecca in the early days of television wrestling.

The 46th Ward hosts stunning art, for both the living and the dead. Alta

Vista Terrace, a one-block masterpiece east of Seminary between Grace and Byron, holds undisputed claim to historic designation. The small, homey block of varied townhouses, each duplicated at the opposite diagonal end of the street, wins many votes for the prettiest block in Chicago.

A small German cemetery, Wunder's Cemetery, and a Hebrew cemetery lie south of Irving Park between Clark and Seminary. North of them is the jewel of Chicago graveyards. Graceland Cemetery is a burial place featuring a Who's Who of Chicago historical figures, many with graves marked by breathtaking sculptures. Marshall Field, the Potter Palmers, *Daily News* publisher Victor Lawson, George Pullman, baseball star "Cap" Anson, and heavyweight champion Jack Johnson are among those interred in Graceland Cemetery. An eerie Lorado Taft death sculpture, *Eternal Silence*, guards their souls.

REDISTRICTING: The 46th Ward was not affected by the 1986 ward remap.

MAYORAL: Even though the 46th Ward had one of the weakest regular organizations in the city, slated candidate Jane Byrne managed to capture the ward in the 1983 Democratic primary. She won 42 percent of the vote to 31 percent for Richard Daley and 27 percent for Harold Washington.

Democratic nominee Washington picked up some of that Byrne and Daley vote in the general election. He captured 47 percent against Republican nominee Bernard Epton—Washington's best showing in any of the six Lakefront wards. Washington saw his best totals in Heart of Uptown. Epton carried high-rise precincts plus Wrigleyville.

Harold Washington won this ward in the 1987 Democratic primary, his largest percentage (52) of any Lakefront ward. Although losing the high-rise vote, he fared well in Heart of Uptown and carried enough of the Wrigleyville vote to defeat challenger Jane Byrne.

Washington also carried the ward in the general election, with 51 percent of the vote. The similarity in numbers between the mayor's primary and general election totals hints that Republican Don Haider's 10 percent of the vote came from those who might have supported Edward Vrdolyak rather than from Washington supporters. Vrdolyak received 39 percent.

CENSUS DATA: Population (1980): 59,843. 52.95 percent white, 14.55 percent black, 22.18 percent Hispanic, 10.32 percent Asian and other. Voting age population: 59.47 percent white, 13.10 percent black, 18.32 percent Hispanic, 9.11 percent Asian and other.

CENSUS TRACTS: See ward map.

Community newspapers:
El Dia, 2648 S. Kolin (227–7676) (Spanish)
El Imparcial, 3610 W. 26th St. (376–9888) (Spanish)

El Informador, 1821 S. Loomis (942–1295) (Spanish)
Impacto, 3507 W. North Ave. (486–2547) (Spanish)
La Opinion, 2501 S. East Ave., Berwyn (Spanish)
La Voz de Chicago, 8624 S. Houston (221–9416) (Spanish)
Lake Shore News, 108 S. Michigan (346–6884)
North Center/Irving Park Booster, 1647 W. Belmont (281–7500)
Ravenswood/Lincolnite, 7519 N. Ashland (761–7200)
Uptown News, 7519 N. Ashland (761–7200)

ALDERMAN: Helen Shiller. Elected 1987. Born 1947. President, Justice Graphics.
Committees: Housing (vice-chairman); Budget and Government Operations; Buildings; Capital Development; Historical Landmark Preservation; Finance; Health, Human Rights and Consumer Protection; Intergovernmental Relations; Zoning.
City hall telephone: 744–6831, 744–5694.
Ward office: 1218 W. Wilson (871–5650).
1987 election:

Jerome M. Orbach	7,476 (41%)	Nancy Kaszak	3,766 (21%)
Helen Shiller	6,878 (38%)	Gerald Pechenuk	215 (1%)

1987 runoff:

Helen Shiller	9,751 (51%)
Jerome M. Orbach	9,253 (49%)

DEMOCRATIC COMMITTEEMAN: Jerome M. Orbach. Elected 1984. Born September 8, 1946. Career: B.A., University of Illinois, 1968; J.D., Loyola University, 1971; ward secretary to Ald. Ralph Axelrod; legislative assistant to State Sen. Cecil Partee; supervising attorney, Housing Court.
Ward office: 4141 N. Broadway (327–4400)
1984 election:

Jerome M. Orbach	7,146 (56%)
Paul Waterhouse	5,685 (44%)

Mayoral elections:
1983 Democratic primary:

		1987 Democratic primary:	
Jane Byrne	8,211 (42%)	Harold Washington	9,294 (52%)
Richard Daley	6,043 (31%)	Jane Byrne	8,598 (48%)
Harold Washington	5,246 (27%)		

1983 general:

		1987 general:	
Bernard Epton	11,543 (53%)	Harold Washington	9,944 (51%)
Harold Washington	10,251 (47%)	Edward Vrdolyak	7,564 (39%)
		Donald Haider	1,844 (10%)

4️7th Ward

A TEAM OF BUSINESSMEN examined the land near the current site of Clark and Leland in 1869. According to legend, they heard the cawing of ravens from a nearby woods and named their newly bought suburban land Ravenswood.

Originally the boundaries of Ravenswood extended only from what is now Montrose to Leland. Over the years the unofficial boundaries of Ravenswood have grown to include an area from Foster south to Belmont, Ashland west to the Chicago River. The area roughly coincides with the 47th Ward.

The easiest way to learn the history of Ravenswood is to look at a mural at the corner of Lincoln and Leland. Its left side depicts Lincoln Avenue extending to a distant Fort Dearborn, a reminder of the days when the avenue connected Waukegan and Chicago and was known as Little Fort Road. A double-deck Chicago Motor Coach bus and two electric trolleys travel along the avenue. One of the buildings they pass is the Krause Music Store (now Arntzen-Coleman Funeral Home) at Wilson and Lincoln, Louis Sullivan's last commissioned work.

The right half of the mural shows vignettes of the neighborhood in an earlier day: produce farms with a woman selling lettuce and pumpkins, depicting the days when the area was a truck farming center; the Bach brickwork plant, which used clay from the nearby river; a spacious victorian home representing the gracious houses still visible in eastern Ravenswood; the statue of Abraham Lincoln and the German Lombard lamp at Lincoln Square (Western, Lincoln, and Lawrence).

"Reflections of Ravenswood" also includes pictures of Riverview, the gone-but-not-forgotten amusement park at Western and Belmont. Pictures of a smiling Aladdin guarding a funhouse, the Bobs (world's fastest rollercoaster), and the parachute jump evoke memories of what was the world's largest amusement park until its 1967 demolition. A police headquarters and a shopping center now occupy the former Riverview site.

Nearby are two other well-known Chicago institutions. Lane Technical High School (Western and Addison), with a campus larger than that of many colleges, is widely considered to be the best public high school in the city. One block west is the WGN television studio, home of Chicago's "superstation" which is seen throughout the country. Bradley Place is renamed Frazier Thomas Place here, in honor of the late and beloved host of the Garfield Goose and Bozo's Circus programs.

The area bustles. Western Avenue here is the used car capital of Chicago. Lincoln Avenue's business strip from Wilson to Lawrence thrives, in part due to the 1978 conversion to a mall of the avenue between Leland and Lawrence. Small factories along Ravenswood Avenue once given up for dead are staging a comeback.

Germans particularly contribute to the prosperity. At one time a highly German area, Lincoln Avenue still hosts delis, gift stores, bakeries, and restaurants featuring goods from the old country. The Davis Theatre (Lincoln and Wilson) offers German-language films two Saturdays a month.

Saturday nights the Lincoln Avenue strip teems with action, although the flavor may not be what Lakefront yuppies have in mind. German bars and clubs predominate, but Greek and Croatian entertainment may also be found. Ravenswood even boasts the King's Manor (Lawrence and Hamilton), a club which features Henry VIII-style food and entertainment.

But on the whole, the atmosphere in Ravenswood is that of a quiet, pleasant, residential community, as tranquil as the name would imply. Often the local wildlife is noisier than the local residents, be they raccoons scurrying near the river, squirrels barking from a rooftop, or crows cawing from a treetop. Pigeons cooing from local ledges make this area their home; Ravenswood hosts the largest pigeon population of anywhere outside the Loop. Even seagulls show up from time to time.

Catholic churches play a major role here (Queen of Angels at Sunnyside and Western was a meeting ground for local anti-Marcos Filipinos). Yet this may be the only nonblack ward in the city with more Protestants than Catholics. Those Protestant churches take on many forms, those on Hermitage being an example: the yellow Carpenter's Gothic All Saints Episcopal Church at Wilson, a Korean Presbyterian Church at Cullom, and a Spanish Baptist Church at Montrose.

Ravenswood also scores high on two other "quality of life" standards. The Conrad Sulzer Regional Library (Lincoln and Sunnyside), named after the first white settler, provides the best facilities of any branch library in the city. One of the most active local historical societies meets here.

Across the street from Sulzer lies Wells Park. Whatever one's recreation preference, Wells likely offers it. Baseball and soccer fields may be found here, as well as lighted tennis courts, horseshoe pits, chess tables, swings, sandboxes, outdoor and indoor basketball courts, an indoor swimming pool, gymnasium, and a well-equipped weight room. An active seniors' club meets here. Recreation classes for special children also are available. In short, Wells Park is the gem of the park district, everything a small park can be. Wells has also served as a political hot potato, which eventually led to the decline and fall of the 47th Ward's most powerful politician.

That politician was Edmund Kelly, still the local Democratic committeeman but no longer the park superintendent. Kelly, a prep basketball star, started his parks career at Wells in the 1940s. He worked his way up in the system and nearly left in 1968 to assume a management position with the Milwaukee Bucks. But Mayor Richard Daley wanted Kelly to resurrect the moribund 47th Ward Democratic organization. Kelly accepted the mayor's offer and took over as committeeman.

Alderman at that time was John Hoellen, a crusty and outspoken Daley foe. Hoellen, alderman since 1947, was the most visible of the city council's Republicans. By the end of his career, he was the only one.

Hoellen started his career with a bang—literally. On the day he filed in 1947, a small-time hoodlum tried to shoot him with a shotgun. He was saved only because the shotgun shell had been wet.

He was a man of many ideas, some of them eccentric. Hoellen proposed a Chicago poet laureate and battled to exempt church bells from the city's antinoise ordinance. When the now famous Picasso sculpture was unveiled in 1967, Hoellen suggested it be scrapped and replaced by a statue of Ernie Banks. Other ideas had considerably more merit and/or success. He battled for a three-digit emergency telephone number years before it came about. He called for city public bodies to give advance notice for meetings, and for competitive bidding for contracts.

Most of all Hoellen, a Republican, opposed Chicago's Democratic organization. Even before Daley's time, he created an emergency crime committee which exposed gambling and police corruption. When Daley assumed power, Hoellen blasted the mayor for his bulging patronage army and the administration's corruption. No other alderman provided more visible irritation to the mayor.

Hoellen ran three times for Congress, barely losing in 1966. But he won easy reelection to his aldermanic seat until 1975. By then, Daley was declining in power. But he still was stronger than anyone the Republicans could have offered. Hoellen, who became the only Republican alderman when two colleagues resigned after 1973 scandals, was put in charge of a candidate search committee. Several people were offered GOP slating for mayor, including Daley biographers Mike Royko and Len O'Connor. All declined.

Since no one else was willing to go on the obvious suicide mission, Hoellen accepted the party bid. County Republicans made him funding promises which were never kept, and Hoellen was stuck with a campaign debt that took more than five years to repay.

Hoellen also sought reelection as alderman. Daley and Kelly showed him no mercy. Kelly assumed control of the parks in 1972 and used his position to build a strong patronage army. Kelly's workers spread rumors through the ward that Hoellen favored (black-occupied) public housing in the 47th—a highly unpopular position in this conservative ward. More important, Daley cut off services from the ward. Hoellen was unable to fulfill the nuts-and-bolts duties which are the life blood of an alderman.

The result was a disaster for the twenty-eight-year incumbent. He polled only 43 percent of the vote against precinct captain and Kelly aide Eugene Schulter. Hoellen won the Republican mayoral primary against undistinguished opposition. But he failed to attract 20 percent against Daley, losing every ward.

After Daley died, Kelly lobbied for the party chairmanship. When he failed to gain that title, he returned to full support of the organization. Kelly's 47th was the only North Side ward to go for party-backed incumbent Michael Bilandic in 1979.

Jane Byrne won that election, and she soon forced Kelly into her fold. The superintendent entertained aloud thoughts of running for mayor. Byrne equally publicly threatened to oust Kelly as park superintendent, and later openly suggested that park board president Ray Simon move to curb Kelly's powers. Kelly acquiesced by offering money to Byrne's campaign fund.

Kelly's handling of the parks came under fire from a number of directions. He pointed to the numerous athletic programs of the Chicago Park District and claimed that those programs helped keep youths out of trouble. Parks advocacy groups and others charged that Kelly used the system to create a patronage empire filled mainly with 47th Ward allies (figures released in 1986 showed that 8 percent of the park's full-time workers were members of Kelly's ward). Minority leaders pointed to Wells Park and the disparity between its facilities and those of parks located in predominantly black and Hispanic neighborhoods. A 1982 Justice Department suit charged that the park district systematically shortchanged those minority neighborhoods. The park district the following year signed a consent decree agreeing to spend more money on parks in black and Hispanic areas, although Kelly never admitted to discrimination.

Ed Kelly's ouster was one of the earliest campaign promises of 1983 mayoral candidate Harold Washington, and one that he fought hardest to keep. Kelly, in turn, became the first major Democrat to switch parties and endorse Republican nominee Bernard Epton after the primary.

EDMUND KELLY (second from left) with Eugene Schulter (left), Bruce Farley (right), and friend.

Even after Washington won, he was unable to unseat the veteran parks boss. Only the parks board can remove a superintendent, and the board was stacked with Kelly allies. They stayed on the board even after their terms expired, because a hostile city council would not act on Washington's nominations of the replacements.

That situation changed after 1986 special elections provided Washington with twenty-five council votes (enabling him to cast a tiebreaker). Two Washington nominees, architect Walter Netsch and museum director Margaret Burroughs, received immediate confirmation from the newly aligned council. Washington allies also persuaded board member William Bartholomay to vote with Netsch and Burroughs in exchange for a promise to retain him on the board.

This trio, a majority on the five-person board, did not oust Kelly. Instead the board stripped him of his powers that June by creating the post of executive vice president and putting administrative powers in that position. Washington ally Jesse Madison was named executive vice president.

Kelly fought back. When Madison reported for his first day on the new job, he found the office's locks had been changed. Kelly made a number of last-minute transfers and promotions, and paper shredders destroying personnel and other records were running so often that "the motors are burning out."

Kelly filed a suit which charged that the meeting which appointed Madison was not a legal one. Park district attorney Michael Hennessey circulated a memo advising executives not to cooperate with Madison.

The park district upheaval even threatened to turn Springfield into Council Wars South. Kelly's major legislative ally, State Representative Bruce Farley, introduced a bill aimed specifically at restoring full parks control to Kelly. This bill was closely tied to one which would have given Republicans control over O'Hare Airport expansion. Only intensive lobbying by Washington and Democratic candidates who needed his support killed the package.

Kelly's lawsuit failed, and he resigned in July. Speculation immediately arose as to his political future. A longtime Chicago political rumor had Kelly bolting to the Republican party and running for mayor on that ticket. Instead, he stayed with the Democrats and supported Jane Byrne (his rally for her just before the primary was the largest of her campaign).

During its prime, Kelly's ward organization was known as the "Fighting 47th." But after the Democratic primary, most of the organization's fighting took place within itself. Kelly came out for Chicago First party candidate Thomas Hynes, but a number of renegade precinct captains instead backed Solidarity party candidate Edward Vrdolyak.

There was one other very important defection. Eugene Schulter, Kelly's eternal supporter in the city council, broke ranks and endorsed Washington a week before the election. After the election, he supported Washington's city council reorganization and received the chairmanship of the Committee on Beautification and Recreation.

Seeing an increased movement of Hispanics, Asians, yuppies, and other unpredictable votes into his ward, Schulter campaigned hard for reelection. Although generally mute during council meetings (his most notable legislation was an ordinance setting time limits for nonalcoholic "juice bars"), he has performed admirably as a "nuts-and-bolts" alderman. Schulter took credit for the Lincoln Square Mall; a new Belmont police station; the Levy Senior Citizens Center (Lawrence and Damen); and the Silent Cooperative Apartments (Belmont and Campbell), the first housing development in the country for hearing impaired senior citizens.

Schulter, with 77 percent, easily beat three rivals: Paul R. T. Johnson, a Republican; Lyndon LaRouche backer Joan Macaluso; and Tom Forte, a former Kelly precinct captain. Forte, with only 3 percent of the vote, became the only aldermanic candidate to receive fewer votes than a LaRouchie.

Hoellen, an attorney and CTA board member, was one of very few Republican committeemen who fielded local candidates and supported the party's countywide and statewide slate. He played the role of loyal opposition in 47th Ward politics—and invariably lost. The aging Hoellen resigned after the general election, and precinct captains voted Johnson to replace him.

Internal politics appeared fiercer here than in any other ward following the mayoral election when Schulter hinted a challenge of Kelly for committeeman. That situation cooled when the alderman proclaimed his support for

Kelly in August 1987. Kelly announced his reelection bid for Democratic committeeman later in the year, instead of making the Republican switch that has been predicted for much of the decade.

REDISTRICTING: No changes were made to 47th Ward boundaries by the 1986 remap.

MAYORAL: Despite the legends of Ed Kelly's political strength, the 47th Ward has not gone solidly for the organization-backed candidate in recent elections. Byrne won it in the 1983 Democratic primary, with only 55 percent of the vote. State's Attorney Richard Daley finished second with 40 percent. Harold Washington trailed with only 5 percent.

Washington fared slightly better in the general election, picking up 13 more percentage points. Nonetheless, Kelly's strong support for Epton gave the Republican 82 percent of the vote.

As Asians, Hispanics, and refugees from the Lakefront have created a soft underbelly for the regulars in the ward's eastern tier, so has Harold Washington's percentage increased. The mayor received 20 percent of the vote in the Democratic primary here, one of his largest percentage increases over 1983 in any ward.

Despite the dispute among precinct captains, they united behind Vrdolyak on election day. He won the ward with 68 percent of the vote. Washington received 22 percent, mostly from eastern precincts. Don Haider got 10 percent from one of the few wards with a real Republican organization.

CENSUS DATA: Population (1980): 60,005. 71.26 percent white, .60 percent black, 19.44 percent Hispanic, 8.70 percent Asian and other. Voting age population: 76.05 percent white, .55 percent black, 16.39 percent Hispanic, 7.01 percent Asian and other.

CENSUS TRACTS: See ward map.

COMMUNITY NEWSPAPERS:
Good News Weekly, 4710 N. Lincoln Ave. (878–7334)
North Center/Irving Park Booster, 1647 W. Belmont (281–7500)
Ravenswood/Lincolnite, 7519 N. Ashland (761–7200)

ALDERMAN: Eugene C. Schulter. Elected 1975. Born 1948. B.A., Loyola University; aide to State Rep. Bruce Farley and Democratic Committeeman Edmund Kelly; appraiser, Cook County Assessor's office.
Committees: Beautification and Recreation (chairman); Buildings; Finance; Local Transportation; Municipal Code Revision; Special Events and Cultural Affairs; Streets and Alleys.

City hall telephone: 744–3180, 744–4021.
Ward office: 1951 W. Lawrence (728–6300).
1987 election:

Eugene C. Schulter	15,699 (78%)	Joan Macaluso	739 (4%)
Paul R. T. Johnson	3,249 (16%)	Thomas M. Forte	569 (3%)

DEMOCRATIC COMMITTEEMAN: Edmund Kelly. Elected 1968. Born 1924. Career: U.S. Marine Corps; Chicago Park District, 1948–69; assistant superintendent, Chicago Park District, 1969–73; acting superintendent, Chicago Park District, 1972–73; general superintendent, Chicago Park District, 1973–86.
Ward office: 1951 W. Lawrence (728–6300).
1984 election:
Edmund Kelly, unopposed.

MAYORAL ELECTIONS:

1983 Democratic primary:

Jane Byrne	13,053 (55%)
Richard Daley	9,504 (40%)
Harold Washington	1,308 (5%)

1987 Democratic primary:

Jane Byrne	16,244 (79%)
Harold Washington	4,132 (20%)

1983 general:

Bernard Epton	20,403 (82%)
Harold Washington	4,515 (18%)

1987 general:

Edward Vrdolyak	13,008 (68%)
Harold Washington	4,161 (22%)
Donald Haider	1,896 (10%)

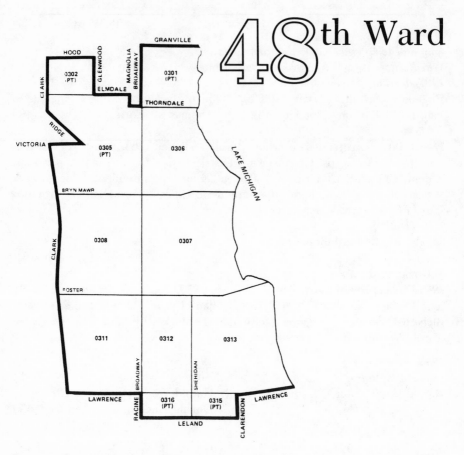

"I WAS TREATED WITH GREAT WARINESS," Marilou McCarthy Hedlund remembers. "I was a new breed. The day after the election, Dave Stahl, who was then deputy mayor, called my husband and said, 'I just want you to know the first two assignments I have on my desk this morning are to install a new bathroom in the city council chambers, and to order a sign that says "Women." I don't know if I like this.'"

People got used to the idea of women in the city council after Hedlund was elected in 1971. She became the first one to be sworn in as alderman (beating Anna Langford by a few hours). And if women are not visible in the council anywhere near their numbers in the general population, at least they are no longer so few as to be considered oddities.

Hedlund's ward, the Lakefront 48th, has led the way in electing women to the legislative body. Of the thirteen who have served as alderman, nearly a quarter (3) have been from the 48th Ward, including incumbent Kathy Osterman.

The relative success of women here is no accident. Regular party organizations have been, for the most part, "old boy" networks which did not slate women for significant positions. Such party organizations traditionally have been weak in this ward. Likewise, independent political organizations have not taken hold here. That leaves community-based organizations as a source of political talent, and women have been more able to attain leadership positions within such groups. One such group is the Edgewater Community Council. Critics charge that the Edgewater council is the most powerful political group in this ward. It is a claim not without validity; the last two 48th Ward aldermen have been ECC presidents.

Hedlund, a former *Tribune* reporter, was the first female candidate to receive endorsement from the Regular Democratic Organization. Even so, it was considered a token effort because of the ward's Republican leanings. She was deemed to have little chance against opponent Robert O'Rourke. Yet Hedlund prevailed. The reason might have been gender pride evoked from her one-word campaign button: "Alderwoman."

Despite her work on "women's" issues such as establishment of rape trauma centers and elimination of pay toilets from public places, Marilou McCarthy Hedlund was no militant feminist. She was a loyal Daley backer, and independents kept her at arm's length.

Hedlund retired after only one term, leaving the 1975 election wide open. Democratic regulars put up the closest thing they had to a blue-ribbon candidate—Arnold Levy, deputy director of the Mayor's Office of Manpower and Education. Attorney and civic leader Dennis Block received both Independent Voters of Illinois and Republican backing. There were two other candidates: Seymour Weiss, an investigator with the Department of Revenue; and Marion Kennedy Volini, president of the Edgewater Community Council.

Block won that election. With the defeat of 47th Ward alderman John Hoellen, he was the closest thing the city council had to a Republican alderman. Yet Block was never comfortable with that designation, calling himself instead an independent Republican.

The Republican party needed a sacrificial lamb to run in the 1977 special election that followed Daley's death. And if Block was not much of a Republican, he was the best the party had to offer. Block accepted the nomination and was squashed by Democratic nominee Michael Bilandic. The hapless Republican received only 23 percent of the vote, in an election where only 38 percent of registered voters bothered to cast ballots. Disgusted by lack of party support, Block quit the city council and moved out of town.

Democratic regulars cooled their heels in setting up a special election after Block quit, since it made little sense to enfranchise a ward likely to elect an independent alderman. Only after 46th Ward alderman Chris Cohen also resigned did they call special elections, which were held in 1978.

The regulars slated Ross Harano, a Japanese-American businessman who was born in a detention camp during World War II. Volini received independents' backing. A third candidate forced them into a runoff, which Volini won.

She was reelected in 1979 and 1983, but not by landslides. The latter election produced a margin of only 811 votes between her and a machine-backed teacher, Sharon Rae Bender.

Block's and Volini's wins came despite the efforts of Martin Tuchow, a county board member and the ward's Democratic committeeman since 1972. Tuchow was anything but a successful ward boss; in his twelve years leading the ward's regular organization, he failed every time to elect an ally as alderman.

But then, testimony at his 1984 trial indicated that he was not the type to engender loyalty. Tuchow was characterized as an all-purpose shakedown artist who billed city workers who fell behind in buying dinner and raffle tickets and who once hit upon a tavern owner for a set of golf clubs. He was convicted for taking payoffs to help contractors obtain needed permits to repair an Uptown building.

The 1984 committeeman election proved to be a standard regulars-versus-independents contest. Harold Washington ally Robert Remer, a Roosevelt University professor, articulately spelled out such party reforms as opening up the slating process and requiring precinct captains to live in the ward. He proved equally adept at mentioning opponent Glen Kaufman's name and Tuchow's in the same sentence. Remer, thanks to Volini's support as much as Washington's, won a close election.

Volini's main citywide contribution as alderman was her work to toughen prostitution laws. On a local level, she succeeded in halting the proliferation of halfway houses in her already overburdened ward, creating a recreational facility from an old armory on Broadway and Thorndale, and engineering the conversion of the Viatorian mansion (Sheridan and Granville) into a cultural center. For the most part, she was more interested in providing ward services than engaging in citywide politics.

No other alderman became entangled in Council Wars more involuntarily than Volini, especially when the 1986 special elections made her vote a deciding one. She was a predictable Washington supporter when her minority-bloc vote was of little importance. Afterward, she tried to move to the political center and appease all people. Instead, she ended up irritating them.

True-blue Harold Washington supporters never entirely forgave her for supporting Richard Daley for mayor in the 1983 Democratic primary. Volini also bolted the Washington bloc on two other occasions. When her pivotal vote was needed to confirm a park board nominee who would help oust Washington foe Ed Kelly, Volini declined to support the mayor. She also refused a plan that would remove Washington antagonist Ed Burke as Finance Committee chairman.

Yet she stayed with the mayor's faction on a vote of prime importance— an $80 million property tax increase. That vote did little to endear her to the Lakewood-Balmoral area homeowners who formed her political base. She was beset from all sides. Even so, it was somewhat of a surprise when Volini announced that she would not seek reelection.

The variegated nature of the ward would have promised a wide-open election anyway. Politically, the 48th may be divided into four parts: the northern end of Uptown at the southern end of the ward, with large Hispanic and Asian populations; the Winthrop-Kenmore corridor, two densely packed streets that are home to most of the ward's black community; the high rises along Sheridan Road, home to some of Chicago's richest and most conservative voters; and the Lakewood-Balmoral and Edgewater areas in the north and west of the ward, with single-family homes.

Volini's retirement made the aldermanic race a free-for-all. Eleven candidates from all over the political spectrum rushed to succeed her. From political left to right, they were Adrian Capehart, program director for the Chicago Metro History Fair and the only black candidate; attorney Mike Radzilowski, a founder of the Organization of the North East (O.N.E.) community group; Remer, who like Capehart and Radzilowski was a firm Washington backer; Kathy Osterman, director of State's Attorney Richard Daley's community relations office and Edgewater Community Council president; Brendan Clancy, a twenty-two-year-old communications student; Tom Shaw, the self-proclaimed "only political scientist in the race"; former restaurant owner John Gorman, who proposed to solve lakeshore erosion by building offshore islands which would support an extension of Lake Shore Drive; Bender, whom enemies dubbed the "Ed Vrdolyak-Marty Tuchow candidate"; attorney John McNeal, a Republican, who passed out autographed bananas; tavern owner Jane McDougall, the only open Byrne supporter and "the woman who got woman bartenders in Chicago"; and Judith Acheson, a Lyndon LaRouche backer.

Harold Washington declined to endorse any of the candidates, and his hesitancy might have cost him a city council vote. Remer, Capehart, and Radzilowski together polled 32 percent of the vote—more than any other candidate. But the trio split their votes evenly. Volini-backed Osterman (26 percent) and party regular Bender (18 percent) advanced to the runoff.

There was little doubt as to the outcome. Osterman was more suitable to the ward's Washington followers than Bender, and she received 55 percent of the runoff total. Bender, as before, claimed her best results on the lakeshore high rises. Osterman held her Lakewood-Balmoral base, plus capturing the Kenmore-Winthrop precincts where Capehart, Remer, and Radzilowski did well in the primary.

Osterman sided with the Washington bloc on city council realignment, but her allegiance to that bloc ended with the mayor's death. She gravitated immediately to the white ethnic aldermen who ended up supporting Alderman Eugene Sawyer instead of Washington floor leader Timothy Evans. Political pundits speculated on a number of reasons for Osterman's choice: the greater likelihood that a Sawyer victory might lead to a reduction of Washington's proposed property tax increase, negative reaction of the ward's large Jewish population to campaigning on Evans's behalf by Rev. Jesse Jackson, antipathy toward neighboring alderman (and Evans backer) Helen Shiller, and the perception that Osterman ally Richard Daley would find Sawyer a less formidable opponent should Daley enter the 1989 special mayoral election. Most likely, the answer is all of the above.

Kathy Osterman has no shortage of issues to deal with in her own ward.

Concerns here vary from immigration laws to property taxes, lakefront erosion to housing. Senior citizen issues cannot be ignored; the 48th has one of the highest, if not the highest percentage of seniors.

The 48th Ward extends from Lawrence to Granville, Clark Street to the lake. Far from monolithic, it presents a variety of attractions. Uptown's northern third encompasses the southern third of the ward. This part of Uptown contains its most historic buildings. The Spanish-style Uptown and Riviera theaters are here, near Broadway and Lawrence. A block east lies the Moorish-inspired Aragon Ballroom. For years a nationally famous big band ballroom, the Aragon was resurrected in the 1960s as the Cheetah, a psychedelic nightclub. It now hosts Latino acts.

Another bit of history lies two blocks east. The Peoples Church at Sheridan and Lawrence describes itself as "liberal and non-sectarian. Here science and religion are friends." Rev. Preston Bradley preached to overflow crowds. Activist performers such as singers Holly Near and Ronnie Gilbert sometimes perform here.

In days gone by, America's best-known actors performed at Argyle and Glenwood. The Essanay Studio there was a film capital in the early days of silent pictures and even produced television's "Wild Kingdom." Today the building is the location of St. Augustin College, a bilingual (Spanish-English) school.

Uptown is the setting for a lively present as well as a past. Chinese merchants started a second Chinatown at Broadway and Argyle, although Vietnamese stores and restaurants now outnumber Chinese ones. Nearby, on Broadway, is the headquarters of Combined Insurance, a multimillion dollar company thanks to the Positive Mental Attitude of founder W. Clement Stone.

The Saddle and Cycle Club lies at Foster and Sheridan. The only private country club along the Chicago lakeshore, it also serves as a buffer between Uptown and the Sheridan Road high rises.

These high rises, often buffeted in recent times by Lake Michigan waves, nonetheless have attracted some of Chicago's wealthiest citizens. The most obvious symbol of that wealth was the Edgewater Beach Hotel, for years a gathering place for the nation's famous at Sheridan and Balmoral.

Between Sheridan and the Howard elevated tracks are Winthrop and Kenmore Avenues, otherwise known locally as the Winthrop-Kenmore Corridor. Developers in the early 1900s built multistory buildings, anticipating a boom that never came. During World War II and afterward, those buildings were divided into smaller apartments or rooming houses, and often served as homes for mental patients. Small residential hotels remain, especially south of Foster.

The corridor, especially north of Foster, is undergoing redevelopment. Winthrop-Kenmore has become a battleground between those who want to rehab formerly moribund houses and apartment buildings, and those who fear that the renovations will serve to drive longtime low-income residents from the area.

Broadway forms the center spine of the ward. West of there and north of Foster lies a residential, upper-middle-class neighborhood. Lakewood-Balmoral bills itself "a nice place to live". Its suburban style houses, often stucco-covered with bright trim, are the sort of places which might contain a wishing well or a gazebo in the back yard. Large Protestant churches may be found here, reminders of the days when this was a predominantly German and Swedish area.

That Scandinavian influence is still evident (and carefully nurtured) along the ward's western boundary. Clark Street is the main street of Andersonville, the latest of Chicago's Swedish settlements. In years past a whistle sounded here at 10:00 A.M., advising local merchants to sweep the streets in front of their stores. Swedish shops are still there but now are joined by Middle Eastern restaurants and Filipino grocery stores.

Lakewood-Balmoral residents, unhappy about the connotations of Uptown, "seceded" from Uptown in 1980. The area between Foster and Devon, Ravenswood and the lake became the separate community of Edgewater, the only new officially designated community (except for newly annexed areas near O'Hare Airport) to be created since the communities were established in the 1930s.

Two other ward sites deserve mention, as signs of the eclectic nature of the ward. Senn High School at Thorndale and Glenwood teaches students who represent more than fifty different nations. The 48th also contains a most unusual monument, at the intersection of Hollywood, Ridge, and Wayne. A small post, draped by evergreens, wishes peace to Chicago, Illinois, the United States, and Earth. The post was installed when the Great Peace March of 1986 passed through Chicago.

REDISTRICTING: No changes were made in the 48th Ward by the 1986 redistricting.

MAYORAL: Jane Byrne, backed by Tuchow, won this ward, although with a lower percentage (41 percent) than in any Lakefront ward other than the 42nd. Richard Daley, supported by Alderwoman Volini, received 33 percent. Byrne and Daley were strong in the Condo Belt and Lakewood-Balmoral. Harold Washington trailed with 26 percent of the vote, capturing Uptown and Kenmore-Winthrop.

Republican Bernard Epton captured the ward in the general election with a comfortable but not overwhelming 56 percent of the vote Washington again appeared strongest in Kenmore-Winthrop and Uptown precincts.

Harold Washington and Jane Byrne nearly split the ward in the 1987 Democratic primary, Washington winning it with 52 percent. His totals in black Kenmore-Winthrop precincts offset those of Byrne closer to the lake.

Washington posted an almost identical total in the general election (his 8,789 votes were only 19 less than in the primary) and carried the ward, 48 percent to 41 for Edward Vrdolyak. Donald Haider took 11 percent of the vote in his home ward.

CENSUS DATA: Population (1980): 60,135. 55.41 percent white, 15.64 percent black, 15.06 percent Hispanic, 13.87 percent Asian and other. Voting age population: 60.93 percent white, 14.31 percent black, 12.73 percent Hispanic, 12.03 percent Asian and other.

CENSUS TRACTS: See ward map.

COMMUNITY NEWSPAPERS:
Lake Shore News, 108 S. Michigan (346–6884)
Rogers Park/Edgewater News, 7519 N. Ashland (761–7200)
Uptown News, 7519 N Ashland (761–7200)

ALDERMAN: Kathy Osterman. Elected 1987. Born 1944. Career: Bloom Junior College; supervisor of Community Unit, Cook County State's Attorney's Office, 1981–.
Committees: Beautification and Recreation (vice-chairman); Aging and Disabled; Capital Development; Economic Development; Education; Energy, Environmental Protection, and Public Utilities; Human Rights and Consumer Protection.
City hall telephone: 744–6860, 744–6834.
Ward office: 5457 N. Broadway (784–5277).
1987 election:

Kathy Osterman	4,413	(26%)	John E. McNeal	1,012	(6%)
Sharon Rae Bender	3,046	(18%)	John P. Gorman	890	(5%)
Robert B. Remer	1,927	(11%)	Jane McDougall	460	(3%)
Adrian Capehart	1,868	(11%)	Tom Shaw	199	(1%)
Michael Radzilowsky	1,672	(10%)	Judith Acheson	128	(1%)
Brendan T. Clancy	1,475	(9%)			

1987 runoff:

Kathy Osterman	9,061	(55%)
Sharon Rae Bender	7,559	(45%)

DEMOCRATIC COMMITTEEMAN: Robert B. Remer. Elected 1984. Born 1946. Career: hospital administrator; professor, Roosevelt University; member, Chicago Library Board.
Ward office: 5602 N. Ridge (275–0480).
1984 election:

Robert B. Remer	6,528	(53%)
Glen Kaufman	5,687	(47%)

MAYORAL ELECTIONS:

1983 Democratic primary:

Jane Byrne	8,160	(41%)
Richard Daley	6,385	(33%)
Harold Washington	5,024	(26%)

1983 general:

Bernard Epton	12,269	(56%)
Harold Washington	9,433	(44%)

1987 Democratic primary:

Harold Washington	8,808	(52%)
Jane Bryne	8,159	(48%)

1987 general:

Harold Washington	8,789	(49%)
Edward Vrdolyak	7,348	(41%)
Donald Haider	1,966	(11%)

49th Ward

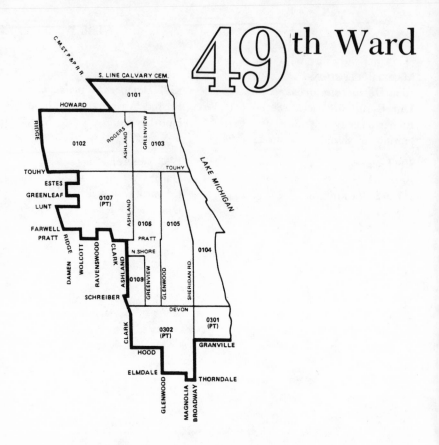

IRISH-BORN SETTLER Phillip Rogers established a home in the 1830s, on a ridge ten miles north of Fort Dearborn. The site appeared to be a good one. He was located within a ten-mile strip of land recently ceded by the Potawatomi Indians. Nearby ran an Indian trail which would become Green Bay Road, the major route between Fort Howard (on the bay) and Fort Dearborn.

The 1,600 acres Rogers purchased from the government included land between the ridge and Lake Michigan. Rogers developed much of his land but made little use of the marshy property near the lake. That once swampy land is now the Chicago neighborhood known as Rogers Park. The uninhabited area, now one of the most densely populated in the city, roughly coincides with the 49th Ward.

Chicago's northeastern cornerstone, the 49th is also one of the most cosmopolitan wards in the city. No ethnic group ever dominated this area. American-born and English settlers were the first to move here. Then came Germans and Irish.

By 1910, Russian Jews made their first inroads. They founded Congregation B'nai Zion (Pratt and Greenview), Chicago's first Conservative congregation. Other Jews flooded here from racially changing Lawndale in the 1950s (even forming a political group, the Donkey Club, composed of alumni from Lawndale's 24th Ward Regular Democratic Organization).

English-, German-, and Irish-Americans are here in diminished numbers; their descendants for the most part have fled to the suburbs. Russian Jews still abound (a restaurant called Troika at Broadway and Devon shows the Russian influence), although they are an aging population.

Ethnic groups from a myriad of origins have infused new blood into Rogers Park. Assyrians (Christians from what is now Iraq) are particularly visible near Clark and Devon. Indians, Koreans, and other Asians are scattered throughout the ward. In recent years, the northeast corner of Rogers Park has taken on a black Caribbean flavor. Howard Street east of the el terminal boasts Caribbean bakeries and a Haitian-Jamaican restaurant (El Dinamico Dallas). The Skokie-Evanston Cricket Club, promoting a popular West Indian pastime, stands at Clark and Jarvis. The blocks north of Howard host a sizeable number of Haitians, Jamaicans, and Belizeans.

Two closely affiliated universities anchor the southeastern corner of the ward. Loyola University, a Jesuit school, transferred here from the Near West Side in the 1920s. Mundelein College, operated by the Sisters of the Blessed Virgin Mary, opened in 1930. The Loyola and Sheridan neighborhood they occupy is the closest thing Chicago has to a college town ambience.

Even without the colleges, Rogers Park retains two busy symbols of a more laid back time. The Heartland Cafe (Glenwood and Lunt) offers natural food, plus what might be considered a counterculture souvenir shop. Across the street lies No Exit, a coffeehouse and gallery.

High-rise buildings (many converted to condominiums in the 1970s) line the lakefront north of the colleges and east of Sheridan Road. Many small beaches dot the shorelines near the buildings. These beaches are all open to the public, yet are jealously guarded by local residents.

Multiunit apartment buildings form much of the central section of the ward. Chicagoans were lured to this outlying area by its excellent train and el connections to downtown. Developers took advantage of this demand in the 1920s, erecting high rises and courtyard buildings. Because of this congestion, parking has long been a major problem here.

Clark Street, the former Green Bay Road, is a major business area. West of Clark is much of the ward's single family housing. Clark and Rogers (the old Indian boundary) intersect near Potawatomie Park, whose field house contains two canyonlike racquetball courts.

Howard Street separates Chicago from Evanston in the western half of the 49th Ward. East of the Milwaukee Railroad, the 49th contains a section north of Howard and south of Calvary Cemetery. This is an area once known as Germania, and it originally belonged to Evanston. But the suburb was unable to provide necessary services to the neighborhood, which was annexed to Chicago in 1915. After World War II, the area's Juneway and Jonquil Terraces were allowed to decline. The area became known as the Juneway Jungle. The most notable attraction there now is Biddy Mulligan's (Sheridan and Rogers), a blues bar which is also the northernmost bar in Chicago.

Liquor (or absence thereof) has played a role in Rogers Park. In its early years Rogers Park remained dry because it fell within the four mile limit south of Northwestern University. Spirits could not be sold north of Devon until after the repeal of Prohibition.

When liquor became legal, enterprising souls wasted no time in lining Howard Street with taverns. "On 'Maid's Night Off,' domestics from all the swank North Side and suburban homes come there to get drunk and picked up, and the boys are waiting to help them," according to a lurid 1950s account.

If the ward itself appears to be a crazy quilt, its politicians reflect that mixture. The 49th in recent years has produced reformers and rascals, pro-Richard Daley and anti-Daley (and at least one who was anti-Daley and later pro-Daley), some who have served in higher office and some who have served time in prison.

Paul Wigoda was first elected in 1959 and served as alderman for fifteen years. A shrewd mind and excellent orator, Wigoda was considered second only to Tom Keane among city council powerhouses during the Daley years. He introduced more successful legislation than any other alderman during his time.

The courts, not the voters, proved to be Wigoda's undoing. The veteran alderman was convicted in 1974 of income tax evasion stemming from the rezoning of the former Edgewater Country Club. Wigoda's conviction was part of a triple blow to Daley's administration. The day before, Keane was convicted of mail fraud. Earl Bush, Daley's press secretary, was convicted of mail fraud the day after Wigoda. U.S. Attorney (now governor) James Thompson led the legal assault.

A similar fate befell Frank Keenan, longtime (1936-57) Democratic committeeman. Keenan, a onetime political cartoonist, served as county assessor (1954-58) and used his office to hone up his artistic skills. He sketched downtown buildings whose owners, desirous of favorable tax assessments, gladly bought those sketches for prices that were the envy of full-time artists everywhere. Such shakedowns earned Keenan a prison term for income-tax evasion.

Keenan's artwork was one of his least offensive traits to Mayor Richard J. Daley. The assessor was the only Democratic committeeman to support the renomination of Martin Kennelly instead of Daley in 1955. A year later he backed Republican Benjamin Adamowski for state's attorney. Keenan switched parties in early 1957 and was convicted later that year (on charges he claimed would not have been made had he remained in Daley's good graces). He refused to vacate the assessor's office because the case was on appeal and had to be carried out bodily in his chair.

Esther Saperstein bridged two generations with her 1975 election as alderman. In 1955, running as an independent, she lost to machine-backed David Hartigan. Twenty years later she won, this time with the blessing of Democratic committeeman Neil Hartigan, lieutenant governor and son of the former alderman.

Saperstein came to the council after eight years in the state senate. Her main cause there was the Equal Rights Amendment; she briefly threatened

DAVID ORR

not to resign from the senate until the General Assembly passed the ERA. Saperstein finally left Springfield, the amendment not having passed.

Her departure caused some stir. Legislators in those days were allowed to receive their full two-year salary in advance. Saperstein took advantage of that custom. Even after resigning to become alderman, Saperstein claimed that she was entitled to the legislative money, and that it was immaterial whether or not she performed constituent services. A court ruling forced her to repay most of that salary.

Hartigan tried to dump the seventy-four-year-old Saperstein before the 1979 election, but she refused to budge until the last minute. Finally she was lured away by a lucrative position with the Department of Human Services.

The regulars had cause to worry about that seat; independent Mike Kreloff lost by only 415 votes in 1975. They slated an impressive candidate, Loyola psychology professor Homer H. Johnson. It became a battle of academics. David Orr, an assistant professor of history at Mundelein, ran as an independent.

Orr, the only WASP alderman, won that election and has been reelected twice. He defeated organization-backed Nancy Kelly by 4,000 votes in 1983, even carrying Committeeman Michael Brady's home precinct.

A solid Harold Washington supporter in an increasingly pro-Washington ward, Orr did not attract a strong challenge in 1987. State Representative (and Democratic committeeman) Lee Preston declined to enter the race. Instead, the Democratic organization supported Jack Fleming, an assistant state's attorney. Two other candidates entered: Howard Spinner, a Republican, and Grady Humphrey, a black candidate with organization ties (who failed to attract significant numbers of black votes from Orr).

David Orr has led the council in two major Washington era reforms. He was the chief supporter of a 1987 comprehensive ethics ordinance which limits campaign contributions and requires financial disclosures. The ordinance was less than universally popular, even among Washington-bloc aldermen (one called Orr a "Mr. Goody Two Shoes" for his efforts on behalf of this good-government bill). Orr forced a vote on the measure before the February election, reasoning that while some aldermen were not overjoyed by an ethics ordinance, they would be afraid to vote against a Washington-backed measure so close to an election.

His other major cause was a tenants' bill of rights, which he advocated ever since his first election. It was a particularly appropriate cause for an alderman representing a ward with one of the highest percentages of renters in the city. This ordinance, stalled like the ethics bill by the anti-Washington council majority, passed after the mayor gained a friendly majority on the city council.

He also serves as vice mayor, a position that until late 1987 was considered largely a ceremonial one. Orr was selected for the post (which provides a budget and patronage jobs but seemingly few responsibilities) for several reasons: he shared Washington's reform philosophy, he was white (Orr as vice mayor served both to showcase the Washington administration's "rainbow coalition" and to prevent jealousy among black aldermen who might covet the post) and he had no ambition (and given his unpopularity among fellow aldermen, no chance) to become mayor. While Harold Washington was alive Orr was invisible as vice mayor, even discontinuing predecessor Richard Mell's practice of providing bagels and sweetrolls for council meetings.

In retrospect, the choice of Orr for vice mayor was an excellent one. He presided calmly as interim mayor during the mourning period for Washington, babysitting the mayoral position until an acting mayor could be named. Alderman Burton Natarus commended Orr for his handling of the job during the council's memorial service for Washington.

Natarus might have wished to retract that praise a few hours later. Orr, a backer of Timothy Evans for acting mayor, was accused of calling only on Evans supporters during the marathon council meeting which chose Washington's successor.

However, Orr was more than fair. When only white ethnic aldermen were present in the council chamber before the meeting, Orr could have gaveled it closed for lack of quorum, thus buying the time needed to convince hesitant candidate Eugene Sawyer to withdraw. He didn't. Orr claimed that he called on Evans allies because he wanted to assure that they had a chance to discuss the Natarus resolution concerning the rules of the acting mayor selection (conceding, though, that such discussion also served to provide fuel for a possible legal challenge to the Sawyer election).

Orr's personal popularity in the ward has not transferred to other independent candidates. The Democratic committeeman office has remained in party regulars' hands. Hartigan, committeeman since 1968, stepped down in 1980. His choice for successor was Ed Rosewell, the county treasurer.

Mayor Jane Byrne had other ideas. She was not willing to concede the position to a Hartigan-backed ally of likely 1983 challenger Richard M. Daley. Byrne persuaded former state legislator Michael Brady, her legislative liaison and influential advisor, to move into the ward and run for the office. Brady won the election.

Brady's loyalty to Byrne exceeded his loyalty to the 49th Ward Democratic organization. He resigned shortly after Byrne's 1983 defeat. Ward precinct captains chose State Representative Lee Preston to take Brady's place. This transfer of power ignited Kreloff, who ran a losing committeeman campaign in 1980. Kreloff charged that the Preston selection was illegal. "(Preston) could call himself the King of Siam, but that doesn't make him king," he commented. Voters had their choice the following spring and elected Preston to a full term.

There is no love lost between Preston, a representative best known for his child abuse legislation, and Orr. When Washington foes in 1985 tried to force the mayor to openly condemn the controversial Rev. Louis Farrakhan, Preston sent a letter to 49th Ward residents saying that Orr voted against the denunciation. Orr countered that his vote was a procedural one and charged that Preston (and opposition leader Ed Vrdolyak) were using the Farrakhan denunciation to drive a wedge between blacks and Jews.

Yet Orr did not field a candidate against Preston in the 1988 committeeman election. Neither did anyone else; Preston won without opposition.

REDISTRICTING: There were no changes made in the 49th Ward boundaries by the 1986 ward remap.

MAYORAL: Be it changing demographics or general satisfaction with the administration, Harold Washington enjoyed increased support here over four years ago. In the 1983 primary, Jane Byrne (supported by Committeeman Brady) won 45 percent of the vote. (Hartigan-backed) Daley won 33 percent, and (Orr-supported) Harold Washington, only 22 percent.

This ward became a major question mark in the general election; would Jewish voters support liberal Democrat Harold Washington or Jewish (and, not incidentally, white) Republican Bernard Epton?

The Jews went for Epton. But other groups in the ward (particularly blacks in northeast precincts) gave Washington a lot of backing. Washington took 43 percent of the vote in the general election, nearly doubling his primary total, in what proved to be a close election in many precincts. Epton carried the area west of Clark Street. Washington again carried the Juneway area.

The ward race was extremely close in the 1987 primary (a difference of less than 400 votes out of more than 17,000 cast). This time Washington carried the ward with 51 percent. He saw increases along the lake, perhaps due to his quick work in reopening Lake Shore Drive after February flooding.

Lakeshore favorite son Donald Haider, with his 10 percent of the vote, prevented either of the other candidates from obtaining a majority in the general election. Washington, with his 47 percent, carried the ward.

CENSUS DATA: Population (1980): 60,231. 70.21 percent white, 9.91 percent black, 10.96 percent Hispanic, 8.92 percent Asian and other. Voting age population: 75.55 percent white, 8.29 percent black, 9.26 percent Hispanic, 6.90 percent Asian and other.

CENSUS TRACTS: See ward map.

COMMUNITY NEWSPAPERS:
Northtown News, 7519 N. Ashland (761–7200)
Rogers Park/Edgewater, 7519 N. Ashland (761–7200)

ALDERMAN: David D. Orr. Elected 1979. Born October 4, 1944. Career: B.A., Simpson College, 1966; M.A., Case Western Reserve University, 1968; researcher, Ralph Nader's Congress Project; assistant professor of history and urban affairs, Mundelein College, 1969–79.
Committees: vice-mayor; Special Events and Cultural Affairs (vice-chairman); Budget and Government Operations; Buildings; Education; Finance; Housing; Local Transportation; Police, Fire, and Municipal Institutions; Streets and Alleys; Zoning.
City hall telephone: 744–3067, 744–3080.
Ward office: 6925 N. Ashland (764–3617).
1987 election:

| David D. Orr | 9,964 | (57%) | Howard E. Spinner | 1,054 | (6%) |
| Jack Fleming | 5,858 | (34%) | Grady A. Humphrey | 573 | (3%) |

DEMOCRATIC COMMITTEEMAN: Lee Preston. Appointed 1983. Born February 6, 1944. Career: B.S., University of Illinois, 1966; J.D., DePaul University, 1972; attorney; teacher, Chicago public schools and Richards High School, Oak Lawn; U.S. Army; administrative assistant to Lt. Governor Neil Hartigan, 1974–76; assistant corporation counsel for license revocation prosecutions, 1976–79; Illinois House of Representatives, 1979–.

Ward office: 1522 W. Devon (262–2611).
1984 election:

Lee Preston	7,377	(54%)
Michael Kreloff	6,311	(46%)

MAYORAL ELECTIONS:

1983 Democratic primary:

Jane Byrne	9,630	(45%)
Richard Daley	7,111	(33%)
Harold Washington	4,757	(22%)

1983 general:

Bernard Epton	12,815	(57%)
Harold Washington	9,719	(43%)

1987 Democratic primary:

Harold Washington	8,716	(51%)
Jane Byrne	8,333	(49%)

1987 general:

Harold Washington	8,269	(47%)
Edward Vrdolyak	7,496	(43%)
Donald Haider	1,809	(10%)

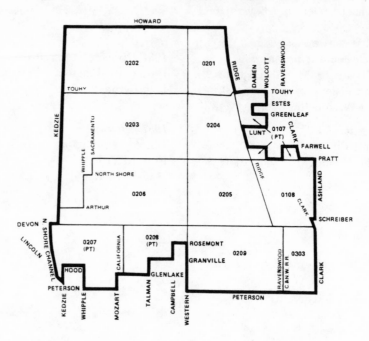

CHICAGO'S JEWISH COMMUNITY is nearly as old as the city itself. The first settlers, German Jews, arrived in the late 1830s and early 1840s. They settled first in the downtown business area, moving after the 1871 fire to the Near South Side area that became known as the "Golden Ghetto."

Already well established and assimilated by 1880, the German Jews looked down upon the second Jewish wave—eastern Europeans from Poland and Russia who congregated in the Near West Side around Halsted and Maxwell Street. If the Germans saw themselves as urbane intellectuals who formed their own high-class social and intellectual societies, the eastern Europeans were considered to be village rustics who made their living dealing goods from the packs on their backs. Yet the eastern Europeans survived and occasionally thrived in their often unfriendly surroundings.

German Jews moved increasingly south to the Grand Boulevard (now King Drive), Englewood, South Shore, Kenwood, and Hyde Park neighborhoods. Black encroachment pushed them from all but the latter neighborhood; their descendants live either in Hyde Park or the suburbs.

Eastern European Jews also migrated through the city. From Maxwell Street some moved north to Albany Park or Sheridan Road. The largest number migrated to the West Side Lawndale neighborhood. There, along Douglas

Boulevard and Independence Drive, they built schools, service organizations, and synagogues as massive as cathedrals.

They fled Lawndale in the late 1940s and early 1950s, ahead of an inevitable black influx. The favorite relocation area was little-developed West Rogers Park. The neighborhood, bounded by Peterson, Kedzie, Ridge, and Howard, roughly coincides with the present day 50th Ward.

For years this was a semirural area inhabited mainly by Luxembourgers, best known for its brickyard and greenhouses. Now West Rogers Park (also known as West Ridge or North Town) is the most heavily Jewish area of the city. The Jewish population of West Ridge (the community name of West Rogers Park) was only 2,000 in 1930. It grew to 11,000 in 1950. By 1963 the Jewish population had mushroomed to 48,000—about three-quarters of the West Ridge community.

In one respect, the Jewish population remained stable despite its travels. Congregations sold their buildings when Jews left the old neighborhoods and lent their names to synagogues in the new ones. Thus many synagogues founded a century ago on Maxwell Street made their way to Lawndale and now may be found in West Rogers Park.

California Avenue between Peterson and Touhy is the Jewish cultural center of Chicago. This area, with comfortable single level houses and manicured yards that make it more reminiscent of suburban Skokie or Lincolnwood than adjacent Chicago, includes a religiously oriented high school (Ida Crown, at Pratt), the Bernard Horwich Community Center (Touhy and Sacramento), offices of various Jewish organizations, and a number of synagogues.

Devon (locally pronounced as duh-VAHN, not DEV-on) is the major cross street here. The Jewish influence is noticeable throughout. One can see it in The Ark, a crisis center at Claremont; the Chicago Hebrew Bookstore (Sacramento); and any number of delis and Jewish bakeries and even a kosher pizzeria just off Devon at California. The preferred fish is gefilte, not catfish or trout.

Yet Devon is not merely a Jewish avenue. Some call it the most cosmopolitan street in Chicago, and with reason. The stretch between Kedzie and Western yields Indian food stores, Pakistani and Indian video stores, Chinese gift shops, a Greek bank, a Middle Eastern general store, Thai and Italian restaurants, and the Midwest's largest selection of *sari* palaces. Further east, at Clark, is the Assyrian-American Association, meeting place for the Iraqi Christians who are one of Chicago's newest ethnic groups.

Gentiles live here, too. Angel Guardian Center at Devon and Ridge, with its tall red brick church, provides the most visible example of Catholic influence. Originally an orphanage, Angel Guardian now hosts a senior citizens center, a home for retarded children, and a gym where the Chicago Bulls practiced.

Two 50th Ward parks deserve mention. Indian Boundary (Lunt and Rockwell), one of the city's best-kept secrets, contains a Tudor field house and a small zoo with animals loaned from Lincoln Park Zoo. Warren Park encompasses most of the land between Western and Damen, Arthur and Pratt. At one time the Edgewater Country Club was located here. Community pressure squelched plans of developers who planned to build high-rise condominiums on the former club site. Now Warren contains a nine-hole golf course, a new field house, and a sledding hill, among other amenities. Democratic committeeman Howard Carroll holds his annual Taste of the 50th Ward food fest here.

In years past the 50th Ward was represented by members of the "economy bloc"—aldermen (often Republicans) from outlying wards who opposed the Democratic machine for fiscal, not social reasons. One of the most respected economy bloc members was Jack Sperling, who served the 50th Ward from 1955 to 1973. Colleagues praised him as a colorful orator, one of the brightest and wittiest of aldermen.

Sperling was elected as a Republican, and twice spurned the GOP mayoral nomination because he felt party leaders would not put out a strong enough effort in his behalf. Nonetheless he claimed, "Independence is the middle name of Jack I. Sperling." He angered party hard-liners by his refusal to back a nondescript Republican U.S. Senate candidate in 1970, and the ward's Republican committeeman refused to endorse him in 1971.

Unlike some Richard Daley foes of the era, Jack Sperling carefully chose those topics on which to oppose the mayor; he became known as a budget watchdog. Although generally allied with the council's Republicans and independents, he won the respect and occasional backing of Democrats. Daley rewarded his loyal antagonist by sponsoring him for a judgeship in 1973.

Sperling's victories were due to personal popularity, not a strong ward Republican organization. Thus regular Democrats were able to capture the aldermanic seat in the 1973 special election. Jerome Huppert, one of the few Luxembourgers to hold local public office, had been Democratic committeeman since 1956. Huppert, Finance Committee chairman of the county board, declined to take the aldermanic seat himself. Instead he chose Bernard Stone, a real estate supervisor with the Cook County Sheriff's office.

Stone won the special election in a runoff, and has been reelected four times by comfortable margins. He received two-thirds of the vote in the 1987 election against attorney Michael Moses and Lyndon LaRouche backer Sander Fredman.

Huppert and Stone clashed almost immediately. Stone moved out of the Huppert ward office on three different occasions and conducted aldermanic business from his Howard Street law office. But when State Senator Howard Carroll beat Stone in the 1980 race to succeed Huppert as committeeman, the two soon made peace.

Nobody ever accused Bernie Stone of being colorless. During his first election campaign, he promised to set up a mobile office if elected. He serviced constituents from a mobile home after the election. During the 1979 snowfall, he promised not to shave until his ward was properly plowed. Two aldermanic allies finally held him down and separated him from his nascent beard.

Independents remember Bernie Stone for two three-word phrases. When Alderman Martin Oberman tried to make a point during the Council Wars

BERNARD STONE

years, Stone interrupted loud and long. The usually dignified Oberman turned to his fellow council member and shouted, "Shut up, Bernie!"

During a 1986 session, freshman alderman Luis Gutierrez riled Stone and council ally Ed Vrdolyak by reading aloud their property tax bills. A choleric Bernard Stone screamed "You little pipsqueak!" and brushed aside Alderman David Orr, who was trying to act as a peacemaker.

Although sometimes boisterous, Stone is no buffoon. He took the lead on one of the most important issues of 1985: the proposed 1992 World's Fair. Stone's opposition stemmed from more than a Washington-Vrdolyak power play; the mayor himself gave only lip service to the fair. As chairman of the Special Events Committee, he insisted that fair organizers consider alternative sites to the downtown Burnham Harbor proposal. He questioned the financial feasibility of such a fair, predicting it would put the city into debt. When the *Tribune* published a poll that 66 percent of Chicagoans would like a fair, and 42 percent of those favoring it would be willing to pay higher taxes for it, Stone pointed out that the poll showed only 28 percent of all surveyed would accept a tax increase to help a fair. If House Speaker Michael Madigan's recommendation against it put the final nail in the fair's coffin, Stone helped place the body there.

A onetime solid "Vrdolyak 29" member, Stone became one of the "pragmatic 12"—former Vrdolyak bloc aldermen who voted with Washington forces for a new city council alignment after the 1987 election. Like most others, he received a chairmanship: that of the Committee on Historical Landmark Preservation.

Stone jumped to the Republican party in late 1987 in return for party slating for recorder of deeds. He pulled another surprise the day of the city council election to replace Harold Washington. Stone announced his candidacy for mayor that morning and released a statement showing his position on key issues (something neither Eugene Sawyer nor Timothy Evans did). Some called the announcement a publicity ploy for his recorder campaign. Nonetheless he received the support of fellow Republican Victor Vrdolyak (and presumably that of some aldermen whose constituents would demand a vote for any white candidate over any black one). Stone later withdrew his candidacy in favor of the ultimate winner, Sawyer.

REDISTRICTING: The 50th Ward received no alterations as a result of the 1986 redistricting.

MAYORAL: Although located next to one of the most liberal Lakefront areas, West Rogers Park has not shared Rogers Park's enthusiasm for Harold Washington. Jane Byrne won a majority of votes (51 percent) in the 1983 Democratic primary. Richard Daley finished second (43 percent) and Harold Washington, with 6 percent, finished a distant third.

Washington tripled his vote in the general election, but it came out to only 18 percent against Republican Bernard Epton.

In 1987, just like 1983, Jane Byrne took the Democratic primary, this time by a three-to-one margin against her only major opponent. Harold Washington failed to show real strength anywhere.

Edward Vrdolyak likewise beat the mayor by better than a three-to-one margin in the 50th Ward during the general election, 69 to 21 percent. Donald Haider won 10 percent of the vote, roughly equal to his North Side average.

CENSUS DATA: Population (1980): 59,916. 84.71 percent white, 1.01 percent black, 4.83 percent Hispanic, 9.45 percent Asian and other. Voting age population: 88.65 percent white, .92 percent black, 4.18 percent Hispanic, 6.25 percent Asian and other.

CENSUS TRACTS: See ward map.

COMMUNITY NEWSPAPERS:
Northtown News, 7519 N. Ashland (761–7200)
Rogers Park/Edgewater News, 7519 N. Ashland (761–7200)

ALDERMAN: Bernard L. Stone. Elected 1973. Born November 24, 1927. Career: B.A., DePaul University, 1949; J.D., John Marshall Law School, 1952; claims adjuster, State Farm Mutual Auto Insurance Co., 1952–54; attorney; real estate supervisor, Cook County Sheriff's office.

Committees: Historical Landmarks Preservation (chairman); Aging and Disabled; Budget and Government Operations; Buildings; Finance; Land Acquisition, Disposition, and Leases; Zoning.

City hall telephone: 744–6855, 744–6016.

Ward office: 6347 N. Sacramento (764-5050).

1987 election:

Bernard L. Stone	13,653	(67%)
Michael Charles Moses	6,285	(31%)
Sander P. Fredman	501	(2%)

DEMOCRATIC COMMITTEEMAN: Howard Carroll. Elected 1980. Born July 28, 1942. Career: B.S. and B.A., Roosevelt University, 1964; J.D., DePaul University, 1967; attorney; Illinois House of Representatives, 1971-73; Illinois Senate 1973–.

Ward office: 2705 W. Howard (243–0500).

1984 election:

Howard Carroll, unopposed.

MAYORAL ELECTIONS:

1983 Democratic primary:

Jane Byrne	12,526	(51%)
Richard Daley	10,440	(43%)
Harold Washington	1,553	(6%)

1983 general:

Bernard Epton	22,368	(82%)
Harold Washington	5,002	(18%)

1987 Democratic primary:

Jane Byrne	15,446	(76%)
Harold Washington	4,858	(24%)

1987 general:

Edward Vrdolyak	14,673	(69%)
Harold Washington	4,385	(21%)
Donald Haider	2,155	(10%)

The
Race
for
Mayor
PART II

POLITICAL WRITER PAUL M. GREEN summed up the fragile state of Chicago politics in a September 1987 television interview. "If Harold Washington dies," Green said, "all hell breaks loose."

His words proved prophetic. Harold Washington died November 25. And politically speaking, all hell broke loose.

It started out as a normal day for the mayor. He broke ground for a South Side housing development, joking and bantering in his usual style. Then he returned to his office. Shortly before 11 a.m., he slumped over his desk. Advisor Alton Miller claimed he thought at first the mayor was groping for something under the desk.

Washington suffered a massive cardiac arrest. He was taken to Northwestern Memorial Hospital and pronounced dead at 1:36 p.m., although most likely he was brain dead before he was removed from city hall.

Harold Washington, it turns out, was a heart attack waiting to happen. Grossly (more than 100 pounds) overweight and a former smoker (who reportedly sneaked a few puffs every now and then), he thrived on a junk food diet, seldom if ever exercised, worked around the clock in a high-stress job, and never took vacations (although, ironically, he mentioned plans to leave that day and take a few days off). His arteries were "ninety to ninety-five percent" clogged, and his heart was three times the normal size.

Washington's death showed amazing parallels to that of Chicago's other dominant modern politician, Richard J. Daley. Both died suddenly of heart attacks, just before holidays (Washington the day before Thanksgiving, Daley a few days before Christmas in 1976). Both carried on a normal schedule the day they died. Both died at Northwestern Memorial Hospital, and the same doctor (John Sanders) worked to save both political titans.

And both left political confusion in their wake. In Daley's case, it was utter chaos. No one was certain who should preside over the city council in his absence. Black alderman Wilson Frost claimed the honor, but white Daley allies literally locked him out of that office. A compromise put in 11th Ward alderman Michael Bilandic as acting mayor.

Daley's death prompted the council to set up a short-term replacement for a deceased mayor, creating the position of vice mayor. Mild-mannered Alderman David Orr held the title, which before November 25 had almost always been prefaced by "largely ceremonial." Orr would preside until a city council meeting in which aldermen would choose one of their own to serve as acting mayor.

Even then, the succession problem raised questions. Would the acting mayor serve until the next regularly scheduled mayoral election in 1991? Until the next scheduled municipal election in 1989? Would a special election date be set? "Election law here is so vague that six different people could look at it and come up with seven different answers," Green commented. Election officials finally determined that 1989 would be the next mayoral election date, although various groups threatened to go to court for an earlier special election.

Washington at his death had reached the zenith of his powers. Faced at last with a cooperative city council, he was virtually assured passage of any of his initiatives. Granted, there were enough issues to fill any agenda: a proposed $84 million property tax increase (a figure definitely open to compromise); continuing school crises (a nineteen-day strike paralyzed classes that September, and the mayor was notable for his inaction. He later organized a "summit" of school, union, business, community, and civic leaders to recommend educational changes); proposed taxicab deregulation; a proposed gay rights ordinance; a proposal to allow night games at Wrigley Field; proposed revision of the city's ethics ordinance; proposed new stadia for the Bears and White Sox; a proposed new central library; a proposal to designate part of the Clybourn Avenue corridor as a protected manufacturing district; a proposed revision of the city's zoning code; proposed redevelopment of Navy Pier and the north Loop; continued deterioration of Chicago Housing Authority projects; funding to prevent lakeshore erosion; an ever-mounting waste disposal problem; battles for neighborhood development between forces who wished to gentrify neighborhoods and those seeking to install low- and moderate-income housing; and a possible municipal takeover of some or all Commonwealth Edison electricity facilities once that utility's franchise expires in 1990.

But the election to succeed Washington revolved around politics, not issues (with the possible exception of the property tax). And the "electorate" was fifty, not three million.

While confusion reigned at Northwestern Memorial (the press was kept in a virtual blackout, and Washington's death was not announced until nearly an hour after the fact), various factions began working to line up aldermanic votes for a Washington successor. By the time of a 3:00 P.M. prayer service led by Aldermen Danny Davis (29th) and George Hagopian (30th), most had been contacted by forces representing one or more contenders.

Most aldermen maintained a discreet silence about their plans, ostensibly out of respect for the recently departed mayor. Not Richard Mell of the Near Northwest Side 33rd Ward. Mell declared to all who would listen that he had twenty votes lined up and had to be considered the front runner to replace Washington.

Few considered him that. From the outset the succession race became a battle between two black Washington allies, Timothy Evans (4th) and Eugene Sawyer (6th).

Evans and Sawyer had many similarities. Both were longtime aldermen (Sawyer sixteen years, Evans fourteen) who had come up through the regular party organization. Both switched to Harold Washington and achieved high positions in the city council (Evans as chairman of the Finance Committee, Sawyer as president pro tempore and chairman of the Rules Committee).

Yet the candidacies showed the divisions in the Washington bloc which had always been evident to insiders. Evans quickly picked up the support of "movement" blacks such as Bobby Rush (2nd) and Dorothy Tillman (3rd) and white Lakefront liberals Helen Shiller (46th) and Orr. He had another set of important backers—the Washington administration, especially chief of staff Ernest Barefield and intergovernmental affairs advisor Jacky Grimshaw.

Sawyer, on the other hand, gained immediate support from those blacks whose alliance to Washington stemmed less from love of his agenda than fear of reprisal (and some of whom barely concealed their joy at the mayor's death)—aldermen such as William Beavers (7th), Robert Shaw (9th), and especially William Henry (24th), who became Sawyer's unofficial campaign manager.

While former mayor Jane Byrne said of her late foe, "May he share his Thanksgiving with God," others made themselves visible. Davis mentioned that he would accept a draft, and fellow West Siders Ed Smith (28th) and Percy Giles (37th) fell behind him. White independent Larry Bloom, a rival of Evans for influence among Washington bloc aldermen, let his availability as a compromise candidate be known. The four Hispanic aldermen—Jesus Garcia (22nd), Juan Soliz (25th), Luis Gutierrez (26th) and Raymond Figueroa (31st)—announced that they would vote as a bloc and remain independent of any candidate.

White ethnic aldermen must have been gleeful as they watched the Washington bloc disintegrate before their eyes. Yet they lacked the votes to elect one of their group mayor. Mell and longtime 32nd Ward alderman Terry Gabinski both claimed the allegiance of the white ethnic bloc (and this group, unlike blacks, remained a bloc), but neither could penetrate into the ranks of blacks and Hispanics to capture the votes needed to pull themselves over the top.

By the time the election was over nearly one-third of the aldermen would be considered for acting mayor, including such unlikely souls as ultraliberal Jesus Garcia, ultraconservative William Banks (36th), and ultra-anonymous Michael Sheahan (19th) and Patrick O'Connor (40th). Some people (mainly political writers, not aldermen) openly pondered the possibility of an alderman such as Gabinski or the 20th Ward's Ernest Jones stepping down to make way for a high-profile compromise candidate, such as 32nd Ward committeeman Dan Rostenkowski or 20th Ward committeeman Cecil Partee. Orr nipped such ideas in the bud, noting that he had the power of aldermanic appointments while he was interim mayor and that he would have no part of such "chicanery."

One person never seriously considered for acting mayor was Orr himself. The interim mayor immediately took himself out of the running, not that his statement made much of a difference. Orr's squeaky clean image and adherence to his tough ethics ordinance made him anathema to too many other aldermen.

Grimshaw called for a meeting of aldermen to discuss the mayoral succession, a call unheeded by everyone. Instead, the aldermen gathered in small caucuses or warmed their telephones with calls among themselves.

Jacky Grimshaw and other Washington staff likewise burned the telephone lines. Among those called was one Jesse Louis Jackson, a presidential candidate who was on a fact finding tour of the Middle East.

While most Chicagoans were preparing for a Thanksgiving Day of feasting and football, David Orr packed a gym bag and headed downtown. "I have no idea when I'll be home," he told his wife. Later on she and a handful of family and friends witnessed his private swearing in ceremony as Chicago's interim mayor.

The new chief executive then held a press conference to discuss the transition period. He announced a city council meeting for the following Tuesday, one which would serve solely as a memorial service. Foes who accused Orr of being a puppet to Barefield and Grimshaw reinforced their beliefs when Barefield whispered phrases to him on numerous occasions during the conference. Barefield, calm and collected up to this time, could not hold back tears when announcing the funeral schedule.

By now it appeared to be an Evans-Sawyer contest, with Mell, Gabinski, and Davis looming only as dark horses. Among the black community, there was little doubt as to preference. Radio call-in shows, the most visible gauge of public opinion, clearly favored Evans (one poll showed Evans over Sawyer, 400–8).

But radio talk-show callers couldn't vote in this particular election, and those that could (the aldermen) seemed to be leaning toward Sawyer. He became the preferred candidate among the anti-Washington bloc for several reasons. First, he was considered easier to get along with (and some charged, to manipulate) than Evans, who was considered part of a "palace guard" that kept many of them from the former mayor. More important, Sawyer was considered easier to defeat in an upcoming election. It also didn't hurt that Sawyer's 6th Ward organization got out the vote better than any other black organization, and that kind of activity could split the black vote enough to allow a white politician to win an upcoming Democratic primary.

The fate of the aldermen became ironic. Evans supporters touted their man, the Finance Committee chairman and floor leader, as the true heir to the Washington legacy even though some foes charged he covertly supported Byrne against Washington in 1983. Sawyer was labeled a machine pawn even though he was the first alderman to support Washington's 1983 bid (foes claimed he made that endorsement only because any other action would destroy his own reelection bid in his black middle-class ward).

A 3:00 P.M. Friday ecumenical prayer service at Daley Plaza honored the late mayor. While thousands shivered through the cold, wet weather to hear a plethora of eulogies, an airplane landed at O'Hare International Airport. Out stepped the Rev. Jesse Jackson, Chicago's most visible pre-Harold Washington black man and now Chicago's most visible post-Harold Washington one. A number of prominent black and Hispanic figures, including Evans, Sawyer, Garcia, Rush, Tillman, Congressman Charles Hayes, and Judge Eugene Pincham appeared to greet him.

Not everyone rushed to the airport. Davis stayed behind, indicating that he had conferred with the civil rights leader many times in the past. Henry issued statements to the effect that election of a new mayor was the aldermen's duty and that Jackson should mind his own business.

Jackson appeared officially neutral. But the picture at the airport told the story. Sawyer appeared near tears, while Evans looked as though he was sitting on a million dollar lottery ticket. Jackson held five separate meetings at the airport terminal, and speculation arose that Sawyer would withdraw from the race in return for chairmanship of the Finance Committee.

Washington's body lay in state throughout the weekend, and hundreds of thousands of Chicagoans displayed a genuine outpouring of grief unmatched for years if not decades. Doors to city hall opened at 4:40 P.M., and the Chicagoans who were lined up for five blocks had a chance to view their mayor. By the time the viewing period ended at midnight Sunday, more than 200,000 persons had paid their respects to Harold Washington. Among those in line were former mayor Byrne and her daughter Kathy, who declined preferential treatment for three hours before finally accepting a police escort to the front of the line.

The Jackson entourage, which now also included Davis, Alderman Anna Langford (16th), and Congressman Gus Savage, entered city hall late in the afternoon, joined hands, and poignantly sang "We Shall Overcome." Then they adjourned to a side room to hold one of many meetings closed to whites and reporters that attempted to unify the black and Hispanic aldermen. Jackson's meetings caused Garcia to miss one he had scheduled with Smith and white aldermen Bloom, Kathy Osterman (48th), Ed Eisendrath (43rd), and Mark Fary (12th)—all unaligned aldermen who could have proven to be key votes. Eisendrath at that meeting attempted to promote Bloom's candidacy.

Jackson's meetings, if not conclusive, proved informative. One alderman later commented, "At one point they asked Sawyer if he really wanted to be mayor, and Sawyer just mumbled something that you couldn't hear. Then Beavers came up behind him and said, 'Speak up, man!'" It was the first of many signs that Sawyer's backers were more interested in his candidacy than was the candidate himself.

Nor was Sawyer encouraged by an Operation PUSH meeting held the next morning. Hundreds of persons attended wearing blue buttons which read "Make no deals," an Evans slogan. At that meeting, radio commentator Lu Palmer warned, "While we are going through a period of mourning, the wolves are on the prowl." Then the candidates were introduced. Sawyer received applause that barely could be described as polite. Evans got a standing ovation, so thunderous that even Sawyer joined in the standing and the applause. It must have been a heartbreaking rejection for Sawyer, the first alderman to back Harold Washington and now being implicated as one who made deals with the "wolves." Sawyer and his allies later complained that the PUSH meeting was packed with Evans supporters in an attempt to pressure him out of the race.

Henry took no chances. Sensing Sawyer's uneasiness, he put twenty-four-hour guards on the candidate—not so much out of fear for his safety as from the worry that someone might get to Sawyer and dissuade him from running.

Jackson hoped for a knockout punch, a display of populism and power that could unite black aldermen behind one candidate (Evans). The ploy didn't work. Sawyer did not exit the race. In fact early indications had him with a majority of the black aldermen: himself, old-line Democratic regulars Henry, Beavers, Shaw, and Allan Streeter (17th); three newly elected aldermen with regular organization ties, Keith Caldwell (8th), Ernest Jones (20th), and Lemuel Austin (34th); and rookie aldermen Jesse Evans (21st) and Sheneather Butler (27th). Evans had himself, Rush, Tillman, the four Hispanics, Shiller, and Orr. Davis retained himself plus West Side allies Smith and Giles. Two other black aldermen, Marlene Carter (15th) and Anna Langford (16th) were uncommitted but believed leaning toward Sawyer.

On the other hand, the Jackson efforts had an effect—an adverse one on Evans. Whites, particularly Jews, let their aldermen know that "Jesse Jackson" candidate Evans was not suitable to them, a point most of those aldermen realized anyway. As he had so many other times in his career, Jackson served as a lightning rod (and convenient alibi) for whites. Banks said, "I don't think the decision on who should be made mayor should be determined by Jesse Jackson, and that will be easy to explain in my community," although nothing in Banks's background indicated that he would support a candidate running on a Harold Washington agenda, whether that candidate was supported by Jesse Jackson or not.

White aldermen held a meeting at Alderman Joseph Kotlarz's (35th) house, as closed to blacks, Hispanics, and reporters as Jesse Jackson's previous night's meetings were closed to whites and reporters. Newsmen, however, could peer through the picture window. They spotted Gabinski, Mell, Eisendrath, Osterman, Fary, O'Connor, Sheahan, Hagopian, Banks, Fred Roti (1st), John Madrzyk (13th), Ed Burke (14th), Robert Kellam (18th), Thomas Cullerton (38th), Anthony Laurino (39th), Roman Pucinski (41st), Bernard Hansen (44th), Patrick Levar (45th), Eugene Schulter (47th), and Bernard Stone (50th). Also represented were 23rd Ward committeeman William Lipinski (representing his alderman, William Krystyniak), committeemen Ted Lechowicz (30th), Thomas Lyons (45th), and Howard Carroll (50th), and state representatives Al Ronan and William Laurino. Alderman Victor Vrdolyak (10th) also phoned in his support.

One white alderman was notable by his absence—Burton Natarus of the 42nd Ward. His committeeman, George Dunne, like Jesse Jackson, rushed from out of town to influence the election. Dunne insisted that a black alderman be elected acting mayor while at the same time complaining about the influence of Jesse Jackson—a sure sign that he favored Sawyer.

The white aldermen were united by their irritation at Jesse Jackson's presence, yet still lacked numbers to elect one of their own as mayor. Burke took himself out of consideration. Mell and Gabinski both sought the group's endorsement; both met with less than total support. Gabinski expressed the belief that he could also get the votes of Natarus and at least one Hispanic. Mell stated that he could win over Bloom and an Hispanic (although the Hispanics vowed to stay together, and Figueroa announced that he would not support Mell).

It was by no means certain that this white bloc would hang together come election time. In Pucinski's case there was his daughter Aurelia, recently slated candidate for clerk of the circuit court. The younger Pucinski was endorsed for the post by Washington shortly before he died, a move that irked many blacks. Already considered an underdog to former mayor Byrne in that race, she (or her father) could barely afford to alienate a large bloc of votes. Fred Roti, in a multiethnic ward, faced potential electoral danger no matter what move he made. And who knew what those unpredictable Lakefronters, Osterman and Eisendrath, would do?

The white aldermen made an astute move. Osterman and Eisendrath were designated the spokespersons of the group. On the one hand, the presence of these independents helped diffuse the image of the old "Vrdolyak 29." At the same time, giving them a role might have leaned their votes in the whites' direction.

Those spokesmen had little to say. The Kotlarz meeting broke up with no definite result. Those at the meeting agreed to meet at Osterman's office Sunday afternoon, and to reconvene at Kotlarz's house Sunday night.

The Hispanic bloc, meanwhile, showed signs of cracking. It soon became evident that Gutierrez, Garcia, and Figueroa, despite their claims of neutrality, were firmly in the Evans camp. Soliz, feeling duped by the others, ended up caught between his desire for Hispanic unity (and fear of fallout from his community if he broke from that unity) and his own desires to influence the outcome. As a result, no one tallied his vote with any certainty in anyone's column.

But as Saturday turned into Sunday, few aldermen seemed willing to commit themselves even to the time of day. Sawyer, Evans, Gabinski, and Mell all claimed that between firm votes and votes leaning their way they had enough to win. But most aldermen hedged their bets by allowing their names to appear on more than one candidate's list. Roti's and Soliz's names appeared on all four lists.

It became a political horse race. The first person to gain twenty-six votes would declare himself the winner by getting three of his allies to call a special council meeting for the sole purpose of electing an acting mayor. Orr, as interim mayor, had the power to call such a meeting himself, but he showed no inclination to do so.

Someone else was busy Saturday night, breaking into Orr's ward office. Orr claimed that nothing had been taken from the office.

Mell came out of the Saturday Kotlarz meeting telling reporters, "We made no deals." But later stories showed that if deals had not been made, it was not for lack of trying. Many of those would-be deals were attributed to Mell himself. Gutierrez disclosed that Mell offered him vice mayor or chairman of the Local Transportation Committee, Hispanic control of the park district, and a Hispanic chief of staff. Soliz could get "anything you want for your community." Mell offered former 43rd Ward alderman William Singer corporation counsel if he could win over Eisendrath's vote. The alderman dangled in front of Bloom a package that would put many baseball free agents to shame: corporation counsel, at $85,000 per year; a six-figure partnership in a downtown law firm; and retirement of the $140,000 debt he accrued during his 1986 state's attorney campaign. Or, if he preferred, Bloom could move to the 33rd Ward, and Mell would see to his election as alderman from there.

Others also did their share of wheeling and dealing. Henry told Eisendrath, a former teacher and present uncommitted vote, "You want education? We'll take care of you." Evans people wooed Hagopian with the Local Transportation Committee chair (which Washington forces had stripped from him after the 1986 special elections). Soliz, too, was offered a chairmanship, to make sure he stayed in the fold. But the one alderman who was most closely identified with a particular issue (Hansen, an outspoken opponent of lights at Wrigley Field) claimed that no promises had been made in return for his vote.

Thousands of Chicagoans watched the Bears defeat the Green Bay Packers that Sunday afternoon. Among them were several Chicago aldermen who congregated at Osterman's office. Pickets outside the office carried "No deals!" signs and accused the aldermen of violating the Open Meetings Act, a state law which prohibits a quorum of a quorum (in this case, 13 of 26) from gathering in private to discuss public business. The aldermen later claimed that they made sure no more than twelve were in any room at any one time, and that others were watching the game in an adjacent room.

While public attention was distracted by the Osterman gathering, Mell and Sawyer met at O'Connor's house. The purpose of each was simple—to stare down the other and get him to withdraw gracefully. Neither blinked. If Mell had more open desire for the job, Sawyer also had his weapon—votes of black aldermen unwilling to face certain death at the polls by supporting a white candidate. Mell later conceded that while whites could unite behind a black for mayor in this election, the reverse was not true ("I could support a black man, but Sawyer in his community could not support me"). Yet he did not back down at the time because Sawyer did not have signatures of black aldermen committed to his candidacy.

Mell kept other options. The four Hispanics met at a downtown hotel and again proclaimed their unity, although many felt Soliz could be pulled away from the other three. Soliz hinted that he could go for a white candidate if Natarus also went. Mell and Lipinski went to Dunne, asking for Natarus's vote. Dunne remained firm that Washington should have a black successor.

Jackson, who had all but anointed Evans over the previous two days, was now stepping back. He described his role as "a senior member of the family who convenes the leaders of the family" after a death. "I am not a kingmaker. I am a peacemaker and a mediator," he declared.

Kotlarz held another meeting Sunday night. This time newspapers and plastic sheets covered the windows. By now it appeared that Sawyer must be the group's choice. Gabinski and Mell had failed to move either Natarus or

Soliz. Aurelia Pucinski warned that failure to select a black mayor could jeopardize the county ticket (most specifically, her chance for clerk of the circuit court). Even Burke, considered a racist by many blacks during the Washington administration, argued that it would be improper for aldermen to install a white mayor after a black mayor had been duly chosen in the last election. His comments caused State Senator Jeremiah Joyce to call him a "fraud" for selling out white candidates.

Stone popped a surprise on the Kotlarz gathering—announcement of his own candidacy for mayor. He told the others that Victor Vrdolyak was backing him. The meeting adjourned with most of the aldermen signing up with Sawyer (those who did not sign—Madrzyk, Sheahan, Krystyniak, Cullerton, Levar—represented wards where voting for a black candidate if a white were available would be just as disastrous for them as would be a vote by blacks for Mell or Gabinski).

After the meeting, Mell and Ronan took a ride. They met Shaw in the parking lot of the Town and Country Restaurant at North Avenue and the Kennedy Expressway in the early hours of Monday morning. Shaw let the Near Northwest Side legislators see his list of eleven committed black aldermen. They, in turn, showed him their list of sixteen whites. That was it; Sawyer had the votes. All his allies had to do was keep Sawyer's nerve up. It would not be an easy task.

A council meeting had been scheduled for that day. Orr canceled it because of the Washington funeral. Instead, limosines awaited the aldermen in front of city hall to transport them to the Far South Side funeral site. Seating was prearranged, but the council members ignored such arrangements and hopped wherever they wanted, presumably to politic on the way to the funeral.

They saw a crowd estimated at 30,000 waiting outside the church, hoping for one of the few available seats. But political celebrities and other dignitaries dominated the funeral. "All them VIPs didn't know Harold Washington, and half of them didn't like him," one mourner complained.

The funeral, like most other events of the last few days, carried political overtones. Evans sat on the podium; Sawyer did not. Gutierrez dropped thinly veiled hints that Sawyer's black allies were selling out the Harold Washington ideals when he said, "No one should cross a line in death that they would not cross in life."

After the funeral, the procession made its way to Oak Woods Cemetery. Thousands of mourners en route cheered, shouted "Harold! Harold!," and threw flowers. A twenty-one gun salute hailed the recently fallen mayor and a drum and bugle corps played "Taps" before the casket was lowered into the ground.

The afternoon of the funeral, a group of note made an endorsement. The Black Task Force for Political Empowerment, a civil rights committee that helped elect Washington in 1983, threw its weight behind Evans. The group's name appeared elsewhere in the day's events. Dr. Conrad Worrell, the Task Force director, was one of those in charge of "The People's Salute to Harold

Washington: The Man, the Message, and the Vision," what was billed as a nonpartisan memorial service at the University of Illinois at Chicago pavilion. The event's other organizers were Washington advisor Walter "Slim" Coleman and former Washington campaign director Joseph Gardner.

Sawyer's advisors remembered the Operation PUSH meeting and vowed not to be set up again. They realized that their man's feet were cold enough already without throwing him into another hostile crowd. Sawyer kept a healthy distance from the pavilion that night.

While activists and mourners streamed into the pavilion, politicians downtown kept busy. White aldermen congregated at the Palmer House, awaiting action from their black allies. That action came just before 5:30 P.M. Three aldermen—Langford, Caldwell, and Butler—formally requested a special meeting for the sole purpose of electing an acting mayor. When the white aldermen heard the news, they scrambled over each other rushing to city hall to sign a resolution indicating their support. That resolution, to the dismay of some, was not binding. Signatures, even notarized ones, did not an election make. The aldermen had to make their voices known, in front of possibly angry constituents. A council meeting still was required for Sawyer to be acting mayor.

The Sawyer camp's fears were grounded in reality. Even if Monday night's memorial service had not been planned that way, it nonetheless became an Evans political rally. Evans supporters alternated cries of "We want Evans" with shouts of "No deals!" Sawyer supporters, present in small numbers if at all, remained silent.

At first the program consisted of speaker after speaker quoting the late mayor's statements on various issues with all the verve of professors reciting position papers. But two announcements charged the audience. One was the message that the special council meeting had been called. The second was word of a television news report that Burke, Ed Vrdolyak, and Byrne advisor Charles Swibel had met the afternoon of Washington's death and discussed how to install Sawyer as mayor.

And if those announcements were not enough, *Sun-Times* columnist and WLS-TV commentator Vernon Jarrett ignited the audience with a speech so emotional that some observers thought he might suffer a heart attack onstage. Jarrett compared the black aldermen siding with former Washington foes to elect Sawyer with slaves who, being freed, chose to return to the plantation. "You have black people who call themselves black people but are Negroes who are no longer men and women. . . . Do not let these fools drag us down!" he proclaimed. "Treat those black enemies like you treat the Ku Klux Klan."

No speech in recent Chicago history aroused more controversy. Evans backers saw it as the verbal outpouring of a civil rights crusader afraid of seeing his life's work going down the drain. Enemies charged that it was blatantly racist (Ed Vrdolyak, who had a score to settle with the *Sun-Times* dating from the previous spring's election, went on television to urge viewers to call the newspaper in protest. It was one of the few public gestures made by Vrdolyak during the election period). Most journalists, whatever their views, questioned the ethics of a writer making such a partisan political statement.

Gutierrez and Jackson continued the appeal, urging those present to attend the Tuesday council meeting. "We must surround city hall because it is ours!" Gutierrez said.

Jackson called to the podium those who could be considered pro-Evans: Rush, Tillman, Evans, Davis (who gave up his own candidacy), Smith, Garcia, Gutierrez, Figueroa, and Shiller. Streeter was there, having switched his vote (reportedly on the advice of minister Louis Farrakhan). Bloom, Giles, and Orr were not present but were considered reliable.

Sawyer, nonetheless, said Monday evening, "The votes are signed, sealed, and delivered" for his election.

Thus the stage was set for a Tuesday confrontation, a faction described by its foes as the forces of Ed Burke, Ed Vrdolyak, and Charlie Swibel versus a group described by its enemies as the side of Jesse Jackson, Vernon Jarrett, and Louis Farrakhan. It promised to be an interesting meeting.

Stone began the day's activities by announcing his candidacy at a 10:00 A.M. press conference. He presented reporters with his stands on everything from tuition tax credits to city council committee restructuring in the form of answers to a seven-page questionnaire (both Sawyer and Evans remained silent on issues, and almost everything else, during this "campaign"). Stone challenged his rivals to a debate, a request the frontrunners ignored. Few took Stone's candidacy seriously; many saw it as a publicity ploy for Stone's upcoming recorder of deeds election.

As the day progressed, signs appeared that the Sawyer coalition was beginning to break. A noon newscast had Jesse Evans and surprisingly, Bob Shaw, slipping over to the Tim Evans column. The newscast claimed Sawyer had seventeen white votes (Roti, Fary, Burke, Hagopian, Gabinski, Kotlarz, Banks, Cullerton, Laurino, O'Connor, Pucinski, Natarus, Hansen, Levar, Schulter, Osterman) and nine black ones (Sawyer, Beavers, Caldwell, Carter, Langford, Jones, Henry, Butler, Austin) and Evans with fifteen votes (Rush, Tillman, Tim Evans, Bloom, Shaw, Streeter, Jesse Evans, Garcia, Gutierrez, Smith, Davis, Figueroa, Giles, Shiller, Orr). Seven white aldermen (Vrdolyak, Huels, Madrzyk, Kellam, Sheahan, Krystyniak, Stone) were not committed to the Sawyer bloc and would likely back Stone, but would not fall behind Evans under any circumstances. The remaining two aldermen, Soliz and Eisendrath, were considered too unreliable to be placed into anyone's camp.

The afternoon memorial meeting gave many of the aldermen a chance to eulogize the late mayor (Bloom called him "a master tactician." Rush compared black pride with Washington to the pride Irish felt with John F. Kennedy or Poles with Pope John Paul II). Others used it to make political statements (Shiller claimed, "Harold Washington's coalition was not the ward bosses and the slatemakers, it was the people" and decried those "meeting in backrooms to destroy the coalition." Langford commented, "Don't destroy Harold Washington's city with hatred. My life has been threatened, my office picketed, and I was cussed," remarks met with jeers from the gallery). But most used the meeting to converse with each other, shoring up the spirits of fainthearted allies and attempting to sway opponents, scurrying about with frequency hinting that Sawyer's vote was anything but etched in concrete.

Some switched sides. Jones moved into the Evans column. Shaw, once away from a television camera, reverted to Sawyer. Others refused to budge. Hansen not only refused to change his vote when confronted with his ward's independent organization, but demanded the tape from a local newspaper reporter trying to record his comments. Soliz remained enigmatic, claiming he was still united with the other Hispanics but that he wanted to assure that Hispanics got something for their community if Sawyer appeared a sure winner.

Natarus closed the memorial meeting by congratulating Orr on his performance, and the council rendered the interim mayor a standing ovation. The memorial meeting adjourned shortly after 3:00 P.M.

Activity took place outside city hall. The Better Government Association filed a lawsuit charging that any results from a Tuesday city council meeting be declared invalid because of the aldermen's weekend meetings allegedly held in violation of the Open Meetings Act. A judge continued the case.

The special meeting was set for 5:30 P.M., but aldermen ignored that call. Evans supporters took heart at this delay, reasoning that if Sawyer indeed had the votes his supporters would call for the election immediately.

If aldermen were nowhere to be found, many other people heeded the Gutierrez and Jackson call. Some five thousand people, almost all of them Evans supporters, crowded outside city hall and filled the lobby. Evans foes and much of the media lost no opportunity to call the gathering a "mob," although by all accounts those gathered were orderly.

Some aldermen showed up in the council chamber—the white ethnic ones. Blacks, Hispanics, and pro-Evans Lakefront whites were nowhere to be seen. Sawyer remained in his Rules Committee office, with followers working hard to persuade him to accept his election. Sawyer, however, had his doubts. He wanted to postpone the council meeting until Friday to try and convince the black community that he was not the "white man's candidate."

A postponement was exactly what Evans's camp wanted. Already Caldwell, Jones, and Jesse Evans had succumbed to public pressure and switched from Sawyer to Evans. A day or two more might cause other black aldermen to change votes, or even move the none-too-certain Sawyer to give up a candidacy which appeared to have little popular support.

White aldermen also realized that time was of the essence and were taking no chances. They looked for alternative candidates in case Sawyer should falter. Gabinski's name was brought up again, and so was Larry Bloom's. Soliz reportedly came up short by one vote; his fellow Hispanics would not vote for Soliz unless the alderman also could get black support, and blacks were not willing to follow a nonblack candidate.

Evans and Sawyer met at about eight o'clock, each asking the other to yield. Sawyer offered to "give" Evans the council. Evans tried to show Sawyer that his candidacy was thwarting the will of the community. Burke broke up the meeting by screaming at Sawyer and all but ordering him to accept the mayorship. Other aldermen described Burke's manner as demeaning to anyone, much less his supposed choice for the city's chief executive.

Talks halted without results. Evans walked into the chamber shortly after 8:30, smiling and waving his fists high, looking like a man who just won an election instead of one whose hopes remained in doubt.

The council chamber, meanwhile, erupted with open shouting matches between Sawyer followers and the more numerous Evans backers. Several Sawyer-leaning aldermen—Carter, Langford, Butler—reported death threats. Henry let everyone know that he was wearing a bulletproof vest. The raucous atmosphere produced a result. Police soon outnumbered aldermen in the chamber.

Sawyer met in the committee hearing room with his coalition of black and white aldermen, in what was described as a cross between pep rally and revival meeting organized by Burke. The aldermen held hands and prayed. They jumped up and down and cheered. Burke told Sawyer that men had spent millions of dollars on mayoral campaigns, and that he was being handed the job on a silver platter. Mell told him, "It's now or never!"

The cheerleading worked. Sawyer, his pleas for delay rejected, told the aldermen, "All right. Let's go out on the floor and do it." A gleeful Mell ran out of the room shouting, "We've got a mayor!" (He later confessed, "I came screaming like a goof.")

But just as he left the room, Sawyer spotted Mary Ella Smith, the late mayor's fiancee. His knees began to buckle. "I can't do this," he told her. "I can't do it. This will divide the community. This is not what (Harold Washington) would have wanted."

Sawyer and Henry walked out to the chamber at 9:15, and Orr convened the meeting. From the first, there was friction. When Jones asked for an invocation, Orr suggested that Davis give the opening prayer. But one alderman suggested Rabbi Solomon Gutstein (himself a former alderman) and another wanted the Rev. Willie Barrow. "Invocation Wars" was settled with both Barrow and Gutstein bestowing blessings.

Caldwell immediately moved to adjourn. The move was defeated along factional lines which remained more or less constant all night. That vote gave heart to Sawyer supporters, now assured they had the numbers if they could keep the candidate.

They nearly lost him. Sawyer stepped out of the council chamber, having (as one unkind columnist put it) "flunked his umpteenth gut check of the night." Burke immediately called for a recess to revive his candidate's flagging spirits.

By now no one could be certain what would happen. Rumors flew that the meeting would be postponed until Friday, although even Sawyer's most ardent backers questioned whether his tenuous coalition could remain together that long.

But if Sawyer's remaining black supporters entertained ideas of switching, they hid those thoughts well. Henry, commenting on alleged death threats, said, "I'm not like Martin Luther King. If people slap me, I'm gonna slap them back."

Langford offered even saltier commentary. She told members of the gallery that her community would gain more if she voted with the winning side. When one observer criticized her, she shot back, "I owe you no allegiance. I've got nobody in my ward who looks like you." When someone questioned her commitment to the reform movement, she retorted, "—the movement. I've got to vote with politicians."

Demonstrators in the gallery, boisterous all night, stepped up their criticism of Sawyer allies during the recess. Pucinski, explaining to a reporter how threats were a common part of political life, was met with cries of "Dump the slate in '88," the black threat to boycott his daughter's candidacy. "See what I mean?" he smiled.

At one point they turned on Butler with cries of "How much, Sheneather, how much?" waving dollar bills at the rookie alderman. She taunted the crowd by waving bills back at them. Someone threw quarters, which hit Gabinski. He demanded that the offender be ejected from the chamber. The alleged perpetrator's allies huddled around him, shouting "No way!" When a different person was hauled from the room the same group shouted, "Police brutality!"

Sawyer remained holed up in his Rules Committee office. Dunne called and encouraged him. So did Rev. Addie Wyatt. Evans, meanwhile, held court with reporters. Sawyer watched his opponent claiming on television that he lacked the necessary votes for election.

That comment triggered Sawyer. He told aides shortly before midnight, "That's it. Let's go to the floor. I'm mayor."

From there it was a matter of time—as it turned out, four hours' time. Sawyer opponents knew the vote was lost unless they could play for time, and they resorted to procedural moves to postpone what appeared to be an inevitable defeat. Motions to adjourn alternated with procedural motions which likewise would have delayed a vote.

Natarus introduced a measure (he called it a declaration rather than a resolution) outlining rules for selecting a new mayor. His proposal was important for three reasons: it stated that a simple majority of those present, not a majority of the whole council was needed to select an acting mayor (Austin, hospitalized, did not attend the meeting. Therefore only 25 votes were needed, instead of 26, a difference that could be important if one or more black aldermen decided to abandon Sawyer); it ruled that the mayoral seat was vacant (assuring that Orr, as acting mayor, could not cast a tie-breaking vote); and it required that the aldermen vote until a mayor was selected (thus averting an impasse which might lead to an adjournment).

Bloom claimed that Natarus's resolution had no connection with the meeting, and Orr sided with him. Natarus claimed it lay within the purview of the meeting. The council sided with him and overturned Orr.

Tim Evans then moved that the Natarus motion be referred to the Rules Committee, stating that the Natarus motion could only be handled by a suspension of rules, and that such a suspension required a two-thirds vote (which Sawyer forces did not have). Natarus argued that since his was a declaration, not a resolution, no two-thirds vote was needed. The motion to refer to committee failed.

Bloom offered a substitute to the Natarus motion, which would have called a recess and then allowed the council to return as a committee of the whole and question all candidates. The motion was tabled.

Gutierrez moved to adjourn. The motion failed. Rush moved to refer the Natarus motion to the Finance Committee. That motion failed. Jesse Evans moved to adjourn. That too, failed. Smith proposed a motion that at least twenty-four hours elapse between the close of nominations and the election. Failed.

The Evans faction strategy became painfully evident to Sawyer-backing aldermen, whom Orr blatantly failed to recognize. Mell at one point shouted out, "What a sham! What a sham!" and then stood on his desk, waving papers. He still was not recognized.

If filibuster or indefinite delay was Orr's game plan (Orr later stated he merely wished to assure that all sides had their say), he made a mistake. Either tired from the whole process or having run out of allies, he called on Eisendrath. The Lincoln Park alderman moved the question. The Natarus resolution (or declaration) passed.

At 1:50 A.M. Wednesday, December 2, the names of Timothy Evans and Eugene Sawyer (but not Bernard Stone) were placed in nomination. The candidates both declined to speak on their own behalf. Instead supporters of each made supporting speeches, the kind which play well to television cameras but seldom change one vote.

Davis declared, "The people are shouting, 'We want Tim.' There is nothing better to do than to give the people what they want." Langford implored the council, "Don't let us sink back into those (Council Wars) years," in a speech for Sawyer that met with mixed boos and cheers.

Gutierrez commented, "I have to have a candidate I can trust. I have to have a candidate I can look in the eye. I have to have a candidate who I can not only call 'Mr. Mayor,' but also say 'You are honorable.' The only candidate I can call honorable is the honorable Timothy Evans. We are elected to serve as public servants, not as public thieves." Henry retorted that Sawyer could "stand up for the programs of the great Harold Washington."

Rush commented, "There are aldermen who fought the first black mayor tooth and nail. When you see the same individuals rallying behind a black man, you know a deal has been cut." Figueroa compared Sawyer supporters to vultures, while Stone decried "the rule of mob" and praised the women who stood up to death threats.

Tillman declared, "Mayor Washington fought those suckers for four years. We intend to hang together for fourteen more months. God is on our side."

Smith added, "I may not have E. F. Hutton, but when people in my ward talk, I listen. If I vote against Tim Evans tonight, I'll be a stranger in my own house." Shaw, however, announced the results of a poll he said he took, in which his constituents backed Sawyer by a 3,000-to-2,000 margin. Natarus perhaps summed things up best: "I don't believe Harold Washington tapped anyone for the job. I believe he would have wanted people to fight it out."

Finally came Eisendrath, the unknown vote. The Lincoln Park alderman rambled on about the relative merits of the two contenders (hinting that he was less than thrilled with both) before declaring, "For the sake of continuity, I'll support Tim Evans." He added, "If the vote doesn't go that way, and I believe I can count, then I'll vote to make it unanimous."

Eisendrath could count. Sawyer got twenty-nine votes (an ironic number considering the former Vrdolyak bloc which formed his base): those of Roti, Sawyer, Shaw, Vrdolyak, Fary, Madrzyk, Burke, Carter, Langford, Kellam, Sheahan, Krystyniak, Henry, Butler, Hagopian, Gabinski, Mell, Kotlarz, Banks, Cullerton, Laurino, O'Connor, Pucinski, Natarus, Hansen, Levar, Schulter, Osterman, and Stone. Evans received nineteen votes: Rush, Tillman, Tim Evans, Bloom, Beavers (a last-minute switch who voiced his vote at a barely audible level), Caldwell, Streeter, Jones, Jesse Evans, Garcia, Soliz, Gutierrez, Smith, Davis, Figueroa, Giles, Eisendrath, Shiller, and Orr. Huels abstained. Eugene Sawyer was declared mayor at 4:01 A.M.

Sawyer in his speech sought to bring all sides together. "I thank all of my colleagues who voted for me and extend my hand in friendship to those who ,did not support me," he said. "The reform movement initiated by Mayor Harold Washington shall remain intact and go forward. . . . I shall continue to unite black and white and Hispanic, Slav and Jew, Christian and Asian, white ethnics and new immigrants. . . . Patronage as we know it is dead, dead, dead."

The meeting adjourned at 4:16 A.M., with little more apparent unity than could be seen a few hours earlier. Aldermen refused to make the Sawyer vote unanimous. People remaining in the lobby, a fraction of the thousands who had congregated earlier, shouted, "Sawyer, Sawyer, you can't hide, you committed suicide." Evans greeted them shortly before 5:00 A.M. with "You will be mine in eighty-nine!"

All hell had indeed broken loose. Peace and unity appeared distant dreams.

Appendix

1988 COMMITTEEMAN ELECTIONS

Black voters sent undeniable messages to aldermen who supported Eugene Sawyer over Timothy Evans for acting mayor in 1987, and Republicans came to life—sort of. These were the main trends in the 1988 ward committeeman elections.

Four black aldermen with ties to Sawyer lost committeeman elections by decisive margins to comparative upstarts. Most prominent of these was William Henry, 24th Ward committeeman, who fell to community activist Jesse Miller. Henry, considered the mastermind of the Sawyer campaign, tried to wrap himself in the Washington mantle. He brought out his campaign troops in full force (including some who tossed sticks and stones at cars celebrating a mock funeral of the 24th Ward machine organized by Miller), but they took home only 31 percent of the vote.

Another incumbent, William Beavers, was a leader of the Sawyer drive. The burly ex-cop squeaked a barely audible vote for Evans during the December Council meeting—one that foes claimed he cast only after the election was safely in Sawyer's hands. He lost to educator Alice Palmer.

Two other black Sawyer allies lost bids to capture committeeman positions. Incumbent Rickey Hendon defeated Alderman Sheneather Butler in the 27th Ward, despite a Butler flier that hinted at support from the Rev. Jesse Jackson (falsely, since Jackson made no committeeman endorsements). Alderman Marlene Carter in the 15th Ward finished a distant third behind Dane V. Tucker, a firefighter, and Leon Jones.

Sawyer himself was unopposed on the ballot in his 6th Ward reelection campaign for committeeman (a write-in candidate, Roy P. Oliver, received 236 votes). However, in what might be considered a Sawyer referendum, 6th Ward voters cast a majority of their votes in the 36th District state representative race for incumbent Monique Davis over Peggy Montes, who was strongly endorsed by Sawyer.

On the other hand, a black alderman was rewarded for his Tim Evans vote. Jesse Evans of the 21st Ward at first leaned toward Sawyer but cast his vote for Tim Evans after community pressure. The community thanked him with two-thirds of the vote against Monique Davis and incumbent committeeman Niles Sherman.

Only one black Sawyer aldermanic ally indirectly won a committeeman election. State Representative William Shaw, twin brother of alderman Robert, defeated Salim Al-Nurridin, a deputy sheriff and ally of Shaw's chief foe, retiring committeeman Perry Hutchinson. Robert Shaw provided by far the most bizarre moment of any of the committeeman campaigns when he appeared on television during election night and charged that his brother's opponent was running a harem full of welfare women.

Aside from the Sawyer-related races, the committeeman elections showed other trends. All four Hispanic aldermen consolidated power in their wards by winning committeeman races. Jesus Garcia defeated real estate investor Peter Sandoval for reelection in the 22nd Ward with 71 percent of the vote—by far his best election showing to date. Fellow Harold Washington ally Luis Gutierrez beat former Park District official Omar Lopez handily in the 26th Ward. Raymond Figueroa surprised some veteran observers with an easy win over incumbent Joseph Berrios in the 31st Ward. Juan Soliz gravely wounded the 25th Ward Regular Democratic Organization by defeating incumbent committeeman Marco Domico.

In addition to the Garcia, Gutierrez, and Figueroa elections, there were other regular-versus-independent races that produced mixed results. Incumbent 10th Ward committeeman Clem Balanoff defeated Edward Vrdolyak ally and former state senator Glenn Dawson, thus foiling the former committeeman's hopes of maintaining influence in both parties' ward organizations. (Vrdolyak ally Sam Panayotovich ran unopposed for Republican committeeman).

But party regulars also claimed victories. Despite a spirited Republican committeeman contest in his ward, 18th Ward incumbent John Daley defeated challenger Eldora Davis. Alderman Terry Gabinski faced no real challenge from former Washington advisor Walter "Slim" Coleman in the 32nd Ward. The only question was whether Gabinski would ignore the Coleman candidacy or move to crush it. The alderman chose the latter course. He mustered an army of precinct workers on election day and overwhelmed Coleman with 82 percent of the vote.

Regulars gained committeeman seats in the 46th and 48th wards over two black challengers. County treasurer Ed Rosewell, who moved into the ward only days before the filing deadline, defeated Chuck Kelly, an officer with the Independent Voters of Illinois–Independent Precinct Organization. Party regulars tried successfully to make the committeeman election a referendum on controversial alderman Helen Shiller.

Kathy Osterman became the first lakefront ward alderman in memory to also be elected committeeman following her victory over hospital administrator James Exum in the politically confused 48th Ward. Exum was the candidate of the 48th Ward Democratic Organization, which consisted of outgoing committeeman Robert Remer and other liberal types. This group was not to be confused with the 48th Ward *Regular* Democratic Organization (the old Marty Tuchow-Sharon Rae Bender group), most of whom supported Osterman. (County party chairman George Dunne first endorsed Exum, thinking him to be the regular party candidate. When he learned that Osterman, not Exum, was the choice of party regulars, he shifted his endorsement—to the vocal criticism of Exum.)

Unlike the near civil war that highlighted the 1984 committeeman elections in which former mayor Harold Washington vowed to oust then-chairman Vrdolyak, the 1988 Democratic committeeman elections ended on a peaceful note. County chairman George Dunne was reelected unanimously.

Republican committeeman elections in the past were little more than the subject of political footnotes, since many of the Republican committeemen held office only at the whim of their more powerful Democratic counterparts. But 1988 showed renewed city interest in the G.O.P. More Republicans than Democrats ran for committeeman (although Democratic primary voters far outnumbered Republicans in every ward). And for once it was the Republicans, not the Democrats, who had a visible battle for the post of party chairman.

The winner turned out to be James Dvorak, right hand man of Sheriff James O'Grady and until recently a Democrat. He defeated incumbent Donald Totten, a conservative ideologue. Dvorak, newly elected committeeman of the Southwest Side's 18th Ward, was considered an upstart by many of the more senior suburban committeemen. But the endorsement of Governor James Thompson (never a Totten fan) turned the chairman election in his favor.

A chief complaint of many suburban Republicans was the reputed influence of Democrat-turned-Republican Vrdolyak on Dvorak and O'Grady. Vrdolyak was the most vocal Republican before the primaries. He broadcast radio ads blasting County Board president (and Democratic party chairman) George Dunne for approving county tax increases and distributed brochures in several North Side wards criticizing several erstwhile aldermanic allies for supporting a 1988 budget that called for property tax increases.

Vrdolyak claimed credit for increased interest in the Republican primary, noting that twice as many voters chose Republican ballots as in 1984. The claim sounds impressive until one realizes that singularly few voters chose Republican ballots that year. In the 50th Ward, where Alderman (and recently converted Republican) Bernard Stone faced an uncertain primary fight for Recorder of Deeds, Democratic ballots cast outnumbered Republican by a six-to-one margin.

The unofficial Dvorak/O'Grady/Vrdolyak slate achieved mixed results. Dvorak won his 18th Ward election handily. Attorney John McNeal won in the 48th Ward, and Michael Caccitolo took the 23rd Ward. But allies Gino Naughton, Joseph Hornowski, and Sal Terranova lost in the 19th, 30th, and 41st wards. Winners in those wards were believed to be aided by crossover votes encouraged by the Democratic ward organizations.

Black wards, for the most part, appeared immune from Republicanmania. The winning Republican candidate received fewer than 100 votes in nine black wards. Three wards with huge black majorities but pockets of whites (15th, 27th, 29th) have white Republican committeemen.

The Hispanic-majority 25th Ward also elected a white Republican committeeman—Stanley Wozniak, member of a family that owns a local bar and bowling alley. Domico put up both Wozniak and Mexican-American Fred Davila for that office, fueling speculation that the 25th Ward Regular Democratic Organization might transfer en masse to the G.O.P. should Domico fail to win reelection as Democratic committeeman.

In the 47th Ward, Democratic Committeeman Ed Kelly saw two former allies dethrone longtime Republicans. Thomas Corcoran defeated Kenneth Hurst, a perennial candidate for higher office, in the 39th Ward. Arthur Fitzgerald, an assistant to one of Kelly's top precinct captains, defeated Paul R. T. Johnson in the 47th Ward. Johnson was the protégé of John Hoellen, ardent Richard Daley foe and the last authentic Republican in the City Council. The Johnson/Hoellen loss marked the fall of the last genuine Republican organization in Chicago.

DEMOCRATIC COMMITTEEMAN RESULTS:

	N	%
1st Ward		
John D'Arco, unopposed		
2nd Ward		
Bobby Rush	7,954	72
William Barnett	3,156	28
3rd Ward		
Dorothy Tillman, unopposed		
4th Ward		
Timothy Evans, unopposed		
5th Ward		
Alan Dobry, unopposed		
6th Ward		
Eugene Sawyer, unopposed		
7th Ward		
Alice Palmer	5,831	60
William Beavers	3,972	40
8th Ward		
John Stroger, unopposed		
9th Ward		
William Shaw	6,560	53
Salim Al-Nurridin	5,912	47
10th Ward		
Clement Balanoff	4,105	46
Glenn Dawson	2,364	27
Gerald Garcia	1,594	18

	N	%
Marion Fisher	441	5
Murell Farmer	327	4
11th Ward		
John Daley	10,067	79
Nicholas Flores	2,634	21
12th Ward		
Robert Molaro, unopposed		
13th Ward		
Michael Madigan, unopposed		
14th Ward		
Edward Burke, unopposed		
15th Ward		
Dane V. Tucker	4,652	43
Leon Jones	3,636	34
Marlene Carter	2,551	24
16th Ward		
James Taylor	5,163	47
Osie Carr	4,268	39
Eular Portman	1,556	14
17th Ward		
Allan Streeter, unopposed		
18th Ward		
John Daley	10,901	56
Eldora Davis	8,714	44
19th Ward		
Thomas Hynes, unopposed		

DEMOCRATIC COMMITTEEMAN RESULTS:

	N	%
20th Ward		
Cecil Partee	7,232	72
Inez Gardner	2,054	20
Glenn Wharton	770	8
21st Ward		
Jesse Evans	11,964	66
Monique Davis	3,736	20
Niles Sherman	2,558	14
22nd Ward		
Jesus Garcia	3,163	71
Peter Sandoval	1,296	29
23rd Ward		
William Lipinski, unopposed		
24th Ward		
Jesse Miller	8,749	69
William Henry	4,021	31
25th Ward		
Juan Soliz	3,400	54
Marco Domico	2,936	46
26th Ward		
Luis Gutierrez	4,072	67
Omar Lopez	1,969	33
27th Ward		
Rickey Hendon	3,376	48
Sheneather Butler	2,065	29
Willie Burrell	1,615	23
28th Ward		
Ed Smith	6,366	72
Kenneth "Butch" Campbell	2,161	24
Renado Hardy	358	4
29th Ward		
Danny K. Davis, unopposed		
30th Ward		
Thaddeus "Ted" Lechowicz, unopposed		

	N	%
31st Ward		
Raymond Figueroa	4,097	57
Joseph Berrios	3,103	43
32nd Ward		
Theris Gabinski	7,702	82
Walter Coleman	1,658	18
33rd Ward		
Richard Mell, unopposed		
34th Ward		
Wilson Frost, unopposed		
35th Ward		
Joseph Kotlarz, unopposed		
36th Ward		
William J. P. Banks, unopposed		
37th Ward		
Percy Giles, unopposed		
38th Ward		
Thomas Cullerton, unopposed		
39th Ward		
Anthony Laurino, unopposed		
40th Ward		
Patrick O'Connor, unopposed		
41st Ward		
Roman Pucinski, unopposed		
42nd Ward		
George Dunne, unopposed		
43rd Ward		
Ann Stepan, unopposed		
44th Ward		
John Merlo, unopposed		
45th Ward		
Thomas Lyons, unopposed		
46th Ward		
Edward Rosewell	5,587	60
Charles Kelly	3,788	40

DEMOCRATIC COMMITTEEMAN RESULTS:

	N	%		N	%
47th Ward			49th Ward		
Edmund Kelly, unopposed			Lee Preston, unopposed		
48th Ward					
Kathy Osterman	5,160	58	50th Ward		
James Exum	3,754	42	Howard W. Carroll, unopposed		

NEW COMMITTEEMEN (OTHER THAN ALDERMEN ALSO ELECTED COMMITTEEMAN):

Alice Palmer, 7th Ward. Born June 20, 1939. Career: B.A., Indiana University, 1966; M.A. Roosevelt University, 1972; Ph.D., Northwestern University, 1979; Director of Special Services, Malcolm X College; Coordinator of English Language Component, Education Program, University of Illinois; Associate Dean of Students and Dean of African-American Affairs, Northwestern University; Director of Voter Registration Program, Citizens Action Committee; Director of Youth-in-Government Program, YMCA.

William "Bill" Shaw, 9th Ward. Born July 31, 1937; Career: Aldermanic Administrative Assistant; Assistant Director, Department of Supportive Service; State Representative, 1983- .
Ward office: 723 W. 123rd St. (785–3200)

Dane V. Tucker, 15th Ward. Born November 17, 1952. Career: Kennedy-King College; Welder, Republic Steel; Sales Manager, Target Marketing; Firefighter, Chicago Fire Department.
Ward office: 1959 W. 59th St. (925–5030)

James C. Taylor, 16th Ward. Born: February 8, 1930. Career: University of Illinois, Monticello College; veteran, Korean conflict; State Representative, 1969–81, 1983–85; State Senator, 1981–83; Department of Streets and Sanitation, 1962–80; Deputy Chief of Staff to Mayor Jane Byrne, 1980–83.

Jesse Miller, 24th Ward. Born June 7, 1942. Career: Manager, W.F. Hall Printing Company, 1961–84; Staff Member, Southern Christian Leadership Conference, 1966; Community Organizer, Lawndale Peoples Planning and Action Conference, 1968–83; Executive Director, LPPAC, 1983- .

Edward Rosewell, 46th Ward. Born December 8, 1926. Career: B.A., DePaul University, 1961; U.S. Army; Executive Director, Illinois State Toll Highway Commission, 1964–69; Vice President, Continental Illinois National Bank & Trust Company, 1969–74; Commissioner, Chicago Park District, 1972–74; Cook County Treasurer, 1974- .
County Building telephone: 443–6200.

Index

Photos appear on pages indicated in italics.
(See also mayoral section and election results for each ward.)

Burroughs, Margaret, 314
Bush, Earl, 328
Butler, Jerry, "Iceman," 66
Butler, Jesse, 15, 182
Butler, Sheneather, 15, 182, *194*, 348, 352, 353, 355, 356, 357, 358, 359
Byrne, Jane, 10, 14, 16, 18, 71, 77, 80, 86, 102, 117, 126, 131, 136, 153, 173, 182, 189, 220, 226, 227, 232, 238, 239, 242, 253, 255, 266, 274, 275, 276, 282, 286, 287–8, 294, 300, 301, 305, 313, 331, 345, 346, 347, 349; and ward remap, 8–9, 205–6; declares mayoral candidacy, 11; opposes gay rights bill, 11; calls Puerto Ricans aliens, 14; campaign in black community, 15; challenges Washington to debate, 15; attempts to defeat Streeter, 121; replaces Kuta, 205
Byrne, Kathy, 347
Byrne, William, 253

Cabrini-Green, 274, 278
Cacciatore, Victor, 248–9
Caccitolo, Michael, 361
Caldwell, Billy, 252
Caldwell, Keith, 66, 348, 352, 353, 354, 355, 358
Caldwell, Lewis, 66
Campbell, Kenneth, 135, 136
Capehart, Adrian, 321
Capone, Al, 24, 130, 284
Capparelli, Ralph, 266
Carey, Bernard, 36, 300
Carothers, William, 189
Carroll, Howard W., 17, 336, 348
Carter, Marlene, 110, 348, 353, 355, 358, 359
Casey, Daniel, 286
Casey, Thomas, 242
Castro, Ray, 60–1
Catania, Susan, 13
Cermak, Anton, 84, 147
Chevare, Gloria, 15, *174*
Chew, Charles, 120
Chicago Defender, 24
Chicago Free Press, 247
Chicago Post, 220
Chicago Reader, 272
Chicago Sun-Times: published Sullivan report, 8; urges Vrdolyak to withdraw from campaign, 17; claims Vrdolyak met with mob boss, 18; sued by Vrdolyak, 18; criticizes Hynes withdrawal, 19; shows environmental problems, 75; comments on McGowan residency, 192; describes Anthony Laurino, 254; location of, 272
Chicago Tribune: discloses Vrdolyak-Republican talks, 5; discloses "Skip" Burrell tapes, 6, 37; editorial on street repairs, 7; describes Patrick Huels, 86–7; describes John Madrzyk, 97; describes Lawndale, 158; complains about 26th Ward election, 173; location of, 272; Freedom Center, 213
Chico, John, 59
Chronis, James, 26
City Council: increased number of committees, 5; meeting to determine successor to Harold Washington, 354–8

Clancy, Brendan, 321
Clark, Mark, 184
Claudio, Felicita, 175
Clements, George, 42
Clewis, Richard, 300
Cody, John Cardinal, 60, 108
"Coffee rebellion," 77, 237
Cohen, Chris, 305, 319
Cole, Frankie, 285
Coleman, Johnnie, 225
Coleman, Mattie, 181
Coleman, Walter "Slim," 5, 215, 304–5, 306, 307, 352, 360
Collazo, Migdalia, 207
Collin, Frank, 108
Collins, Brian, 286
Collins, Cardiss, 194, 243
Collins, George, 159
Committeeman, role of, viii
Communities and neighborhoods: Albany Park, 254, 258; Andersonville, 258, 259, 323; Archer Heights, 89, 92; Austin, 195, 236, 242; Avalon Park, 65; Avondale, 230; Back of the Yards, 93, 100–1; Belmont-Cragin, 198, 236; Beverly, 142, 225; Beverly Hills, 132; Bowmanville, 259–60; Brighton Park, 89, 92; Bucktown, 212; Buena Park, 304; Burnside, 65; the Bush, 59; Canaryville, 83; Chatham, 53; Chicago Lawn, 111; Chinatown, 23; Dunning, 236; East Side, 76; Edgebrook, 252, 253, 268; Edgewater, 321, 323; Englewood, 114–5, 116; Forest Glen, 252; Fuller Park, 85; the Gap, 31; Garfield Park, 187–8, 189, 242; Garfield Ridge, 152; Gold Coast, 283; Grand Boulevard, 35; Greater Grand Crossing, 136; Greektown, 23; "new" Greektown, 259; the Grove, 124; Heart of Uptown, 304; Hegewisch, 76; Humboldt Park, 9, 175, 208, 241; Irondale, 74; the Island, 196; Jefferson Park, 299; Jeffrey Manor, 76; Kensington, 70; Kenwood, 42–3; Lake Meadows, 30; Lake View, 291, 299; Lakewood-Balmoral, 320, 321, 323; Lawndale (North Lawndale), 157–9, 334; Little Village (South Lawndale), 9, 146–7; Logan Square, 9, 208, 218; McKinley Park, 83; Montclair, 236; Morgan Park, 132, 225; Mt. Greenwood, 132; Near North Side, 271–4; New Town, 291; North Park, 253; North Town, 258, 335; Norwood Park, 268; Oakland, 42; Old Town, 272, 282, 292; Palmer Square, 208; Park Manor, 53; the Patch, 183; Pill Hill, 76; Pilsen, 9, 27, 162–4; Prairie Shores, 30; Pullman, 69–70; Ravenswood, 258, 310–1; Rogers Park, 326–8; Roseland, 70, 225; Sauganash, 252–3; Sheridan Park, 304; Skid Row, 24, 180; Slag Valley, 74, 76; South Chicago, 58–9, 75; South Deering, 76; South Shore, 47–8, 59; Stony Island Heights, 60; Ukrainian Village, 211; Uptown, 303–4, 320, 322; the Valley, 24; Washington Heights, 141, 142, 225; Washington Park, 135; West Englewood, 111; West Pullman, 70, 225; West Town, 9, 175; Wicker Park, 175; Woodlawn, 136. *See also* Bridgeport; Hyde Park
Community Development Bloc Grants, battle over, 6–7

ynes, Thomas,—*continued*
dacy, 13; portrays himself as boring, 14; attacks Washington, 17; hints Vrdolyak met with mob boss, 18; withdraws, 18

ackson, Claude, 110
ackson, Jesse, 14, 43, 285, 321, 346, 346-7, 348, 353, 354, 359; influence on acting mayor election, 347-8, 350; hostility from whites, 348
aksy, Kenneth, 109
ambrone, Joseph, 189
anulus, Charles, 97
arrett, Vernon, 352, 353
iminez, "Cha Cha," 305
ohn Paul II, visits to Chicago churches, 154, 163
ohnson, Johnny, 243
ohnson, Leif, 255
ohnson, Maurice, 132
ohnson, Paul R. T., 315, 362
ohnson, Wallace, 12
ones, Art, 97
ones, Ernest, 137, 345, 348, 354, 355, 358
ones, Excell, 41
ones, Gerald, 60
ones, Leon, 359
ones, Sheila, 16
ones, Virgil, 110
oyce, Jeremiah, 13, 131, 132, 351
urek, Joseph, 234

aplan, Nathan, 260
ardzionak, John, 205
arganon, Alan, 293
aszak, Nancy, 306
aufman, Glen, 320
eane, Adeline, 204-5
eane, George, 204
eane, Thomas E., 26, 49, 77, 85, 203-6, 242, 260, 305, 328; draws ward map, 9, 205-6, 232, 242, 276; power as alderman, 203-4; conviction, 204; ruled ward through others, 204-5
eane, Thomas Jr., 204, 293
eane, Thomas P., 203
eenan, Frank, 328
ellam, Robert, 3, 9, 125, 126, 348, 353, 358
elley, Clifford, 4, 8, 77, 135, 136-7, 172; humor, 136; involvement in Operation Incubator, 137
elly, Chuck, 307, 360
elly, Edmund, 5, 11, 153, 275, 312, 313, *314*, 314-5, 316, 320, 362; ouster as park superintendent, 10; dissension within organization, 18
elly, Edward, 84-5, 130, 159
elly, Nancy, 329
enna, Michael "Hinky Dink," 25, 254
ennedy, Eugene, cited, 85
ennelly, Martin, 85, 101, 130, 159, 203, 328
enner, Tyrone, 4, 36-7
ennison, David, 284
ing, Martin Luther Jr., 108, 116, 356; compared Chicago and Mississippi, 108; settled in West Side, 158; riots following death, 187

King, William Jr., 61
Kluczynski, John, 109
Koen, Rev. Charles, 110
Kolasa, Emil, 265
Kolk, Thomas, 267
Kotlarz, Joseph, 3, 194, 233-4, 348, 349, 350-1, 353, 358
Kozubowski, Walter, 15, 138, 232
Kramer, John, 13
Kreloff, Mike, 329, 331
Kriska, Joseph, 108
Krystyniak, William, 3, 154, 348, 351, 353, 358
Kunicki, Richard, 249, 267
Kusper, Stanley, 13, 266
Kuta, Chester, 205, 207
Kuta, Frank, 153
Kwak, George, 90

Langford, Anna, 4, 108, 109, 116, 117, 118, 318, 348, 353, 355, 357, 358; work with Ald. Francis Lawlor, 108-9; as perennial candidate, 117; support for Eugene Sawyer, 348, 352, 356
LaPietra, Angelo, 25
LaRouche, Lyndon, 16, 223; allied candidates, 16, 48, 132, 255, 267, 315, 336; headquarters, 260
Laskowski, Casimir "Casey," 232
Lathrop, Ross, 49, 285
Laurino, Anthony, 3, 254, 255, 348, 353, 358
Laurino, Margie, 255
Laurino, William "Billy," 255, 348
LaVelle, Michael, 192
Lawlor, Francis X., 108-9, 117
Lechowicz, Thaddeus "Ted," 200-1, 348
Leopold, Nathan, 75
Levar, Patrick, 300-1, 348, 351, 353, 358
Levy, Arnold, 319
Lewis, Benjamin, 159
Ligon, Krista, 142
Lipinski, William, 17, 19, 153-4, 348, 350; led non-partisan mayoral vote campaign, 111
Loeb, Richard, 75
Lopez, Omar, 172, 175, 360
Louis, Joe, 85
Lozano, Emma. *See* Rico, Emma Lozano
Lozano, Rudy, 147, 148, 215
Luetgert, Adolph, 213
Lyons, Thomas, 17, 300-1, 348

Macaluso, Joan, 315
McAuliffe, Roger, 248, 249
McClain, Clarence, 7-8, 117-8
McCutcheon, John Barr, 285
McDermott, James, 101, 102
McDougall, Jane, 321
McFolling, Tyrone, 120-1
McGowan, Iola, 192-3
McKee, Ronald, 91, 92
McLaughlin, Gerald, 3, 300, 301
McMahon, Edwin, 200
McMillan, Thomas, 9, 121
McMullen, Jay, 77; describes Tom Keane, 204
McNeal, John, 321, 361
McVoy, Fredrick, 41
Madigan, Michael, 96, 97, 337